Brodsky Abroad

Brodsky Abroad

Empire, Tourism, Nostalgia

Sanna Turoma

THE UNIVERSITY OF WISCONSIN PRESS

Publication of this volume has been made possible, in part, through support from the Andrew W. Mellon Foundation.

The University of Wisconsin Press
1930 Monroe Street, 3rd Floor
Madison, Wisconsin 53711-2059
uwpress.wisc.edu

3 Henrietta Street
London WCE 8LU, England
eurospanbookstore.com

5 4 3 2 1

Printed in the United States of America

Library of Congress Cataloging-in-Publication Data
Turoma, Sanna.
Brodsky abroad: empire, tourism, nostalgia / Sanna Turoma.
p. cm.
Includes bibliographical references and index.
ISBN 978-0-299-23634-2 (pbk.: alk. paper) — ISBN 978-0-299-23633-5 (e-book)
1. Brodsky, Joseph, 1940–1996—Travel. I. Title.
PG3479.4.R64T87 2010
811′.54—dc22

2009040639

for

Tony, Anniina, and Mummi

Contents

Acknowledgments

In 1995 Joseph Brodsky visited Finland and read his poetry at the Helsinki Festival. *Watermark*, his book-long essay on Venice, had just been translated into Finnish. I was present at a press conference and witnessed the nervous fingering of cigarettes and idiosyncratic English, which had by then become his trademark.

Years later I took up the task of writing a dissertation on Brodsky's poetry. This book is an outcome of that work. The first steps of the work were taken under the guidance of Professor Pekka Pesonen and Professor Natalia Baschmakoff. I am grateful to both for their help and support. The discussions and activities shared by the junior and senior research staff at the Department of Slavonic and Baltic Literatures and Languages at the University of Helsinki were a necessary starting point for my further explorations in the field. A major bulk of the research for this book was conducted at Columbia University in New York, where I had a chance to work with the graduate community at the Slavic Department in 2000–2003. I benefited greatly from the rigorous academic environment at the Columbia graduate school, some of whose members have remained close colleagues and friends. I especially wish to thank Professor Boris Gasparov, my instructor, for his scholarly generosity and guidance. The two examiners of my dissertation, Professor David Bethea and Doctor Aleksandra Smith, shared with me their enlightened ideas about Brodsky and their invaluable commentary on my work. I am especially indebted to Professor Bethea for his encouragement and support in turning the dissertation into a book. Professor Bożena Shallcross, one of the reviewers of the manuscript, made important suggestions, as did Dr. Kirsti Simonsuuri, whose support throughout the book project was invaluable. Several scholars have read parts of the manuscript at its various stages and shared their experience and insights with me. I am grateful to them all. I would especially like to thank Jost van Baak, Arja Rosenholm, Liisa Byckling, Ben Hellman, Jopi Nyman, Irina Sandomirskaja, Evgenii Bershtein, Pekka Kuusisto, Carol Ueland, Jon Kyst, Jonathan Platt, Kirsten Lodge, Tench Coxe, Rebecca Pyatkevich, Margo Rosen, Sergei Zavialov, Olga Timofeeva, and Paul Graves. Gwen Walker of the University of Wisconsin Press offered me sound and thoughtful advice on the last stretch of the work. I would also like to thank the two young Finnish colleagues with whom I shared an office space while the book was in progress. Mari Raami's and Ulla Hakanen's tolerance of the *khudozhestvennyi besporiadok* (artistic disorder) I created in that space was extensive, as were, outside that space, the resources of Dr. Kirsti Ekonen's collegial support. My warmest thanks go to them and all the other members of the unofficial Helsinki Women Slavists' lunch club.

The research for this book project has been funded by the Finnish National Graduate School for Literary Studies, the Academy of Finland, and Wihuri Foundation. I am thankful of their financial support. I am also grateful to *Russian Literature*; *Ulbandus, The Slavic Review of Columbia University*; and *Slavic Almanach: The South African Year Book for Slavic, Central and East European Studies* for granting me the permission to reprint some of my previously published articles. Some of chapter 1 was published in Russian in *Novoe Literaturnoe Obozrenie* and in Finnish in *Nostalgia: Kirjoituksia kaipuusta ja ikävästä*, ed. Riikka Rossi and Katja Seutu (Helsinki: SKS, 2007). I would also like to thank Alan Myers for sharing with me some valuable information about the translations he made with Joseph Brodsky. Finally, there was a sense of homecoming and great pleasure in getting the book ready for print as a visiting scholar at the Harriman Institute of Columbia University.

Note on Translations and Abbreviations

Throughout the book Joseph Brodsky's name is spelled in the English form he adopted after his emigration. Exception is made when the name is quoted in a reference to a Russian publication, i.e., Iosif Brodskii, *Stikhotvoreniia i poemy*. Brodsky's poetry is quoted in Russian originals and in English translations. I have used Brodsky's own English versions of his Russian poems or authorized translations as they appear in *Collected Poems in English* (New York: Farrar, Straus and Giroux, 2000). When there was no English translation available (as is the case with many of the poems quoted in chap. 1), the quotes are rendered in interlinear translations in brackets. The quotations of Brodsky's Russian poetry are from his collected Russian works *Sochineniia Iosifa Brodskogo*, 7 vols. (St. Petersburg: Pushkinskii fond, 1997–2001) unless otherwise indicated. In reference to the Russian *Sochineniia* I give the number of the volume followed by page number, that is, 2:67, and in references to the English *Collected Poems* I give the page number. In text references, *Collected Poems in English* is abbreviated as *CP*. Brodsky's collections of essays *Less Than One* and *On Grief and Reason*, and the essay on Venice *Watermark*, are abbreviated in the text as *LTO*, *GR*, and *W*, respectively. The essays I discuss in more detail, "A Guide to a Renamed City" and "Flight from Byzantium," are included in *Less Than One*; and "After a Journey, or Homage to Vertebrea" and "A Place as Good as Any" are included in *On Grief and Reason*. I use the Library of Congress system of transliterations with diacritical marks omitted. An exception from the LC system is made in some well-known authors' names, that is, Dostoevsky, Mayakovsky, Viazemsky, which are spelled in the form more familiar to the English-language reader. In the endnotes, ST refers to Sanna Turoma.

Brodsky Abroad

Introduction

In the 1989 documentary film *Joseph Brodsky: A Maddening Space,* there is a scene where the filmmakers arrange a viewing of photographs taken seventeen years earlier in Leningrad on the day of Brodsky's departure from the Soviet Union. The obviously moved and somewhat emotionally distressed Brodsky is asked to comment on photographs of himself taken at the moment of his departure, as well as on photographs of his family and friends taken immediately after he had left the country. The pictures take Brodsky back to the moment of his departure, forcing him to reflect on and articulate both the personal loss and the cultural significance of his decision to emigrate. The interviewer directs the conversation to Brodsky's reception in Russia (the documentary was made after Brodsky had received the 1987 Nobel Prize in Literature, and some of his works were being published for the first time in Soviet journals and magazines). When asked how he sees himself in terms of the Russian readership, and whether he now consciously addresses his new readers in Russia, Brodsky says that the attention of state publishing houses and young readers "might tickle my ego," but "I really don't care what the new generation thinks." "One's affinity, sentiment," he affirms, "is for the generation to which one belongs."[1]

From this and other interviews, as well as the many dedications, allusions, and references in Brodsky's works, one is inclined to conclude that his imaginary reader, apart from the dead poets' society he affectionately created in his literary essays, was a group of Leningrad friends and acquaintances, some of whom he sees in these photographs. But despite this pronounced loyalty to an intimate circle of readers, Brodsky became an immensely important figure for many Russians outside it; he was one of the leading public figures of Soviet emigration in the Cold War period, and his role as a model for the constructing of Russian cultural identities in the last years of the Soviet Union was, and still is, extremely important. Svetlana Boym, writing about Brodsky and Venice in an honorary and personal essay in *The Future of Nostalgia*, reflects on Brodsky's importance as a cultural figure, not only for the author herself but for many educated Russians, for whom Brodsky's burial place in the Venetian graveyard of San Michele has become a site of cultural pilgrimage:

> On the day of Brodsky's funeral in Venice, his widow and his friends discovered that the lot prepared for the poet was next to that of Ezra Pound. They immediately protested, refusing to bury Brodsky in the close proximity to the poet whom he despised for both artistic and political reasons. Now Brodsky lies not far from Stravinsky, another modernist cosmopolitan. Still, there is poetic justice in the fact that Brodsky is buried not in Petersburg, but in Venice. At the end, the "Penelope of a city" received her erring hero.[2]

The outrage caused by the initial burial place, which Boym artfully weaves into the patterns of Russian cultural mythologies, invokes the question of Brodsky's position as the successor of the "modernist cosmopolitans," some of whom, such as Ezra Pound, he audaciously criticized, while affectionately affiliating with some others through his bold self-fashioning in poetry and prose—W. H. Auden comes to mind first.[3]

The question this book sets forth concerns the belatedness of Brodsky's position. What did it mean to be a successor of modernist cosmopolitanism in the last decades of the twentieth century, when the ideological foundations of the very position were being challenged by postindustrial globalization and global migration, on the one hand, and postmodern concepts of subjectivities, on the other. Rather than taking Brodsky's canonical position as a descendant of the major Russian- and English-language modernists as given, this book reconsiders this commonly accepted presumption from the perspective of Brodsky's travel poetry and prose. Another commonplace of Brodsky scholarship this study challenges has to do with the concept of exile, which has so far been the biographical and conceptual point of departure for most scholarly discussions of Brodsky's works. Shifting the focus away from exile, the book discusses Brodsky's travel poetry and prose not so much *against* as *outside* the modernist discourse on exile, relocating their analysis in the diverse context of contemporary travel and the literary and cultural criticism that has evolved around the study of travel and travel writing in recent years. The aim is not to undermine the cultural significance of Brodsky's status as an exiled writer or the tragic underpinnings of his emigration; whether we look at Brodsky's life as the tragic fate of an individual under a totalitarian regime or as one of exile's success stories, his works remain as an unambiguous testimony to the painfulness of personal choices and the difficulties of external circumstances that informed these choices. Instead, the book aims at setting Brodsky in a dialogue with leading representatives of postcolonial and postmodern theories in order to recontextualize the scholarly investigation of his travel poetry and prose. This dialogue offers previously unexplored perspectives for analyzing the geopolitical, philosophical, and linguistic premises of Brodsky's poetic imagination; it allows Brodsky's major themes to be examined from the viewpoint of their worldly rather than metaphysical or transcendent associations. Travel writing offered for Brodsky a discursive space for negotiating his own transculturation, while it also offered him a discursive space for making powerful statements about displacement, culture, history and geography, time and space—all major themes of his poetry.

The idea of geographical space emerged as a powerful creative impetus in Brodsky's early poems inspired by geological expeditions, and in his later works it was imagined through an increasing awareness of imperial histories, while it also became explicitly associated with creativity and masculinity. Eventually, history and geography, time and space, were the concepts through which Brodsky represented the division between East and West, the metropolitan and the third world, cultural signification and nonsignification. Apart from inserting his lyric subject and traveling author into European and non-European landscapes through his geographical imagination, Brodsky also situated them in the historical narrative of travel and colonization. Brodsky's travel poetry and prose written in emigration address the postwar moment when the irrevocable impact mass tourism had on travel and travel writing had become widely recognized by many Western travel writers and cultural critics. The "traveler" (*puteshestvennik*), which emerges as a complex autobiographical trope in Brodsky's post-1972 travel texts, communicates the author's nostalgia for the mythic gentleman traveler and for the lost opportunities of authentic travel, adventure, and exploration in the postcolonial era; it signifies his nostalgic attitude for the aesthetic and existential isolation of modernist subjectivity. Brodsky's travel writing was, then, a response not only to the exilic but to the tourist condition, and above all, to the postmodern and postcolonial landscape, which initially shaped the writing of his travel poetry and prose.[4]

One of Joseph Brodsky's great contributions to Russian literature from the latter half of the twentieth century is the wide geographical scope of his poetic and prose works. Brodsky was not a *travel writer*, but he was a *traveling writer* who wrote a considerable number of poems that relate to his trips and travels in the Soviet Union and outside it. After his emigration Brodsky traveled extensively in the West at a period when most Soviet citizens and writers were unable to travel abroad or to describe countries and territories beyond the Soviet space. The travel experience Brodsky gathered during this period in his life is reflected in poems he wrote about European countries and cities, an essay he wrote about Venice, and three travel accounts, which relate to his trips outside Europe and North America—the poetic cycle of Mexico titled "Meksikanskii divertisment" ("Mexican Divertimento"), and two essays titled "Posle puteshestviia, ili Posviashchaetsia pozvonochniku" ("After a Journey, or Homage to Vertebrae") and "Puteshestvie v Stambul" ("Flight from Byzantium"), which reflect his trips to Rio de Janeiro and Istanbul, respectively.[5] These two prose travel texts—"Flight" is included in *Less Than One* and "After a Journey" in *Grief and Reason*—represent travel writing in the sense the term is used conventionally: they present the author's account of a trip to a specific place and of the foreign manners and people he encounters there, while they also introduce the author's highly subjective historical and geographical imaginings inspired by that encounter. Meanwhile, the Venetian essay *Watermark* illuminates another important aspect of travel writing—the fact that travel writing is always a form of autobiography.

The book at hand covers a number of travel poems Brodsky wrote in the Soviet Union, but the focus is, however, on the prose and poetic travel texts he wrote after emigrating from there in 1972. Apart from the essays on Brazil, Turkey, and Venice, it will discuss the retrospective travel guide to Leningrad titled "A Guide to a Renamed City" (included in *Less Than One*) and "A Place as Good as Any," an English-language essay (included in *Grief and Reason*) that reflects the author's accumulative tourist experience.[6] Out of Brodsky's numerous post-1972 travel poems, this study focuses on the 1975 "Mexican Divertimento" and the poems Brodsky wrote about Venice between 1973 and 1995. These are "Laguna" ("Lagoon"), "San Pietro," "Venetsianskie strofy (1)" and "Venetsianskie strofy (2)" ("Venetian Stanzas 1" and "Venetian Stanzas 2"), "V Italii" ("In Italy"), "Lido" ("Venice: Lido"), "Posviashchaietsia

Dzhirolamo Marchello" ("Homage to Girolamo Marcello"), and "S natury" ("In Front of Casa Marcello"). The Mexican cycle and the Venetian poems create a contrast between Brodsky's European and non-European imaginings, while a parallel reading of the Russian-language Venetian poems and the English-language Venetian essay provides a productive point of departure for discussing Brodsky's troubled but successful transculturation from a Soviet emigrant and Russian-language poet into an English-language essayist and a Nobel Prize winner, which, in turn, foregrounds the question of displacement, integral to all travel writing.[7]

Defining travel writing in terms of a literary genre is difficult, a fact illustrated, for instance, by the editors of the recent *Cambridge Companion to Travel Writing*, who include a wide range of discursive practices from poetic to theoretical in their historical outline of travel literature in Western canonical culture: biblical tales (Exodus, the punishment of Cain); journeys of antiquity (the *Odyssey*, the *Aeneid*); medieval travel tales (Marco Polo, pilgrimages, and crusades); seamen's, merchants', and scientists' travel accounts (from sixteenth-century explorers to Charles Darwin and Alexander von Humboldt); forgeries and travel parodies (*Gulliver's Travels*); Romantic literature; the modern flâneur (Baudelaire); Thomas Cook's tours and travel journalism; travel literature by the late nineteenth-century and modernist writers (Flaubert, D. H. Lawrence, Graham Greene, W. H. Auden); political travel writing (George Orwell); contemporary best-selling travel books (Bruce Chatwin, Paul Theroux); and theoretical approaches to travel (postcolonialism, gender studies).[8] The survey is Anglocentric, by the editors' own admission, but it is useful for the purposes of discussing Brodsky's travel writing for two reasons. First, it points at some of the sociohistorical changes, as well as the evolvement of literary conventions, which inform Brodsky's imaginings of travel: the Ulysses narrative, "Sternism," the Romantic poets, the emergence of mass tourism, and Anglo-American modernist literature. And second, it invites the reader to approach travel writing in terms of a rather loose conception of a discursive practice rather than in terms of a strict definition of a literary genre.

Viewed from this perspective, travel writing encompasses not only travel essays but also reflections on travel represented by means of lyric poetry. Travel writing, then, as the term is used in this book, refers to Brodsky's poems and prose that either relate directly to a specific trip he made or reflect his travel experience on a less specified level. Furthermore, I occasionally also use travel "text" in the course of the discussion in order to emphasize the theoretical foundations of the scholarly position. This position draws from the acknowledgement that literary texts are "events" or "worldly," since texts are "a part of the social world, human life, and of course the historical moments in which they are located and interpreted," as Edward Said writes with the assertion that they are so "even when they appear to deny it."[9] Besides the meanings that the word "writing" (as a translation of the French *écriture*) has acquired in the theoretical formations of recent decades, the word's commonsensical meanings denote a process rather than a completed action, which captures the Saidian perception of a text's being-in-the-world, its "worldliness," and which, in turn, points a way to the contextualizing approaches applied to Brodsky's works throughout the book.

A brief outline of the history of Russian travel writing gives the impression of a literary practice as heterogeneous as the Anglophone overview outlined above. The first Russian travel narratives were medieval reports of pilgrimages (*khozhdenie*). The best-known secular medieval travel text was the fifteenth-century merchant Anafasii Nikitin's description of his journey to Persia and India. The sixteenth-century diplomats' reports (*stateinye spiski*) kept to diplomatic affairs; later they also touched on topics interesting to the court, such as gardening, theater, and hospitals. Some of the young men who were sent to Europe to receive an education—a practice initiated by Boris Godunov but continued more successfully by Peter I and Catherine II—turned their experiences to written travel accounts, the best known of which is P. A. Tolstoi's travel diary. An important change in Russian travel practices took place during Peter III's reign, when the nobility was freed from the obligation to serve the court, and members of the upper classes were able to take a full advantage of travel abroad. Princess E. P. Dashkova's diaries and D. I. Fonvisin's letters reflect this change. N. M. Karamzin's *Letters of a Russian Traveler* (1791) and A. N. Radishchev's *Journey from St. Petersburg to Moscow* (1790) established, as Andreas Schönle has recently put it, the Russian "fashion and genre," modeled after such European successes as Sterne's *A Sentimental Journey* and Charles Dupaty's *Letters on Italy* with their subjective and personal observations and emotional responses to travel and, in Karamzin's case, foreign lands.[10] At the beginning of the nineteenth century, travel writing became a popular and lucrative form. With the Russian Empire expanding, the new territories captured the Russian literary imagination. The travel narrative set in the Caucasus became a central topos of Russian Romantic literature, and, working on "Journey to Arzrum" in 1835, Pushkin, one of the champions of the poetic topos in the 1820s, was able to parody its prose outgrowth, the Russian Oriental journey.[11] In the nineteenth century there also emerged yet another subgenre of imaginary travel, the belletristic *progulka* (stroll) along the streets of Petersburg.[12] The writers later recognized as the elite of Russian modernism produced a mass of travel writing: Aleksandr Blok, Andrei Belyi, Nikolai Gumilev, Boris Pasternak, Osip Mandelstam, and Vladimir Mayakovsky reflected on their travel experience in both poetry and prose.[13] Italy was central to the Russian modernist imagination, but Gumilev and Belyi, for instance, also wrote about their trips to African countries, and Mayakovsky about his American experience.[14] The topic of travel flourished in early Soviet literature, ranging in the 1920s and 1930s from Boris Pil'niak's reflections on his trip to the United States in *O'kei: Amerikanskii roman* (*OK: American Novel*) to reportage and fiction by less well-known Soviet writers about industrial and agricultural progress within the Soviet state.[15] The highly personal, literary, and artistically ambitious treatment of travel, such as Mandelstam's travelogue *Journey to Armenia* (1930), would not have been published in the more rigid Stalinist years that followed, which is not to say that there were no travel accounts written or published: Il'f and Petrov's 1936 *Odnoetazhnaia Amerika* (*One-Storied America*) was one example.[16] In the Stalinist period traveling was, however, strictly controlled by the state, and while borders abroad were closed, domestic tourism was encouraged; Soviet *turizm* was patriotic tourism, which contributed to the construction of the Soviet identity.[17] In the post-Stalin period domestic travel became more laxly controlled.[18] It is this historical moment that Brodsky's traveling subject enters. Before and after the forced journey to the northern Norenskaia, the site of his eighteen-month internment, Brodsky took advantage of the various forms of the unofficial practices of post-Stalin travel, which informed the representation of travel in 1960s Soviet literature, film, and popular song, and which were reflected in Brodsky's poems set on geological expeditions, on the Baltic shore of Soviet Lithuania, and in the southern tourist resorts by the Black Sea.[19]

As these historical outlines of Russian and Anglophone travel literature indicate, the evolvement of Russian travel writing, in contrast with English-language travel literature, has been defined by restrictions and constraints on travel implemented by czarist rule and Soviet regimes, and consequently, the distinction between narratives of coercion and narratives based on voluntary displacement is seminal to any study of Russian travel writing. But while it is important to make the distinction between these two types of narratives, it is equally important to mark the peculiar dialectics between them in Russian cultural practices. Pushkin's exile by the Black Sea is a seminal model for fashioning a literary identity in collision with authoritarian rule in Russian cultural formations, while his *iuzhnye poemy* (southern poems) and the stanzas of Onegin's travels, written in the southern exile, drew from his opportunity to travel in the Caucasus and the southern regions of the Russian Empire; they were seminal to the evolution of Russian travel literature. In Pushkin's case the exilic identity is inseparable from the introduction of the lyric identity in a non-Russian setting, and both are equally important for Russian cultural mythologies. Brodsky's poetry and prose manifest this peculiar Russian dialectics of displacement transposed to the Cold War environment; while it is difficult to disassociate Brodsky's poems written in the northern internment (*ssylka*) from the significations of exile (*izgnanie*) in Russian intellectual formations, his travel accounts written in emigration outside the borders of the Soviet Union exhibit questions of displacement that is as much voluntary as coercive. The freedom to travel and to exploit non-native territories for literary purposes was granted to Brodsky by the coercion of exile, and it is the experience of exile and tourism—two major forms of displacement, often perceived as conflicting human conditions—that creates the crux of much of Brodsky's post-1972 writing.

During the decades Brodsky lived in emigration and performed a bulk of travel writing, the topic of travel attained increasing attention in Western academia and emerged, to quote the editors of *The Cambridge Companion*, as "a key theme of humanities and social sciences."[20] Together with scholarly interest in the concept of travel and the metaphorics of travel, which this interest induced in theoretical formations, there emerged a growing body of academic research focused on travel writing, on individual writers' travel accounts, and on the treatment of travel in literature in general.[21] The theoretical approaches to travel gained much from the scholarly experience provided by postcolonial and feminist critiques, for which the contribution of such critics as Edward Said, Gayatri Spivak, and Homi Bhabha has been paramount. Note that the theoretical foundations of these approaches, which have mostly evolved around the critique of the Euro- or Anglocentric positions of the Euro- or Anglocentric travel writing they explore, seem to fit poorly the study of a Russian poet's works, especially someone like Brodsky's, whose marginalized position in the Soviet empire does not conform to the paradigm of Eurocentric imperial power and its resistance, which these approaches presuppose.[22] Then again, applying these approaches to Brodsky's post-1972 works discloses the connection of his representational strategies to those that were dominant and shared by Russian and Euro-American metropolitan discourses; the articulation of the traveler's authoritative vision in Brodsky's travel narratives was shaped, especially in his non-European travel accounts, by Russian, Soviet, and European imperial knowledge.[23] By the same token, asking, as Dennis Potter does in his investigation of European travel writing, whether travel writing presents "an effort to overcome cultural distance through a protracted act of understanding" or whether it functions as a "vehicle for the expressions of Eurocentric conceit or racist intolerance" is not, despite that conceit's idiosyncratic functions in Russia, an entirely inappropriate point of departure in investigating Russian travel writing in general and Brodsky's travel writing in particular.[24]

Besides "understanding" and "intolerance," which Potter recognizes as the two basic attitudes to the "others" that travel writing inevitably produces, Patrick Holland and Graham Huggan have suggested a paradigm of a different kind. In their investigation of contemporary English-language travel writing they set forth to answer the question of "what happens to travel writing in an age of what Homi Bhabha calls 'transnational dissemination,' at a time when the idea of a national culture, or even 'culture' is under threat." They end up pointing at two major responses:

> At least two, more or less diametrically opposed, sets of responses are possible. First, travel writing can recognize the conflictedness of cultural origins, focusing not so much on encounters between the traveller and the target culture (or cultures) as on process of transculturation—of mutual exchange and modification—that takes place when different cultural forms collide or intersect. . . . The second set of responses involves the recognition of belatedness. It is no longer possible to tout a view of, say, "the English gentleman abroad" as if this gentleman—naturally, white—existed other than in myth. Yet this myth, precisely, matters and is adhered to with a vengeance, even though its effect is largely comic and its power obviously in decline. . . . These two responses are symptomatic of a "postimperial" era that has yet to deliver itself from the recrudescence of its beliefs.[25]

Brodsky's travel writing often discloses the processes of his own transculturation, while he also often focuses on the "conflictedness of cultural origins." *Watermark* exhibits the first of these tendencies remarkably; the travelogue to Istanbul is a powerful manifestation of the second. At the same time, much of Brodsky's travel writing falls into the category of belatedness and its recognition, as discussed by Holland and Huggan; what is more, Brodsky's belatedness, unlike that of his contemporary British and North American writers, was doubly felt. Brodsky's transculturation into the English language and North American academic environment was a transition from a stagnant imperial state, with a monolithic cultural hegemony over its domain, into a West where Europe's imperial domination of its former colonies was coming to an end and where the modernist canon, in many ways intertwined with metropolitan Europe's imperialism, had been challenged by a set of polemic aesthetical practices.[26] Coming from a Soviet Russian subculture, in which the concept of "postimperial" would have evoked an entirely different set of nostalgic meanings from what was emerging in his contemporary West, and in which the modernist values signified dissent from prevailing imperial realities and official aesthetic practices, Brodsky encountered a contemporaneity, which did not match his experience of the relation between the imperial and the aesthetically nonconformist. Brodsky's response to Western travel illustrates this incisively; he is constantly negotiating between the authentically imperial Eurocentric past and the present imperial realities of his two contemporary superpowers, Soviet and American; between the aesthetic norm of the neoclassical past and the contemporary absence of such a norm; and between the modernist singularity and the postmodern disintegration of the unique subject. The realization of these absences—Europe's imperial past, the neoclassical aesthetic norm, the modernist subject—induces the ironic yet utterly nostalgic attitude characteristic of Brodsky's travel writing. Underscored by a textual attitude, as well as by an awareness of the unavoidability of such attitude, Brodsky's travel poetry and prose appears to draw from a multitude of masculine identities seminal to the literary travel canon: the gentleman traveler, introduced to Russian-language literature by Fonvizin, Karamzin, and Radishchev; the lyric identity of Russian romantic poets construed against the backdrop of the Caucasus and the Black Sea; the Russian literary tourist in Europe, especially in Italy, from Viazemsky to Khodasevich; and the Anglophone modernist traveling writer, such as John Dos Passos, Ernest Hemingway, and W. H. Auden. The lyric subject of Brodsky's travel poems and the traveling male author of his travel prose are shaped by these literary identities.

Questions of empire, tourism, and nostalgia are foregrounded in one way or another in Brodsky's travel writing performed in emigration. I explore these concepts in regard to his travel texts through the study of tropes, strategies of identity construction, and politics of representation. My understanding and use of empire as a conceptual frame draws from those theoretical formations that foreground it as a discursive practice; my focus is not on the concept as defined in economic, military, or political terms but on how empires are imagined and articulated in literary and cultural practices.[27] Nostalgia appears in Brodsky's travel texts as a response to the many absences he encounters in the postcolonial/postmodern world outside the Soviet Union, and it is often accompanied with irony. Irony and nostalgia, as Linda Hutcheon reminds us in her essay on the uses of the two in postmodern aesthetics, often go hand in hand, while neither is a "quality of an object" but a "response of a subject—active, emotionally and intellectually engaged subject."[28] In Brodsky's case nostalgia appears to be a primary response, whereas irony often occurs as a response to nostalgia; his irony is an intellectual strategy and a representational means of encountering what Susan Stewart has recognized as the "necessarily insatiable demands of nostalgia."[29] The ironizing of nostalgia in Brodsky's travel writing is his way of responding to the belatedness of his subject position; it is a response to the realization that the position of a literary exile and traveling writer, which occupied a central role in modernist high culture, is challenged in the era of postmodern tourism and global mass migration.

The topic of nostalgia invokes the question of Brodsky's place in the modernist/postmodernist paradigm, a question several scholars have addressed from the viewpoint of Russian cultural practices, some of them rejecting postmodernism as a framework for discussing Brodsky's works, while others recognize in Brodsky the "forebear" of Russian postmodernism.[30] My approach to the topic of postmodern/ism is concerned more with placing Brodsky's in the *postmodern context* rather than in the *context of postmodernism*, an approach Thomas Epstein points at when he wonders whether "postmodernism as such [is] a part of a larger cultural paradigm, the Postmodern, marked by a sense of fragmentation and historical breakdown or transition, to which artists of various stripes (Joseph Brodsky is but one telling example) have reacted, each in his or her own way."[31] In other words, when questions of postmodern/ism are concerned, this book deals mainly with the ways Brodsky reacted to the postmodern condition he encountered in the West and how this encounter was reflected in his travel writing.[32]

Grounded on these methodological and theoretical guidelines, chapter 1 traces the development of modernist and postmodernist discourses on displacement and explores how the modernist metaphorics of travel informed

Brodsky's poetic imagination and his subject position since his early poetic output. In the poetry Brodsky wrote while still in the Soviet Union, his lyric identity was construed through images that were informed by Romantic and modernist conceptions of individualism and estrangement, while in his post-1972 travel texts the individualism and singularity of his authorial identity is repeatedly challenged by his encounters with the contemporary tourist condition. The rhetoric of amnesia he invokes, for instance, in his Brazilian travelogue "After a Journey, or Homage to Vertebrae" is just one exam-pleof Brodsky advancing the idea of the tourist condition threatening the condition of literature and the writing subject's creativity, a thought that concludes "K Evgenii" ("To Evgeny"), the penultimate poem in the cycle "Mexican Divertimento."

The relation between the concepts of empire and tourism, seminal to contemporary literary tourism, is manifest in Brodsky's travel writing, especially in the texts related to his encounters with non-European territories, which bring forth the dynamics between metropolitan discourses and the nonmetropolitan world. The aesthetic ideals and cultural mythologies that Brodsky rejuvenated in "A Guide to a Renamed City," analyzed in chapter 2, derive from the Russian eighteenth-century imperial discourse, informed by a conviction of the preeminence of Europe's cultural achievements and Russia's ability to catch up with these achievements. These ideological premises of Brodsky's dissenting politics of imperial nostalgia are displayed from an altogether different angle when he transposes them on the territories outside Europe and the United States in his poetic travelogue of Mexico and prose account of Brazil. In these Latin American encounters, discussed in detail in chapters 3 and 4, Brodsky constantly negotiates between two sets of imperial knowledge—the nostalgic embracing of the Russian and Euro-imperial and the rejection of the Soviet, and it is the tension between these two that creates the crux of his encounters with postcolonial realities. In "Cuernavaca," the first poem in the Mexican cycle, Brodsky refashions the Russian nineteenth-century elegiac identity in a postcolonial location. The postcolonial elegy historicizes the elegiac genre, and through the nostalgic attitude toward elegy, the poem also constructs a nostalgic attitude toward the colonial and imperial age, and what is more, it creates a nostalgic attitude toward imperial knowledge, in the production of which elegy participated in Europe's and Russia's imperial age. In "After a Journey" the lament for Europe's colonial past is articulated through representational strategies that bear striking affinity with what Mary Louise Pratt has termed as "the grumpy metropolitan discourse" of the "third-world blues," established in Western travel literature in the 1960s and 1970s, coinciding with the decolonization of African countries and liberation movements in the Americas.[33] What sets Brodsky's author apart from his European and North American contemporaries, however, is the historical perspective gained through the experience of a post-utopian society in the Soviet Union, which, in this instance, provides him with the doubly authoritative viewpoint to the "third world." This is a viewpoint he assumes in his creation of his metropolitan authorial subjectivity, a creation marked with ambiguity due to the awareness that because of his Soviet Russian background his own legitimacy as a metropolitan man of letters may be a subject of dispute in some Western metropolitan communities.

The theme of "historical lack" is a central theme of the metropolitan travel discourse in the postcolonial era, and Brodsky conjures it up in one playful line in the occasional verse titled "Rio Samba," in which Brazil is imagined as space with no historical signification. This metaphor is central to "Flight from Byzantium," Brodsky's travelogue of Istanbul and Turkey, and one of his most controversial essays. My reading of Brodsky's Oriental journey in chapter 5 is informed, above all, by Edward Said's *Orientalism*, which was, as I argue, the point of departure for Brodsky's polemic essay. When Brodsky turns his representational powers to describe Istanbul, his ironic detachment from what he sees and experiences is juxtaposed with his polemical engagement with the tradition of Russian and Western accounts of the Orient as well as with debates about Russia's place on the Orient-Occident axis. Despite the self-ironic play with literary conventions and the constant discursive conflicts that characterize Brodsky's writing, the author's assertive voice and authoritative vision reconstructs a coherent imaginative geography and history of "East" and "West," in the metaphysical hierarchy of which West equals time and East equals space—a reoccurring theme of the Orientalist myth. Eventually, Brodsky's irreverent appropriation of the Eurocentric conceit brings forth his own identity construction on what emerges as an imaginative "contact zone" of two metropolitan cultures, Eastern and Western.[34] Aware of the fact that Russia challenges the East-West dichotomy, the author of Brodsky's essay uses the liminality of his own Russian identity to *validate* his opinions about both East and West and to *invalidate* the critique of this dichotomy as expressed by Said and others.

If Brodsky's identity creation was most notably contested in his encounter with Istanbul, his textual encounters with Venice provided him with a discursive space where he could negotiate his hyphenated identity through culturally affirmative models. Brodsky's Russian poems about Venice rejuvenated the Russian *Venetophile* discourse, quoting a term the British historian John Pemble has coined in his study of British perceptions of Venice. Brodsky's appeal for the preservation of the city in *Watermark* performed the act of preserving the cultural significations invested in Venice in Russian and Euro-American metropolitan formations. But more than the collective significations related to the "world's heritage," Brodsky explores in *Watermark* the private meanings the city had for him. The narrative of longing, which Brodsky creates in the essay through his detailed recollections of his first encounters with Venice in the Soviet Union, demonstrates how the Acmeist formula of *longing for world culture* was transformed into a *longing for Leningrad culture*: the self-reflective reaching from peripheral Russia to the centers of Western culture made a full circle and turned from a longing for the postcolonial, popularized, decanonized, and deconstructed West into a longing for an ideal Russia of (Western) canons, hierarchies, and fixed identities. The Russian poems Brodsky wrote about Venice between 1973 and 1995 create a narrative of his transformation from a Soviet emigrant and a Leningrad poet into a Russian-American writer and metropolitan intellectual, and *Watermark*'s fragmented autobiography narrates this transformation in English-language prose. Drawing on Homi Bhabha's theoretical thinking, chapter 6 presents an analysis of each Russian-language poem Brodsky wrote about Venice with a focus on the abundance of intertextual allusions and references, which exhibit the speaker's cultural knowledge and which, when read next to *Watermark*, display the English-language essay's arresting and troublesome translation, in which cultural differences are staged rather than transcended. In the geopolitical landscape of postcolonial postmodernity, Venice became the site of the unique reinvention of Brodsky's lyric self; his Venice in *Watermark* emerges as the space in-between, a "third space," quoting Homi Bhabha's term, it is a site of rediscovery and reinvention where a fixed identity is transformed into a hybrid and more fluid subjectivity.[35]

1

Exile, Tourist, Traveler

The first critical approaches to Brodsky's post-1972 travel texts were overshadowed by the modernist mystification of exile.[1] Taking their cue from Brodsky's own poetic similes, the critics would repeatedly make the same literary analogies and cultural references: Ulysses, Ovid, Dante, Pushkin, Mandelstam—the canonized prototypes of Western and Russian literary exiles. Peter Vail's review of what he calls Brodsky's *zhanr puteshestviia* (travel genre) outlines this approach: "The thing is that Joseph Brodsky is not only a traveler [*puteshestvennik*] but also an exile [*izgnannik*] (the literary orientation is again, after all, the citizen of the Eternal City, Ovid)."[2] George L. Kline discusses Brodsky's poetic travel texts inspired by European cities from the same perspective and observes, quoting Lev Loseff, how in these "poems of exile,"[3] "the local color of all these places—with special stress of their architecture—appears in one or another of his [Brodsky's] poems. But, as Loseff has noted, the role and status of a traveler or tourist is quite different from that of an exile, even though both are 'away from home.' The traveler looks around him with greedy eyes; the exile looks rather within himself at the receding image of his homeland,' the traveler sees many countries, the exile sees only one: '*non*-homeland.' Despite Brodsky's planetary displacements since June 1972—Loseff concludes—he has not traveled but has simply *lived in exile*."[4] In a brief account of Brodsky's poetic cycle "V Anglii" ("In England"), Gerald Smith does not emphasize Brodsky's exilic viewpoint but is eager to point out that the viewpoint is not that of a tourist, either. Smith rejects this reading by observing that "we are hearing from someone who has penetrated into the fastnesses of ordinary English life rather than being in the country as a tourist."[5] Writing about Brodsky's Istanbul essay, "A Flight from Byzantium," David Bethea observes how "Brodsky comes to Istanbul not as a Western tourist or journalist but as a belated representative of Mandelstam's Hellas."[6] While Bethea's observation is a valid assessment of Brodsky's identity creation and its roots, the comparison between Brodsky and Mandelstam foregrounds Brodsky's status as a Russian writer in exile and successor of the modernist tradition, but it also overlooks the significance of Brodsky's travel account of Istanbul as an articulation of contemporary literary tourism.

Apart from the *biograficheskii fakt* (biographical fact) of Brodsky's exile, these readings of Brodsky's travel texts draw from a modernist understanding of literature, in which exile, literature, and authorial subjectivity are inseparably associated with each other. In this modernist conception, literature is perceived as a metaphysical country and writers as its displaced citizens, whose very displacement functions as the ideological premise informing their art, while their art informs their displacement; in other words, exile conditions literary creativity. Malcolm Bradbury outlines this metaphysics of modernism and exile in "The Cities of Modernism," an essay included in the 1976 anthology *Modernism: 1890–1930*, published in the Pelican Guides to European Literature:

> Much Modernist art has taken its stance from, gained its perspectives out of, a certain kind of distance, an exiled posture—a distance from local origins, class allegiances, the specific obligations and duties of those with an assigned role in cohesive culture. . . . Thus frequently it is emigration or exile that makes for membership of the modern country of arts, which has been heavily traveled by many great writers—Joyce, Lawrence, Mann, Brecht, Auden, Nabokov. It is a country that has come to acquire its own language, geography, focal communities, places of exile—Zürich during the First World War, New York during the Second. The writer himself becomes a member of a wandering, culturally inquisitive group—by enforced exile (like Nabokov's after the Russian revolution) or by design and desire. The place of art's very making can become an ideal distant city, where the creator counts, or the chaos is fruitful, the *Weltgeist* flows.[7]

Brodsky himself appropriated this geographic trope of modernism extensively. One such instance was the public letter published in the *New York*

Times Magazine in October 1972, a few months after he had settled in the United States at the University of Michigan. The letter, one of Brodsky's first attempts to reconcile with his recent emigration and exilic condition in published form, was part of an eight-page feature article, which introduced Brodsky to the American audience with an excerpt from Frida Vigdorova's transcript of Brodsky's 1964 trial in Soviet court and three photographs of the poet. The feature was titled with a quotation from Brodsky's letter: "A Writer is a Lonely Traveler." The text underneath the two photographs of Brodsky next to the headline read: "Traveler: Brodsky in 1964 (*top*) during internment on a farm near Archangel, and at the University of Michigan where he is now poet-in-residence"; the latter shows Brodsky flying a Frisbee on an American university campus. The letter itself is a touching account of the author's recent emigration with its unavoidably tragic underpinnings disclosing the posture that became a hallmark of Brodsky's future émigré works. It evokes the posture of a "foreigner," or "dissident," as Julia Kristeva imagined the displaced intellectual in the 1984 "A New Type of Intellectual: The Dissident"; aloof, seemingly indifferent and arrogant in his effort to hide the "secret wound," the "foreigner," as Kristeva writes, "holds to what he lacks, to the absence."[8] Meanwhile, the letter also shows how Brodsky made provocative use of modernist imagery of displacement and vocabulary of travel:

> I have come to America and I am going to live here. I hope that I will be able to do my work, i.e., write poetry, as before. I have seen a new land, but the sky is the same. Of course, the future inspires greater concern than ever before. Because if I could not write before it was explainable by internal rather than external circumstances. The doubts which possessed me and led to silence from time to time are, I think, familiar to every serious writer.—But I also foresee another reason for paralysis: the presence of a different linguistic environment.—In order to write well in a language you have to hear it—in taverns, buses and grocery stores. I have not yet invented a way to fight this. But I hope that a man's language travels with him. And I hope that I will take the Russian language wherever I go. In the final analysis it is all God's will. To paraphrase a German writer who found himself in a similar situation 35 years ago, "Die Russische Dichtung ist da wo ich bin."[9]

The reference to Thomas Mann (the German writer Brodsky paraphrases) evokes the canon of twentieth-century European displaced writers and literary exiles, which, together with the modernist metaphorics of travel, reveals the makings of Brodsky's authorial position—his representation of his authorial identity and exile draws on the modernist discourse of displacement, the conflation of writing, travel, and exile.[10] The *New York Times* publication marked Brodsky's entrance into the high-cultural exilic canon, and both Brodsky's own text and the feature article edited by the magazine participate in the production of the modernist trope of exile.

In "The Condition We Call Exile," a speech written for a conference of émigré writers fifteen years after the letter to the *Times*, and published in *On Grief and Reason*, Brodsky attempts to redirect his approach away from the significations exile has in canonical literature and to situate the exilic experience in the context of global migration and the displacement of peoples. An exilic writer is no longer a traveler but a privileged immigrant. In this speech Brodsky seems to take up the challenge that Edward Said, Brodsky's contemporary and another American immigrant intellectual, set forward a few years earlier in "Reflections on Exile," published initially in *Granta* in 1984 and many times since. Said's essay is one of the most influential reassessments of the exilic condition in recent decades. It starts out as a critique of the humanistic understanding of exile, advocated, for instance, by George Steiner, who looks at exile as aesthetic gain and a seminal experience in producing twentieth-century Western literature. Said challenges Steiner's concept of Western literature as "extraterritorial" (that is, "unworldly," in Said's own idiolect) and sums up the cultural and social changes that have made it necessary to rethink the position of an exiled writer in relation to the contemporary world:

> In other ages, exiles had similar cross-cultural and transnational visions, suffered the same frustrations and miseries, performed the same elucidating and critical tasks—brilliantly affirmed, for instance, in E. H. Carr's classic study of the nineteenth-century Russian intellectuals clustered around Hertzen, *The Romantic Exiles*. But the difference between earlier exiles and those of our own time is, it bears stressing, scale: our age—with its modern warfare, imperialism, and the quasi-theological ambitions of totalitarian rulers—is indeed the age of the refugee, the displaced person, mass immigration.[11]

The crux of Said's essay is to think of exile outside the canonized literary discourses: "To concentrate on exile as a contemporary political punishment, you must therefore map territories of experience beyond those mapped by the literature of exile itself. You must first set aside Joyce and Nabokov and think instead of the uncountable masses for whom UN agencies have been created" (ibid., 175).

Brodsky's "The Condition We Call Exile" starts out as what seems to be an affirmative response to the changes in the social and historico-political circumstances brought up by Said. Brodsky sets out to question the myth of the suffering exiled writer by drawing attention to other forms of contemporary global displacement, referring to those whom "nobody has ever counted . . . and nobody, including the UN relief organizations, ever will: coming in millions, they elude computation and constitute what is called—for want of a better term or higher degree of compassion—migration."[12] But after this initially radical gesture Brodsky takes a more conventional stance. Despite his attempt to approach the concept of exile in the contemporary global context and outside the realm of literature, he remains imprisoned in his Arnoldian understanding of the ethical hierarchy between literature and society: "We must somehow maintain that literature is the only form of moral insurance that a society has" (*GR*, 23). In order to agree with Brodsky one has to accept his canonical definition of "literature" and share his firm belief in the moral supremacy of that canon: Keats, Miłosz, Musil, Ovid, Dante, Joyce—these are the names that constitute "literature" for him in this essay and elsewhere.[13] Literary high culture and its practitioners, himself included, are Brodsky's primary interest and concern, not the "territories of experience beyond those mapped by the literature of exile itself," as Said demands. Brodsky's point of departure is Said's critique of the modernist concept of exile, but unlike Said he does not challenge the concept as a discursive practice or an ideological position. Instead of re-politicizing or re-historicizing modernist exile, Brodsky de-politicizes and de-historicizes it by concluding: "For the . . . truth of the matter is that exile is a metaphysical condition" (*GR*, 25). Brodsky, then, reaffirms the Steinerian viewpoint of exile as aesthetic gain, whereas Said seeks to radically alter it.[14] Aware of the historical changes in the exiled writer's position, Brodsky's response to it is an ironic lament: "Whether he likes it or not, *Gastarbeiters* and refugees of any stripe effectively pluck the orchid out of an exiled writer's lapel" (*GR*, 23). All in all, Brodsky's essay bespeaks nostalgia for an era when writers, and especially writers in exile, had an elitist position in Western societies. The essay bespeaks nostalgia for the privileged position literature enjoyed in Western society before literature had "taken on the dimensions of a demographic phenomenon" (*GR*, 28), as he writes. In other words, Brodsky's nostalgia is directed toward the Western literary scene dominated by high modernism, which, to follow Fredric Jameson's outline, prevailed until the 1960s, by which time it had become established in academic institutions and challenged by the new aesthetic practices recognized as postmodernist art and literature.[15] And even further than that, Brodsky's nostalgia encompasses the era of *The Romantic Exiles,* which offered the models for modernist literary and exilic identities.

The modernist conceptions of exile and literature, which inform both the critical reception of Brodsky's works and his own understanding of literature and authorial subjectivity, draw from and contribute to the hierarchy of twentieth-century literary displacements.[16] In this literary hierarchy the exile occupies the top, and the traveler is a good contender, whereas the tourist hardly qualifies. The voice of the "refugees of any stripe" is seldom heard. The anti-tourist discourse occupies a solid place in these formations, drawing from the literary practices of the Romantic era. One of the first instances of the dismissive attitude toward "tourists" in European literature was in William Wordsworth's 1799 poem "The Brothers," which relates to the popularity of the Lake District among English travelers: "These Tourists, heaven preserve us! Needs must live / A profitable life: some glance along, / Rapid and gay, as if the earth were air, / And they were butterflies to wheel about / Long as the summer lasted."[17] In George Sand's *Lettres d'un voyageur,* written in 1834, she directs her scornful wit at the English "touristes pneumatiques."[18] Prince Viazemsky reflects the general unpopularity of English visitors to Italy when he writes in his Venetian journal that a head had been cut out of a painting in one of the Trevisa churches—"no one knows by whom and how, but they suspect English tourists."[19] Some fifty years later in a diary entry on his 1913 stay in Constantinople, Nikolai Gumilev makes a distinction between authentic travel experience, manifested in his desire for adventure, and "tourist" behavior, associated with commerce and sightseeing: "I am not a tourist. What do I care after Hagia Sophia for the buzzing bazaar with its tempting silks and beads, coquettish peers, or even the incomparable cypresses at the graveyard. I'm going to Africa."[20] The assertive self-definition through a negation, "I am not a tourist," in Gumilev's diary entry illuminates the modernist moment, which Helen Carr, writing from the viewpoint of English-language literature, situates in the early years of the twentieth century, when it became an increasingly common trait in travel accounts "to put a distance between [the author] as traveler and the burgeoning droves of tourists."[21]

The negative meanings invested in tourism in modernist discourses acquire particular significance in Russia, where the discourse on tourism evolved somewhat differently from that in the West and acquired specific Soviet significations. In the late 1920s *turizm* became appropriated as a "Soviet" project, and by the 1960s it had become a mass movement. In the Stalinist era travel was supposed to "create a correct understanding of the 'socialist homeland' by investing historical sites and 'exotic' spaces with Soviet significance," as Anne Gorsuch describes the patriotic endeavors of Soviet *turizm* and its contribution to the construction of the Soviet identity.[22] "Through hilly paths / Through swamps and bushes / Tourists force their way / Through unknown places" as the lyrics march on in V. I. Lebedev-Kumach's "Pesnia turistov" ("Tourists' Song").[23] In the post-Stalin period semi-official travel practices were common among the intelligentsia, while millions of Soviet citizens traveled on trips and excursions arranged by Soviet tourist officials. The word *turist* was reserved for these masses; it functioned as a model for the sporty and active Soviet citizen, a model that carried over to the popular romantic *bard* culture, as captured in the youth magazine *Yunost'*: "They [bards] were young, clear, fresh voices. And [the songs] were sung not by artists but by students, engineers, teachers, who in their free time were tourists, scuba divers, and travelers."[24]

Although the socioeconomic structure and ideological framework of the Soviet tourist phenomenon differed from postwar Western tourism, the two did have something in common: Tourism concerned masses of people. In the West this meant that by the 1970s tourism had become an object of anthropological research; in the now classic *The Tourist: A New Theory of the Leisure Class* (1976), Dean MacCannel lays out a semiotic approach to the tourist experience and creates a historical narrative of tourism, which in many points coincides with the history of travel writing:

> Self-discovery through a complex and sometimes arduous search for an Absolute Other is a basic theme of our civilization, a theme supporting an enormous literature: Odysseus, Aeneas, the Diaspora, Chaucer, Christopher Columbus, *Pilgrim's Progress*, Gulliver, Jules Verne, Western ethnography, Mao's Long March. . . . It grows and develops, arriving at a kind of final flowering in modernity. What begins as the proper activity of a *hero* (Alexander the Great) develops into the goal of a socially organized *group* (the Crusaders), into the mark of status of an entire social *class* (the Grand Tour of the British "gentleman"), eventually becoming *universal experience* (the tourist).[25]

MacCannel's semiotic approach was partially a response to the anti-tourist discourse, which the emergence of mass tourism after World War II prompted, and in which the word "tourist" had negative connotations similar to those it had in nineteenth-century travel literature. One of the characteristics of this discourse is the denigration of the tourist at the traveler's expense. Daniel J. Boorstin's *The Image; or, What Happened to the American Dream*, the influential 1961 study of American postwar society, included a chapter on tourism titled "From Traveler to Tourist: The Lost Age of Travel."[26] What characterizes tourist behavior, Boorstin argues, is tourists' fascination with the inauthentic and the superficial, with what he calls the "pseudo-event." Since Boorstin Western tourism has been repeatedly associated with inauthenticity, as, for instance, by Umberto Eco in the 1975 American travelogue *Travels in Hyperreality*, where the exploration of the "fake" and the "imitation" begins when you go "beyond the Museum of Modern Art and the art galleries, and you enter another universe, the preserve of the average family, the tourist, the politician."[27] This type of critique of tourism often reveals a nostalgic longing for the age of "real" travel made impossible by tourism.

The American literary critic Paul Fussell's popular 1980 study of Anglo-American interwar literary travel draws from this nostalgia (inspired by Evelyn Waugh's 1946 travel book, *When the Going was Good*) and sums up its basic stance: "I am assuming that travel is now impossible and tourism is all we have left."[28] The "now" refers to the end of the 1970s, and the "we" to Americans and, presumably, other Westerners of Fussell's educational background and social status. For Fussell the "golden age of travel" was the 1920s and 1930s, when British and American writers such as Graham Greene, Aldous Huxley, George Orwell, John Dos Passos, Ernest Hemingway, and the Auden generation of poets traveled extensively and, in terms of travel literature, prolifically. Jonathan Culler's 1981 article "Semiotics of Tourism" critiques Boorstin and Fussell and follows MacCannel's semiotic approach. Culler attacks the anti-tourist discourse and claims that "the repetition and displacement of the opposition between tourist and traveler suggests that these are not so much historical categories as terms integral to tourism. The historical explanations are excuses for what travelers always do: feel superior to other travelers."[29] But despite these critical voices, the semiotic embrace of tourism has not abolished the popular hierarchies where the tourist always appears lesser than the traveler. Neither has it abolished those modernist discourses where this dichotomy functions as a powerful ideological metaphor. Brodsky is among those authors whose travel writing proves this point.

To explore the works of a Russian exile writer not only in the context of an exilic but also a touristic experience disturbs the popular hierarchies outlined above in a way that may at first seem unacceptable. Caren Kaplan's investigation of the modernist and postmodernist discourses of exile and tourism may help in understanding why this is so:

> The commonsense definitions of exile and tourism suggest that they occupy opposite poles in the modern experience of displacement: exile implies coercion; tourism celebrates choice. Exile connotes the estrangement of the individual from an original community; tourism claims community on a global scale. Exile plays a role in Western culture's narratives of political formation and cultural identity stretching back to the Hellenic era. Tourism heralds postmodernism; it is a product of the rise of consumer culture, leisure, and technological innovation. Culturally, exile is implicated in modernist high art formations while tourism signifies the very obverse position as the mark of everything commercial and superficial.[30]

In Kaplan's view, tourism and the travel industry typically represent the postmodern consumer society, which Fredric Jameson described in his widely anthologized 1982 essay.[31] The collectivity and conformity of the masses associated with tourism challenges the modernist understanding of the subject's individuality and uniqueness, as Kaplan writes:

> Euro-American Modernisms celebrate singularity, solitude, estrangement, alienation, and aestheticized excisions of location in favor of locale—that is, the 'artist in exile' is never 'at home,' always existentially alone, and shocked by the strain of displacement into significant experimentations and insights.[32]

Viewed against this modernist position, the tourist condition, as discussed by Kaplan and analyzed by MacCannel, seems to incorporate the "end of individualism" as envisioned by Jameson.[33]

Due to a long history of oppressive regimes and implementation of travel restrictions, the concept of "exile," the Russian *izgnanie* (banishment, expulsion, exile) or *ssylka* (internal exile, deportation), plays an exceptionally important role in Russian narratives of cultural identity.[34] Aleksander Pushkin is the mythical key figure in these formations. The comparisons between

Brodsky and Pushkin in critical literature write Brodsky into these narratives and establish his place in the Russian literary canon, an exercise that Brodsky himself instigated by his poetics of intertextuality.[35] This approach, when applied to Brodsky's travel texts, however, produces the type of criticism that cuts these texts off from their time and place, and relates them solely to the metaphysical discourses on exile. And yet, Brodsky's post-1972 travel texts, with their reflections on contemporaneity, are a response as much to an exilic as to a tourist condition. But in order to analyze Brodsky's textual responses to Western travel practices, and in order to consider how the tourist condition is reflected in Brodsky's representation of his traveling identity, his travel texts have to be read against the concepts of travel, exile, and authorial subjectivity as represented in Brodsky's poetry written in the Soviet Union.

Traveling the Soviet Union: Expeditions, *Autsaiderstvo*, and Exilic Pose

In the post-Stalin era of the late 1950s and the 1960s, the era of Brodsky's literary coming-of-age, the territory of the Soviet empire offered a multiethnic and multicultural space for Soviet tourists and travelers to exploit. The dream of travel and the liberalization of travel practices informed Russian high and popular culture in many ways, while the opportunities of creating contacts with Westerners traveling to Russia also widened the cultural space of Russian intellectuals. Travel was a popular topic in Soviet film and literature, as well as in the popular *bard* songs in the "epoch of movement," as Petr Vail' and Aleksander Genis refer to this period in their memoir, *60-e: Mir sovetskogo cheloveka* (*The '60s: The World of the Soviet Man*).[36]

The geological expedition, popular among Soviet youth, was a form of travel that involved certain bureaucratic formalities but was not dependent on a steady job, as trips to tourist camps and rest homes usually were. One of the popular films of the Thaw period, Mihail Kalatozov's 1959 *Neotpravlennoe pis'mo* (*Unsent Letter*) captures a group of young Soviet expeditionists on the Siberian tundra and their doomed fight with nature, found to be "alien to socialist humanism" by the more conservative Soviet critics.[37] *Dikie*, that is "wild" travelers, referred to a common practice of traveling alone without *putevka*, a pass or voucher to a tourist camp or sanatorium, while *tvorcheskaia kommandirovka* (artistic work assignment) was practiced by members of the creative intelligentsia, who were able to take advantage of official permissions and funds in arranging trips to places out of reach for most Soviet citizens.[38] Anatolii Naiman captures this form of travel in a memoir of his 1967 trip to the Black Sea, on assignment from the Moscow journal *Pioner* and partially in the company of Joseph Brodsky, who, according to Naiman, was also on assignment from the equivalent Leningrad journal, *Koster*:

> All the newspapers and magazines had special funds they could use to send a writer to some part or other of the Soviet Union in order to do a piece about it. As a rule, the editors specified exactly what they wanted. Sometimes, though, as with me, they let the writer choose. Many of my friends and colleagues had taken advantage of these relatively scanty perks to travel the length and breadth of the country. When you got back you had to account for your expenditures and plop some sort of article on the editor's desk. Which didn't mean they had to publish it, of course.[39]

This type of literary travel, then, offered Soviet intellectuals a discursive space for reflecting on the Soviet Union and its realities while negotiating the borders of what was officially accepted.[40] The travel experience gathered on geological expeditions, the *tvorcheskaia kommandirovka,* and the voluntary flights to the Soviet south and the Baltic seafront—all these forms of Soviet travel are reflected in Brodsky's 1960s poetry.[41] Mapping out Brodsky's trips and travels through the geographical points of references of his early 1960s poetry creates an imaginative space, which covers a large part of the Soviet territory, with Leningrad as its center and the following places as the outer regions: Yakutsk, Kazakhstan, Estonia, Moscow, the Karelian isthmus, Irkutsk, Tarusa, Baltiisk (Pillau), Kaliningrad, Pskov, and, finally, Norenskaia, the site of Brodsky's internment in the Arkhangel'sk region.[42] Some of these poems relate to the speaker's immediate environment or the idea of travel only through their dating. "Pamiati E. A. Baratynskogo" ("In memory of E. A. Baratynskii") and "Vitezslav Nezval" are dated "June 19, 1961, Yakutsk" and "June 29, 1961, Yakutia," respectively, as if to manifest the speaker's detachment from his actual environment, contrasted with the European and Russian literary space that the poems' subject matter, unrelated to travel, conjure up. At the same time, "Uezzhai, uezzhai, uezzhai" ("Away, away, away"), a poem with the same date and place as the one dedicated to the Czech writer Vítěslav Nezval, addresses the theme of travel and sets the speaker in the geographical space of Kazakhstan. Such early poems as "Pesenka o Fede Dobrovol'skom" ("A song for Fedia Dobrovol'skii") and "Vospominania" ("Memories") set the speaker on expeditions by the White Sea.[43] In the undated "Kniga" ("Book") the expedition experience serves as an impetus for an ironic comparison of life to a book with a happy ending; the conspicuously optimistic first line, "Putshestvennik, nakonets, obretaet nochleg" (The traveler, finally, finds a place to stay overnight), is debunked immediately with the following line: "Chestniaga-blondin raspravliaetsia s podletsom" (The honest blond has to deal with [or lie down with] a villain). This sets the tone for the rest of the poem's sardonic conclusions about the facts of life, such as:

> Экономика стабилизируется,
> социолог отбрасывает сомненья—
> Все самолеты благополучно возвращаются на аэродром.
> Все капитаны
> отчетливо видят землю.
> Глупцы умнеют. Лгуны перестают врать.
> У подлеца, естественно, ничего не вышло.[44]
>
> [The economy is being stabilized, / sociologists give up doubts—All airplanes successfully return to airports. / All captains / see the land clearly. / Fools get wiser. Liars stop lying. / And nothing, of course, came out of whatever the villain was up to.]

Apart from the actual travel experience Brodsky gathered on geological expeditions and *kommandirovkas*, the representation of travel in his poetry was informed by post-Stalin Soviet cultural practices, as well as readings of Russian and Western canonical literature. The 1959 "Pilgrimy" ("Pilgrims") anticipated the unconventional, from the Soviet viewpoint, framework of cultural references Brodsky's poetry was headed for—the poem's epigraph is a quotation of two lines from Shakespeare's Sonnet 27: "For then my thoughts, from far where I abide, / Intend a zealous pilgrimage to thee." Meanwhile, the text itself captures the overall sense of movement emblematic of Soviet culture of the time:[45]

> Мимо ристалищ, капищ,
> мимо храмов и баров,
> мимо шикарных кладбищ,
> мимо больших базаров,
> мира и горя мимо,
> мимо Мекки и Рима,

синим солнцем палимы
идут по земле пилигримы.
(1:21)

[Past stadiums, sanctuaries, / past temples and bars, / past luxury graveyards, / past large bazaars / past the world and sorrow / past Mecca and Rome, / scorched by the blue sun, / the pilgrims travel across the earth.]

This early eulogy of movement and representation of the enthusiastic "pilgrims" has, however, a double-edged meaning: The pilgrims move on with "eyes filled with sunset" and "hearts filled with sunrise," while the landscape they leave behind communicates a perception contradictory to the apparent optimism of the march onward: The "deserts behind them sing," and the "birds around them cry out" that "the world remains the same," "deceptive," "eternal," "perhaps comprehensible, but nevertheless, endless," which leads to the poem's concluding thought:

. . . И, значит, остались только
иллюзия и дорога.
И быть над землей закатам,
и быть над землей рассветам.
Удобрить ее солдатам.
Одобрить ее поэтам.
(1:21)

[And, so, there remained only / illusion and the road. / And let there be sunset in the world, / and let there be dawn in the world. / Let soldiers fertilize the earth. / Let poets make it famous.]

This early poetic realization of reality, specifically Soviet reality, being an illusion, grew into a more explicitly articulated sentiment of the lyric subject's disillusion and displacement in such early 1960s poems as "Liubi proezdom rodinu druzei" ("Love the homeland of friends while passing through"), "Ia kak Uliss" ("I'm like Ulysses"), and "Instruktsiia opechalennym" ("Instructions to those who grieve"). The first and third stanzas of "Love the homeland" capture in an elegiac tone the boredom of travel and the monotony of Soviet provinces:

> Люби проездом родину друзей.
> На станциях батоны покупая,
> о прожитом бездумно пожалей,
> к вагонному окошку прилипая.
>
> Отходят поезда от городов,
> приходит моментальное забвенье,
> десятилетья искренних трудов,
> но вечного, увы, неоткровенья.
> (1:70)
>
> [Love the homeland of friends while passing through. / Buying a bread loaf at the station, / feel sorry for the past thoughtlessly, / sticking to the train car's window. // The trains leave towns / and momentary oblivion arrives, / decades of sincere labor, / but, alas, eternal non-revelation.[46]]

The speaker's relation with *rodina* (homeland) is communicated through the uncommon combination of words in "rodina druzei" (homeland of friends). This dissociates the speaker from the patriotic discourse that "liubi rodinu" (love your homeland) invokes. In the fourth stanza the boredom with travel grows into a realization of travel not providing discoveries but disclosing life's disillusionment:

> Да что там жизнь! Под перестук колес
> взбредет на ум печальная догадка,
> что новый недоверчивый вопрос
> когда-нибудь их вызовет обратно.
> (1:70)
>
> [And what about life! Out of wheels' tapping / a sad thought gets into one's head / that a new distrustful question / will some time call them back.]

In the final stanza this skepticism turns, however, into something the speaker full-heartedly embraces as a position in life, and the desire for travel, for constantly moving on, is acknowledged as the lyric subject's sense of permanent displacement:

Так, поезжай. Куда? Куда-нибудь,
скажи себе: с несчастьями дружу я.
Гляди в окно и о себе забудь.
Жалей проездом родину чужую.
(1:70)

[So, set off. Where to? Somewhere, / Say to yourself: I'm friends with misfortunes. / Glance out of window and forget about yourself. / Feel sorry for the strange homeland while passing through.]

The "homeland" is no longer that of "friends," but it is "strange," and with that the speaker dissociates himself from the provincial Soviet country. The Romantic "kuda?" (where to?) and the elegiac displacement disclose his alienation from his native land. A similar desire to travel and sense one's displacement is conveyed in the 1961 "I'm like Ulysses":

Зима, зима, я еду по зиме,
куда-нибудь по видимой отчизне,
гони меня, ненастье, по земле,
хотя бы вспять, гони меня по жизни.

Ну, вот Москва и утренний уют
в арбатских переулках парусинных,
и чужаки по-прежнему снуют
в январских освещенных магазинах.
(1:136)

[Winter, winter, I travel through winter, / to somewhere through the visible fatherland, / chase me, bad weather, along the earth, / even if backwards, chase me through life. // Well, here's Moscow, its early morning coziness / on Arbat's canvas lanes, / and strangers as always dash about / in January's lit-up stores.]

This is one of Brodsky's early 1960s poems about Moscow, and the observations of Moscow's street life, more cosmopolitan than in Brodsky's native Leningrad, soon turn into a contemplation of the lyric subject's sense of non-belonging and of his impatience with his own restlessness:

И желтизна разрозненных монет,
и цвет лица криптоновый все чаще,
гони меня, как новый Ганимед
хлебну зимой изгнаннической чаши

и не пойму, откуда и куда
я двигаюсь, как много я теряю
во времени, в дороге повторяя:
ох, Боже мой, какая ерунда.
(1:136)

[And the yellow of odd coins, / and the color of my face is all the time more krypton-like, / chase me, like a new Ganymede / I drink down (endure) in the winter from the cup of exile // and do not understand from where and to where / I move, how much I lose / in time on the road repeating: / oh, my God, such nonsense.]

The image of "chasha" (the cup) refers to the myth of Ganymede, a Trojan youth famed for his beauty, whom Zeus abducted from Phrygia. Once on Olympus, Ganymede was made the cupbearer for the gods. Rather than the homoerotic connotations that the myth, through Ganymede's association as Zeus's lover, invokes, and that Ovid, for instance, makes use of in *Metamorphoses*, the poetic self-fashioning focuses on Ganymede's exilic displacement on Olympus. In the sixth stanza the speaker finds a point of cultural reference in the Romantic canon of English poetry:

Мелькай, мелькай по сторонам, народ,
я двигаюсь, и, кажется отрадно,
что, как Улисс, гоню себя вперед,
но двигаюсь по-прежнему обратно.
(1:136)

[Flash by, flash by on the sides, people, / I move, and, it seems pleasingly, / that like Ulysses, I drive myself forward, / but move, as before, backward.]

The "Uliss" (Ulysses) most likely refers to Alfred Tennyson's poem of the same name.[47] Brodsky's poem seems to respond particularly to the following lines of Tennyson's poetic monologue, in which Odysseus articulates his decision to leave Ithaca:

> I cannot rest from travel: I will drink
> Life to the lees: All times I have enjoy'd
> Greatly, have suffer'd greatly, both with those
> That loved me, and alone; on shore, and when
> Thro' scudding drifts the rainy Hyades
> Vext the dim sea: I am become a name;
> For always roaming with a hungry heart
> Much have I seen and known; cities of men
> And manners, climates, councils, governments,
> Myself not least, but honour'd of them all;
> And drunk delight of battle with my peers,
> Far on the ringing plains of windy Troy.
> I am a part of all that I have met;
> Yet all experience is an arch wherethro'
> Gleams that untravell'd world whose margin fades
> For ever and for ever when I move.
> How dull it is to pause, to make an end,
> To rust unburnish'd, not to shine in use![48]

Tennyson's late-Romantic desire to travel and move is captured almost word for word by Brodsky's imagery of movement: Tennyson's "I will drink / Life to the lees" and the "plains of windy Troy" are recaptured by Brodsky's Trojan Ganymede and "drinking down (or enduring) the winter by the exilic bowl." Tennyson's thrust forward in "How dull it is to pause, to make an end" is transformed in Brodsky's poem into a sense of aimless and purposeless wandering, which discloses the futility and disillusion of travel in the lyric subject's concluding realization that he is "moving, as always, backwards."

In the 1962 "Instructions to those who grieve," the metropolitan speaker experiences the Soviet provinces of Siberia with the stale water and moldy snacks at the airport cafeteria, acknowledging his "fathomless solitude" and dreaming of an escape:

> Я ждал автобус в городе Иркутске,
> пил воду, замурованную в кране,
> глотал позеленевшие закуски

в ночи в аэродромном ресторане.
Я пробуждался от авиагрома
и танцевал под гул радиовальса,
потом катил я по аэродрому
и от земли печально отрывался.
И вот летел над облаком атласным,
себя, как прежде, чувствуя бездомным,
твердил, вися над бездною прекрасной:
все дело в одиночестве бездонном.
(1:172)

[I was waiting for a bus in the city of Irkutsk, / drinking water, imprisoned in the tap, / gulping down moldy snacks / at night in the airport restaurant. / I woke up to the aerothunder / and dancing to the rumble of a radio waltz, / then I bowled past the airport / and parted from the earth in grief. / And there I was flying above the silky clouds / feeling, as before, homeless, / and kept repeating, hanging above the beautiful abyss: / it's all about fathomless solitude.]

In the final four lines of the poem the speaker's experience of geological expeditions and sense of geography give rise to the poem's central paradox of the vastness of Soviet space being a cul-de-sac for an individual inhabiting it:

Не следует настаивать на жизни
страдальческой из горького упрямства.
Чужбина так же родственна отчизне,
как тупику соседствует пространство.
(1:172)

[One shouldn't insist on having a life full of / suffering out of bitter obstinacy. / Foreign land is related to homeland, / as space neighbors a dead end.]

In all these poems, the dream of travel and freedom, the sense of geography, and Soviet travel *romantika,* as Vail' and Genis refer to the Soviet version of Byronic romanticism familiar from school anthologies, coincide with Soviet post-utopian disillusion and a modernist sense of urban displacement. The poems capture the existential *autsaiderstvo,* a word Brodsky used in a letter to

Irina Tomashevskaia written from his internment, to describe his position in Soviet society at the time of his arrest: "I lived differently and that is why I am not so dismayed by all that happened to me. I do not even think about the reasons. In my opinion, nobody is to be blamed. It seems that my *autsaiderstvo* was too enormous."[49] The sense, in Brodsky's poems of the early 1960s, of displacement and elegiac disillusion pronounced through reflections on travel conducted outside the officialdom of Soviet *turizm* is clearly contrary to the Soviet mainstream. The sense of urban displacement and restlessness manifest in Brodsky's early poetry was something he must have recognized in the works of Anglo-American writers, such as Ernest Hemingway and John Dos Passos, who formed the popular reading material for Brodsky's generation of young Soviet intellectuals, and who introduced in their early works a modernist male subject whose travels were motivated by existential displacement and desire for the exotic, accompanied with sexual desire and/or simply boredom.[50] T. S. Eliot, whose poetry Brodsky discovered in the early 1960s, was obviously a source of the modernist sense of displacement, too. "Journeying and displacement" were reoccurring motifs in Eliot's works, as Mary Carr writes, and it is easy to see how Eliot's "sordid metropolis, fragmentation, tawdry present, jumbled cultures, the flotsam and jetsam of a decayed civilization, nostalgia for an earlier, lovelier world," encapsulated in *The Waste Land,* influenced Brodsky's early and mature poetic imagination.[51]

The 1962 "Ot okrainy k tsentru" ("From the outskirts to the center") is not a travel text, but it is, nevertheless, illustrative in terms of how Brodsky's early poetic self-fashioning was modeled after the existential displacement typical of the modernist male subjectivity. The poem presents a Leningrad parallel to such Moscow-based films as *Mne dvadtsat' let* (*I Am Twenty*) and the later and less subversive *Ia shagaiu po Moskve* (*I Walk around Moscow*) in its articulation of maturation, both intellectual and erotic, and the Thaw period's fascination with Western culture.[52] In this early declaration of poetic self-creation Brodsky maps out the region of Malaia Okhta, the semi-industrial wasteland of factories and Soviet apartment blocks of Brodsky's contemporary Leningrad. The first line, "Vot ia vnov' posetil" (So, again I visited), evokes Pushkin's "Vnov' ia posetil" ("Again I visited"), an elegy reflecting Pushkin's 1835 visit to Mikhailovskoe, his native estate and the site of his exile; during his visit Pushkin complained in letters to family and friends about not being able to write, and this waning of creative powers, or the anticipation of it, is the crux of the elegiac mode of Pushkin's poem.[53] Pushkin's lyric subject in the 1835 elegy is parting with his past and reflecting on it from the viewpoint of a resigned older poet, whereas Brodsky's poem presents the lyric subject at a point when he is parting with memories of first love, adolescent hopes and convictions, and entering into a new stage of self-awareness with the confidence and self-assurance of a young poet:

> Вот я вновь пробежал Малой Охтой сквозь тысячу арок.
>
> Предо мною река
> распласталась под каменно-угольным дымом,
> за спиною трамвай
> прогремел на мосту невредимом,
> и кирпичных оград
> просветлела внезапно угрюмость.
> Добрый день, вот мы встретились, бедная юность.
>
> Джаз предместий приветствует нас,
> слышишь трубы предместий,
> золотой диксиленд
> в черных кепках прекрасный, прелестный,
> не душа и не плоть—
> чья-то тень над родным патефоном,
> словно платье твое вдруг подброшено вверх саксофоном.
> (1:201)
>
> [And again I took the same route through Malaia Okhta through the thousands of arches. // In front of me there was the river / spread out underneath the smoke of stony coal, / behind my back a streetcar / rattled on a sturdy bridge / and a red brick fence / suddenly enlightened by gloominess. / Good day, again we meet, my poor youth. // Suburban jazz is greeting us, / you can hear the suburban pipes, / golden dixieland / beautiful in black caps, delightful / no soul no body— / someone's shadow on the native gramophone, / like your dress all of a sudden blown up by the saxophone.]

Reconstructing the lyric plot of the poem from an autobiographic fragment in one of Brodsky's later English-language essays, one may conclude that the speaker, twenty-two years old at the time of writing the poem, is remembering a time when he was fifteen or sixteen and either worked or spent some time in Malaia Okhta, where he also had a girlfriend, indicated by the dress in the poem.[54] But the poem not only acknowledges the speaker's transformation from adolescence to manhood but also declares his artistic individualism and creative transformation, which the crossing of the bridge expresses on a symbolic level. The poem is a proclamation of a new poetic identity: "I congratulate myself / For this early discovery, for you / I congratulate myself / for my amazingly bitter fate."[55] The early discovery of the outskirts, and the individualism he identifies with that discovery, lead him to renounce the discourse of the collective optimism of Soviet society: "Whether the place toward which we are running / is a hell or a paradise, is not known, / dear country, / the constant object of praise." Meanwhile, his renouncement of all patriotic affiliations reveals a sense of displacement: "Thank God I remained on the earth without a fatherland" (1:203–4).

The need to rejuvenate the canonical image of the Russian lyric hero is highlighted by the choice of the Pushkin subtext. The rural setting of Pushkin's poem is replaced by the industrial landscape of a Soviet suburbia. Pushkin's wilderness of "kholm lesistii" (forested hill) is replaced by the "peninsula of factories, paradise of work shops and arcadia of mills," where the lyric subject is encountered not by Pushkin's "three pine trees" but by three street-lights: "Is it really not me, / lit-up by three street-lights . . . Is it really not me? Something here has changed forever" (1:203). Brodsky's discovery of the liminal Leningrad echoes the symbolist fascination with the liminal Petersburg, but instead of the decadent borderland *kabak*, Brodsky embraces an entire borderland neighborhood. The displaced visionary wanderers of Russian modernist literature—Mandelstam's "Peterburgskii roman" ("Petersburg romance") and Gumilev's "Zabludivshiisia tramvai" ("Straying streetcar") come to mind—certainly provided models for Brodsky's lyric subject; at the same time, this subject, who is not a "zhilets" (inhabitant) or "mertvets" (dead man) but "kakoi-to posrednik" (some sort of a middleman) and "sovershenno odin" (absolutely alone) is also modeled after the urban heroes of the existentially oriented Western modernist literature:

Слава Богу, чужой.
Никого я здесь не обвиняю.
Ничего не узнать.
Я иду, тороплюсь, обгоняю.
Как легко мне теперь,

> оттого, что ни с кем не расстался,
> Слава Богу, что я на земле без отчизны остался.
> (1:204)
>
> [Thank God, [I am] a stranger. / I don't accuse anyone here. / There is nothing to find out. / I walk, I hurry, I pass people by. / How relieved I am now / that I have not parted with anyone. / Thank God that I have been left on the earth without a fatherland.]

The creation of urban *autsaiderstvo* takes place through images of jazz music and the bridge, the *Bol'sheokhtinskii most* connecting the Smolny side of the city with the neighborhood of Malaia Okhta. It was built at the beginning of the twentieth century, and it is the only bridge in Petersburg with a double arch spanning both lanes for cars and railroad tracks, making it resemble some of the modernist iron bridges common in North America. The bridge and the "jazzy" industrial pipes—the jazz tunes are also captured through the poem's rhythm, which imitates improvisation—create a framework of references pointing to the urban American landscapes that were established in the English-language modernist canon by the novels of John Dos Passos and other writers popular in Brodsky's Leningrad circles in the early 1960s.[56]

Brodsky's invention of the 1960s Leningrad identity in "From the outskirts to the center" owes both to American popular culture and English-language modernist literature. It showcases Brodsky "celebrating his own marginalization," to quote David Bethea's phrase, used in discussing Evgenii Rein's influence on Brodsky's early poetry; or, perhaps more to the point, these lines capture Brodsky *creating* this marginalization.[57] The creation of the urban *autsaiderstvo*, interwoven with the articulation of the coming-of-age of a masculine identity, reminds one of the connection David MacFadyen makes between Brodsky's fascination with the "bravado of certain Soviet poets, such as Boris Sluckii or the romantic Éduard Bagrickii" and the "universal concerns of Western, existentially driven masculinity" of such writers as "Hemingway, Dos Passos, Joyce, Salinger, and others."[58] Valentina Polukhina has quoted these lines to argue how "the image of a man in exile—appeared in [Brodsky's] early poetry long before his exile," which she then reads into the Pushkinian poet-prophet discourse as Brodsky's "prediction." But rather than the poet prophesying, the lines disclose a "modernist construction of authorship through displacement," to quote a phrase Caren Kaplan uses in another context. This modernist device was central for Brodsky's early identity creation, as the poems discussed above manifest.[59]

In February 1964 Brodsky was arrested, tried for *tunciadstvo* (parasitism), and sent for internment to the Arkhangelsk region. In the poems written during his forced stay in Norenskaia—in his Russian *Works* from March 1964 to September 1965—Brodsky depicts the region and his immediate environment, but he also reflected on the trips and travels made before the arrest; the two Kaliningrad poems, the 1962 "Otryvok" ("Fragment") and "Einem Alten Architekten in Rom," and a poem related to Pskov, "Pskovskii reestr (dlia M. B.)" ("The Pskov Register [for M. B]"), were written there.

After the forced stay in Norenskaia the poetic exploration of the Soviet territory resumes with an increasing awareness of that territory as an imperial space.[60] Roman imperial culture and Russian romantic era with its imperial imaginings formed the framework through which Brodsky imagined Soviet space and located himself in it. Brodsky's post-Norenskaia poetry includes such regions and cities as Sevastopol, Palanga, Moscow, Yalta, Kaliningrad, Koktebel, and Odessa. The "Lithuanian" poems "V Palange" ("In Palanga"), "Anno Domini," "Elegiia" ("Elegy") dedicated to M. B., and the seven individual poems of the 1971 "Litovskii divertisment" ("Lithuanian Divertissement") form what Thomas Venclova has called Brodsky's "Lithuanian cycle."[61] The group of poems that relate to Brodsky's trips to the Black Sea region form an equally prominent cycle, with altogether ten poems written between 1967 and 1971. These include "Morskie manevry" ("Nautical maneuvers"), the 1968(?) "Elegiia" ("Elegy") dedicated to A. G. Naiman, "Zimnim vecherom v Yalte" ("On a Winter Evening in Yalta"), "Posviashchaetsia Yalte" ("Homage to Yalta"), "V al'bom Natal'i Skavronskoi" ("For the album of Natalia Skavronskaia"), "S vidom na more" ("With a view to the sea"), "Pered pamiatnikom A. S. Pushkinu v Odesse" ("In front of A. S. Pushkin's statue in Odessa"), "Science Fiction," the 1970 "Sonet" ("Sonnet"), and "Vtoroe Rozhdestvo na beregu" ("A second Christmas by the shore").[62] The poems, with their southern location associated with tourism, erotic encounters, and literary exile, anticipate Brodsky's poems about Venice written later in emigration; this parallel will be discussed in more detail in chapter 6.

In these late 1960s poems Brodsky's traveling subject was transformed from the youthful identification with Tennyson's Odysseus and the metropolitan expeditionist into the postexile, celebrated, and scandalous poet of the 1967 "Anno Domini," dated "January 1968, Palanga":

И я, писатель, повидавший свет,
пересекавший на осле экватор,
смотрю в окно на спящие холмы
и думаю о сходстве наших бед:
его [наместника] не хочет видеть Император
меня—мой сын и Цинтия. И мы

мы здесь и сгинем.
(2:214)

And I, a writer who has seen the world,
who has crossed the equator on an ass,
look out of the window at the hills asleep
and think about the identity of our woes:
the Emperor won't see him [the Governor-general],
I won't be / seen by my son and Cynthia. . . . And we,

we here shall perish.
(*CP*, 6)

Now the lyric subject, who has "seen the world" and "crossed the equator on an ass" and who has withdrawn from "the capital" to the "provinces" to ponder in a Propertian manner on his relationship with the authorities and his mistress (whom he calls Cynthia, the name of the addressee of Propertius' love elegies), refers to himself self-assertively and unapologetically as "pisatel'" (a writer), and makes an ironic parallel between himself and the "Governor-general" of the province.

The ironically elegiac, and exilic, identity exhibited in "Anno Domini" becomes established as the lyric subject's recurring pose in Brodsky's late 1960s and early 1970s poems. The sixth poem of "Lithuanian Divertissement," titled "Palangen" (German for Palanga), conjures up a desolate scene with the lyric subject, "putnik" (traveler), alone at a beach in the Lithuanian resort, contemplating his personal losses; without home or family, distant from his son, he projects himself ironically onto the image of an exiled king through biblical references:

Только море способно взглянуть в лицо
небу; и путник, сидящий в дюнах,

опускает глаза и сосет винцо,
как изгнанник-царь без орудий струнных.

Дом разграблен. Стада у него—свели.
Сына прячет пастух в глубине пещеры.
И теперь перед ним—только край земли,
и ступать по водам не хватит веры.
(2:420)

[Only the sea is capable of looking into the face / of the sky; and a traveler, sitting on the dunes, / casts down his eyes and sucks plonk / like an exiled king without stringed instruments. // His home has been pillaged. His herd has been taken away. / His son is hidden by the shepherd in the cave. / And now in front of him there is only the edge of the earth, / and for walking on waters he has too little faith.]

The poems set in the Black Sea region are taken from the literary convention of an exiled poet traveling by the sea with references to Pushkin's southern exile. The Odessa poem "In front of A. S. Pushkin's statue in Odessa" thematizes the biographical parallel between the two poets, while the 1968 "Elegy" dedicated to Naiman and the 1970 "Sonnet" dedicated to Evgenii Rein, both written on Yalta, rework the Pushkinian topos by transposing the elegiac identity seminal to Russian Romantic poetry onto a Soviet tourist site. In "Elegy" Brodsky strikes the Pushkinian posture by evoking the *vot ia snova* (here again I) convention, while in "Sonnet" the speaker projects the topos onto the future by anticipating another poem on the southern coast, where "in the dull fumes of a semi-basement café"

—не раз
Еще, во всяком случае, я буду
Сидеть в своем углу и без тоски
прикидывать, чем кончится все это.
(2:392)

[many times / still, in any case, I will / sit in my corner and without longing / ponder how this will end.]

In these poems, as in the pre-Norenskaia ones related to the Karelian Isthmus, the literary topos is invested with autobiographical meanings. In the case of Finland, cultural significations are taken from Baratynskii, Mandelstam, and Akhmatova—consider, for instance, the Baratynskian landscape in the 1962 "Utrenniaia pochta dlia A. A. Akhmatovoi iz goroda Sestroretska" ("Morning mail for A. A. Akhmatova from the town of Sestroretsk") with its first two lines, "In the bushes of immortal Finland / where pinewoods reign sternly" (1:212). In the case of the Black Sea region they draw, above all, from Pushkin and his "southern exile" with Ovidian significations.

The Ovidian theme entered Brodsky's poetry as early as in the 1963 "Polevaia ekloga" ("Eclogue on a field"), written in anticipation of the consequences of the official reproach targeted at him. There he rejects the Ovidian exile: "No, he is not an exile . . . who filled with visions / begins to sink in floods / like Naso by murky waters" (1:278–79). But despite the fact that the speaker rejects the Ovidian model, Ovid does, however, remain the archetypal exile against whom other modes of exilic existence are assessed and defined. In 1965 Brodsky embraced the Ovidian position fully in a poetic adaptation titled "Ex ponto (Poslednee pis'mo Ovidiia v Rim)" ("Ex Ponto [Ovid's last letter to Rome]"). After this the Ovidian topos reappears in the Black Sea poems and the 1972 "Pis'ma rimskomu drugu" ("Letters to a Roman Friend"). The latter anticipates emigration and is inspired by Ovid's *Epistulae* and its Pushkinian evocations, with the first lines establishing the Ovidian topos of an imperial province by a sea: "Now it's windy and the waves are running crisscross," reinforced by the speaker addressing a friend in the capital: "Postumus, I'm sending books, I hope you'll like them. / How's Imperial Rome?—A soft bed, hard to sleep on? / How fares Caesar? What's he up to? Still intriguing?" (*CP*, 58).

As this commentary on Brodsky's travel poems written in the Soviet Union illustrates, the tropology of travel evolved in Brodsky's poetry together with the creation of his poetic identity. In his late-1960s and early-1970s poems the romantic and modernist high-cultural models of literary exile gradually replace the Soviet travel *romantika* and the discovery of modernist urban displacement. But despite Brodsky's use of the rather obvious Russian lyric conventions and models from Pushkin and Baratynskii to Mandelstam, it seems that the term *liricheskii geroi* (lyric hero), used in traditional literary criticism to connote the lyric subject of Romantic and modernist poetry, describes Brodsky's manifestly anti-heroic lyric pose poorly. I do not refer to the "anti-heroic" here as an antagonistic position in relation to the socialist hero, but as the construction of a self-deprecating poetic identity prone to infamous behavior, which toward the end of the 1960s becomes more and more manifest, of which the Dostoevskian voice from the underground in "Rech' o prolitom moloke" ("Speech over Spilled Milk") is just one example.[63] At the same time, however, the subject of Brodsky's poetry is a "lyric hero" in the sense Lydiia Ginzburg defined the term in her 1964 study of lyric poetry, in discussing Russian Romantic poets: the biographical materials related to the lyric "I" create a poetic *siuzhet*, a plot or a narrative, which, in the case of Brodsky's works, is structured through the theme of travel and displacement.[64] Moreover, "lyric hero," a term taken from Romantic and modernist critical discourses, is a fitting concept for describing Brodsky's lyric subject in the sense that Brodsky constructs his poetic identity by fixing it on the canonized formations of Russian and Western literature through Greek mythology, Latin poetry, and the poets of the Romantic era. Most of all, his lyric hero, especially the pose exhibited in the Lithuanian and Black Sea poems written before his actual exile, comply with Caren Kaplan's description of the literary identity of the "modernist exile" who "is 'never at home,' always existentially alone"; and, as Kaplan points out, "even more importantly, the modernist exile is melancholic and nostalgic about an irreparable loss and separation from the familiar or beloved."[65] Consider the speaker's estranged, arrogant, and indifferent attitude to his environment, the Soviet holiday resort, in Brodsky's "Elegy" dedicated to M. B. and dated "1968, Palanga":

> Подруга милая, кабак все тот же.
> Все та же дрянь красуется на стенах,
> все те же цены. Лучше ли вино?
> Не думаю; не лучше и не хуже.
> Прогресса нет. И хорошо, что нет.
> (2:249)

> [My darling, the bar is still the same. / The same old dirt prettifies the walls, / the prices are the same. Is the wine better? / I don't think so, not better or worse. / There is no progress. And it's just as well that there isn't.]

The arrogant indifference is soon, however, turned into an expression of melancholia and sense of loss, articulated through explicit autobiographical references in the last stanza, in which the speaker refers to the beloved's deception, which has caused the irreparable parting:

> Зачем лгала ты? И зачем мой слух
> уже не отличает лжи от правды,
> а требует каких-то новых слов,
> неведомых тебе—глухих, чужих;
> но быть произнесенными могущих,
> как прежде, только голосом твоим.
> (2:249)

> [Why did you lie? And why is it that my hearing / can no longer tell the difference between lies and truths, / but requires some kind of new words, / unknown to you—distant, strange; / but words that can be pronounced, / as before, only in your voice.]

The desire to hear "new, resonant, strange words" was soon to be realized by way of emigration.

But what happens to Brodsky's elegiac lyric hero and exilic pose, a pose established and poetically mature, after he leaves the Soviet Union? What happens to this modernist masculinity that "celebrates singularity, solitude, estrangement, alienation, and aestheticized excision of location in favor of locale," to quote Kaplan's description of the modernist male writer—what happens to Brodsky's modernist subjectivity, constructed through images of displacement, when the poet is actually exiled from the Soviet Union and encounters Western travel practices and the postmodern tourist condition?

Exile as Tourist: Nostalgia for the Modernist Traveler

> I know I've not the least chance of survival
> Beside the major travellers of the day.
> I am no Lawrence who, on his arrival,
> Sat down and typed out all he had to say;
> I am not even Ernest Hemingway.
>
> —W. H. AUDEN, "Letter to Lord Byron"
> from *Journey to Iceland*, 1936

Brodsky's attitude toward travel in his post-1972 travel writing is best described as ambivalent. The penultimate poem of the Mexican cycle, "K Evgeniiu" ("To Evgeny") written after five years in emigration, is instructive in this sense. The postcard-like upbeat greeting, with which the poem begins, "I've been in Mexico, clambered up the pyramids," descends by the end of the poem into an expression of boredom with things seen and done:

Скушно жить, мой Евгений. Куда ни странствуй,
всюду жестокость и тупость воскликнут: «Здравствуй,
вот и мы!» Лень загонять в стихи их.
Как сказано у поэта, «на всех стихиях . . . ».
Далеко же видел, сидя в родных болотах!
От себя добавлю: на всех широтах.
(3:100)

Life is a drag, Evgeny mine. Wherever you go,
everywhere dumbness and cruelty come up and say, "Hello,
here we are!" And they creep into verse, as it were.
"In all the elements . . ." as the poet has said elsewhere.
Didn't he see quite far, stuck in the northern mud?
In every latitude, let me add.
(*CP*, 95)

The title of the poem is a reference to Pushkin's "To Evgenii," written in southern exile and inspired by Gavriil Derzhavin's poem by the same title, and usually read against Pushkin's increasing impatience with Russian autocracy and the Byronic dreams of travel and escape.[66] Brodsky's use of the verb "stranstvovat'" (translated in the English version, not as the exact "wander," but as the more colloquial "go") together with the allusion to Pushkin evoke the romantic concepts of travel and *Wanderlust*. Brodsky used "stranstvovat'" and "stranstvie" (the former is the verb "to wander" and the latter the noun "wandering") with references to specific poems by Pushkin, in his poems written by the Black Sea. In the 1968 "Elegy" dedicated to Anatoli Naiman, the lines "Moi drug ne sushe zakhlebnulsia melkoi / no gor'koi lozh'iu sobstvennoi; a ia / pustilsia v *stranstviia*" (2:251) (My friend choked on dry land of petty / but bitter lie of his own; / but I / set out to wander) evoke Pushkin's "I nachal *stranstviia* bez tseli . . ." (And began to wander aimlessly) from *Eugene Onegin*, and "odin pustilsia *stranstvovat'*" (alone set out to wander) from *Andželo*, another narrative poem by Pushkin. Brodsky's "In front of A. S. Pushkin's statue in Odessa" opens up with an ironic reference to *Wanderlust* and travel:

> Не по торговым странствуя делам,
> разбрасывая по чужим углам,
> свой жалкий хлам,
> одна зжды поутру
> с тяжелым привкусом во рту
> я на берег сошел в чужом порту.
> (2:338)
>
> [Wandering not on trading business, / loitering in strangers' rooms / my pitiful stuff / once in the morning / with a bad after-taste in my mouth / I went to the shore in a strange port.]

A response to Pushkin's famous "K moriu" ("To the Sea"), the poem is also a parodic narrative of the lyric subject walking in the streets of Odessa on an early winter morning after a party. Imprisoned in his Soviet *byt,* as he imagines Pushkin once was in his Southern exile, the speaker ends up releasing his hangover by Pushkin's statue, in other words, by the Soviet representation of Pushkin: "I was there too, and I too vomited there in the snow" (2:339).

In "In front of A. S. Pushkin's statue in Odessa," the use of "wander" in the first line opens up the discourse of Pushkinian travel with the unavoidable questions of freedom and exile. In the Mexican poem, however, the function of the verb "wander" is quite different from what it is in the pre-1972 poems. In the Mexican poem, evoking *Wanderlust* and the romantic sublimation of travel does not lead to a meditation on emigration or freedom, rather, the citation creates an ironic contrast between Pushkin's position and the speaker's own contemporary touristhood.[67] He has gone beyond the Pushkinian situation; he is no longer imprisoned in his Soviet living, but is faced by questions of contemporary Western travel, which, and this may be the worst, threatens the condition of literature and that of the writing subject, the poet's creativity, by "creeping into the verse." As Caren Kaplan rephrases the complaint common in modernist discourses of travel: "tourism causes the destruction of 'real' travel and (implicitly) the end of 'good' writing."[68] Ironically, then, the exilic pose projected onto Soviet tourist resorts appears belated and superfluous in actual exile.

In the 1977 "Kvintet," which Brodsky later worked into the English "Sextet," adding a sixth stanza to the English version, accumulated travel experience grows into an expression of overall discontent with travel, displacement, the contemporary world, and life at large:

Веко подергивается. Изо рта
вырывается тишина. Европейские города
настигают друг друга на станциях. Запах мыла
выдает обитателю джунглей приближающегося врага.
Там, где ступила твоя нога,
возникают белые пятна на карте мира.

В горле першит. Путешественник просит пить.
Дети, которых надо бить,
оглашают воздух пронзительным криком. Веко
подергивается. Что до колонн, из-за
них всегда появляется кто-нибудь. Даже прикрыв глаза,
даже во сне вы видите человека.
(3:151)

An eyelid is twitching. From the open mouth
gushes silence. The cities of Europe mount
each other at railroad stations. A pleasant odor
of soap tells the jungle dweller of the approaching foe.
Wherever you set your sole or toe,
the world map develops blank spots, grows balder.

A palate goes dry. The traveler's seized by thirst.
Children, to whom the worst
should be done, fill the air with their shrieks. An eyelid twitches
all the time. As for columns, from
the thick of them someone always emerges. Even in your sweet dream,
even with your eyes shut, you see human features.
(*CP*, 263)

The poem evokes a lyric plot with the speaker on a train in Europe in a half-asleep, nervous state (the twitching eye), disturbed by children's loud voices. The thirsty "puteshestvennik"/"traveler" of the second stanza appears as a metaphor simultaneously for the speaker and any traveler in general, while travel itself emerges as a metaphor for human existence, a way of existing in space.

Space is imagined in the poem both as an abstract and as a geographical concept. The poetic thought disclosed in "wherever you set your sole . . .

the world map develops blank spots" exhibits Brodsky's fascination with the ontological paradox of a subject's presence in space, which simultaneously implies an absence of something that the subject's presence excludes. John Givens has traced Brodsky's fascination with this paradox in this particular poem back to the American poet Mark Strand's influence—the English version of "Kvintet/Sextet" is dedicated to Strand, whose first collection of poems, *Sleeping with One Eye Open*, is evoked in the image opening Brodsky's poem: "an eyelid is twitching."[69] The intertextual connection to Strand's poetry highlights the idea of abstract space, central to both poets' creative imagination, and especially germane to Brodsky's 1987 collection *Uraniia* (*To Urania*), in which "Kvintet/Sextet" initially appeared. The dilemma of Strand's two-line "wherever I am / I am what is missing" is paraphrased in the collection's title poem by Brodsky's exilic maxim: "da i chto voobshche est' prostranstvo, esli / ne otsutstvie v kazhdoi tochke tela?" (And what is space anyway if not the / body's absence at every given / point?) (2:248; *CP*, 281). In the next line of "To Urania" the speaker expands this to involve the conceptions of geography and history, represented by means of Classical mythology: "That's why Urania's older than sister Clio." Space controls time, history, and individuals.

The idea of the vastness of space as something that time ultimately cannot conquer, the idea of geography always ruling over history, is central to Brodsky's creative imagination. The only means an individual has at his disposal to control space is language and writing. The act of writing, then, is an invasion of geographical space. Here Brodsky addresses the equation between spatial and textual invasion, which has been at the core of the critique of travel writing in contemporary theoretical formations.[70] But Brodsky's stance on the matter is not critical, it is affirmative. The "Strandian" lines in the first stanza of "Kvintet/Sextet," apart from thematizing an individual's relation with abstract space, evoke space as a geographical concept. The poetic thought in "wherever you set your sole . . . the world map develops blank spots" is a reversal of the high-imperial impetus of mapping the "blank spots" of the non-European continents. For the contemporary traveler there are no such spots left; the "blank spot" communicates the idea of the traveler's presence having no impact on a place: it is equivalent to him never having been there. Thus this reversal of the imperialist urge communicates a lament for the absence of that urge, or, to be more precise, it communicates a lament for the fact that such an urge cannot occur in the postimperial world. Brodsky's poem recalls Mark Strand in thematizing abstract space, but the concerns of geographical space, history, and travel are also similar to those prompted by Elizabeth Bishop. Unlike Brodsky, though, Bishop addresses the ethics of travel and imperial/ist impetus directly: "Should we have stayed at home and thought of here?" and never invaded the "imagined places."[71]

In section 3 of "Kvintet/Sextet" the figure of the *puteshestvennik*/traveler acquires autobiographical features with the section recounting some of the main aspects of Brodsky's biography:

> Тридцать семь лет я смотрю в огонь.
> Веко подергивается. Ладонь
> покрывается потом. Полицейский, взяв документы,
> выходит в другую комнату.
> (3:152)

> For thirty-six years I've stared at fire.
> An eyelid is twitching. Both palms perspire:
> the cop leaves the room with your papers . . .
> (*CP*, 264)

The first stanza of this section states his age, thirty-seven at the time of writing the poem, and addresses his encounters with authorities, presumably the Soviet ones, though border formalities on European railroads may also be referred to. The next stanza of the section brings up Brodsky's civil status as a nonmarried man: "Night. With your hair quite gone, you still dine alone, / being your own grand master, your own black pawn." And the final stanza of the section establishes his past in the "Eastern bazaars," metonymically representing the Soviet Union and/or his travels in Soviet Central Asia. Apart from this autobiographical reference to the "Eastern bazaars," the stanza also records Brodsky's ill health and heart condition with the image of the "traveler" gasping for air near his hotel.

> Я понимаю только жужжанье мух
> на восточных базарах! На тротуаре в двух
> шагах от гостиницы, рыбой, попавшей в сети,
> путешественник ловит воздух раскрытым ртом:
> сильная боль, на этом убив, на том
> продолжается свет.
> (3:152)

I comprehend only the buzz of flies
in the Eastern bazaars! On the sidewalk, flat
on his back, the traveler strains his sinews,
catching the air with his busted gills.
In the afterlife, the pain that kills
here no doubt continues.
(*CP*, 264)

In this third section of the poem, then, the initially anonymous *puteshestvennik*/traveler acquires a specific reference to the speaker; it is the lyric subject's self-portrait. In the fifth section the speaker's exhaustion from life, travel, and displacement gives him an impetus to imagine himself in pure space without time:

Теперь представим себе абсолютную пустоту.
Место без времени. Собственно воздух. В ту
и в другую, и в третью сторону. Просто Мекка
воздуха. Кислород, водород. И в нем
одинокое веко.
(3:153)

Now let us imagine an absolute emptiness.
A place without time. The air *per se.* In this,
in that, and in the third direction—pure, simple, pallid
air. A Mecca of it: oxygen, nitrogen. In which
there's really nothing except for the rapid twitching of a lonely eyelid.
(*CP*, 265)

In "Kvintet/Sextet" everything moves toward nonexistence and emptiness, and the ontological reversal is accompanied by a reversed evolution. Everything is imagined as going backward on the evolutionary ladder—the traveler turns into a fish, the monkey in the first stanza of section 2 has no time to become human; a similar imaginative principle underlies "Novyi Zhul' Vern" ("The New Jules Verne") written at about the same time. The nullification of evolution, biological and cultural alike, and of the self, is brought together in the final stanza of the Russian poem:[72]

Это—записки натуралиста. За-
писки натуралиста. Капающая слеза
падает в вакууме без всякого ускоренья.
Вечнозеленое неврастение, слыша жжу
це-це будущего, я дрожу,
вцепившись ногтями в свои коренья.
(3:153)

These are the notes of a naturalist. The naughts
on nature's own list. Stained with flowerpots.
A tear falls in a vacuum without acceleration.
The last of hotbed neu-roses, hearing the
faint buzzing of time's tsetse,
I smell increasingly of isolation.
(*CP*, 265–66)

The English poem pushes this even further, imagining the speaker's absence in space as death, a thought captured in the first two Audenesque lines of the last stanza:

When you are no more, unlike the rest,
the latter may think of themselves as blessed
with the place so much safer thanks to the big withdrawal
of what your conscience indeed amassed.
And a fish that prophetically shines with rust
will splash in a pond and repeat your oval.
(*CP*, 266)

The general sense of exhaustion from travel and life at large, which the poem thematizes, and the recognition of the fact that there is no more space to be conquered, which it proposes, do not, however, entirely overturn the impetus for travel and adventure; "taking part in geography" is, after all, as the speaker of "Kvintet/Sextet" proposes, a "better" choice than "participating in history":

Лучше плыть пароходом, качающимся на волне,
участвуя в географии, в голубизне, а не
только в истории—этой коросте суши.

> Лучше Гренландию пересекать, скрипя
> лыжами, оставляя после себя
> айсберги и тюленьи туши.
> (3:151–52)

> Better sail by steamer, horizon's ant,
> taking part in geography, in blueness, and
> not in history, this dry land's scabies.
> Better trek across Greenland on skis and camp
> among the icebergs, among the plump
> walruses as they bathe their babies.
> (*CP*, 263–64)

Brodsky's fascination with geography and his articulations of this fascination, in this poem and elsewhere, point in several directions. Apart from the metaphysical, or ontological, operations described above, "Kvintet/Sextet" also communicates more worldly significations that space and geography invoke in Brodsky's poetry. The autobiographical source for his fascination with geography, as he pointed out himself, was his father, who "held two degrees: in geography . . . and journalism" (*LTO*, 461).[73] That Brodsky associated geographical space with bravery and adventure, characteristics of a stereotypical epic masculinity, is apparent in a remarkable passage in "A Guide to a Renamed City," where he re-evokes the imperial myth of Peter the Great. The representation of the czar resembles the stereotypical male hero of an adventure-novel: "A man of sober mind, though of frightful drinking habits, he regarded every country where he had set his foot—his own included—as but a continuation of space. In a way, geography was far more real for him than history, and his most beloved directions were north and west. In general, he was in love with space, and with the sea in particular" ("Guide," 72; see also chap. 2, pp. 76–77 in this book). It is not unjust in this instance to suggest that apart from the portrait of Peter the Great, the author's self-portrait does not loom far away, at least when it comes to the author's fascination with geography and the sea, which this extract illustrates. Geography is associated with literary creativity later in the essay, when, discussing the emergence of Petersburg literature, Brodsky states that "the reason for this sudden outburst of creative power was again mostly geographical. In the context of the Russian life in those days, the emergence of St. Petersburg was similar to the discovery of the New World: it gave pensive men of the time a chance to look upon themselves and the nation as though from outside" ("Guide," 79).

Brodsky's poetic semantics of geography, then, convey meanings that have to do with an idealized heroic masculinity, discovery, travel, movement, and literary creativity. The meanings Brodsky invests in the concept of geography lead to the idea of space as something to be conquered, and the equation of spatial invasion with textual invasion is never far away in travel writing. Brodsky's extensive travels and numerous poetic and prose texts, which reflect this travel in his post-1972 works, speak of an intense desire to "take part in geography." To be sure, his poetry of the 1970s and 1980s demonstrates an increasing fascination with abstract space and the notion of one's absence in space—or even an inclination to give space authority over the subject to define the subject's existence, as in the Nobel Prize acceptance speech, "from space's point of view, anyone's presence is incidental in it" (*GR*, 60). Nevertheless, there is also a strong desire to imagine the poetic self in geographical space, assert himself into that space, and have control over that space by means of textual representation.

Moreover, while Brodsky's post-1972 travel texts exhibit his desire to "take part in geography," inserting the lyric subject into geographical space, they also insert him into historical time. As detached as the speaker of "Kvintet/Sextet" desires to be from history and time, Brodsky's post-1972 travel poetry and prose illustrate an acute awareness of his place, not only in space and geography, but also in time and history, and more specifically, in the chronology of travel and travel writing. The prose travel texts Brodsky wrote in emigration are particularly illustrative in this sense. Brodsky's first travel text in prose, "After a Journey, or Homage to Vertebrae" (co-translated with Alexander Sumerkin from the Russian "Posle puteshestviia, ili posviashchaetsia pozvonochniku"), was written in 1978, six years after he left the Soviet Union, and inspired by a trip to a PEN conference in Rio de Janeiro. It is a record of touristic anxieties underscored with the rhetoric of amnesia. The author does not want to remember places, events, or people. His unwillingness to remember the trip culminates in his hoping to erase it from his memory:

> What it boils down to is that I didn't see the place. I wonder whether I even saw what I remember myself looking at. . . . A round trip is an awful psychological trap: the return portion robs you of any chance of psychological investment in the place. The best outcome of such travel is a

> snapshot of your sweet self against some corny backdrop, and indeed Stella Polaris [the name Brodsky calls his female companion] and I took several pictures of each other in the Botanical Garden. Still, the camera was hers. Which spares me at least one more, albeit small, indignity, removing thus one more, perhaps the last, proof of my ever having been to Brazil. ("After a Journey," 77)

The essay is an anti-travelogue, whose title anticipates the author's ambivalence about travel. The seminal observation the author makes is that he realizes he has indeed fallen prey to the tourist condition. This realization grows into a lament over the lost opportunities of what the author seems to perceive as "real" travel:

> There is something revolting in all this drifting along the surface, a camera in your hands, with no particular goal in mind. In the nineteenth century one could still do a Jules Verne or a Humboldt: in the twentieth, flora and fauna should be left to their own devices. ("After a Journey," 69)

The geographical space no longer offers opportunities for adventure; the tourist condition has put an end to heroic masculinity and its deeds. This is the metanarrative meaning the title conveys: apart from conveying the meaning of boredom and recognition of travel's nuisance through the ironic "Homage to Vertebrae," the title also communicates the general recognition of the era in which the author travels being an era of "after travel." The grand narrative of travel is over, to put it in Lyotardian terms.[74] The fast travel of the "round trip" in the jet-plane era denies the passage of time provided by traditional transportation (train, ship), and introduces the "phenomenon of speed," antithetical, as Patrick Holland and Graham Huggan note, to the notion of hardship and adventure.[75]

Brodsky's lament echoes the realization voiced by Claude Lévi-Strauss in the first chapter of *Tristes Tropiques*, titled emblematically "An End to Journeying":

> Then, insidiously, illusion began to lay its snares. I wished I had lived in the days of *real* journeys, when it was still possible to see the full splendour of a spectacle that had not yet been blighted, polluted and spoilt; I wished I had not trodden that ground as myself, but as Bernier,

> Tavernier or Manucci did. . . . In short, I have only two possibilities: either I can be like some traveler of the olden days, who was faced with a stupendous spectacle, all, or almost all, of which eluded him, or worse still, filled him with scorn and disgust; or I can be a modern traveler, chasing after the vestiges of a vanished reality.[76]

Lévi-Strauss's writing anticipates the ironic, yet nostalgic, lament for the lost opportunities of European exploration in the tropics, which Brodsky articulates in his Brazilian encounter and which reflects the realization of the end of travel and adventure as perceived by Westerners and Europeans at the end of the colonial era. "Do[ing] a Jules Verne," a desire denied, as the author laments, for the contemporary traveler, is possible only in terms of the poetic imagination of a contemporary writer, as "Novyi Zhul' Vern" ("The New Jules Verne"), a poem Brodsky wrote two years before the Brazilian encounter, manifests. There Brodsky takes the reader on an exploration of the seas and its depths, an exploration that seems to be inspired by Brodsky's youth of adventure novels and the successes of Soviet oceanography.

"Flight from Byzantium," Brodsky's 1985 travel essay about Turkey, begins with the author assuming the same anti-travel attitude as that seen in "After a Journey." At the beginning of the second chapter, the author declares: "My desire to get to Istanbul was never a genuine one. I am not even sure whether such a word—'desire'—should be used here" ("Flight," 393). He then moves on to explain his decision to travel to Turkey by referring to the promise he made to himself, when still in Leningrad, to visit all the places on the same latitude and longitude as his hometown. He also lists a number of other reasons for his trip. One of them is the wish to find in Istanbul an historical atmosphere: "I always felt, for some reason, that here, in apartments, shops, and coffeehouses, I should find intact an atmosphere that at present seems to have totally vanished everywhere else" ("Flight," 394). For him, Istanbul represents the past, not the present or the future. This projection of the past on the image of the "East" is one of the many Orientalist clichés Brodsky deploys in "Flight from Byzantium" (see chap. 5 in this book). At the same time, the desire to "find intact an atmosphere that at present seems to have totally vanished everywhere else" expresses a lament over the homogenization of the contemporary world and a nostalgia for historical authenticity and authentic travel.

The narrative of travel that Brodsky's historical imagination produces follows, then, the narrative Paul Fussell outlined in *Abroad*. According to Fussell, the travel writing performed by some of the leading Anglo-American modernist male writers between the two world wars still bore signs of adventure characteristic of exploration, which for Fussell is the historical model of travel: "Before tourism there was travel, and before travel there was exploration. Each is roughly assignable to its own age in modern history: exploration belongs to the Renaissance, travel to the bourgeois age, tourism to our proletarian moment."[77] In this narrative, exploration is associated with the historical period of the European discovery of other continents; travel coincides with the height of colonization; and tourism with the postwar collapse of European control over the colonies. In other words, Fussell's longing for "real" travel implies longing for the Western colonial past, a longing not entirely absent in Brodsky's evocations of Latin American realities either.

As all these examples show, Brodsky's travel texts reveal not only exilic nostalgia but also a nostalgia for Europe's imperial past, of which we will say more in the following chapters, as well as touristic nostalgia for an authentic travel experience. The era of Byronic escapes, heroic exploration, and adventure is over, and all that there is left to do, as Brodsky's Brazilian travelogue contests, is to parody one's own touristhood, which the author does by describing how the "traveler," as he refers to the first-person narrator in this passage, has his wallet stolen on Copacabana Beach, thus causing the trip he planned down the Amazon to be cancelled. On the other hand, as he remarks, "it would have been quite amusing for a Russian author to kick the bucket in the jungle: this hadn't happened in a while" ("After a Journey," 69). In other words, the clichéd tourist condition in the postimperial era denies him the chance even to *imitate* exploration and adventure, while, and perhaps most remarkably and lamentably, it also denies him the opportunity to fulfill a historically significant and meaningful authorial fate, to participate in making literary history.

The coda of the tourist condition as represented in Brodsky's travel writing is the 1986 English-language prose text "A Place as Good as Any," a lament and a celebration of a contemporary tourist experience played against the fading sense of exilic nostalgia. Written some ten years and many trips after the Brazilian encounter, and included in *Grief and Reason*, it is a description of a travel experience represented in the framework of a nightmare. The text introduces the "traveler," who "is either pursued or pursues somebody" in a city, whose features belong "to several places at once," resembling "the town of one's last year's, or the year before's, sojourn." The topography of the city-hybrid is taken from the landmarks of an urban tourist route: the airport, the train station, taxi stands, restaurants, museums, shopping malls. On this route the "traveler" encounters the mundane concerns of leaving the right tip, finding a urinal, getting a bargain, not knowing the local language, rating attractions, and following the guidebook. At the same time, the narrative keeps breaking into a catalogue of tourist sights, which the author takes an obvious pleasure in recounting, as in listing the European train stations. What eventually emerges from the nightmare is an ideal city-hybrid with urban features sanctioned as sublime by Brodsky in his other writings, features of Venice in particular. Represented as a nightmare, the text sets out to critique the tourist condition, but deconstructs its own critique and acts out a celebration of the condition. Meanwhile, the "traveler," challenged by the tourist condition, remains unable to relate to or identify with anyone but his own double: "So if you find somebody in the hotel bar, it's most likely a man like yourself, a fellow traveler. 'Hey,' he'll say, turning his face toward you. 'Why is this place so empty? Neutron bomb or something?'" ("Place," 42).

Finally, the description of a tourist experience grows into a critique of contemporary culture and society. The nightmare culminates in the realization that the image of the city is not an image of the city itself but of its reproduction: "We know these vertical things [well-known tourist attractions] before we've seen them. What's more, after having seen them, we retain not their three-dimensional image but their printed version. Strictly speaking, we remember not a place but our postcard of it" ("Place," 37). In other words, the countless reproductions of tourist sights, or *markers* as Dean MacCannel calls them—that is, postcards, posters, miniatures, and other tourist memorabilia, have engulfed the original sight. The hybrid images our unconscious mind produces, Brodsky seems to be saying, are images of reproductions, signs of signs with a fleeting referent. Brodsky's vision of the de-hierarchization of the original and the copy—the "reduction or swapping" ("Place," 37), is not, however, the celebration of the blurring of the difference it first appears to be. This becomes apparent when Brodsky expands his critique to concern contemporaneity as a whole, and when read against the conception of history the text produces, Brodsky's position resembles Jean Baudrillard's Platonic lament over the loss of the referent, the historically legitimate and ethically superior original: "Small wonder, too, that a traveler reveres ancient ruins many times over the modern ones left in the center of your city by its fathers for didactic purposes: a traveler, by definition, is a product of hierarchic thinking" ("Place," 39).[78] The hierarchy between the past and the present, that is, between the "ancient" ruin and the "modern" ruin, is based not on an aesthetic but an ethical choice; the historical designates the original and the authentic, the modern and contemporary the unoriginal and the inauthentic. Hence Brodsky's open hostility to contemporary art and architecture, ubiquitous in his travel writing. The pace at which we experience reality is accelerated by technological innovation, which, according to Brodsky, obscures our perception of historical details; observed from a speeding car, a statue of a "great local eighteenth-century military or civic genius" is demoted to "some skin-clad William Tell or other" ("Place," 39–40). To sum up his lament, Brodsky reverts to one of his favorite binary oppositions, the one between history and geography: "history long since exited your city, yielding the stage to the more elementary forces of geography and commerce" (ibid.).

The word "traveler" is repeated so many times in the course of "A Place as Good as Any" that it emerges as a textual anomaly, which estranges the reader and prompts an inquiry into the significations of the word. It appears again in *Watermark*, where the opening passages, with the author recollecting his first arrival at the Venetian train station, the nocturnal walk to the lodgings under the guidance of a local, and awaking in the sunlight the following morning, evoke Boris Pasternak's travel notes from his trip to Venice in *Safe Conduct*. The repetitious use of the world "traveler" and the chronotope of a train station on a winter evening also evoke Italo Calvino's play with the travel convention in *If on a Winter's Night a Traveler*. In the first memoiristic passage of *Watermark*'s fragmentary narrative, Brodsky depicts the "traveler" in a detailed fashion, giving him specific features and an outlook that functions as a self-portrait of the author on his first trip to Venice:

> In the unlikely event that someone's eye followed my white London Fog and dark brown Borsalino, they should have cut a familiar silhouette. The night itself, to be sure, would have had no difficulty absorbing it. Mimicry, I believe, is high on the list of every traveler, and the Italy I had in mind at the moment was a fusion of black-and-white movies of the fifties and the equally monochrome medium of my métier. (*W*, 4)

The nostalgia underlying this autobiographic fragment points two ways. On the one hand, it exhibits a young man's nostalgic ideal of what a traveler on a trip to Italy should look like, and on the other hand, it exhibits the more mature author's nostalgia for the nostalgia experienced as a young man. The mention of the "black-and-white movies" evokes the fascination with Italian neorealist films of the Soviet *shestidesiatniki* (the generation of the 1960s), while "London Fog" and "Borsalino" signify the travel aesthetics of the past. But the fragment exhibits yet another level of nostalgia. it represents the author at a time when his idealistic perception of an authentic and individualistic travel was not challenged by the awareness brought up by the later tourist experience of "mimicry" being "high on the list of every traveler." In other words, the fragment speaks of the author's longing for the innocence he has lost as a traveler. This longing implies the notion of the original and the authentic, which, in turn, points to the utopian nature of nostalgic longing; the authenticity of travel is a lost ideal, and this is what the figure of the "traveler" in *Watermark* ultimately signifies. Brodsky's nostalgia in *Watermark* is self-conscious, ironic nostalgia. The retrospective stylization shows the author's amused detachment from his past and himself: "winter thus was my season; the only thing I lacked, *I thought,* to look like a local rake or carbonaro was a scarf" (*W*, 4–5, emphasis added). The ironic representation of the author's own nostalgia provides the author an aesthetic tool to respond to the irresolvable state of his nostalgic position, to its state of melancholia.[79] Finally, the "traveler" together with the essay's descriptions of Brodsky's repeated trips to Venice, the chronology of return and parting, discloses the author's nostalgia for the mythic homecoming of antiquity; the fragmented passages of *Watermark* disclose the author's longing for the authenticity of Odysseus' narrative. This bridges the essay with the numerous poetic instances in which Brodsky used the Odysseus narrative to imagine his life-story, perhaps the two most moving instances being the 1972 "Odissei Telemaku" ("Odysseus to Telemachus") and the 1993 "Itaka" ("Ithaca").

Apart from the personal meanings Brodsky nostalgically invests in the figure of the "traveler" in his travel writing, larger cultural significations are also very much at issue. The nostalgia exhibited in Brodsky's travel writing is directed toward the modernist traveling and writing subject, the mythic modernist "traveler" shaped by the models of Romantic writing and reinvented by the European and American writers a generation before Brodsky, the generation Paul Fussell nostalgically discusses in his study of English-language travel writing. The "traveler" appears frequently in English-language travel writing: it is the mythic gentleman figure that Mary Louise Pratt recognizes as one of the major forces in the production of the nineteenth-century Euroimperial myth of colonial geographies. This model still informs the adventurous male in modernist formations, as Caren Kaplan argues. She pins down the "traveler" as

> the mythic figure produced through a myriad contradictory practices and discourses. In modernity, this "traveler" . . . is produced in popular culture as well as in high art. An ideal figure, the "gentleman traveler" populated the imaginative faculties of the era that produced him, and provided the model for Indiana Jones and the inspiration for Paul Theroux.[80]

In this list one could add Brodsky's "traveler," too, with his roots fixed in Russian travel writing. Brodsky's *puteshestvennik* emerges from a canon laid down by Karamzin's and Radishchev's travelogues at the turn of the eighteenth and nineteenth centuries, Pushkin's and the other Romantic poets' elegiac identity constructed around the Caucasus, and Russian and Anglo-American modernist gentleman-travelers and their Soviet and Western incarnations in popular culture.

The Byronic model is important for these identities. As Susan Layton has observed, in the romantic period Byron "acquired a Russian reputation as the travelling author *par excellence*."[81] Byron's figure was important for modernist writers, too, with Auden's "Letter to Byron" coming to mind here. The poem was initially published in *Letters from Iceland*, a travelogue compiled mostly from letters in prose and verse—the best-known being Auden's "Letter to Lord Byron" and "Journey to Iceland."[82] Among the chapters based on the poems and letters there is a chapter called "For Tourists." This chapter is written in a bureaucratic prose style with practical advice concerning passports, transportation, accommodation, and so on. The "tourist," then, is contrasted with the "traveler"; the latter appears as a reference to the authors themselves—for instance, in the opening lines of "Journey to Iceland," and as a reference to other authors of other travel books—for instance, in "Letter to Lord Byron." The "traveler" is a representation of the lyric subject, an individual and literary subjectivity separate from the representation of the "tourist." Consider the first stanza of Auden's "Journey to Iceland" with its writer/traveler longing for a place equal to his sense of artistic displacement:

> And the traveler hopes: "Let me be far from any
> Physician"; and the ports have names for the sea;
> The citiless, the corroding, the sorrow;
> And North means to all: "Reject!"

Letters from Iceland was based on Auden and MacNeice's trip to Iceland in 1936, and according to Valentina Polukhina's chronology of Brodsky's life,

Brodsky made a trip to Iceland in July 1978 in Auden's steps. In an interview with Solomon Volkov, Brodsky explained what kind of role Auden's "Letter to Byron" played in his life:

> By the end of my existence in the Soviet Union—the late 1960s and early 1970s—I knew Auden more or less decently. That is, for a Russian, I knew him better than anyone, I think. Especially one of Auden's works, his "Letter to Lord Byron," which I labored over mightily, translating it. For me, "Letter to Lord Byron" became an antidote for every kind of demagoguery. Whenever I was pushed over the edge, I would read this poem by Auden.[83]

The Audenesque Byron, a modernist model of a traveler/poet, rooted in Romantic narratives of displacement and dissent, informed, then, Brodsky's identity creation in the 1960s Soviet Union.

To conclude, drawing on romantic and modernist models of travel and exile, the "traveler" emerges as a nostalgic autobiographical trope in Brodsky's post-1972 works. When Brodsky, in "Flight from Byzantium" (1985), writes that "I'm not a historian, or a journalist, or an ethnographer. At best, I'm a traveler, a victim of geography. Not of history, be it noted, but of geography" ("Flight," 443–44), he is seeking to tone down the effect of his provocative opinions about Turkey and Islamic cultures, while he also uses "traveler" to downplay the drama of exile, much the same way as he did earlier in the 1972 *New York Times* letter. On the other hand, the "traveler" has now grown into an autobiographical figure: it has become the "lyric hero" of Brodsky's travel texts, the hero of the narrative of his life, of the autobiographical *siuzhet* (plot) that Brodsky's post-1972 travel writing produces. As such it signals the modernist individuality and singularity of the poet's experience, his unique subjectivity as an author. The ironizing of nostalgia in Brodsky's travel writing is his way of responding to the realization that the position of the literary exile and adventurous male traveling writer, which occupied a central role in modernist high culture, is challenged in the era of postmodern tourism and global mass migration. It is a belated position. In a larger cultural context, Brodsky's travel writing illustrates the crisis of the modernist subject, while it also manifests the drift that underscored much of Brodsky's writing performed in emigration, that is, the drift, or incompatibility, between Soviet Russian logocentric culture, which nurtured the making of Brodsky's authorial identity, and the radical change in Western aesthetic and literary practices, which signaled the emergence of those cultural practices that became labeled as postmodern. The ironic nostalgia of Brodsky's travel writing presents, then, a response to what Fredric Jameson envisaged as the "end of individualism," an individualism that the "great modernisms" produced. Integral to modernist thinking, in Jameson's view, was the idea that "the modernist aesthetics is in some way organically linked to the conception of a unique self and private identity, a unique personality and individuality, which can be expected to generate its own unique vision of the world and to forge its own unique, unmistakable style" (114). This is what the tourist condition challenges, and it is the challenge that Brodsky takes issue with in his travel texts.

Apart from responding to the landscape of postmodernity, Brodsky's travel texts also respond to the geopolitical landscape of postcoloniality. His travel poems and prose about Mexico and Brazil place his traveling author outside Europe, and it is in these encounters that the belatedness of his modernist position, and its links with Europe's imperial era, become irrevocably exposed. These encounters also foreground the seminal role the concept of empire played in Brodsky's creative imagination. Before examining how imperial themes, and attitudes, were articulated in Brodsky's Latin American imaginings, we shall look at how he rejuvenated Russian imperial mythologies and imperial aesthetics in the retrospective travel guide to Leningrad.

2

A Travel Guide to Imperial Mythologies

Leningrad

The concept of empire emerges in Brodsky's works as one of the essences structuring his historical and geographical imagination, as well as his understanding of cultural signification. Brodsky's experience of Soviet Union, and his understanding of the country as an empire, was crucial to his understanding of empire both as a historical fact and a metaphysical concept. In his creative imagination empire was a cultural given, which provided the conditions necessary for a civilization with its arts, philosophy, and moral order to develop, while it could also exhibit the "human negative potential," as was the case, in Brodsky's view, with the Byzantine empire, imagined in "Flight from Byzantium" as the historical predecessor of the Soviet empire (*LTO*, 422).[1] Brodsky's fascination with imperial histories is felt throughout his works: imperial Rome, the British Empire, and the Venetian Republic were in different ways pivotal sites in his creative imagination. In the poems Brodsky wrote before emigrating from the Soviet Union, he often turned to the historical framework of imperial Rome when satirizing Soviet life, as, for instance, in the 1970 "Post aetatem nostra," with the section "Bashnia" (Tower) anticipating the play *Mramor* (*Marbles*), written in emigration. But despite Brodsky's use of Roman references to depict the absurdity or moral unruliness of the authoritarian Soviet empire, or his marginalized position within it, Brodsky never questioned the historical legitimacy of the Roman Empire, the significance of the imperial culture it produced, or the authority of its cultural heritage. Brodsky's treatment of the imperial theme in the 1981 play *Marbles* is instructive in this sense. The play presents an ambiguous vision of empire as an ideal social order and a utopian human community, as well as an anti-utopia with its citizens as prisoners.[2] The description of the morbid conditions under which the play's two main characters Tullius and Publius live was clearly informed by Brodsky's personal experiences and knowledge of the Soviet disciplinary system—at the end of the play Tullius, the intellectual of the two, submits himself to the soporific the empire provides for free. With the terrifying features of totalitarian society, the empire and its metaphoric counterpart, the prison-tower, where Tullius and Publius reside and where the action takes place, remains the only world imagined in the play; it is impossible, as Valentina Polukhina points out, "to escape from this prison, for the Empire is everywhere."[3] At the same time, empire is the only point of origin and cultural reference in the play. It is represented as the only meaningful world; the space beyond the borders of the empire/tower is anonymous and unvoiced, without power to produce meanings. With the play's referents firmly fixed in ancient Greece and Rome, the semiotic border between the empire/tower and the space beyond evokes the classical and culturally persistent dichotomy between "civilization" and "barbarians."[4]

By his ardent advocacy of Roman writers and their poetic forms, and by his saturated use of imperial Rome as the means of his intertextual poetics, Brodsky fixed the semantic groundwork of his poetic imagination on the archive of knowledge informing all European as well as Russian imperial discourses. This said, the view that Brodsky, while still in the Soviet Union, took of the empire in his imaginings of antiquity was a view from the provinces; it was a view defiant of the imperial center.[5] Ovid and Propertius, the two seminal figures for Brodsky's poetic self-fashioning, offered him a model for representing a poet's political—and in the case of Propertius, also amatory—marginalization.[6] Then again, the view from the provinces was still a view informed by Russian metropolitan formations, by a Leningrad awareness of the cultural significance of Petersburg's imperial past. To strike the pose of the margins, Brodsky set his lyric subject in Lithuania or on the Black Sea shore, the real borderlands of the Soviet, and in the case of the Black Sea, historical Russian, empire.

Once in emigration, the topic of the provinces and marginality subsided in Brodsky's Roman imaginings, and in the prose and poems on Roman themes written in the 1980s and 1990s, the view from the provinces was transformed into the author's assertive desire to situate himself at the center of the imperial space and history of classical Rome. This new orientation was introduced in "Roman Elegies" (1981). While the speaker expresses a sense of dispossession and marginality, conveyed in the image of the "Jewish broken *r*" in "Elegy II," there is also a sense of the lyric subject having found his place in midst of the Roman ruins:

> Для бездомного торса и праздных граблей
> ничего нет ближе, чем вид развалин.
> Да и они в ломаном «р» еврея
> узнают себя тоже . . .
> (3:227)

> To a homeless torso and its idle, grabby
> mitts, there's nothing as dear as the sight of ruins.
> And they, in their turn, see themselves in the broken Jewish
> *r* no less gladly . . .
> (*CP*, 274)

The lyric subject's identification with the ruins in Rome is an ironic reflection on his physical state, while it also conveys a sense of him having found a point of cultural reference for his displacement, ethnic and existential. Rome's ancient ruins appear as displaced in time as the lyric subject does in space and time. This perception is accompanied by the speaker affiliating himself with Rome's cultural and literary heritage, which is conveyed in the first line of "Elegy IX." He presents a catalogue of the female recipients of Roman love elegies for the purpose of poetic self-fashioning: "Lesbia, Julia, Cynthia, Livia, Michelina. / Bosoms, ringlets of fleece: for effects, and for causes also" (*CP*, 278). The line, which contains Catullus's Lesbia, Ovid's Julia, Propertius's Cynthia, and Livia, the second wife of Emperor Augustus, is extended by Brodsky's own muse, the Roman acquaintance Michelina.[7] Even if the metrical anomaly of the four-syllable "Michelina" contrasted with the four rhyming dactyls of "Lesbia, Julia, Cynthia, Livia," sets Michelina ironically apart from the canonized Roman mistresses, and accordingly, the author from his literary predecessors, this assertion of the author's biography into Roman historical space points the way to a qualitatively different way of imagining Roman antiquity and the lyric subject's relation with it, than was the case in Brodsky's poetry before emigration. The poem "Biust Tiberiia" ("The Bust of Tiberius") and Brodsky's two major essays on antiquity written in English, "Homage to Marcus Aurelius" (1994) and "Letter to Horace" (1995), continue this orientation.

Brodsky's "Letter to Horace" represents an imaginative journey in time and space, with the author situating himself, and Russian poetry, on the map of classical heritage. The poem that triggers off the writing of the letter is Horace's ode to Titus Valgius (Ode 9 in Book 2), in which Horace maps out the imperial space of his contemporary Rome.[8] In the essay, Brodsky is struck by Horace's mentioning "the Scythians" (the Geloni), since "my people—well, in a manner of speaking—aren't mentioned that often by the great poets of Roman antiquity" (*GR*, 429). From there on the author defines his own geographical, historical, and cultural position from the imagined viewpoint of the Roman poet. The mention of *mare Caspium* in Horace's ode serves as the geographical point of departure for the fragmentary autobiography, which Brodsky narrates through his affection with Latin poetry, fixing the turning points of his life-story on the map of the Roman Empire. The first encounter with Roman poetry is associated with the Caspian Sea and the author's participation on a Soviet expedition there as a young man, whereas the latest encounter, the writing of the essay, takes place in an "unimaginable (for you) [Horace] place," that is the United States, to where he was "brought . . . from Hyperborea," that is, the Soviet Union, or Russia ("northern Scythia").[9] Eventually both the United States and the Soviet Union, and the historical Russia, are referred to as "outskirts of Pax Romana."

The view from the provinces, or the "outskirts," still defines this instance of Brodsky's authorial positioning, but at the same time, the point of the Roman identification is no longer Ovid or Propertius, the elegists of the margins, but the odic Horace and his poetics of empire, which Brodsky's historical and geographical imagination appropriates to situate himself in imperial space, encompassing the historical empires of Rome and Russia, and the more contemporary Soviet and American empires. Moreover, speculating on the exotic appeal of the *mare Caspium* for the Roman poets, Brodsky concludes: "The main thing, though, about 'Caspium' is that this word is dactylic" (*GR*, 442). By the end of the letter, in an extraordinary authorial identification with Horace, he reprehends Horace and Virgil for their loyalty to Caesar, but refrains from "reproaching you more venomously . . . because I am not your contemporary: I am not he, because I am almost you. I've written in your meters [dactyls], and in this one particularly. That, as I've said, is what makes me appreciate 'Caspium, Niphaten,' and 'Gelonos' sitting there at the end of your lines, expanding the empire" (*GR*, 450).[10] By "expanding the empire" the author seems to refer to the actual depiction of imperial space through the dactylic names, which is the task Horace's speaker performs, and, at the same time, the expansion of empire takes place on a metaphorical level; the "empire of poetry" expands by later cultures adopting the originally Roman poetic meters. Meanwhile, the metaphoric meaning of the expression, the idea of poetic meters "expanding the empire," invokes the perception, common in contemporary cultural criticism, of language being the fundamental factor in building, maintaining, and articulating empires. In postcolonial critique since Edward Said's *Orientalism* this insight has been used in a Foucauldian fashion as a theoretical point of departure for uncovering the discursive power of language to produce knowledge, which supports imperial and colonial domination. But Brodsky approaches it from the ideologically opposite end. He transcends the cultural products of imperial antiquity, classical metrics above all, to a metaphysical foundation of eternal cultural values: "Tetrameters are tetrameters, no matter when and no matter where. Be they in Greek, Latin, Russian, English. So are dactyls, and so are anapests. Et cetera" (*GR*, 441). In this way Brodsky comes to endorse imperial Rome and its cultural products as a source of Western, as well as Russian, imperial discourses. For Brodsky, then, poetic meters represent a timeless entity of all imperial discourses, and their cultural value remains unchanged, regardless of the historical context.

Despite the shift in Brodsky's poetic self-fashioning from provinces toward the imperial center of the imaginary Rome, the sensibility of imperial outskirts continued to inform his understanding of imperial culture and his own position within the English-language literary scene. This was a position not unlike that of some postcolonial writers—something Brodsky's 1983 review on the poetry of the Anglo-Caribbean writer Derek Walcott implies:

> Because civilizations are finite, in the life of each of them comes a moment when centers cease to hold. What keeps them at such times from distintegration is not legions but languages. Such was the case with Rome, and before that, with Hellenic Greece. The job of holding at such times is done by the men from the provinces, from the outskirts. Contrary to popular belief, the outskirts are not where the world ends—they are precisely where it unravels. (*LTO*, 164)

Though Brodsky is writing here about Walcott, whose entry into English literature was entirely different from Brodsky's own, and whose native competence was never questioned the way Brodsky's, the non-native latecomer's, was many times, this extract seems to refer not only to Walcott but to Brodsky himself and his personal experience of imperial cultures.[11] When writing the review on Walcott in 1983, Brodsky occupied the position of a Russian poet in the process of acquiring an English-language authorial identity, an identity on the "outskirts" of a language, which, despite the fact that the British Empire no longer set a norm for its usage, was still, and perhaps increasingly, a global language with its post- or neoimperial center recognized mostly as North American but displaced in the postindustrial world. Moreover, the cultural importance Brodsky assigns to imperial outskirts stems from his experience as a Soviet *literator* and a native of a city, which, though once a capital of the Russian Empire established on its outskirts, had then lost its centrality and been transformed into the outskirts again, this time of the Soviet empire. Meanwhile, it also echoes his re-evocations of the Silver Age parallel between Petersburg and the Hellenistic Alexandria he had appropriated, for instance, in an earlier essay on Osip Mandelstam. But despite this sensibility of the imperial outskirts exhibited in the extract, Brodsky's writing is an expression of a legitimizing attitude toward imperial culture, and imperial centers at that: Outskirts do not threaten or deconstruct imperial power; on the contrary, the dynamics between imperial center and outskirts supports the power by revitalizing its cultural products. Imperial centers may collapse, as Brodsky seems to be saying, but imperial culture lives on, in poetry, if nowhere else; "England . . . still an empire and fully capable . . . of ruling waves," as Brodsky penned with a reference to "Rule Britannia!" in the 1976 "York," referring to the English language and its poetic achievements personified for him by the poem's addressee, W. H. Auden. In "On 'September 1, 1939' by W. H. Auden," one of his two essays on Auden, Brodsky explicated his nostalgic attitude toward what he perceived as imperial languages, and toward the English language as the language of an empire, in particular:

> Because what Auden had in mind from the very outset of his poetic career was the sense that the language in which he wrote was transatlantic or, better still, imperial: not in the sense of the British Raj but in the sense that it is the language that made an empire. For empires are held together by neither political nor military forces but by languages. Take Rome, for instance, or better still, Hellenic Greece, which began to disintegrate immediately after Alexander the Great's own demise (and he died very young). What held them for centuries, after their political centers collapsed, were *magna lingua Grecae* and Latin.

> Empires are, first and foremost, cultural entities; and it's language that does the job, not legions. (*LTO*, 309)

Again, Brodsky invokes the idea of language being the fundamental factor in building, maintaining, and articulating empires, and, again, he does so without apparently taking into account what in contemporary critical formations has often been viewed as the fatal intertwining of language's discursive power and imperial/colonial domination. In Brodsky's essays of Leningrad and Petersburg culture, the ideological premises of his dissenting politics of imperial nostalgia are foregrounded through his re-adaption of Russian imperial mythologies. In his essay "In a Room and a Half," a touching account of his parents and of his family's life in a Leningrad *kommunalka* (communal apartment), Brodsky traced his fascination with imperial histories back to Russian soil, to his native city, and on a more personal note, to his father's profession. Brodsky's recollections of his father's wartime experience in the Soviet Navy, the subsequent job he held at the Navy Museum in Leningrad, and the impression the father's naval uniform made on the young author, break into a eulogy on Peter the Great, the Russian navy, and Russian imperial history:

> It is my profound conviction that apart from the literature of the last two centuries and, perhaps, the architecture of the former capital, the only other thing Russia can be proud of is its Navy's history. Not because of its spectacular victories, of which there have been rather few, but because of the nobility of spirit that has informed its enterprise. Call it idiosyncrasy or even psycho-fancy, but this brain child of the only visionary among Russian emperors, Peter the Great, seems to me indeed a cross between the aforementioned literature and architecture. Patterned after the British Navy, but less functional than decorative, informed more by the spirit of discovery than by that of expansion, prone rather to a heroic gesture and self-sacrifice than to survival at all costs, this Navy indeed was a vision: of a perfect almost abstract order, borne upon the waters of the world's oceans, as it could not be attained anywhere on Russian soil. (*LTO*, 466)[12]

There are two intellectual operations at work here. First, the benign character Brodsky projects on the Russian Empire's military undertakings by playing down its navy's military force allows him to divorce the historical and political realities of the empire from its aestheticized ideal. And second, the observation of the Russian Navy being "patterned after the British Navy" summons the Russian awareness of the Petrine Empire being modeled after European imperial powers. In the Petrine and post-Petrine periods this idea was promoted through ideologically affirmative imagery; it became a seminal myth reflecting the Petrine Empire's break from the old *Rus,* while it also promoted the European orientation of the reforms initiated by Peter the Great.[13] In later intellectual formations the comparison of the Russian Empire with European powers acquired new interpretations, most notably in Chaadaev's *Philosophical Letters,* which advanced the perception, informed by Romantic organistic thought, of Russia as an "infant" nation, which had not gone through its "adolescence," let alone achieved "maturity"—unlike the European nations.[14] In the 1969 "Konets prekrasnoi epokhi" ("The End of a Beautiful Era"), Brodsky captures these views, seminal to Russian self-definitions, by calling the Russian Empire "vtorosortnaia" (second-rate) in lines with the lyric subject defining his marginalized position in the Soviet Union:

> Потому что искусство поэзии требует слов,
> я—один из глухих, облысевших, угрюмых послов
> второсортной державы, связавшейся с этой,—
> не желая насиловать собственный мозг,
> сам себе подавая одежду, спускаюсь в киоск
> за вечерней газетой.
> (2:311)

> Since the stern art of poetry calls for words, I, morose,
> deaf, and balding ambassador of a more or less
> insignificant nation that's stuck in this super
> power, wishing to spare my old brain,
> hand myself my own topcoat and head for the main
> street: to purchase the evening paper.
> (*CP*, 38)

The "vtorosortnaia derzhava" (literally, second-rate power) appears to have a double meaning in that it refers to the imperial Russia, conveying the historical perspective of Russia as an empire modeled after the European imperial powers (not a first-rate, "mature" nation but the Chaadaevian "infant"), while it also refers to the Soviet Union, reflecting the speaker's imperial awareness informed by the Kafkaesque absurdity and chaos of Soviet realities.[15] Next to the false and inauthentic Soviet power, the historical Russian power emerges, then, as an authentic imperial power, even if "second-rate" in comparison with its European models. In David Rigsbee's English translation, which is included in *Collected Poems* and which Brodsky himself revised, the Russian "second-rate power" has been rendered as "a more or less insignificant nation," while the use of the Russian pronoun "eta" (this), referring to the Soviet Union, is replaced by the more transparent "super power," borrowed from Cold War jargon. The translation thus foregrounds Brodsky's perception of Russia as a "nation" separate from the Soviet "power"; the "insignificant nation" imprisoned by the "super power" implies, then, a perception of that nation as a victim of the Soviet regime, a perception Brodsky would later expand on in "Flight from Byzantium." In the Russian original this distinction is achieved by the use of the word "posol" (ambassador), which fixes the historical Russian Empire as the primary signified of the double-edged "power," and which, despite the seemingly pejorative "second-rate," reveals the speaker's nostalgia for that imperial power and its cultural products, its literature and literary identities above all. This nostalgia conveys the same congenial view of Russian imperial history as the extract from "In a Room and a Half"; it is a Soviet metropolitan view oriented toward an aestheticized perception of the Russia Empire's cultural past.

This dissenting politics of imperial nostalgia also encompassed a linguistic nostalgia, a nostalgia for a Russian language as it was before the Soviet jargon, something Brodsky's Brazilian travel account spells out, when the author comments on the Bulgarian and East German delegates at the conference. "She spoke English," Brodsky writes, "he German and French." He concludes, "And as a result, on hearing them speechify, one (or at least I) had a most extraordinary sense of the soiling of civilization." Hearing the two representatives of the communist regimes speak gives rise to the author's comments: "It was particularly painful to listen to all this homeland-made drivel in English, since English is somehow entirely unfit for this stuff—although, who knows, some hundred years ago one might have had the same reaction in Russian" ("After a Journey," 72–73). This points clearly to the significance the English language had for Brodsky as the language free of Soviet jargon, which, as the reasoning in the quotation goes, had corrupted his native Russian. This passage discloses Brodsky's nostalgia for a Russian language that he imagines here as sort of a linguistic innocence lost, a language that a hundred years ago was not submitted to the Soviet idiom.

In "A Guide to a Renamed City," the retrospective travel guide to Leningrad Brodsky wrote and published in *Vogue* in 1979, the author's antagonistic position toward the Soviet regime produces an idealized aesthetization of Russia's imperial history; in his defiant attitude toward the Soviet era Brodsky glorifies and legitimizes the city's imperial past. Brodsky endorses the imperial beginnings of Russian canonical literature by anchoring his historical narrative of Russian literary culture on the widely accepted view of Russian *vysokaia slovesnost'* (canonical high literature) being established at about the same time as the extensive building of the Russian Empire got under way. He locates the emergence of Russian poetic language in Petersburg, assigning it to Lomonosov and Derzhavin, the poets whose works gave an articulation to the Russian imperial aspirations, achievements, and splendor. In what probably is one of the most quoted passages of the essay, Brodsky creates a narrative of the Russian, as well as his own, poetic genealogy, combining the two realms in which Russian imperial discourses evolved in the Petrine and post-Petrine periods—architecture and literature:[16]

> Every criticism of the human condition suggests the critic's awareness of a higher plane of regard, of a better order. Such was the history of Russian aesthetics that the *architectural ensembles of St. Petersburg,* churches included, were—and still are—perceived as the closest possible incarnation of such an order. In any case, a man who has lived long enough in this city [St. Petersburg] is bound to associate virtue with proportion. This is *an old Greek idea;* but *set under the northern sky, it acquires the peculiar authority of an embattled spirit* and, to say the least, makes an artist very conscious of form. *This kind of influence is especially clear in the case of Russian or, to name it by its birthplace, Petersburgian poetry.* For two and a half centuries this school, from Lomonosov and Derzhavin to Pushkin and his pleiad (Baratynsky, Vyazemsky, Delvig), to the Acmeists—Akhmatova and Mandelstam in this century—has existed under the very sign under which it was conceived: *the sign of classicism.* ("Guide," 83–84; emphasis added)

Here Brodsky draws on a cluster of Russian cultural mythologies that all originate in eighteenth-century imperial discourse. Brodsky's sources are, however, primarily the appropriations of these imperial myths in the "Silver Age" period: the glorification of the architecture and urban space of St. Petersburg, the significance of Petersburg for Russian literary practices, Russia's identification with the North, and Russia's affiliation with antiquity. Apart from these cultural mythologies, Brodsky's "Guide" clearly owes to the tradition of the Petersburg literary guides, the literary *progulka*, a tradition in which these mythologies have partially evolved, and which Julie Buckler has recently outlined in the following terms:

> These more loosely conceived Petersburg literary guides developed as a tradition from Konstantin Batiushkov's elegant 1814 stroll to the Academy of Arts, through the satirical urban travel notes of declassed gentry writers like Dostoevsky and Nekrasov, who wrote feuilletons for ready cash in the 1840s, and thence to all comers—late-imperial popular journalists like Nikolai Zhitov, nostalgic postimperial memoirists such as Anatoly Koni, and contemporary literary time travelers charting the byways of Petersburg cultural history.[17]

Buckler includes in these literary guides of Petersburg the preservationist movement's works, and especially Nikolai Antsiferov, whose legacy, as Buckler argues, informed Soviet interpretations of Petersburg/Leningrad, even if his works were no longer favored in official cultural practices, while his legacy also had a great impact on dissident and émigré imaginings of Petersburg.[18] Articles by such scholars as Yuri Lotman and Viktor Toporov on the urban phenomenology of Petersburg and its literature demonstrate the theoretical end of the Antsiferovian influence, whereas Brodsky's "Guide" presents one of the Antsiferov legacy's most successful manifestations in Russian essayistic writing.[19]

One of the seminal ideas of Russian imperial and aesthetic thought, which Brodsky reintroduces in the essay, and which has been promoted in literary guides to Petersburg many times before him, is the idea of the uniqueness of St. Petersburg next to the European capitals that served as its models. This idea, in turn, derives from the perception of the exceptional unity of Petersburg's classical architecture. In the Petrine and post-Petrine periods, classical iconography and its use in sculpture and architectural ensembles were to demonstrate the Petrine Empire's European affiliations.[20] The heterogeneous influences on Petrine Baroque, including its Dutch, Danish, and Swedish orientation, with the addition of the late Italian Baroque and French Empire styles, later came to coexist with what is usually referred to, and often pejoratively, as the architectural "eclecticism" prevailing at the end of the nineteenth century. But despite the diversity of styles, there developed an idea of the exceptional architectural unity of Petersburg, which proved to be extremely persistent in Russian imaginings of the city.[21] In the 1814 "Progulki po Akademii Khudozhestv" ("Walks in the Academy of Arts"), Konstantin Batiushkov has a young Petersburg artist proclaim how necessary it is to visit the "ancient" capitals Paris and London "to realize the value of Petersburg. Look—what a unity! How all parts come together to form a whole!"[22] While this must be understood as a reflection of the cultural authority the ideal of classical unity still bore at the beginning of the century, when the eclecticist styles of the later nineteenth century had not yet occurred in the Petersburg cityscape, the twentieth-century pronouncements of the "imaginary classical unity" of Petersburg, to quote Buckler's phrase, are reflections of cultural mythologies and ideological positioning informed by later historical events and developments in Russian thought.[23] The idea was re-established as a popular view held by Petersburg intellectuals at the turn of the twentieth century and promoted most successfully by the preservationist movement led by Aleksandr Benois. The movement was related to a larger interest in both neoclassical aesthetics and architecture in general, manifested, for instance, in the literary practices of the poets involved in the Acmeist gatherings—Mandelstam's architechtural metaphors are probably the best-known instance. The preservationists put into practice their educational propaganda of neoclassical aesthetics through elite cultural outlets such as *Mir iskusstva* (*World of Art*) and *Apollo*, with which many of them were closely associated. Benois and other preservationists were opposed specifically to the eclecticist trends popular at the end of the nineteenth century, as well as to the Russian national revival and *stil' modern* (art nouveau).

The pathos of the campaign to rescue the "old Petersburg," by which the preservationists meant the buildings erected during Alexander I's reign and before, rose from the need to oppose the general cultural prejudice of regarding Petersburg as a city of "barracks and bureaus," advanced in the literature of the latter nineteenth century.[24] In "Zhivopisnyi Peterburg" ("Painterly Petersburg"), an article promoting the movement's cause in *World of Art*, Benois championed "a return to an artistic approach to the neglected Petersburg," encouraging writers and artists to seek inspiration in the eighteenth-century odic poets and landscape artists in representing the exceptional beauty of the city.[25] Brodsky's Petersburg narratives owe much to this moment in Russian cultural history, forgotten in the Stalinist years but recalled in the Thaw and post-Thaw periods in the 1960s.[26]

In his re-narration of the Petersburg myth, Brodsky follows Nikolai Antsiferov's interpretation of it in the 1922 *Dusha Peterburga* (*The Soul of*

Petersburg), which appeared as a YMCA-Press reprint in Paris in 1978, a year before Brodsky wrote his essay.[27] Antsiferov's 1920s literary excursions of Petersburg were unavailable to most readers in the later Soviet periods, but the 1978 reprint by one of the leading émigré publishers ensured that the Antsiferovian readings of the Petersburg cityscape, conceived during the years of the intense evolvement of the cult of Petersburg, continued to live outside the officialdom of Soviet mainstream. Brodsky's "Guide" functions as a metanarrative on the myth celebrated by Antsiferov. Brodsky comments on the myth's basic themes, investing its dualistic potential with affirmative and glorifying meanings, just as Antsiferov did. The city's geographical location and its architecture, the city's character of being antithetical to nature, the human sacrifice of its building, the demonic quality it attained in folklore, Peter the Great's person, its "premeditatedness" (quoting Dostoevsky), its opposition to Moscow—all this acquires a positive interpretation in Brodsky's writing.

The Antsiferovian method of reading the cityscape of Petersburg through literary referents, that is, his way of mapping out the city through literary imagination as much as through factual historical figures and events, is captured and refashioned in a typically Brodskian maxim, in which the viewpoint common among Russian and Soviet literati is represented as a universal truth: "Toward the middle of the nineteenth century . . . Russian literature caught up with reality to the extent that today when you think of St. Petersburg you can't distinguish the fictional from the real" ("Guide," 80). In other words, Brodsky seems to say, the literary myth preconditions the way Petersburg is thought of and represented in popular and artistic articulations—and, in a way, Brodsky's own metanarrative, construed through cultural mythologies and commonplaces, confirms this view. Brodsky updates Antsiferov's famous formulation, "the Bronze Horseman is the *genius loci* of Petersburg," by beginning his essay with an ironic juxtaposition of the Bronze Horseman and Lenin's Statue at the Finland Station; just as the Bronze Horseman is the genius loci of the historical Petersburg, so is the statue of Lenin of the Soviet Leningrad. The two statues are established as symbols of the two periods in the city's history, the Russian and the Soviet, and this juxtaposition sets the tone for the rest of the text and its dissenting politics of nostalgia.

Throughout his essay Brodsky emphasizes the significance of geography and space for the founding of St. Petersburg, echoing both Antsiferov and Benois. In *The Soul of Petersburg* Antsiferov notes, quoting Benois, that the *vlast'* (power) of the city took command of the creativity of foreign architects, resulting in the unique cityscape: "The intention was to turn Petersburg into something Dutch, but the outcome was of something peculiar. . . .

There [in Amsterdam] they have narrow houses, accurate, narrow embankments, crooked streets, facades made of bricks, big windows . . . here we have wide extended low mansions, a vast river with wide shores, straight perspectives, stucco and small windows."[28] Brodsky continues Antsiferov's thought by observing that the spatial dimensions of the Russian territory guaranteed that the "outcome" of imitating "European architectural styles" was "unmistakably Russian." The "overabundance of space," Brodsky writes, "dictated to the builder where to put what on another wing," resulting in the sensation, when looking at the Neva panorama, that "it's not Russia trying to catch up with European civilization but a blown-up projection of the latter through a laterna magica onto an enormous screen of space and waters" ("Guide," 77). Here Brodsky's apotheosis of the Petersburgian space re-evokes the extolling observation Benois makes in "Painterly Petersburg," according to which classical forms "hired" from France, Italy, and Germany came together, forming something "magnificent and utterly distinctive. . . . It seems as if our vast plains, the excessively wide Neva, inspired the foreigners to create absolutely unusual works . . . here there was an empty space, where one could build what one wished and how one wished."[29] In the Mandelstam essay "The Child of Civilization," Brodsky refashions this as "Classicism never had so much room" (*LTO*, 131).

Brodsky's writing manifests how his geographical and historical imagination worked through both the cultural mythologies of Russia's imperial age and through Soviet metropolitan commonplaces. Just how ingrained Brodsky's thinking was in the spatial mythologies of the Soviet era is revealed in "Guide." When preparing the reader for an explanation as to why Peter the Great's decision to build a capital city "on the edge of the land" shocked contemporaries, he claims: "Russia is a very continental country; its landmass constitutes one-sixth of the world's firmament" ("Guide," 71). While it is historically accurate to characterize the late seventeenth- and early eighteenth-century Russia as a "very continental country," to claim that it covered "one-sixth of the world's firmament" is an anachronistic projection of a Soviet textbook mythology on Russian history.[30] A similar concurrence of Russian imperial and Soviet mythologies underscores Brodsky's appropriation of the cult of Peter the Great. Brodsky credits him with the questionable honor of giving "birth to the Russian totalitarianism," but follows this thought immediately with what almost emerges as a justification for Peter's autocracy: "He dealt with the people in exactly the same fashion as he dealt with the land for his would-be capital. Carpenter and navigator, this ruler used only one instrument while designing his city: a ruler. The space unrolling before him was utterly flat, horizontal, and he had every reason to treat it like a map, where a straight line suffices" ("Guide," 73–74). In other words, Peter the Great's actions, which have just been presented as the foundation of Russian totalitarianism, are now viewed as a consequence not of his personal willpower and rational thought but of his natural environment, the space surrounding him. The naturalization of Peter the Great's will to autocratic rule undoes the critique of his actions, and eventually the czar comes to represent the ideal heroic masculinity, which in Brodsky's works was often associated with the love of the sea and fascination with geography: "In general, he [Peter] was in love with space, and with the sea in particular. He wanted Russia to have a navy, and with his own hands this 'Czar-carpenter,' as he was called by contemporaries, built its first boat" ("Guide," 72). Here Brodsky continues to weave his private mythologies (the affiliation of geography with his father) with Silver Age mythologies (Mandelstam's 1912 poem "Admiralteistvo," "The Admiralty"), Soviet textbook legends, and narratives of Russian nationhood; Peter the Great was the czar, as Brodsky concludes, who "united the nation for the first time" ("Guide," 73).[31] Brodsky assigns a similar significance of nation-building to Petersburg literature, which Soviet school children are made to learn by heart, and it is this "memorization," as he continues, "which secures the city's status and place in the future—as long as this language exists—and transforms the Soviet schoolchildren into the Russian people" ("Guide," 93–94). In one imperial move of Brodsky's Soviet metropolitan imagination, the citizens of the multinational Soviet Union represent the "Russian people."

Finally, to return to Brodsky's appropriation of Antsiferov's and Benois's promotion of neoclassicism, Brodsky's exaltation of Petersburg space inverts the idea of inauthenticity, related to the concept of imitation, and implied in the semantics of the "second-rate empire" in "The End of a Beautiful Era." The city of Petersburg emerges in Brodsky's historico-aesthetic conjectures not as a mere copy of the original European model but as its augmented, improved, and idealized adoption—unique and exceptional. In "In a Room and a Half" this perception underlies Brodsky's affectionate recollection of one of Petersburg's most celebrated neoclassical buildings, the Stock Exchange, which housed the Soviet Navy Museum, where his father worked: "The building was that of the former Stock Exchange: a far more Greek affair than any Parthenon, and far better situated as well, at the tip of Basil Island, which juts into the Neva River where it is at its widest" ("Guide," 465). To be sure, passages like this, with Brodsky eulogizing Petersburg architecture and its neoclassical aesthetics, reflect his need to present the Cold War Western reader with his view of Russia's European past and the cultural heritage he affiliated with. At the same time, the insistence on the superiority of the Petersburg buildings over their initial models invokes the imperial attitudes that informed the original cultural models Brodsky draws on. As Katerina Clark reminds us in her discussion of Benois and the turn-of-the-century Russian revival of Empire style, the revival not only signaled a predilection for antiquated styles, but its aesthetic orientation and historical utopianism had specific political and ideological underpinnings; it was not only "about taste" but also about "national aggrandizement." Clark continues, "Neoclassicism is at base a historicism oriented toward the establishment of norms that enact certain values."[32] The values, which the early twentieth-century neoclassical aesthetics enacted and which Brodsky in his essays re-evokes, were those initially articulated in imperial discourses, which evolved in the cultural practices of Europe's imperial powers. While the preservationists sought models of classical aesthetics in ancient Greece and Rome, they also turned to Louis XIV's Versailles, a symbol of imperial splendor and glory but also a product of an absolutist state. Moreover, many of the readers of *World of Art* and *Apollon*, who were sympathetic to the preservationists' cause and sought for change, looked for ways of modernizing Russia also by turning to Peter the Great. The prevalence of the nineteenth-century view of presenting Petersburg as Peter the Great's mistake subsided, and he was advanced as the great Europeanizer: Petersburg and Peter the Great were "twin symbolic heroes." With all this in mind, David MacFadyen's observation of the dialogue between Petersburg and Venice in Brodsky's works, especially in *Watermark*, seems apt—it is the "relationship of both places [Petersburg and Venice] to the theme of empire, to the theme of autocracy, and to the theme of neo-classical aesthetics that both empire and autocracy cultivate."[33]

While Brodsky's imaginings of the Petersburg past, or of Venice, do not exhibit admiration for autocracy, they do exhibit an admiring attitude toward historical, authentic empires as opposed to the inauthentic Soviet empire; they exhibit an admiring attitude toward the cultural products of what the author of the essay perceives as authentic imperial aesthetics. The "national aggrandizement," which the original historical models propagated, could in Brodsky's case be articulated only from the disenfranchised position of a Soviet émigré intellectual; his retrospective glance endorses the aesthetic practices, but not the imperial or colonial actions, of Russia's imperial era.

And yet, the Soviet metropolitan view, which the nostalgic construction of Leningrad Eurocentrism entails, is not far from endorsing the imperial/ist policies of Soviet russification when that view celebrates the memorization of Russian literature about Petersburg in the process of "transform[ing] Soviet schoolchildren," including, presumably, non-Russian schoolchildren, into "the Russian people."

Among the Russian imperial mythologies Brodsky recycles in "Guide," there is Russia's historical identification with the North—I refer to Brodsky's idea of the specifically Petersburgian association of "virtue with proportion," which for him was a manifestation of a "Greek idea . . . set under the northern sky." Russia's affiliation with the North was introduced and incorporated into Russian poetics of empire in the eighteenth-century ceremonial ode in connection with imperial metaphors, which supported Russia's affiliation with Europe; despite its young age, the Russian Empire with its capital, the *Severnaia Palmira* (Northern Palmira), was equal with European powers.[34] The nineteenth-century Romantic poets made the *surovyi sever* (austere North) a popular topos, while they also transformed some of its ideological contents. It no longer symbolized Russia's affiliation with Europe but became a symbol of the uniqueness of Russia's character.[35] In the late Soviet period, as the imaginative geography created by Petr Vail' and Aleksander Genis in *The 60s: The World of the Soviet Man* manifests, the Romantic identification with the North still functioned as a productive commonplace in the Russian intelligentsia's narratives of Russian national, and imperial, identity. In the 1960s every Russian (*rossiianin*), as Vail' and Genis claim, was "aware of the importance of the State," which covered "one sixth of the earth" and a "whole one side of the globe, the North." Vail' and Genis identify the "North" not only with Russia but with Siberia, and the significance they give to Siberia is its role as the space where "russkaia udal'," the reckless boldness thought to be characteristically Russian, has traditionally been played out. In Vail' and Genis's narrative the North is, then, associated—very much in the manner of the Romantic period, with the *surovnost'* (austerity) of Russian national character, especially its male representations, while historical events recognized by historians as a colonizing process of military conquest of Siberia, systematic scientific research (cartography and geology), commercial exploitation, and extensive russification of indigenous peoples are romanticized as empire building founded on individual men's heroic if "despairing bravery."[36] Vail' and Genis's historical conjecture confirms Joost van Baak's observation that in the Soviet era the concept of the North informed the construction of

Russian masculinity both in the official Soviet narratives of the socialist hero and in the counternarratives of the GULAG, and also in the unofficial and dissident narratives in general, as Brodsky's essay illustrates.[37]

The meanings Brodsky invests in the concept of the North in "Guide" are similar to those exhibited in Vail' and Genis's conjecture; he creates a mythopoetic narrative familiar to the readers of his poetry, where the North provides a locus for the emergence of his personal creative powers as well as a setting for a collective male identity.[38] In Brodsky's poetry the qualities associated with the North are not always represented as desirable—as in the humorous lines of "Ekloga 4-ia (Zimniaia)" ("Eclogue 4: Winter"), "For me, other latitudes have no usage. / I am skewered by cold like a grilled-goose portion" (*CP*, 292)—but they are repeatedly conveyed as something that is necessary, morally purifying and affirmative for the lyric subject's existence and masculinity. Within this semantic field the North is associated in his poetry with Norenskaia, the region of Brodsky's internment in Arkhangelsk—see, for instance, "K severnomu kraiu" ("To the northern region"), and with the Baltic region and Leningrad/Petersburg, as in the often anthologized "I was born and grew up in the Baltic marshlands" (*CP*, 101), with its "zinc-gray breakers," opening the cycle "Chast' rechi" ("A Part of Speech"), and affirming the masculinity of the lyric voice that these harsh marshlands, as represented by Brodsky, induce.

In "Guide" Brodsky combines the mythology of the North with a search for cultural value and authenticity by placing the origins of Petersburg culture in ancient Greece, which, in turn, is an oddly belated appropriation of Russian Grecophilia and derives, too, from the eighteenth century. The idea of Petersburg arts and literature as an adoption of Greek classicism was put forward by Brodsky in the cultural-semiotic fictions of the earlier Mandelstam essay "The Child of Civilization." There he defines "civilization" as a "sum total of different cultures animated by a common spiritual numerator," whose "main vehicle—speaking both metaphorically and literally—is translation. The wandering of a Greek portico into the latitude of the tundra is a translation" (*LTO*, 139). This imaginative cultural history echoes strongly Georgii Fedotov's idea in the 1926 article "Three Capitals": "Petersburg is an incarnation of Palladio's dreams on the polar circle, bog paved with granite, Greek porticoes stretched out a thousand versts in the midst of northern birches and spruces."[39] In Brodsky's perception, however, the idea acquires a moral overtone, and Russian classicism, especially its poetry, emerges as an aesthetic norm superior to all other national variants of classicism: "Apart from her metaphors, Russian poetry has set an example of moral purity and firmness, which to no small degree has been reflected in the preservation of so called classical forms without any damage to content" (*LTO*, 142–43). Brodsky's evocation of Petersburg classicism was shaped by his understanding of Mandelstam's Hellenism, itself a modernist interpretation of Russian Grecophilia. What seems to have made an especially strong impact on Brodsky's creative mind is Mandelstam's re-evocation of the Romantic idea of Greek harmony; Skriabin's "harmonic architectonics" represented for Mandelstam the "most extreme revelation of the Hellenistic nature of the Russian spirit possible."[40] In Brodsky's historical imaginings the idealization of Greek harmony is re-evoked again and projected on a naturalized view of Petersburg architecture, which is presented as "a giant-scale embodiment of perfect order," where "iambic beat is as natural as cobblestones" (*LTO*, 132).

Overall, however, as the Roman imaginings in Brodsky's poetry demonstrate, his search for cultural authentication led him more often to Rome than to Athens. He located original and authentic antiquity in Greece but embraced the cultural tradition of the Roman Empire; Roman antiquity provided him with the model of how to write poetry and how to be a poet. His linguistic experience as a Russian poet living and writing in an English-language environment inspired him to advance the idea that the Russian language bore particular affinity with Latin, the language of Roman antiquity. The "highly inflected" Russian with its "gutta-percha syntax," he writes in "Letter to Horace," is exceptionally suitable for the "translation of the likes of you [Horace]" (*GR*, 430), since Russian "copes with your asclepiadic verse in a far more convincing way than the language I am writing this in [English], for all the familiarity of the latter's alphabet. The latter just can't handle dactyls" (*GR*, 434). Brodsky's source here may have been M. L. Gasparov's introduction to the 1970 Soviet edition of Horace's poetry—possibly the edition Brodsky refers to as the one he has at hand. In the introduction Gasparov points out certain syntactic features, which, according to him, make Russian more adaptable to translating Horace than other languages: "Luckily there are at least some means through which the Russian language allows the translation to achieve greater approximation with the Latin original than other languages."[41] Though his immediate source may have been M. L. Gasparov, and though he is referring not to Greek but to Latin, Brodsky's linguistic remarks in "Letter to Horace" echo one of the most famous articulations of Russian Grecophilia, Lomonosov's claim of Greek influence on the Russian language, as well as Pushkin's use of this claim to prove that "as a literary instrument Slavonic is unquestionably superior to all other European languages."[42] The ideological position remains the same: Brodsky, just as paradoxically as Lomonosov and Pushkin, ends up promoting Russia's superiority over Europe in an attempt to affiliate Russia with Europe's classical heritage.

To return to "Guide": it is a fragmentary text underlined by the author's occasionally ironic and always self-conscious use of Russian cultural mythologies and intellectual commonplaces. From these fragments, imbued with nostalgia toward losses on both the individual and collective planes, one can discern coherent authorial narratives of origins rooted in debates concerning Russian national identity and cultural self-definition, which originated in the eighteenth century but were articulated with the novel enthusiasm and philosophical orientation of the Romantic period, and which merged into the Silver Age mythologies a century later. Writing from a dissenting position with regard to the Soviet Union, though informed by its popular mythologies, Brodsky reintroduces views and attitudes concerning Russian imperial culture, views that originated in a period of intense empire building and were often closely tied up with the real and imaginary construction of the urban space of St. Petersburg. Brodsky dismisses the nineteenth-century literary perception of the city, informed by the negative potential of the dualistic myth of Petersburg expressed in urban folklore; instead, he reworks the turn-of-the-century cult, which evolved as a reaction to the mid- and late-nineteenth-century views. By idealizing Petersburg neoclassical aesthetics and by returning to the myth of the city that evolved in the literary and aesthetic practices of the Silver Age period, such as Antsiferov's *The Soul of Petersburg* and Benois's works, Brodsky draws from the myth promoted initially by eighteenth-century panegyric literature and architecture—the two realms where Russian imperial discourse evolved. The meanings Brodsky invests in Leningrad/Petersburg and its monumental buildings from his Soviet post-utopian, or post-Stalin perspective, produce a nostalgic and affirmative attitude toward Russia's imperial past, which, in turn, reconstructs Petersburg as the center and a major achievement of Russia's imperial power, with the latter emerging as an object of the author's nostalgia, too. Brodsky's dissenting politics of imperial nostalgia produces a perception of the historical Russian Empire as the authentic and legitimate empire, as opposed to the Soviet imperial absurdity he left behind. Poetry emerges from these conjectures as a product of an authentic imperial culture, as well as a means of maintaining it.

The eighteenth-century Russian imperial discourse from which Brodsky's narratives derive were informed by a European belief in the preeminence of Europe's cultural achievements. This conviction underscores the Leningrad Eurocentrism, which Brodsky's authorial position in "Guide" and other Leningrad essays produces. When these imperial imaginings are transposed on non-European territories in the postcolonial era, the ideological positionings of Brodsky's dissenting politics of nostalgia are turned on their heads and displayed from an altogether different perspective.

3

A Postcolonial Elegy

Mexico

If one were to look for historical analogies in Russian writers' encounters with Latin America, Mayakovsky's visit to Mexico in 1925 and Brodsky's in 1975 would provide an interesting one. Both Mayakovsky and Brodsky visited Mexico as successful Russian-language poets, and both were received by leading Mexican intellectuals and artists of their time—Mayakovsky's host was Diego Rivera, and Brodsky's Octavio Paz. Both were restless travelers before and after the Mexican sojourn, and both reflected on their impressions of Mexico in their poetry, Mayakovsky in a cycle called "Stikhi ob Amerike" ("Poems about America"), Brodsky in "Mexican Divertimento."[1]

But despite these apparent correspondences, the analogy also discloses several points of contrasts between the two poets and their careers. Mayakovsky visited Mexico as a celebrated champion of the young Soviet state. Before his trip to the Americas he had established himself in the lucrative business of illustrated commercial verse, with the State Publishing House among his clients, and his privileged position within Soviet cultural politics was also reflected in his easy and frequent travel abroad. Brodsky's literary fame, on the other hand, was being established in emigration outside the Soviet Union, and his success among his Russian readership was partially grounded on his subversive use of the official rhetoric of his contemporary, stagnated Soviet empire; he was personally familiar with the Soviet disciplinary system and continued to deal with the Brezhnevian suppression of intellectuals from abroad.[2] In other words, the two poets came to Mexico at a different historical moment and from a different political position, a fact that is manifested brilliantly in their poems about Mexico.

Mayakovsky's declamatory pathos against imperialism and colonialism, which underscores especially such American poems as "Sifilis" ("Syphilis"), "Blek end uait" ("Black and White"), and "Khristofor Kolomb" ("Christopher Columbus"), was informed by his political convictions and revolutionary enthusiasm, on the one hand, and contemporary Latin American social and political conditions, on the other. However, in the poem titled "Meksika" ("Mexico") the strategies of representation Mayakovsky used for his political agitation draw from the conventions of lyric poetry; he sets out to depict the social injustice of Mexican society from the perspective of his childhood readings. Mayakovsky arrived in Mexico by sea from Cuba and described the anticipation of the arrival in the following terms: "How many miles the screw propeller has dug the water, and the land of Fenimore Cooper and Mayne Reid emerges alive."[3] But instead of the wild and brave "indeitsy" (Indians) romanticized by nineteenth-century literature, their "Blednolitsyi Brat" (Pale-Faced Brother), as Mayakovsky identifies his lyric subject, encounters the misery and social repression of the indigenous people laboring at the harbor of Veracruz: "And Montihomo's Hawk's-Claw picks up the suitcase filled with issues of 'Lef'" (ibid., 344). This initially humorous recognition of Mexican reality not matching his juvenile expectations fed by adventure novels grows into a sardonic observation of the heroic Aztec leader's name now connoting a beer brand: "Heroism is not for now. Montezuma has become a beer brand" (ibid., 347). After expressing his personal disillusion, glorifying Mexico's pre-Columbian past, and condemning the colonizers' descendants still in power, Mayakovsky moves on to make direct political statements through a parallel between Mexico and Latvia, "kindred genres," as he calls them, by which he means that both exemplified for him a bourgeois society: Mexico was "the Latvia of the tropics."[4] In the end the political message grows into the direct propaganda of the last lines with a catalogue of Mexican communists and the final exclamation: "Soon throw a crimson flag over the Mexican melon!" (Mayakovsky, *Sobranie sochinenii*, 350). Reviewed in the context of the early Soviet ideologies of the 1920s, Mayakovsky's poem illustrates the then-dominant Leninist approach to Latin America, in which Latin American countries were placed on the map of capitalist imperialism, and their relations with international capital were seen as parallel with prerevolutionary Russia's, and consequently, their future was identified with that of the new Soviet state.[5]

By the time Brodsky visited Mexico, the Soviet Union's own imperialist mission had become apparent to dissenting intellectuals such as Brodsky, and instead of the two countries' place in the prerevolutionary capitalist world-order, the point of comparison between Mexico and the Soviet state was provided for Brodsky by a militant authoritarian rule, which controlled both. Visiting the mid-1970s monolithic Mexico, led by Luis Echeverriá and the Mexican Institutional Revolutionary Party (PRI), in power since its establishment in 1928, Brodsky recognized in the country the Soviet regime he had left behind:

> I expected to see something similar to our Central-Asian republics. And just as expected, it was just like that. When the plane landed, I saw a huge inscription made of stone or something on a hillside. 'Viva Eccevarria!' [*sic*]. It was the then president Echevarria. Well, this was all familiar and recognizable to me. When we got to the TV station, we went through a couple of stages of security control. Three or four times, before we got to the studio, soldiers with rifles checked our IDs. Back then it was pretty dangerous times in Latin America, and in Mexico, in particular. And it dawned on me that it was not clear whether the armed forces were protecting the station or whether they had taken it over. Which basically amounts to the same.[6]

From Brodsky's metropolitan Soviet viewpoint, Mexico reminded him not of Latvia (which had become "half a Russian province," as Mayakovsky desired in the 1922 poem "The Fifth Internationale") but of one of the Soviet Union's Central Asian republics, exotic and under military control.

The parallel between the Soviet Union and Mexico is implied throughout Brodsky's Mexican cycle and is conveyed, for instance, in the meanings Brodsky gives to the landmarks of Mexico City in "Meksikanskii romansero" ("Mexican Romancero"):

> Вечерний Мехико-Сити.
> Пляска горячих литер
> Кока-Колы. В зените
> реет Ангел-Хранитель.
>
> Здесь это связано с риском
> быть подстреленным с ходу,
> сделаться обелиском
> и представлять Свободу.
> (3:98)

Night. Coca-Cola's burning
message adorns the House
of Lawmaking. Beyond it
the Guardian Angel hovers.

Here he runs a risk
of being shot at random
and pinned to an obelisk
as a symbol of Freedom.
(*CP*, 93)

Apart from a set of generalizations and political commonplaces about Mexico and Latin American countries—random violence, the role of North American cultural imperialism (the Coca-Cola sign)—Brodsky's perception of Mexico is obviously informed by Russian historical events: religious symbols can be replaced by symbols of a socialist, or communist, order without much improvement from an individual's viewpoint.[7] Images of poverty and social injustice are abundant in Brodsky's encounters with Mexico, but he does not make a cause-effect connection between poverty and Mexico's colonial past as Mayakovsky did; rather, he decontextualizes social injustice, presenting it as something integral to the human condition. There are always those in power and those disempowered:

На Авениде Реформы
масса бронзовых статуй.

Подле каждой, на кромке
тротуара, с рукою
протянутой—по мексиканке
с грудным младенцем. Такою

фигурой—присохшим плачем—
и увенчать бы на деле
Памятник Мексике! Впрочем,
и под ним бы сидели.
(3:97)

The Ave. of Reforma forces
eyes to prefer the statues.

Under each one, in the gutter
with hands stretched to the traffic,
sits a Mexican mother
with her baby. A tragic

sight. Let the winning party
carve them both for a Statue
of Mexico, huge and portly.
To cast some shade in the future.
(*CP*, 91)

Whether paved by monuments symbolizing Mexico's historical events, revolutionaries and colonizers alike, as *Paseo de la Reforma* is, or by symbols of inequality and depression, as the speaker sardonically suggests it should be, there will always be beggars looking for shade: the change of statues (power) bears little consequence to social injustice.[8] The last poem of the cycle "Zametka dlia entsiklopedii" ("Encyclopedia Entry") ends on the same fatalist note, with Brodsky's speaker not seeing much hope for Mexico:

. . . В грядущем населенье,
бесспорно, увеличится. Пеон
как прежде будет взмахивать мотыгой
под жарким солнцем. Человек в очках
листать в кофейне будет с грустью Маркса.
И ящерица на валуне, задрав
головку в небо, будет наблюдать

полет космического аппарата.
(3:102)

. . . In the future, population,
beyond a doubt, will keep on growing. Peons
will rhythmically ply the hoe
beneath the scorching sun. A man in specs
will sadly leaf through Marx in coffee bars.
And a small lizard on a boulder, raising
its little head, will passively observe
up there in the blue

a spaceship's passage.
(*CP*, 96–97)

Again, Brodsky's experience of the Soviet Union is projected on Mexico, this time on the country's future, revealing the paradigmatically opposite ideological function to what the parallel offered for Mayakovsky. Instead of revolutionary dreams, Mexico offered for Brodsky a space onto which to project postrevolutionary disillusion. Poverty is not abolished despite intellectuals studying Marx, an irony emphasized by the clash between the spaceship, a symbol of technological advancement, and the lizard, a prehistoric creature symbolizing the reverse development on the evolutionary ladder.

As for European colonialism against which Mayakovsky reacted strongly, Brodsky recognized in it, as articulated in the penultimate poem of the Mexican cycle, "To Evgeny," a lesser evil than the sacrificial rites of the native Mexicans. Studying the clay statues discovered at the ancient sites of the Tehuantepec isthmus, the poem's speaker wonders what they would tell us if they spoke, and in reply imagines them articulating the significance of ancient rituals, among them the "sacrifice of eight young and strong men before dark," which prompts the speaker to comment on the colonization of Mexico in the following terms:

Все-таки лучше сифилис, лучше жерла
единорогов Кортеса, чем эта жертва.
Ежели вам глаза скормить суждено воронам,
лучше если убийца—убийца, а не астроном.
Вообще без испанцев вряд ли бы им случилось
толком узнать, что вообще случилось.
(3:100)

Better syphilis after all, better the orifice
of Cortés's unicorns, than sacrifice like this.
If fate assigns your carcass to the vultures' rage
let the murderer be a murderer, not a sage.
Anyway, how would they ever, had it
not been for the Spaniards, have learned of what really happened.
(*CP*, 95)

As if in response to Mayakovsky, who in "Syphilis," written on the way from Havana to Veracruz, makes the accusation that European exploiters spread the disease among the colonized people, Brodsky argues that, even though colonization was brutal and violent (the phrase "Cortés's unicorns" refers to guns), its European actors gave the colonized a means of knowing about their past, which—by the perverse logic of imperialism's civilizing mission, which Brodsky here re-evokes—means that colonizers first destroyed cultures, but then gave the colonized access to the historical knowledge about the destruction of their cultures.[9]

The title of the final poem, "Encyclopedia Entry," captures the authoritative position that Brodsky's lyric subject takes on Mexico's past and present, history and geography, throughout the cycle. The title anticipates Brodsky's imitation of an encyclopedic discourse, which, no matter how ironic, raises the question of the relation between the speaker and colonial, or imperial knowledge, for the production of which encyclopedias are seminal. The relation with colonial/imperial knowledge, in turn, highlights Brodsky's access to two "native" archives of such knowledge, Russian and Soviet. With the first of these, his relation, as argued in the previous chapter was based on an aesthetic idealization and nostalgia for that empire's cultural achievements; while the second, based on firsthand experience, informed his anti-totalitarian views. In "Encyclopedia Entry" these two sets of imperial knowledge inform the historical analogy, which the speaker puts forward in the third stanza of the poem:

> История страны грустна; однако,
> нельзя сказать, чтоб уникальна. Главным
> злом признано вторжение испанцев
> и варварское разрушение древней
> цивилизации ацтеков. Это
> суть местный комплекс Золотой Орды.
> С той разницею, впрочем, что испанцы
> действительно разжились золотишком.
> (3:101)

> The country's history is sad; however,
> unique is not the word to use. The main
> disaster was, as they insist, the Spaniards,
> the barbarous destruction of the ancient

Aztec civilization—that's the local,
plain version of the Golden Horde complex.
With this distinction, namely, that the Spaniards
did grab, in fact, their little pile of gold.
(*CP*, 96)

The destruction of indigenous people and languages by the Spanish conquistadors, and implicitly, its historico-political consequences felt in postcolonial Mexican society, are summed up in an unexpected move of Brodsky's Soviet/Russian imperial imagination as the "local . . . version of the Golden Horde complex." This parallel of Mongol rule with the Spanish conquistadors ignores, however, the historical fact that the disintegration of the Mongol Empire in the fifteenth century signaled the beginning of those historical processes, which gave way to the emergence of the Russian Empire and its colonial undertakings in the eighteenth century. At about the time the last colonial war was raging in Mexico—and Brodsky makes much use of the events related to this war in the first two poems of the cycle—Russia controlled large non-Russian territories it had acquired in its attempt to become a European-style imperial power. Mexico, on the other hand, never became a colonial power after its colonizers withdrew.

To turn back to the analogy between Brodsky and Mayakovsky—in spite of the obvious differences in the historical circumstances and political sensibilities, which the two poets' responses to their visits to Mexico reflect, not to say anything of the differences in style and versification of their poetic responses, Mayakovsky's "Mexico," bears an affinity with Brodsky's Mexican cycle. Mayakovsky's poem raises questions of the role of a textual attitude—very much at issue in Brodsky's cycle, too—and the sense of belatedness and nostalgia, which a textual attitude can invoke.[10] Mayakovsky's strategy was to reveal the sources of his textual attitude; he lays bare the makings of his Euroimperial knowledge by naming its creators, James Fenimore Cooper and Mayne Reid. But he does this in order to reject the knowledge and to narrate, through this rejection, the development of his lyric subject's social consciousness. The poem narrates the lyric subject's *put'* (road) from being informed by bourgeois adventure novels to being aware of the historical process of bourgeois colonization and its consequences, which he discovers in his real-life encounters with the "Indians," his "childhood friends."[11] In other words, Mayakovsky recognized his own belatedness and used it to make a political statement, even if his personal memories of his childhood games had a conspicuously important role in this statement. Not in tune with the futurist pathos the poem ends on, these memories disclose a nostalgic attitude to a childhood's lost innocence, and, by way of implication, to an idealized colonial past, which provided the fictitious space for the childhood games to be played in—to "beat with arrows Columbus' ships shot from behind flower pots in Kutaisi" (Mayakovsky, *Sobranie sochinenii*, 344). However, the narration of Mexico's colonization with the depiction of the brutal social injustice it brought along undoes this nostalgia, and eventually, if there is a nostalgic undercurrent in Mayakovsky's poem, it is directed not at the colonial era but at Mexico's precolonial past, which emerges as a utopia idealized in a parallel manner with childhood's paradise lost. Moreover, in Mayakovsky's poem nostalgia is something that the lyric subject strives to shake off, even if it informs his lyric position more than the poet would have probably cared to admit, whereas, to finally turn to Brodsky, in his Mexican cycle a nostalgic attitude becomes established as the position from which the lyric subject surveys Mexico's past and present. In the fifty years that separated Brodsky's Mexican trip from Mayakovsky's, there had emerged Russian intellectual dissent against Soviet ideology, and Euroimperial knowledge had acquired a nostalgic status among some dissenting intellectuals, such as Brodsky, something Brodsky's Mexican cycle manifests. The representational strategies that Brodsky uses in the cycle present a re-adoption of Euroimperial, as well as Russian imperial, knowledge to a poetic articulation of an encounter with a non-European territory. Reviewed in the 1970s and the period of decolonization, this re-adoption was doomed to disclose the poet's belated position. "Cuernavaca" (the Russian original is spelled as "Guernavaca," as the name appears in some European sources), the first poem in Brodsky's Mexican cycle, exhibits this position through the utterly ironic yet thoroughly nostalgic evocation of the final episode of Mexico's colonization.

"Cuernavaca" has so far been overlooked in scholarly discussions of Brodsky's elegies, and yet the poem is imbued with elegiac attitude induced through the representation of the lyric subject's exilic condition, as well as through his historical imagination. What makes the poem elegiac is the poet's mourning the absence of home, language, empire, and Europe's colonial past, which the elegy itself, as a historical genre, comes to symbolize.[12] Outlining the history of the Russian elegy in 1973, the Soviet scholar L. G. Frizman posed the question of whether "the Russian elegiac genre exists at the moment," to which he then replied affirmatively by referring to the authors of Soviet textbooks and encyclopedias, who based their view of the genre's exuberance on the example of such early twentieth-century poets as Bryiusov, Mayakovsky, and Blok, and on such later Soviet poets as Simonov and Tvardovskii.[13] It was obviously not possible for Frizman to name any of the post-Stalinist Leningrad poets associated with Joseph Brodsky, even if the elegiac lyrics produced by Brodsky alone before 1973 had proved that the Russian elegy was alive and well. It was the elegiac quality of Brodsky's poetry, the constant lamenting of the absence of dead eras, civilizations, and poets, which contributed to his, if not anti-Soviet then at least non-Soviet, lyric voice. But Brodsky was not only an exceptionally elegiac poet in his contemporary Soviet context, he was also the poet who, as David Bethea argues in his discussion of "Stikhi na smert' T. S. Eliota" ("Verses on the Death of T. S. Eliot"), "reinvented" the genre by rejuvenating it with a new and unexpected cultural import, English-language poetry.[14] Brodsky's 1975 poem "Cuernavaca" shows how Brodsky continued to rejuvenate the Russian elegiac tradition in emigration, not so much by appropriating foreign literary tradition as by setting the native tradition on a foreign land, previously unexplored by a Russian elegiac identity.[15]

The lyric plot of "Cuernavaca" takes place in Jardín Borda, the Borda Gardens in Cuernavaca. The botanical garden, landscaped in the late eighteenth century in Andalusian style, was a well-known tourist site at the time Brodsky visited Mexico. The poem is divided into three sections; the first describes the garden:

В саду, где М., французский протеже,
имел красавицу густой индейской крови,
сидит певец, прибывший издаля.
Сад густ, как тесно набранное «Ж».
Летает дрозд, как сросшиеся брови.
Вечерний воздух звонче хрусталя.

Хрусталь, заметим походя, разбит.
М. был здесь императором три года.
Он ввел хрусталь, шампанское, балы.
Такие вещи скрашивают быт.
Затем республиканская пехота
М. расстреляла. Грустное курлы

доносится из плотной синевы.
Селяне околачивают груши.

Три белых утки плавают в пруду.
Слух различает в ропоте листвы
жаргон, которым пользуются души,
общаясь в переполненном Аду.
(3:92)

Beneath the tree where M., the Frenchmen's pet,
possessed his pearl of sluggish Indian blood,
a poet sits, who's come here from afar.
The garden's dense, like jewels closely set.
A thrush, like eyebrows knit, departs for food.
The evening air's a crystal chandelier.

The crystal, be it noted, smashed to sand.
When M. reigned here as emperor three years,
he introduced them: crystal, champagne, dancing.
For things like that pep up the daily round.
But then appeared the patriot musketeers
and shot poor M. A doleful, haunting

cry of the crane drifts out from dense blue shadows.
The local lads shake down a rain of pears.
Three snow-white ducks are swimming in the pond.
The ear picks out among the rustling shudders
of leaves the lingo tossed around as pairs
of souls converse in hell of things profound.
(*CP*, 87)

The historical events that Brodsky evokes relate to the French intervention in Mexico (1861–67), which from the viewpoint of French history has to do with the period of Napoleon III's colonial policies and efforts to strengthen the French foothold in territories outside Europe. The events evolved as Mexico's economic difficulties accumulated in the mid-nineteenth century, and the country was unable to pay its foreign debt to its European creditors. As a result, England, Spain, and France sent troops to Mexico to collect their claims, and while British and Spanish troops soon withdrew, Napoleon III ordered his to stay, which signaled the beginning of the French occupation of Mexico. Ferdinand Maximilian of Hapsburg, the "M." of Brodsky's poem, an Austrian aristocrat related to several reigning families in Europe, was appointed as the emperor of Mexico, and together with his wife, the Belgium princess Charlotte (Carlota), he set off from Trieste to Mexico to realize upon his arrival in Veracruz that he was not as welcomed by the Mexican people as the Mexican émigré monarchists and their European allies had led him to believe. Negotiating between Mexican liberals and conservatives, Maximilian tried to establish a monarchy in the country, but in a few years his empire had fallen to Benito Juárez's troops.[16]

Introduced in the first section, Emperor Maximilian grows into a central figure of the three-section poem. Brodsky appropriates biographical facts and popular legends of his life, which he must have known from history books, such as Parkes's classic, and travel guides, as well as from painting and films, such as Eduard Manet's *The Execution of Maximilian* and William Dieterle's Hollywood film *Juarez,* with Bette Davis as Carlota. Jardín Borda was the site of Maximilian's summer residence, the beauty "of sluggish Indian blood" refers to the native woman Maximilian had as his mistress, and "crystal, champagne, dancing" and "chandeliers" echo Maximilian's legendary indulgence in lavish European court life.[17] The "patriot musketeers" (literally, the "republican troops") in Brodsky's poem refer to Benito Juárez's men; after being surrounded by Juárez in Querétaro, Maximilian surrendered, and Juárez ordered the emperor to be executed.

From the viewpoint of Mexican decolonization, Maximilian was the last colonial ruler sent to Mexico by Europeans to guard European interests, but the viewpoint Brodsky appropriates in his representation of the historical figure draws from the traditional European stance, in which Maximilian is usually portrayed as a misled idealist and a victim of Napoleon's colonial adventure and manipulation, a "sentimental Viennese prince—to be imposed as emperor over the tempestuous Mexicans," as Henry Parkes writes. Despite the pejorative "Frenchmen's pet" (literally, "French protégé"), as Brodsky calls Maximilian, the speaker sympathizes with Maximilian's fate. The "doleful, haunting / cry of the crane" ("grustnoe kurly"), highlighted by the enjambment between the second and third stanzas following the laconic mention of the emperor's execution, conveys the speaker's position in regard to the emperor's death: the cry of the crane is a metaphor for Maximilian's isolation and tragic fate. Meanwhile, in the poem Maximilian symbolizes a European past represented through the signs of aristocratic *byt,* which the emperor "introduced" to the locals, whose contemporary equivalents now "shake down . . . pears," while the crystal is "smashed." The reminiscences of

European comfort and courtly manners are contrasted to the garden's current overgrown and uncultivated state evoked in the "thrush," the "crane," and the "local lads [shaking] down . . . pears" (literally, "peasants," who "okolachivaiut," literally, "loiter" or "lounge about"—the verb is slangy). The first section ends in an image of a ruined garden, in which the falling leaves resemble the sounds of "hell" (literally, "overcrowded hell"). With the speaker's historical imagination shifting from the colonial past to the postcolonial present, the poem descends from nocturnal to infernal.

Brodsky appropriates Maximilian's historical figure to imagine the last colonial period in Mexico's history, but more significantly, he appropriates Maximilian for a poetic self-fashioning. The speaker's identification with Maximilian is established in the first three lines, in which "'M.,' the Frenchmen's pet" and the "poet . . . who's come here from afar" are paralleled through their displacement; Maximilian is a European displaced in the New World, and this together with the fact that he was not only a European emperor in Mexico but also a German-language lyric poet, forms the basis of the lyric subject's identification with Maximilian. The biographical parallel, implied in the first section of "Cuernavaca," is elaborated on when the speaker in the second section provokes the reader to imagine Maximilian writing a letter to his brother, the Austrian Emperor Franz Joseph I:

Отбросим пальмы. Выделив платан,
представим М., когда, перо отбросив,
он скидывает шелковый шлафрок
и думает, что делает братан
(и тоже император) Франц Иосиф,
насвистывая с грустью «Мой сурок».

«С приветом вам из Мексики. Жена
сошла с ума в Париже. За стеною
дворца стрельба, пылают петухи.
Столица, милый брат, окружена
повстанцами. И мой сурок со мною.
И гочкис популярнее сохи.

И то сказать, третичный известняк
известен как отчаянная почва.
Плюс экваториальная жара.

Здесь пуля есть естественный сквозняк.
Так чувствуют и легкие, и почка.
Потею, и слезает кожура.

Опричь того, мне хочется домой.
Скучаю по отеческим трущобам.
Пошлите альманахов и поэм.
Меня убьют здесь, видимо. И мой
сурок со мною, стало быть. Еще вам
моя мулатка кланяется. М.»
(3:92–93)

Dismiss the palms, let plane trees loom in view.
Imagine M. now laying down his pen;
he flings aside his silken gown and frets
and cogitates on what his kin would do—
Franz Joseph, fellow ruler over men—
and whistles plaintively: "Me and my marmot friend."

"Warm greetings, sir, from Mexico. My wife
went off her head in Paris. Now the palace
walls all resound with shooting, fire sprawls.
Now rebels, brother, choke the city's life.
(My marmot friend and I, we saw the places . . .)
Well, here guns are more in vogue than plows—

And who's to wonder; tertiary limestone
is just like brimstone, a heartbreaking soil.
Just add to that the equatorial heat.
So bullets are a natural ventilation.
Both lungs and kidneys sense this as they toil.
My skin is sliding off me—how I sweat!

Aside from which, I feel like coming home.
I miss the homeland slums, the homeland splendor.
Send current almanacs—I long for them!
This place will likely prove a goodly tomb
for me and my marmot. Gorgeous sends her
due greetings to my royal brother. M."
(*CP*, 87–88)

In this section Brodsky continues to work on some of the historical details of Maximilian's life, such as his ardent correspondence with his brothers and mother.[18] "My wife went off her head in Paris" refers to Carlota's journey back to Europe, where, with her mental health failing, she pleaded to both Napoleon III and the pope, hoping to get them to help Maximilian, who was being threatened by Juárez. The reference to "Moi surok," "Marmotte" or "Ich komme schon," as Beethoven's song, based on Goethe's lyrics from *Jahrmarktsfest zu Plundersweilern* (*Festival in Plundersweilern*), is sometimes referred to, evokes another biographical legend about Maximilian, that is, his fondness of piano music.[19] Meanwhile, it is difficult not to read into these lines, where Maximilian expresses his longing for Europe, the "poet" longing for Russia: "I feel like coming home. / I miss the homeland slums, the homeland splendor. / Send current almanacs—I long for them!" Despite the humorous irony underlying the letter—more than a nineteenth-century epistolary style, the letter resembles the shorthand typical of postcards and telegrams—the allusion to Goethe's entertainer who tours with a marmot as his companion, conveys a portrait of extreme loneliness of both Maximilian and the "poet" in exile. One of the uses of the irony is to de-imperialize and humanize Maximilian's historical figure and to present him as an individual with literary and amorous rather than political concerns, not a colonizer but a northern tourist suffering from the heat ("how I sweat"), though enjoying the erotic license of travel to an exotic place ("moia mulatka," literally, "my mulatto girl or woman").[20]

The historical figure, then, merges with the poem's lyric subject. The letter is written entirely in a double-coded language in which images and cultural references can be traced back either to Maximilian's or Brodsky's biography: Goethe's lyric/Beethoven's song refers to Maximilian's affection for his native European culture, and more specifically, for piano music, while it also evokes the speaker's native competence. The song "I moi surok so mnoi" ("And My Marmot Is with Me"), as Beethoven's song is known in Russian, was a popular children's song in Soviet times. Apart from the reference to popular Soviet culture, the *siuzhet* of Goethe's lyric/Beethoven's song is also associated with Leningrad's Hermitage Museum, where there is a painting by Jean Antoine Watteau that depicts a Savoyard child with a marmot, a scene typical of Goethe's time and similar to the one that apparently inspired his lyric.[21]

Apart from being exiled in an exotic location, where, as Brodsky imagines Maximilian writing to his brother in the Russian version of the poem, "I apparently will be killed," there is also a sense of the poet-Maximilian being imprisoned in it. Maximilian, occupied by piano music and poetry rather than military strategy, is portrayed as a hostage to Napoleon's imperial aspirations and to the violence it provoked in the local rebellious Mexicans, just as the poet is hostage to his emigration: from his "afar" he is free to travel to Mexico but not to home. In the context of Russian poetry Brodsky's treatment of a nineteenth-century exile imprisoned in an exotic landscape, where "bullets are a natural ventilation," evokes another exotic location, the Caucasus, and one of the most powerful myths of Russian imperial era, the myth of a captive, initiated by Pushkin's *Kavkazskii plennik* (*A Prisoner of the Caucasus*).[22] Brodsky transposes this myth on a Latin American setting; in Brodsky's poem the poet-Maximilian emerges not as a captive of the Caucasus but as a captive of Mexico. And with this, there emerges the comparison between the poet-Maximilian cast off in Mexico and the dissenting Russian romantic poets cast off in the Caucasus. The poem is written in iambic pentameter, which further affirms Russian romantic poetry's role as the source of the cultural knowledge informing the writing of the poem; more specifically, the choice of meter points at the role of Russian elegiac tradition, seminal to romantic poetry, as the point of reference for Brodsky's poetic self-fashioning.

Apart from the elegiac subject matter (absence of home, language, Europe, and the colonial past) and apart from the setting (nocturnal garden), the poem invokes the Russian elegiac tradition through its meter. According to M. L. Gasparov, iambic pentameter is the "most 'neutral' of Russian classical meters" in terms of "stylistic and thematic associations."[23] From the viewpoint of the meter's historical evolution, however, the associations the meter induces are nothing but neutral. As Gasparov attests elsewhere, iambic pentameter was introduced to Russian poetry by the poets of the Romantic period, in whose poetic practices it was connected with an interest in German and English poetry and the emergence and popularity of the elegiac genre.[24] In other words, the adoption of iambic pentameter in Russian classical metrics was seminal to the development of Russian elegy and Russian elegiac identity. The meter was used, for instance, by Lermontov in "Son" ("Dream"), the canonical poem about the poet-soldier imagining his beloved at home, who, in turn, imagines the soldier's death in the "midday heat" of a Dagestani valley (as opposed to the "equatorial heat" in which Brodsky's poet-emperor dreams of home). In conclusion, the imperial knowledge on which Brodsky grounds his representation of an exilic and elegiac identity in a non-Russian, non-European, exotic location was provided by Russian romantic identity construed against the backdrop of the Caucasus and the Crimean landscapes.

By making the nineteenth-century emperor-poet Maximilian the point of his lyric identification, Brodsky foregrounds the question of a poet's relation with imperial power. In "1867," the poem that follows "Cuernavaca," Brodsky comments on this by depicting the poet-turned-emperor at the brink of his demise, dancing the tango, while Juárez's troops are plotting a revolution. The following lines are voiced by a parrot following the scene: "Scorn for one's neighbor among those who sniff the roses / may be, not better, but more straight than civic poses" (*CP*, 89). In other words, contempt of others does not become a poet, but it is morally more acceptable than a poet corrupted by power.[25] This subversive position to imperial power is reinforced by the carnivalizing image of the parrot. In "Cuernavaca" a poet's relation with imperial power is communicated in a more complex way. What is significant in "Cuernavaca" is that the relation between a poet and imperial power, represented through a reconstruction of the historical narrative of Maximilian and Mexico, is also communicated through the lyric subject's elegiac posture, the narrator's nostalgic attitude to what he narrates. Discussing the intertwining of imperial power and elegy in the Romantic period, Monica Greenleaf has argued that

> modern elegiac verse has tended to make its appearance as a part of a nation's or city-state's Golden Age, as a correlative of national formation and empire building. Just as the Roman elegiac poets were criticized for trivial, personal pursuits out of keeping with Rome's civic and historical mission, modern elegy appears to rise on the back of political centralization, either as a product of the civilized leisure and education it enables or as a subversive response to the official discourses of public life.[26]

While the development of Brodsky's elegiac identity endorses elegy's function as a subversive poetic stance toward a political centralization, it also communicates a nostalgic attitude toward the imperial age within which the identity was originally articulated. Elegy peaked at the height of Russia's and Europe's imperialist era, and these imperial beginnings of the elegiac tradition become strangely exposed when imposed on a non-European postcolonial territory. No matter how subversive the nineteenth-century elegists' relation with their contemporary imperial power, from Brodsky's late twentieth-century perspective the elegy was among the cultural achievements of Russia's and Europe's imperial age. With Brodsky, then, elegy is simultaneously a subversive gesture toward an imperial reality (Soviet) and a nostalgic gesture to an authentic imperial past (Russian). Through the nostalgic attitude toward elegy, the poem also constructs a nostalgic attitude toward the colonial and imperialist period, and, what is more, toward the imperial knowledge that the elegy communicates.

In Brodsky's treatment, then, elegy becomes historicized and elegy itself emerges as an object of elegiac nostalgia; what is lamented is the elegy as an aesthetic practice of an imperial era. Brodsky's "Cuernavaca" confirms, from the postimperial perspective, Jahan Ramazani's observation that for modern elegists "every elegy is an elegy for elegy—a poem that mourns the diminished efficacy and legitimacy of poetic mourning."[27] Removed from its historical origins, Brodsky's elegy can only articulate a pastiche-like relation with its historical referent.[28] This brings to mind Harsha Ram's recent observation of the genre play typical of Russian romantic poetry, which was "markedly elegiac in tendency but never completely renounced the temptations of odic rapture." This, in turn, corresponded to the "striking coexistence" in Russian romantic poetry between "imperialist sentiment" and "more dissonant currents of disenchantment, alienation, and even open defiance of the state."[29] Brodsky transposes this peculiar dialectics of Russian romantic poetry into a new era with new imperial anxieties.

In the third section Brodsky returns to the lyric situation of the first section and depicts the rainy garden topos and the ruins of European neoclassical architecture:

Конец июля прячется в дожди,
как собеседник в собственные мысли.
Что, прочем, вас не трогает в стране,
где меньше впереди, чем позади.
Бренчит гитара. Улицы раскисли.
Прохожий тонет в желтой пелене.

Включая пруд, все сильно заросло.
Кишат ужи и ящерицы. В кронах
клубятся птицы с яйцами и без.
Что губит все династии—число
наследников при недостатке в тронах.
И наступают выборы и лес.

М. не узнал бы местности. Из ниш
исчезли бюсты, портики пожухли,
стена осела деснами в овраг.
Насытишь взгляд, но смысл не удлинишь.
Сады и парки переходят в джунгли.
И с губ срывается невольно: рак.
(3:93)

July's conclusion merges with the rains
as talkers get entangled with their thoughts
—a thing of rather small concern to you;
back there the past means more than what remains.
A guitar twangs. The streets are out of sorts.
A passerby gets soaked and fades from view.

And everything's grown over, pond included.
Grass snakes and lizards swarm here, the tree crowns
bear flocks of birds, some laying eggs, some eggless.
What ruins all the dynasties, blue-blooded,
is surplus heirs replete with numbered thrones.
The woods encroach, and likewise the elections.

M. wouldn't know the place again. Each niche
is bustless now, the colonnade looks bundled,
and walls are sliding slack-jawed down the cliffs.
The gaze is sated, thoughts refuse to mesh.
The gardens and the parks become a jungle.
And "Cancer!" is what bursts out from the lips.
(*CP*, 88–89)

Here Brodsky moves away from imagining the colonial events from inside the historical moment, but he does not abandon Maximilian; instead, he assumes Maximilian's position and inspects his postcolonial surroundings through the colonizer's imperial gaze: "M. wouldn't know the place again." What he sees through the eyes of the gentlemen-colonizer are the ruins of Europe's colonial presence, ruins that satisfy his aesthetic appetite but prevent thoughts from expanding. The garden has been turned into a "jungle," the emblematic metaphor of the noncivilized in European colonial discourses; the garden's overgrown state is a metaphor of the lamentable absence of Europe's imperial past. This desire to imagine Europe's imperialist past through an aristocrat's viewpoint in a postcolonial setting, discloses the belatedness of Brodsky's position in the era of decolonization, while it also discloses the speaker's nostalgia, conditioned by the poet's experience of what he perceived as Soviet empire, for Russia's Euroimperial past.[30]

Brodsky's nostalgic use of Russian imperial knowledge, as I argued above, drew on the models provided by Russian romantic poetry. But In "Mexican Divertimento" he also used the Spanish poetic tradition, presumably, to authenticize his textual encounters with a Spanish speaking country. He framed the Mexican cycle in poetic forms whose origins were in the imperial culture of the Spanish colonizers. Brodsky comments on these forms in the notes to the English version of the cycle published in *A Part of Speech* with no apparent sensitivity to the historical perspective of colonization the poetic device reconstructs: "This poem [in reference to the cycle as a whole] employs meters that are standard in Spanish poetry." "Mérida," the third poem in the cycle and the name of a Mexican city, was written, according to Brodsky, in "the meter used by the fifteenth-century Spanish poet Jorge Manrique," while "Mexican Romancero," he notes, "has the traditional poetic form of the Spanish ballad." It is in this historical frame that he places the representational strategies of "1867," too: "'1867' is set to the rhythm of 'El Choclo,' an Argentine tango," as he explains.[31] Apart from imitating the rhythm of "El Choclo," or "The Kiss of Fire," as the tango is known in English, the representation of Maximilian and of the historical moment the poem captures, is entirely based on Euro-American and Russian appropriations of Latin American history and culture. Brodsky makes use of Dieterle's film, Manet's painting, and Maximilian's own lyric verse. In general, the poem's images of tango, eroticism, exoticism, and revolutionary action draw from a cluster of commonplaces associated with Latin America in European and Russian popular and high arts.[32] The title of the poem, "1867," the year of Maximilian's execution, highlights the significance of Maximilian's death as a symbol of an era and its end. This is the era that produced the Euroimperial knowledge on which the representations of Mexico, used in the poem, are fundamentally based. The poem "1867" promotes a subversive relation to imperial power, as discussed above, but the textual attitude it exhibits, that is, the cultural references on which Brodsky fixes his representation of imperial subversiveness, communicates a different kind of relation with that power; it is a relationship imbued with nostalgia. In articulating the events seminal to Mexican nineteenth-century history through a nostalgic re-evocation of Euro-American and Russian representations of Latin America, Brodsky also articulates his nostalgia for the imperial beginnings of these representations; he articulates a nostalgic attitude toward the sources of Euroimperial knowledge.

4

The Metropolitan Man and the Third World

Rio de Janeiro

The myth of the gentleman traveler, and his belated desire to resurrect the imperial past, has been recognized by many critics as the dominant tendency in much of contemporary Western travel writing.[1] Discussing the 1960s generation of Soviet intellectuals, Petr Vail' and Aleksander Genis argue that the myth had little use in the Soviet Union. They outline a paradigm of imperial experiences, on one end of which is the myth of the "gentleman-colonizer," which, they claim, "belongs to Anglo-Saxon nations [but] had no room in Russia," where "Kipling's 'white man's burden' became the burden of barbarity, which the [Soviet] empire brought to Europe" (*60-e*, 260). The other end of their paradigm is the Austro-Hungarian Empire and its cultural products, such as Franz Kafka and Jaroslaw Hašek, the masters of the absurd and the surreal. It is this model, Vail' and Genis assert, which their post-Stalin generation of Soviet intellectuals appropriated in their efforts to make sense out of Soviet reality.

Brodsky's poetic responses to his experience of Soviet society support Vail's and Genis's view of the significance of the Austro-Hungarian model for 1960s Soviet culture—the mental asylum of "Gorbunov and Gorchakov" as a metaphor of the Soviet state is just one example of Brodsky's perception of the Kafkaesque absurdity of Soviet surreality. However, responding to travel experience in his post-1972 works, Brodsky's authorial position drew largely on what Vail' and Genis refer to as the Anglo-Saxon model, the gentleman-colonizer. This brings forth the fact that the Anglo-Saxon, or British, and Austro-Hungarian imperial experiences had more in common than Vail' and

Genis recognize; the gentleman-colonizer was a European model, which was well-established in the nineteenth-century German-, French-, English-, and—something Vail' and Genis dismiss—Russian-language articulations of imperial experience: one has only to think of the vast literature on the Caucasus prompted by Pushkin's *A Prisoner of the Caucasus,* where the Russian poet-officer repeatedly colonizes not only land but also women.[2] This myth did not lose its cultural authority in the aesthetic practices of the Soviet era, as Brodsky's transfiguration of it in the Mexican cycle, especially in "Cuernavaca," manifests.[3] Another example of the model's persistence is provided by Andrei Bitov's 1960s and 1970s travel accounts of Armenia and Georgia, in which the author's imperial gaze is framed in a net of textual references to Pushkin and Lermontov.[4]

The lyric subject of Brodsky's Mexican cycle is caught between the two ends of the imperial paradigm as described by Vail' and Genis. The speaker's nostalgia for the Euroimperial era and one of its seminal myths, the gentleman traveler in an exotic location, is conditioned by the poet's experience of the Soviet surreality. It is the tension between these two sets of imperial knowledge and the lyric subject's attitude toward them—the nostalgic embracing of the Russian and Euroimperial and the rejection of the Soviet—that creates the crux of Brodsky's encounters with postcolonial realities. These encounters highlight the complexity of Brodsky's position in regard to the Eurocentric formations that underlie imperial myths, a position whose makings David Bethea has captured in the following way:

> The texts that Brodsky and his generation read in their formative years (Mandelstam, Tsvetaeva, Dostoevsky, the Bible) were precisely the ones that the state was furiously attempting to identify as "anarchic," "irrational," "inferior," and "immoral" and to deposit outside the culture. Moreover, these texts were the ones that reestablished continuity with a worthy past (Russian literature prior to 1917) and with Western culture. The genuinely anonymous and monolithic discourse of the Soviet state wielded massive power, but its efforts to deposit those such as Brodsky outside its midst only *empowered* the latter's language—unique, eccentric, commanding attention because of its difference. In the upside-down world of Soviet-Russian culture, the forbidden texts, which we from our perspective as late-twentieth-century "Euro-" and "logo-centric" intellectuals are apt to see as enforcers in a "hegemonic" canon, emerged as the ones that helped Brodsky and his colleagues become free individuals.[5]

Brodsky's postcolonial encounters with Mexico and Brazil, the latter being the topic of this chapter, add yet another perspective to what, from a Western viewpoint, appears as the "upside-down" Soviet context. They illustrate the incompatibility of Western and Soviet Russian experiences of the relation between the imperial and the aesthetically nonconformist; in the Leningrad counterculture that Brodsky affiliated with, a Euroimperial past was the object of an aesthetic nostalgia, whereas in 1970s Western cultural practices that past was becoming a focus of vigorous critique. Drawing from this Western critical mode, Mary Louise Pratt has detected in much of contemporary Western travel writing a repetition of the nineteenth-century "monarch-of-all-I-survey" scene, whose origins she locates in the nineteenth-century explorers' travel accounts of European colonies. According to Pratt, the imperial vantage point and the rhetoric of natural wonders and geographical discoveries still function as a model for contemporary travel writers and their representations of non-European territories. The rhetoric devices of "aestheticization, density of meaning, and domination" are, as Pratt writes, "transposed into a very different historical moment and a different esthetic key." The nineteenth-century aestheticization of landscape, the beauty and the sublime of non-European territories, is turned into the third-world cityscapes constructed of "ugliness, grotesquery, and decay." What has remained constant, Pratt asserts, is postcolonial metropolitan writers' claim to the "authoritativeness for their vision," which suggests "no sense of limitation on their interpretive powers." Just as the nineteenth-century explorers, these writers "are still up there, commanding the view, assigning it value." Analyzing Alberto Moravia's *Which Tribe Do You Belong To?* (1972), set in Ghana, and Paul Theroux's reflections on Guatemala City in *The Old Patagonian Express* (1978), Pratt asserts that the "monarch-of-all-I survey" scene "gets repeated from the balconies of hotels in big third-world cities" in the works of these "widely read canonical writers," who "are speaking from the 1970s, deep in the postcolonial era of 'underdevelopment' and decolonization," when few new areas of the globe are left for Europeans to discover, and "the myth of the civilizing mission" bears no cultural authority in the old ones.[6]

Some of the representational strategies Brodsky uses in his Mexican cycle, and especially in the prose account of his trip to Brazil, accord in a surprising fashion with Pratt's analysis of the metropolitan discourse of the third world. The title of the fourth poem in Brodsky's Mexican cycle, excluded from the English cycle, "V otele 'Kontinental'" ("In the Hotel 'Continental'"), epitomizes the "balcony convention," while it discloses the speaker's imperial vantage point, the hotel window.[7] The view of Mexico City is depicted through geometrical images: "Mondrian's victory. Behind the [window] glass / a feast of cubic content. The air is either drunk on / ninety degree angles, / or generously poured into a parallelepiped" (3:96). The view, presented as an abstraction, renders the cityscape void of historical references and as such incapable of producing any historically significant meanings. Instead, the geometrical forms frame a view for the speaker's voyeuristic indulgence; apart from the city, he is observing a woman undressing.[8]

But rather than the poetic cycle of Mexico, it is Brodsky's prose account of Brazil that is astonishingly similar to Moravia's and Theroux's representational strategies as analyzed by Pratt. The author's metropolitan approach to Brazil is established at the beginning of the text when he informs the reader that "I had flown in [to Brazil] from England" and that "by the second day I already felt like packing, like going back to New York" ("After a Journey," 62, 69). When he later writes that "the essence of all my travels (their side effect, rather, turning into their essence) is in returning here, to Morton Street—in a more and more minute elaboration of the new meaning invested in my notion of 'home,'" and that "I will probably never return to Liteynyi 27, and 44 Morton is but a last-ditch attempt to get away from perceiving the world as a one-way street" (ibid., 69–70), he not only summarizes the geographic narrative of his exile but also establishes metropolitan authorial subjectivity: he has moved from Leningrad, the historical capital of the Russian Empire and a Soviet metropolitan city, to New York, and more specifically to Greenwich Village, a center of cosmopolitan literati. It is from there that he is now looking back on his "junket" in Brazil made "in the name of international cultural exchange" (ibid., 62). Whether articulated in the original Russian or the translated English, the author's status is clearly, even if self-ironically, pinned down: he is a metropolitan man of letters, a Soviet exile who in an international conference finds himself "fighting like a lion for the creation of a PEN Club section for Vietnamese writers-in-exile" (ibid., 67).

The travel experience is described throughout Brodsky's Brazilian anti-travelogue as something the author relates reluctantly to and would rather forget. This rhetoric of amnesia (see chap. 1) discloses the author's impulse to reject what he sees and to dissociate himself from it. Elaborating at the beginning of the essay on the subtitle "Homage to Vertebrae," he formulates his opinion of the intellectual capacities required from an author of "travel notes and memoirs" in the following way: "the mind there seems to get flat on its back and give up resistance, preparing for a rest rather than for settling scores with reality" (ibid., 62). This skeptical characterization of travel writing as something of an anti-intellectual exercise appears, however, as a mere rhetorical gesture, since he ventures on to describe the realities of his travel experience, the country, and its people with assertiveness, which discloses little doubt in his perceptual capacities or in their authoritative force. If his writing comes across as unimaginative, the fault lies with what he describes, he seems to be saying, not with his capacities to describe it:

> Rio—at least the part I managed to see—is a very monotonous city, with all its riches and its poverty, both by accident and by design. The two- or three-kilometer strip between the ocean and the looming cliffs is entirely overgrown with utterly moronic—à la that idiot Le Corbusier—beehive "structures." As though the vista denies man imagination. Perhaps it does. The eighteenth and the nineteenth centuries are completely wiped out. Occasionally you can bump into the debris of the mercantile style of the turn of the century, with its surreal medley of arcades, balconies, winding stairs, turrets, gates, and whatnot. But this is rare, and of no relief. And equally rare and relief-free are the small three- or four-floor hotels in the back streets behind the concrete-cum-stucco giants, or in the narrow lanes climbing up the hills at a minimum seventy-five-degree angle, winding up into an evergreen forest, the real jungle. There, in these narrow streets, in little villas and cobbled-up tenements, dwells the local population, employed mainly by the tourist outfits: extremely poor, somewhat desperate, but on the whole not overtly protesting. At night, at every ten meters or so, you are offered a fuck, and later the West German consul treated us to the observation that prostitutes in Rio do not take money—or at least do not expect to get any, and are surprised if a client offers to pay. ("After a Journey," 63–64)

The assertiveness with which the author evaluates, gives meaning, and patronizes—the rhetorical power of his condemnation—ascribes to the metropolitan discourse of the third world, which, as Pratt claims, uses repeatedly the rhetorical devices of "negation, domination, devaluation, and fear," which, in turn, produce an "intense 'effect of the real'" (*Imperial Eyes*, 220). The trivialization of the cityscape ("a very monotonous city"), the dehumanization of the locals' living conditions ("the real jungle"), and the threat that the legendary prostitution and sexual promiscuity of the locals poses to the metropolitan author (his knowledge of these is, of course, offered to the reader as second-hand) exemplify the rhetoric Pratt detects in Moravia's and Theroux's descriptions of Ghana and Guatemala, the "rhetoric of triviality, dehumanization, and rejection," which, in Pratt's opinion, informed the "new esthetic key" of metropolitan representations of postcoloniality.

Among the things the author in the passage quoted above condemns is the lack of imperial architecture: "The eighteenth and the nineteenth centuries are completely wiped out." In other words, the signifiers of Europe's colonization are gone. This is in tune with the author's ironic yet nostalgic comments on the lost opportunities of European exploration and adventure in the tropics (see chap. 1). The landscape, as he further laments, is "entirely overgrown with utterly moronic—à la that idiot Le Corbusier—beehive 'structures.'" This is later summarized in a maxim: "Rio is a most abstract place" ("After a Journey," 66)—recalling the view of Mexico City as captured in "In the Hotel 'Continental.'" The natural landscape is void of meaning, too, and incapable of provoking thoughts in the author: "As though the vista denies man imagination." Just as the garden-turned-jungle in "Cuernavaca" prevents thoughts from expanding, the landscape in Brazil denies creative thinking (see chap. 3).

The core of the critique Pratt launches in her discussion of Theroux's and Moravia's works is aimed at these writers' Eurocentric positions. There is, eventually, an ethical imperative in Pratt's critique: the writers she discusses turn a blind eye, she maintains, to the dynamics between the postcoloniality they reject and the metropolitan culture they embrace, by choosing to ignore the colonial relations of subjugation between the cultures they represent and the cultures they describe (*Imperial Eyes*, 218). Not having the historical tie with Brazil that Pratt claims Theroux and Moravia should acknowledge with Guatemala and Ghana, Brodsky creates one—not in order to critique the postcolonial relations of subjugation, but, on the contrary, to claim a right to his metropolitan position: Brodsky invents a European identity, and he does so by way of negation. Because of the strangeness of local vegetation and the absence of colonial architecture, the author of Brodsky's travel account argues, Rio de Janeiro cannot produce any memories "no matter how many years you spend there" (according to the author himself, he spent a week there). "For a native of Europe," he continues, "Rio is biological neutrality incarnate," the local vegetation "neither corresponds to nor echoes any species a European is used to." As for the architecture: "Not a single façade, not one little lane or gateway, evokes any associations. It is a city of this century: nothing colonial, or even Victorian" ("After a Journey," 66). Only a building that reminds him simultaneously of St. Isaac's Cathedral in St. Petersburg and the Capitol in Washington, D.C.—both simulations of classical Greek and Roman architecture and expressions of imperial power—meets the approval of the author, the "native of Europe," "vykhodets iz Evropy" in the Russian text (6:59).

It is instructive to parallel Brodsky's Latin American imaginings with his poems about European cities from the viewpoint of how European identity is constructed in his post-1972 travel writing. The urban highlights of Brodsky's poems of the 1970s and 1980s form a poetic travel guide to Europe, in which the speaker is driven by the touristic urge of "been there, done that": "rain in Rotterdam," "night at San Marco," "December in Florence"; in London he keeps affirming that "the city of London is wonderful"; in Paris he notes in a seemingly nonchalant manner that he had "shown up in the Luxembourg garden"; and in Rome he expresses undisguised gratitude: "I was in Rome. I was flooded by light." In all of these poems, written as if to report back to the readers left in the Soviet Union that he made it to Europe, the speaker seems to seek a confirmation for his presence in culturally and historically significant sites, the topographic landmarks and historical monuments that form the canonical cultural landscape of his desired Western Europe. This reinforcement of his presence among the signifiers of European cultural values inadvertently emphasizes his displacement in relation to their signified; the lyric subject, touring the western parts of Cold War Europe, is writing in Russian, speaking in Russian, articulating his presence in Russian. He is one of Europe's *others*:

> *Я пишу эти строки,* сидя на белом стуле
> под открытом небом, *раздвигая скулы*
> *фразами на родном.*
> Стынет кофе. Плещет лагуна, сотней
> мелких бликов тусклый зрачок казня
> за стремленье запомнить пейзаж, способный
> обойтись без меня.
> (3:240; emphasis added)

> I am writing these lines sitting outdoors, in winter,
> on a white iron chair, in my shirtsleeves, a little drunk;
> the lips move slowly enough to hinder
> the vowels of the mother tongue,

> and the coffee grows cold. And the blinding lagoon is lapping
> at the shore as the dim human pupil's bright penalty
> for its wish to arrest a landscape quite happy
> here without me.
> (*CP*, 308)

This is the last stanza in "Venetian Stanzas 2," where the contrast between "mother tongue" and Venetian environment conveys a sense of displacement and an acknowledgement of the lyric subject's otherness. In "Venetian Stanzas 1" his outsider's position in regard to Europe is conveyed through identification with Shakespeare's "Moor," of which more will be said in chapter 6.

But despite the strong sense of being an outsider, the lyric subject's attitude toward the European cityscapes is always affirmative. He never questions their cultural or historical value. This affirmative attitude toward the urban environment is entirely altered in the texts reflecting Brodsky's encounters with Mexico and Brazil. In the travel texts that relate to his trips to non-European countries, he reconstructs a metropolitan European identity through a denouncement and devaluation of the non-European cityscapes.

The occasional verse Brodsky included in the English version of "After a Journey" (*GR*) presents many of the key motifs of Brodsky's perception of Latin America by means of a playful song, which Brodsky titled "Rio Samba." The poem, written in the tone of a light lyric, appears at the end of the essay and is presented as the sole poetic outcome of the trip, whose significance the author has used the entire essay to undermine. But despite the "doggerel" quality of the lines, a word he uses himself, the lyrics do, however, present some views, which imply that the "vistas" provoked more thoughts than the speaker/narrator is willing to credit to them:

> Come to Rio, oh come to Rio.
> Grow a mustache and change your bio.
> Here the rich get richer, the poor get poorer,
> here each old man is a *Sturmbahnführer*.
>
> Come to Rio, oh come to Rio.
> There is no other city with such brio.
> There are phones by Siemens, and even Jews
> drive around like crazy in VWs.

Come to Rio, oh come to Rio.
Here Urania rules and no trace of Clio.
Buildings ape Corbusier's beehive-cum-waffle,
though this time you can't blame this on the Luftwaffe.

Come to Rio, oh come to Rio.
Here every bird sings "O sole mio."
So do fish when caught, so do proud snow geese
in midwinter here, in Portuguese.

Come to Rio, oh come to Rio.
It's the Third World all right, so they still read Leo
Trotsky, Guevara, and other sirens;
still, the backwardness spares them the missile silos.

Come to Rio, oh come to Rio.
If you come in duo, you may leave in trio.
If you come alone, you'll leave with a zero
in your thoughts as valuable as one cruzeiro.
(*CP*, 461)

Brodsky makes a comparison between the creative impulse triggered by Rio de Janeiro and the country's deflated third-world currency—"If you come alone, you'll leave with a zero / in your thoughts as valuable as one cruzeiro"—appropriating thus one of the series of metropolitan stereotypes about "third world" he casually presents in the poem. References to the fact that many Germans, among them officers of the Nazi army, settled in Brazil after World War II are fused with the European clichéd perception of chaotic third-world traffic and tropical climate. As the author self-ironically observes: "This, of course, could have been written without my leaving Manhattan. As quite a lot of far better stuff was written, even by me. Guilt, as I said, is a better vehicle [than confidence]. Still, I've dipped myself into the southern Atlantic and in general insinuated my body into what until then was just a high-school geography lesson. *Ergo sum*" ("After a Journey," 79). One can easily fill in the missing term of the author's elliptic quotation: "I travel, therefore I am," even if the target, as in the case of Brazil—as the whole text is designed to demonstrate—was barely worth the effort.

But among the apparently amusing puns and word play, which the author presents to the reader, framed in apologetic discursive gestures, there is in

"Rio Samba" a poetic statement that sums up Brodsky's historical and geographical imagination as projected on Brazil. What seems to be the central point of the author's condemnation of the place is his view of Rio de Janeiro having no history: "Here Urania rules and no trace of Clio." In this one line, framed in references to Greek mythology, Brodsky summarizes one of the central themes that informs colonial discourses, the theme of "historical lack."[9] In Brodsky's poetic vocabulary, Urania connotes space and geography, Clio time and history. In other words, space and geography rule in Rio de Janeiro, while time and history have no role to play.[10] This is the major point of Brodsky's Brazilian lament and echoes the prose passage quoted earlier, in which the author observes the absence of the signifiers of colonial history. In the Euroimperial hierarchy Brodsky establishes, Europe equals historical meaning, while the territories and cultures outside Europe equal space, an idea Brodsky develops further, making it one of the key metaphors of his travel account of Istanbul. In "Rio Samba" Brodsky's strategies of representation again coincide with Pratt's description of the third-world discourse, and now in an English-language poem; representing the nonmetropolitan parts of the world as having no history is one of the seminal strategies of Western dehumanization and domination in the contemporary travel accounts Pratt analyzes.[11]

There is, however, a line in the samba that brings forth once more the complexity of Brodsky's Soviet Russian position in regard to what, in Pratt's reading of contemporary travel writing, discloses Euroimperial and Western metropolitan formations in a postimperial era. In the penultimate stanza—"it's the Third World all right, so they still read Leo / Trotsky, Guevara, and other sirens; / still, the backwardness spares them the missile silos"—Brodsky spells out his opinions of the "Third World" in direct and unapologetic terms. But the ideological makeup of these opinions is more intricate than first meets the eye; the word "still" is the key here and points many ways. The first "still" in the quote reconstructs the historical awareness through which to judge the "backwardness" of the underdeveloped "Third World" contrasted with the apparent advancement of the developed world, whose voice the speaker assumes in the poem. But immediately after proposing this view, the speaker seems to skeptically challenge that very advancement; by stating that "still, the backwardness spares them the missile silos," he seems to be saying that the fact of the Soviet Union and the Western powers being caught in the Cold War arms race questions their non-"backwardness," or advancement; the fundamental hierarchy of the developed and the underdeveloped world is momentarily questioned. And yet, read against the Euroimperial hierarchy of time and space Brodsky creates in the poem, the "backwardness" assigned to the "Third World" appears as a rather sincere opinion from the speaker's part, and in fact recalls the contrast between technological advancement and the prehistoric, introduced in last lines of the Mexican cycle where the "lizard" is passively observing a "spaceship's passage" (see chap. 3, p. 88). This, in turn, communicates a complaint about "a kind of esthetic and semantic underdevelopment [which is connected] with the prehistoric," as Pratt sums up this representational device characteristic of the metropolitan discourse.[12]

At the same time, to point out again a distinction between Brodsky and the Western metropolitan writers Pratt analyzes—and to go back to the first use of "still"—the use of the word there reflects the poet's experience of a postrevolutionary country, the Soviet Union, an experience through which he seeks to legitimize his position. The author's Soviet experience, the reasoning seems to go, provides him with the historical perspective to *know* what happens when the works of the "sirens" are put into practice: nothing good comes out of it. It recalls the resigned and disillusioned authorial voice that Brodsky establishes in "Mexican Romancero," "To Evgeny," and "Encyclopedia Entry," and that was contrasted with Mayakovsky's revolutionary enthusiasm in chapter 3. In other words, in "Rio Samba" Brodsky turns the position of a Soviet Russian writer to his speaker's advantage and, in one more move, through his Soviet experience assumes a doubly authoritative position in regard to the "Third World." His denouncement of the "Third World" is that of a metropolitan Westernized writer—the poem is written in English, the global post- or neoimperial language—as well as that of an ex-Soviet citizen, who has the authority provided by his "native" knowledge to call the popularized figures of Marxist ideology "sirens," seductive and destructive at once. Meanwhile, this authorial construction is obviously informed by the author's awareness of his status as a Soviet emigrant, a political underdog of the Cold War world order, and a potential object of Western "monarchic surveys" refashioned after Euroimperial models.[13] The author's condemnation of the "Third World" is, then, informed by his struggle for legitimacy, for an access to the Westernized metropolitan position he creates in the travelogue.

To return to the poem with its perception of the lamentable lack of three factors in Latin America—historical meaning (no trace of Clio), colonial architecture (in the place of which there are Corbusier's "beehives"), and political perceptiveness ("still" reading Trotsky and others)—the poem strikes the reader as a rather melancholic samba. To keep with the musical metaphor, it is kind of a "third-world blues," as Pratt designates the genre she finds characteristic of much of contemporary Western travel writing related to the world outside Europe and North America. The lament that this genre exhibits, Pratt concludes, "seems to remain remarkably uniform across representations of different places, and by westerners of different nationalities. It is a monolith, like the official construct of the 'third world' it encodes."[14] Based on the textual evidence of Brodsky's Mexican and Brazilian encounters, the representational strategies of the discourse concerned not only "westerners of different nationalities" but also metropolitan writers on both sides of the Cold War divisions. As a Leningrad writer Brodsky was, no matter how marginalized within the officialdom of Soviet cultural politics, a Soviet metropolitan man, someone for whom Irgutsk and Lithuania alike were Soviet provinces and Mexico "similar to our Central-Asian republics."

Brodsky formulates this metropolitan position in a Soviet context in a passage in "After a Journey," when, writing about his futile efforts to speak about Russian culture to an international audience, he makes a rather unexpected parallel between himself and the "official messengers of Russian culture," by whom he presumably means writers who would be sent to international conferences as official representatives of the Soviet Writers' Union. He imagines how these official representatives "feel the same way [as the author], particularly when they drag their bones across all kinds of Mogadishus and Ivory Coasts. Because everywhere there is dust, rusty soil, twisted chunks of decaying metal, unfinished buildings, the swarthy multitudes of the local population for whom you mean nothing, just like for your own" ("After a Journey," 80).[15] In this passage Brodsky assumes the Soviet Russian metropolitan view of the underdeveloped world, in this case African third-world countries. Meanwhile, the metropolitan man's lament over the urban decay and over-population of the third world expresses also "the lament of the Intellectual and the Writer" (Pratt's phrase) in the age of mass tourism and mass culture, Western and Soviet alike, when a writer, whether exiled or privileged by his native country, in this case the Soviet Union, does not enjoy the kind of status in his country the author seems to think he, and writers in general, should enjoy. As for the relation between this Soviet metropolitan position and the Eurocentric formations, which Pratt critiques and whose role in the upside-down Soviet world Bethea captures, in Brodsky's case the metropolitan approach to the world outside the metropolis often coincided with a nostalgia for Eurocentric formations and the myths these formations induced. If, indeed, as Patrick

Holland and Graham Huggan claim in their explorations of the works of such popular writers as Bruce Chatwin and V. S. Naipaul, "British travel writing, in the nominally postimperial era, continues to trade successfully in ironically recycled imperial myths,"[16] then Brodsky's case—the case of an Americanized Soviet Russian Nobel Prize–winner—shows that inventively and ironically recycled imperial myths can be successfully traded not only in British but metropolitan travel writing at large. But in order to understand how Brodsky arrived at his idiosyncratic use of Eurocentric/imperial myths, one has to take into account the monolithic Soviet discourse against which his Eurocentric position was formed. Brodsky's Leningrad Eurocentrism was a nostalgic construction shaped by an experience of a cultural environment in which affiliation with Euroimperial canons and cultural values was a sign of an antagonistic attitude toward the hegemony of the official Soviet culture.

5

Time, Space, and Orientalism

Istanbul

Why does Nietzsche challenge the pursuit of the origins (*Ursprung*), at least on those occasions when he is truly a genealogist? First, because it is an attempt to capture the exact essence of things, their purest possibilities, and their carefully protected identities; because this search assumes the existence of immobile forms that precede the external world of accident and succession. . . . However, if a genealogist refuses to extend his faith in metaphysics, if he listens to history, he finds that there is "something altogether different" behind things: not a timeless and essential secret, but the secret that they have no essence or that their essence was fabricated in a piecemeal fashion from alien forms.

—MICHEL FOUCAULT, "Nietzsche, Genealogy, History," 1971

In the system of knowledge about the Orient, the Orient is less a place than a *topos*, a set of references, a congeries of characteristics, that seem to have its origin in a quotation, or a fragment of a text, or a citation from someone's work on the Orient, or a bit of previous imagining, or an amalgam of all these.

—EDWARD SAID, *Orientalism*, 1978

There are two versions of Brodsky's travel account of Istanbul: the Russian-language "Puteshestvie v Stambul" ("Journey to Istanbul") was translated into English by Alan Myers under the title "Flight from Byzantium."[1] Both versions of the essay were published in 1985, the Russian in the Paris-based émigré journal *Kontinent*, and the English in the *New Yorker*, the New York–based magazine popular among the Anglophone Western readership. After the initial appearance the English text continued to feature in high-profile publications. It was included in *Less Than One*, Brodsky's first collection of essays published by Farrar, Straus and Giroux. It was also picked out to be reprinted in *The Best American Essays of 1986*, which marked the inception of the subcategory for essays in the Best American series by Houghton Mifflin. Meanwhile, the Russian version was reprinted in a number of publications, which established Brodsky's fame in Russia in the post-perestroika years. Furthermore, the title of the English text featured as the title of the Italian and German collections of Brodsky's essays, *Fuga da Bisanzio* and *Flucht aus Byzanz*, respectively; both were published soon after Brodsky received the Nobel Prize for Literature in 1987. With all this in mind, it is hardly an exaggeration to claim that the text is one of the most influential pieces of Russian travel writing of the recent past.[2]

From the first reader responses to later academic and critical reflections, Brodsky's "sustained jeremiad" has stirred up sensibilities and provoked emotions in both Russian- and English-language audiences. Within academic criticism these emotions indicate a cultural divide: the American reception has tried to come to terms with Brodsky's idiosyncratic use of cultural and ethnic stereotypes, while the Russian reception has mostly been astonished by what is usually perceived as the essay's stylistic idiosyncrasy.[3] These responses are not, however, mutually exclusive but point to two sides of the same coin. The authorial voice of "Flight from Byzantium" is highly stylized, elusive, ironic, and even parodic; the author dwells on cultural commonplaces, showing off his brilliance in mastering both Russian and Western myths and mythologies of East and West. At the same time, the textual play raises questions about these mythologies and the bias the author projects through them, and, inescapably, it also raises questions about Brodsky's own position in regard to the bias. But rather than tackling the futile question of how close Brodsky's opinions were to those projected in "Flight from Byzantium," we need to look at this perplexing text-event from the viewpoint of literary tourism, that is, travel writing as a discursive practice common in contemporary cultural practices. The Russian and English versions of Brodsky's travelogue belong to two different textual spaces, which conjure up two separate sets of cultural frameworks, as Thomas Venclova has pointed out in "A Journey from Petersburg to Istanbul"; at the same time, there is a discursive space where the Russian and English versions not only collide but also coincide, and that is the space of "Orientalism," a space that any literary journey to the "Orient" inevitably evokes.[4]

The Oriental Journey as a Polemic

As if anticipating the controversial reception of his essay on both the Russian and American sides, Brodsky opens the text to "Flight from Byzantium" with a disclaimer:

> Bearing in mind that every observation suffers from the observer's personal traits—that is, it too often reflects his psychological state rather than that of the reality under observation—I suggest that what follows be treated with a due measure of skepticism, if not with total disbelief. The only thing the observer may claim by way of justification is that he, too, possesses a modicum of reality, inferior in extent, perhaps, but conceding nothing in quality to the subject under scrutiny. A semblance of objectivity might be achieved, no doubt, by way of a complete self-awareness at the moment of observation. I do not think I am capable of this; in any event, I did not aspire to it. All the same, I hope that something of the sort took place. ("Flight," 393)

This opening establishes an authorial voice that is highly self-conscious and self-ironic. It brings forth the question that travel writing irrevocably foregrounds, that of the subject's relation with his environment and the subject's ability to represent that environment objectively. But rather than descending into the Kantian depths of the problem he conjures up, Brodsky uses it as a stepstool for an ironic resignation of all responsibility for his travel notes; he undermines at the outset the authenticity of the narrative and the credibility of its narrator, after which he moves on to undermine the initial impetus to go on the journey he is about to recount:

> My desire to get to Istanbul was never a genuine one. I am not even sure whether such a word—"desire"—should be used here. On the other hand, it could hardly be called a mere whim or a subconscious urge. Let it be a desire, then, and let's note that it came about partly as the result of a promise I made to myself in 1972, on leaving my hometown, that of Leningrad, for good—to circumnavigate the inhabited world along the latitude and along the longitude (i.e., the Pulkovo meridian) on which Leningrad is situated. ("Flight," 393–94)

After revealing this autobiographical motivation, the author immediately downplays its significance by hinting at another, more important motive for his trip, as well as a number of less important ones. The list of what he calls the "secondary and tertiary motives," designated by letters from "a" to "e" (in Russian, from "a" to "d"), are finally followed by what is presented as the main reason leading to the author's trip—that is, a conversation with an "American Byzantinist":

> This "chief" reason represents the pinnacle of fancifulness. It has to do with the fact that several years ago, while I was talking to a friend of mine, an American Byzantinist, it occurred to me that the cross that Constantine beheld in his dream on the eve of his victory over Maxentius—the cross that bore the legend "In this sign, conquer"—was not in fact a Christian cross but an urban one, the basic element of any Roman settlement. . . . The consequences of this move of his were so momentous that, whether I was right or wrong, I felt an urge to see this place. After all, I spent thirty-two years in what is known as the Third Rome, about a year and a half in the First. Consequently, I needed the Second, if only for my collection. . . . But let us handle all this in an orderly fashion, so far as this is feasible. ("Flight," 395)

Again, the author ironically undermines his own authority; he debunks outright the idea he is about to introduce by referring to it as a "pinnacle of fancifulness." The self-conscious and metatextual commentary that opens the next passage—"But let us handle all this in an orderly fashion, so far as this is feasible"—further undermines the author's discursive authority by questioning the possibility, and more specifically, the author's own ability, to have a coherent discussion around the thought he has just introduced. Seeking a Russian pretext for the highly ironic and stylized voice of Brodsky's text, Thomas Venclova writes that the narrative "device" deployed by Brodsky "cannot be termed as 'skaz,' if only because the distance between narrator and author is hard to define. One should speak rather of a specific narrative mode. Among other things, this mode involves constantly checking with the reader or interlocutor, constantly provoking him, aiming at a dialogue that ends without having time to begin."[5] Venclova analyzes Brodsky's text as divided into a "narrative part," which has "the marks of a scholarly philosophical tract . . . packed" with "names, dates and facts" and a "lyrical part . . . dominated by metaphor and metonymy, by the ironic joke, or simply by the cry." Apart from these two, there is the "meta-textual chapter 23 [25 in the English text], where the author expresses his dissatisfaction at the fact that his notes have gotten out of hand" (ibid., 140–41). Another example of metatextuality, in the sense Venclova has in mind, is chapter 37 (35 in Russian), where the author comments on the polemic catalyst that triggered off his writing of the essay, and anticipating the "objections" his essay will arouse in "an art historian or an ethnologist"; Brodsky asserts that "if I hadn't foreseen these objections I wouldn't have taken up my pen" ("Flight," 434–35). The narrative mode, which reminds Venclova of *skaz*, highlights the questions of authenticity and authorial reliability. These questions, seminal to travel writing, were epitomized by Laurence Sterne's *A Sentimental Journey*, which, despite the fact that its early Russian reception "smoothed over" its "sense of playful ambivalence," as Andreas Schönle has recently remarked, had a great influence on Russian travel narratives, not to say anything of the English travel canon.[6] Brodsky's *sternizm* is laid bare right at the beginning of the essay, when his author speculates on the motives of his trip, the "ridiculous notions" as he calls them, echoing Sterne's playful classification of "reasons to travel."[7]

The devices that Venclova describes and that make up the narrative mode of Brodsky's essay are, then, a common trait in travel writing: toying with the idea of travel, textual play and literary parody, the composition of loosely related notes, the ironic play with authorial credibility and the constant addressing of the reader, together with the formal hybridity and the blurring of the boundary between fact and fiction, objectivity and subjectivity, constitute what Patrick Holland and Graham Huggan have termed "discursive conflicts," typical of travel writing. Travel writing functions, they write, appropriating Hayden White's terminology, as "fictions of factual representation." Travel narratives "claim validity—or make as if to claim it—by referring to actual events and places, but then assimilate those events and places to highly personal vision."[8] Brodsky's essay is a display of discursive conflicts typical of contemporary travel writing. The author is represented as an amateur enthusiast in a discipline (Byzantine history) from which he borrows freely, showing sometimes erudition and sometimes a lack of it. His uninhibited interventions into history, geography, ethnography, and anthropology are equaled by the candid subjectivity of the conclusions he draws from them. The occasional attempt at objective analysis is frequently undermined by emotional interventions and by discursive gestures—such as "let us handle all this in orderly fashion, so far as this is feasible," or "what happened next everybody knows: from out of who knows where appeared the Turks," or "I have no clear notion of what was going on in Judea at the time," or "here I should like to admit that my idea concerning antiquity seems somewhat wild even to me." These discursive gestures undercut the seriousness of a scholarly discourse, specifically of history-writing, which the author seems to occasionally strive at, and make the reader wonder whether the author is parodying that discourse. Meanwhile, the alternation between a "semi-ethnographic, distanced, analytic mode" and an "autobiographical, emotionally tangled mode," as Rob Nixon characterizes V. S. Naipaul's travel narratives, points at Brodsky's conscious and ironic play on authorial subjectivity.[9] The elusive voice of Brodsky's author, which could have been heard in "Leningrad and Moscow kitchens in conversations among intellectuals, or rather quasi-intellectuals," as Thomas Venclova contextualizes it, fluctuates between a voice of a pedagogue giving a lecture on Alexandrian elegists, a memoirist remembering his parents, a writer consciously parodying the conventions of his genre, a weary tourist complaining about other tourists, a public intellectual denouncing contemporary culture, or any (male) participant in a private conversation accentuated by anecdotes, jokes, and double-entendre. Periodically, Brodsky also deploys the rhetorical device of ending a passage with a question, leaving the reader with the feeling that, despite the forceful polemic the author launches, he really only offers open ends.

Despite these figures of speech and rhetorical patterns, which make it difficult to pin down the author's position, and which remind one of the rhetorical devices Brodsky used in "After a Journey," the author ventures on to assert opinions and give authoritative meanings to the imaginative geography of "East" and "West" that he creates in the essay. He also creates a narrative of historical events and advances a conception of history, which, despite the ubiquitous irony and play with myths, is fixed firmly on recurring ideas and themes he had introduced in his works before writing the travelogue.[10] When read against the significations that Brodsky gives to such concepts as empire, time and space, history, and geography elsewhere in his poetry and prose, the opinions he launches in "Flight from Byzantium" emerge as having more weight than the reader might assign in his playful appropriations of literary conventions and cultural commonplaces at first blush.

Among the literary conventions Brodsky toys with is the encounter with the "Orient." The Oriental journey was established as a productive subgenre of the Russian travelogue at the beginning of the nineteenth century, so much so that Pushkin, rewriting his "Journey to Arzrum" in 1835, was able to parody the genre.[11] But if Pushkin, through parody, attempted to "disengage himself from Orientalist discourse, both professional and poetic, and clear a space for his own journey in the overpopulated space of literary travel," to quote Monika Greenleaf's formulation of Pushkin's textual play, then Brodsky's text seems to be triggered by the realizations that such a disengagement is impossible and that the only way to encounter the East is to encounter the discourse of it. And he does so by fiercely polemicizing that discourse, both its Russian and English variants.

The English title "Flight from Byzantium" rebukes outright the tradition it refers to by turning on its head the title of W. B. Yeats's "Sailing to Byzantium," one of the seminal imaginings of the Orient in English-language canonical poetry. The reversed movement in Brodsky's title anticipates the reversed approach; what Brodsky rebukes is Yeats's romanticized perception of Oriental (Byzantine) refinement and wisdom, which he replaces with an imaginative history and geography where the Byzantine heritage engenders all that the author considers culturally and morally undesirable. If the historical Constantinople was for centuries "the city of the world's desire," as a recent book title claims, then Brodsky sets out to show that there is very little if anything to desire in the contemporary Istanbul.[12] The author's provocative attempt to write against what he perceives as a Western perception of Byzantium and the "East" is highlighted ironically at the beginning of the essay, when he claims that the impetus for his trip to Istanbul rose from an idea conceived during a conversation with a "friend of mine, an American Byzantinist." Brodsky's provocation did not pass the English-language audience unnoticed. The *New York Times* book critic John Gross anticipated, in a review of *Less Than One* shortly after its appearance, that some readers of Brodsky's "account of [his] recent visit to Istanbul—will no doubt find Mr. Brodsky guilty—of Orientalism, in the pejorative sense."[13] What Gross refers to are the negative remarks aimed at Turkish and Islamic cultures, which, when pronounced in English, repeat the whole gamut of biased misconceptions and negative characterizations informing the Orientalist discourse as described by Edward Said in *Orientalism*, published a few years before Brodsky's essay was written. The following extract from "Flight" is one of the central passages where Brodsky launches his attack of the "East":

> If Byzantine soil turned out to be so favorable for Islam it was most likely because of its ethnic texture—a mixture of races and nationalities that had neither local nor, moreover, overall memory of any kind of coherent tradition of individualism. Dreading generalizations, I will add that the East means, first of all, a tradition of obedience, of hierarchy, of profit, of trade, of adaptability: a tradition, that is, drastically alien to the principles of a moral absolute, whose role—I mean the intensity of the sentiment—is fulfilled here by the idea of kinship, of family. I foresee objections, and am even willing to accept them, in whole or in part. But no matter what extreme of idealization of the East

> we may entertain, we'll never be able to ascribe to it the least semblance of democracy. ("Flight," 417)

Brodsky's essay—with its self-consciously provocative reinforcement of some of the most common generalizations of "Eastern," especially Muslim and Arab societies, as anti-individualistic, anti-democratic, oriented toward profit-making and trade—was a heady intervention into the Orientalist debate; it appears to be aimed at pulling the rug from under Said's argument by approaching it from an ideologically opposite angle with the authority of an exiled Soviet writer.[14] It is as if Brodsky was returning the ticket of Western Orientalization of Russia by assuming a moral upper hand over the knowledge of the Orient's true character; the Oriental origins of Russian despotism, he seems to claim, are even more insidious than the Westerners in their naivety can imagine.[15] In Said's study the Orient comes across as a victim of the discursive power and colonial domination imposed on it by Western countries, but in Brodsky's conjecture it is the West that should be viewed as a victim: the West is a victim of its own metaphysical naivety demonstrated by its "unwitting reduction of its notions of evil"; "by divorcing Byzantium," Brodsky writes, "Western Christianity consigned the East to nonexistence, and thus reduced its own notion of human negative potential to a considerable, perhaps even a perilous, degree" ("Flight," 422).[16] Brodsky projects this demonized, in a very literal sense, perception of the "East" on the Soviet Union, which emerges as the contemporary incarnation of all calamities, ills and corruption engendered by the "East." As a cultural document of the late Cold War period, the English version of Brodsky's essay reads as a sermon to warn the West of the East, which in the form of the Soviet Union is "now by the walls of Vienna" (ibid., 438). This specific reference to the Cold War world order is an addition to the English text. From the English-language perspective the polemic Brodsky raises in "Flight from Byzantium" is twofold. It is directed, on the one hand, against the traditional Yeatsian idealization of the Orient, and, on the other hand, against the more contemporary Saidian position, where the non-Western viewpoint is adopted by Western intellectuals to critique the West's own colonial and representational power over the Orient. In addition, there is a more mundane level in Brodsky's critique put forward in the ironic observation that the fact of Istanbul being so "cheap" for Western tourists "constitutes that celebrated 'fascination' of the East for the northern Scrooge." While there is a sense of self-criticism in the satirical "northern Scrooge" ("severnyi skriaga"), in what follows, included only in the English text, the satire is redirected away from the author and targeted exclusively at other (Western) tourists. The "vulgarity and crassness" of the touristic quest, he writes, "is markedly more innocent, and of better consequence for the locals, than that of some talkative smart-ass Parisienne, or of the spiritual lumpen fatigued by yoga, Buddhism, or Mao and now digging into the depths of Sufi, Sunni, Shia 'secret' Islam, etc." (ibid., 425). This critique of what he calls the Western "mental bourgeois" is directed against many positions but especially against the lefty Western intellectuals, signified by the "Parisienne" and "Mao." In passages like this Brodsky's jeremiad reveals the Spenglerian pathos underlying the essay; the author idealizes the ancient *culture* of the West but condemns its *contemporary civilization*, whose representatives he portrays as, if not morally decaying, then at least politically unsound.

The Russian title does not betray the provocation of the text the way the English title does, but the text itself is equally provocative.[17] Apart from denouncing Russia's Soviet rule, Brodsky's polemic is directed against all Russian formations, which affirm Russia's affiliation with what the author perceives as the "East." Moreover, Brodsky polemicizes with the idea of "holy Russia" and the messianism it entails by defying the significance of Constantinople as a central topos of Russian religious thought and as the "*pium desideratum* of Russian Slavophiles."[18] By the same token, he appropriates the Third Rome mythology, attacking both the political and religious meanings the doctrine acquired in nineteenth-century Slavophile and Russian nationalist thought.[19] Recognizing the messianic impetus of these nineteenth-century formations, Brodsky replaces the patriarchy of Moscow with the Soviet Kremlin and attempts to expose both Russian and Soviet expansionism. The latter, as Alexander Genis and Petr Vail' have demonstrated, was not a wholly unusual dissident appropriation of "Moscow, the Third Rome" in the 1960s; it is reflected in Brodsky's 1973 poem "Na smert' druga" ("To a Friend: In Memoriam"), in which the parallel between Rome and Moscow is turned on its head by rendering Moscow an infernal, perhaps purgatorial, place. When viewed against the culturally affirmative meanings Brodsky invests in Roman antiquity in his poetry, this can only be read as an image of an anti-Rome:[20]

да лежится тебе, как в большом оренбургском платке,
в нашей бурой земле, местных труб проходимцу и дыма,
понимавшему жизнь, как плеча на горячем цветке,

и замерзшему насмерть в параднике Третьего Рима.
Может, лучшей и нету на свете калитки в Ничто.
(3:58)

May you lie, as though wrapped in an Orenburg shawl, in our dry, brownish mud,
you, a tramper through hell and high water and the meaningless sentence,
who took life like a bumblebee touching a sun-heated bud
but instead froze to death in the Third Rome's cold-piss-reeking entrance.
Maybe Nothing has no better gateway indeed than this smelly shortcut.
(*CP*, 212)

This subversive approach, the reversed parallel of Moscow as anti-Rome, is the crux of Brodsky's appropriation of "Moscow, the Third Rome" mythology in "Flight from Byzantium." Brodsky's author locates the origins of "absolute power" in the historical Rome but, nevertheless, invests unquestionably positive value in Roman law and in what later developed into the Roman Church. For him they form the basis of the "ethico-political system" and the "so-called Western conception of state and individual being"; in other words, they form the antipode of the "East" and its latest incarnation, Soviet Moscow, the "Third Rome."[21] Rejecting the historical linkage between the "first" and the "third" Romes, Brodsky focuses on pointing out the ideological resemblance between the "second" (Byzantium/Ottoman Empire) and the "third"; his polemical recapitulation of the Third Rome mythology and Russian Byzantinism in the essay discloses the notion of the ideological heritage the Soviet Union received from Byzantium and, in one move further, its correspondence with Islam, an idea he expressed first in the 1960s poems "Vremia goda—zima" ("The time of year is winter") and "Rech' o prolitom moloke" ("Speech over Spilled Milk"), where the image of "Moscow infected by the Koran" evokes Mandelstam's "Buddhist Moscow" of the early 1930s, a topic I will return to below.[22] In the essay he equates the General Secretary and the Politburo with the Padishah and the Great Divan, the Sultan and the Council of the Ottoman Empire, associating with them "the late M. Suslov," "the late Milyukov," as well as Konstantin Leontiev, all of whom are presented as personifications of the "spirit of the place," the "Byzantine soil," and the East in general; in Brodsky's historical conjecture Byzantium and the Ottoman Empire are indistinguishable; the "Second Rome" equals the "Byzantine soil."[23] Eventually, Byzantine Christianity, Islam, and Soviet ideology are all clustered in one ideological conjecture projected on the concept of the "East" or the "Eastern" value system, invested with nothing but negative meanings. The ideological linkage between them is symbolized by the Soviet flag—the crescent has been transformed into a sickle and the cross into a hammer:

> Didn't one of them, another Selim, say during the conquest of Egypt that he, as Lord of Constantinople, was heir to the Roman Empire and therefore had a right to all the lands that had ever belonged to it? Do these words sound like justification or do they sound like prophecy, or both? And does not the same note ring four hundred years later in the voice of Ustryalov and the Third Rome's latter-day Slavophiles, whose scarlet, Janissary's-cloaklike banner neatly combined a star and the crescent of Islam? And that hammer, isn't it a modified cross? ("Flight," 428–29)

The Ottoman sultans (designated in this passage by the typifying "another Selim" ["odnogo iz nikh, opiat'-taki Selima"]) and the Soviet ideologues are presented as interchangeable in their despotic and violent will to autocratic power, as well as in their militant "fusion between army and state" ("Flight," 429). The reference to Ustrialov as one of the "latter-day-Slavophiles" draws a historical link between Russian nineteenth-century patriotic and nationalist thought and later Bolshevik nationalism.[24] Brodsky's essay ends in an image of the author observing the "aircraft carriers of the Third Rome [the Soviet Union] sailing slowly through the gates of the Second [Istanbul] on their way to the First [Rome/the West]" ("Flight," 446), leaving the idea of the Soviet Union as the Third Rome the culminating and concluding thought.

In positing the source of what he perceives as Russian totalitarianism and anti-individualism in the historical Byzantium, Brodsky's author follows the model established, among others, by the émigré thinker and historian Georgii Fedotov, whose views of Byzantium's historical role in Russian ideological formations were pronounced in New York at the end of World War II:

> Christianity arrived to us from Byzantium, and it seems Byzantinism was in every sense, in the political as well as in others, prepared as the

> natural form for the young Russian nation. But Byzantinism is a totalitarian culture, with the state as a sacred power holding the Church in its not too soft grip. The core of Byzantinism excludes the possibility of any kind of freedom.[25]

The affinity of Brodsky's thoughts with Fedotov's becomes more apparent when Fedotov gets closer to contemporary times. Interpreting Russia's historical position between East and West, Fedotov turns to the traditional Moscow-Petersburg paradigm, where Moscow represents the despotic East, whose origins he places, on the one hand, in the "orientalized Christianity" received by Rus from Byzantium, and, on the other, in the Tatar yoke, which "infected [the Muscovite gentry] with its eastern concepts and the *byt* of the steppe." The rise of the intelligentsia in the nineteenth century with its expression of freedom, both in theory and practice, represented "the island of Petersburg in the middle of the Moscow seas,"[26] but in the contemporary rulers of the Soviet state, and above all in the Soviet citizen, Fedotov detected a reincarnation of the sixteenth-century "Muscovite type," whose "eastern" character was revealed in his willingness to "give his life for the collective":

> The Soviet man is closer to the Muscovite with his proud national consciousness: his country alone is Orthodox, his country alone is socialist—first in the world: the third Rome. He looks at the rest of the world, that is, the Western world, with contempt; he does not know it, does not like it, and is afraid of it. And, as in olden times, his soul is open to the East. The many *ordy*, joining civilization for the first time, are integrated to the Russian cultural stratum, Orientalizing it second-hand [*vtorichno orientaliziruia ego*].[27]

This is Brodsky's claim too: Soviet rule has Orientalized contemporary Russia, and this Orientalization is analogical with Byzantium's historical influence—in this line of thought "Orientalization" is, of course, free of its post-Saidian meanings. And just like Fedotov, Brodsky projects the myth of "Moscow, the Third Rome" on the Soviet regime, lining it up with Byzantine totalitarianism and Muscovite autocracy.[28] Unlike Fedotov, Brodsky's views were not, however, pronounced within the paradigm of Russian religious thought, and while the Byzantine legacy meant for both Fedotov and Brodsky a legacy of militant social rule, for Fedotov it simultaneously signified Russia's uninterrupted connection with the Christian tradition and Greco-Roman culture. The crux of Brodsky's poetic narrative of Russian history is the view that the Orientalized Christianity had lost its vital connection with the Roman concept of law and its respect for the individual. For this part, Brodsky's narrative is a recapitulation of Petr Chaadaev's influential ideas expressed in the *Philosophical Letters*, which initially scandalized the Moscow and Petersburg intellectual scene in the 1820s and 1830s. The historical narrative Chaadaev proposes in his letters is a narrative of separation. In Chaadaev's Romantic thought, nations grew from infancy to maturity, and unlike the mature European nations Russia was still in its infant state, cut off from Europe's historical development and Christian unity, and consequently left outside the desired European fraternity: "Driven by a baneful fate, we turned to Byzantium."[29] While not part of the West or the East, and failing to combine these two great forces, Russia was, as Chaadaev concluded in *The Apology of a Madman*, "simply a country of the North,"[30] whose historical path was determined by the "fact of geography," *fait geographique*:

> There is one fact which absolutely dominates our progress through the ages, which runs through our whole history, which encompasses in a way all its philosophy, which occurs at all periods of our social life and determines their character, which is both the one essential element of our political greatness and the true cause of our intellectual weakness; this fact is the fact of geography.[31]

Similar anxieties underscored Pushkin's prophetic exclamation that "ancient history is the history of Egypt, Persia, Greece, and Rome. Modern history is the history of Christianity. Woe to the country that finds itself outside of the European system!" while the exiled Alexander Hertzen recapitulated Chaadaev's ideas in his assertion that Russia is "more subject to geographical than to historical authority."[32]

Brodsky's essay revoices these nineteenth-century anxieties, without Chaadaev's Christian overtones, in the historical context of the latter half of the twentieth century: Russia, now in the form of the Soviet Union, had found itself outside the European system. In Brodsky's treatment Chaadaev's narrative of separation takes the following form:

> The combination of Roman law, reckoned with more seriously in Rome than in Byzantium, and the specific logic of the Roman Church's inner development evolved into the ethico-political system that lies at

> the heart of the so-called Western conception of the state and of individual being . . . this Western conception drew around itself a kind of circle, which the East, in a purely conceptual sense, never crossed, and within whose ample bounds was elaborated what we term, or understand as, Western Christianity and the world view it implies. ("Flight," 421)

Russia, or "Rus," as Brodsky's thought continues to narrate the history of Russia, was left outside the "circle" of the Western value system and Western Christianity, when it became a "prey of Byzantium":

> If civilizations—of whatever sort they are—do indeed spread like vegetation in the opposite direction to the glacier, from south to north, where could Rus, given her geographical position, possibly tuck herself away from Byzantium? Not just Kievan Rus, but Muscovite Rus as well, and then all the rest of it between the Donets and the Urals. . . . There was nowhere for Rus to go to get away from Byzantium—any more than for the West to get away from Rome. And, just as the West in age after age became over-grown with Roman colonnades and legality, Rus *happened to become the natural geographical prey of Byzantium*. . . . But then its northward expansion took place at a time of growing domination by the crescent, and the purely physical power of the Sublime Porte hypnotized the North in far greater measure than the theological polemics of dying-out scholiasts. ("Flight," 436–37; emphasis added)

Here Brodsky's historical imagination envisions Russia as a victim of Chaadaev's "fact of geography"; Russia, or the historical Rus, was "Byzantinized" due to its geographical location north of Byzantium, between "East" and "West."

Brodsky's appropriation of Chaadaevian thought is simultaneously an appropriation of Osip Mandelstam's essay on Chaadaev; discussing Mandelstam's Hellenicism in "The Child of Civilization," Brodsky quotes Mandelstam quoting Chaadaev, and ascribes the Russian fascination with an "ideal of cultural unity 'out there' [in the West]" to a "cultural inferiority complex," which "Russian has always suffered from"; for Brodsky this is a "Russian version of Hellenicism."[33] Mandelstam was among those who responded eagerly to Chaadaev's views when they reentered the Russian intellectual scene in the 1910s.[34] For Mandelstam, Chaadaev, the "snob of Zamoskvorechie," personified a "new, deepened understanding of nationality as the supreme flowering of national individuality." Even if Mandelstam felt acutely the myth-making force of Chaadaev's West—"only a Russian could invent this West, which is far denser and more concrete than the historical West itself"—Chaadaev's "demand for unity" found resonance in Mandelstam's own Hellenistic conception of culture, while he also responded to Chaadaev's anxieties about Russia's place on the "historical path":

> The fact is that Chaadaev's conception of history excludes the possibility of any *access* to the historical path. In keeping with this conception, one could be on the historical path only prior to any beginning. History was Jacob's ladder, down which angels descended from heaven to earth. It must be called sacred due to the continuity of the spirit of grace that inhabits it. Therefore Chaadaev did not utter a word about 'Moscow, the Third Rome.' In this idea he could see only a sickly fantasy of Kievan monks.[35]

Brodsky, in "Flight from Byzantium," seems to respond to Mandelstam's provocative observation about Chaadaev regarding "Moscow, the Third Rome" mythology as a "sickly fantasy of Kievan monks," while Brodsky's travelogue is also a forceful manifestation of how Brodsky himself constantly engaged in the discussions of Russia's place in European cultural history, and, ironically, of how he grounded his views on an equally idealized conception of Western culture's unity.

Chaadaev is the common source for imagining Russia's place in history in Brodsky's "Flight from Byzantium" and in Mandelstam's *Journey to Armenia*, one of the seminal Russian journeys to the Orient preceding Brodsky's. But while there is a common Chaadaevian undercurrent in Brodsky's and Mandelstam's Oriental journeys, exhibited in the authors' relation to their contemporary Russia and its place in the historical process, the two travelogues differ from one another in other crucial ways. Mandelstam's journey to ancient Armenia, conducted under Stalin's increasing control of literary life, is an imaginative descent on the evolutionary ladder of biology and also Jacob's ladder of history, which he juxtaposed with the "watermelon emptiness" of Russia, the vulgar and profane "Zamoskvorechie," the "Buddhist Moscow," as he writes in a poetic fragment of the same year.[36] Armenia, which "turned away from the bearded cities of the East" was for Mandelstam a country of "tufted eagles with owl-like wings not yet profaned by Byzantium."[37] Mandelstam embraced the Christian Armenia with his newly rediscovered creative powers, enclosing it in the realm of his imaginative cultural unity of Judeo-Christian Hellenism; Brodsky, on the other hand, used the occasion of his trip to Muslim Turkey to express a rejection of the place and to exclude it from his imaginative unity of the West. Mandelstam's "journey" is a metaphoric journey to the origins of Christianity; Brodsky journeys to the historical origins of Russian despotism. Mandelstam's projection of the evolutionary ladder on Armenian nature, with his fascination with "vertebrates" and archaic pottery, can be viewed as a primitivization typical of the Orientalist myth, while his imagining of the Armenian past in terms of Christian origins—manifested in his preoccupation with Armenian manuscripts and church architecture—can be viewed as an equally Orientalizing project. What is conjured up as the "origin" is, after all, an "origin" from Mandelstam's Hellenistic, European viewpoint, no matter how construed through a Russian lens.

Nevertheless, Mandelstam expresses curiosity and willingness to explore otherness, while Brodsky projects his preconceptions of other cultures and ethnicities on Turkey.[38] The broken chronologies of Mandelstam's and Brodsky's narratives correspond to this difference of embrace and rejection: Mandelstam begins his narrative by immersing the reader in the middle of his Armenian experience, while Brodsky postpones the encounter with Istanbul till chapter 9 (11 in the Russian version) to introduce first his ideas of Greek poetry. The etymological fantasies Armenia inspires in Mandelstam, and Turkey in Brodsky, further illustrate the paradigmatic difference between the travelogues. Mandelstam's fanciful comparisons between Russian and Armenian, made in the spirit of Marrian linguistics, are based on examples with affirmative semantic potential, whereas Brodsky's makes parodic use of the commonly acknowledged fact of Turkic languages' contribution to Russian vocabulary by pointing to chance lexical correspondences with either negative or absurd semantic potential, such as *katorga* (forced labor) or the name of the Turkish town *Nigde* ("nowhere" in Russian). Brodsky's casual guesswork of lexical relations between Russian and Turkish is articulated as a reinforcement of his views of the East as the source of all that is negative in Russia:

> In purely structural terms, the difference between the Second Rome and the Ottoman Empire is accessible only in units of time. What is it, then? The spirit of place? Its evil genius? The spirit of bad spells—

> *porcha* in Russian? Where, incidentally, do we get this word *porcha* from? Might it not derive from *porte*? It doesn't matter. It's enough that both Christianity and *bardak* [brothel, mess] with *durak* [fool] came down to us from this place. ("Flight," 427–28)[39]

Finally, we come to the difference between Mandelstam's and Brodsky's discourses of history. Mandelstam, who took issue with positivist science and, in particular, Darwin's evolutionary theory, advanced ideas that drew from the Romantic conception of organic development, Bergsonian philosophy, and neo-Lamarckian biology, with which he was familiar through his acquaintance with the biologist B. S. Kuzin.[40] In Brodsky's case, however, the author is far removed from the sources of Romantic or neo-Romantic thought; in his poetic genealogies and search for origins, Romantic thought is present mainly as patterns of speech, metaphorical expressions, and popularized ideas where "civilizations spread" and "cultures" are "infectious." In Brodsky's hybrid conception of history, genealogical and narrative thinking coexists with typological and structural models. For the traveler of Brodsky's essay, Christianity and despotism manifest the same "essence"; their "structure" alone is different. This argument is put forward in a passage where Brodsky' imagines the transformation of Constantinople's churches into mosques—possibly with the parallel of the Stalinist destruction or transformation of Moscow churches in mind:

> The *tuyrks'*—gradually becoming the Turks'—love affair with Byzantium lasted approximately three centuries. Persistence brought its rewards, and in the fifteenth century the cross surrendered its cupolas to the crescent. The rest is well documented, and there is no need to expand upon it. What is worth noting, however, is the striking similarity between 'the way it was' and the 'way it became.' For the meaning of history lies in the essence of structures, not in the character of décor. ("Flight," 426)

The final sentence in this passage is the reductivist credo of Brodsky's conception of history.[41] In his paradigm of historical "essences" despotism is clustered with expansionism, imperialism, and violence, which is juxtaposed with individualism, democracy, and legality; Christianity, Islam, and totalitarian societies, on the one hand, and language, poetry, and writing, on the other, are their respective "structures." Due to the ironic undermining of conventional historical narratives and of the author's own credibility in creating such narratives—"The rest is well documented, and there is no need to expand upon it"—it is impossible to know whether the author is proposing this essentialist view of history in earnest.

In another instance, the journey to the site of despotism triggers an apocalyptic vision of history as a disintegrating tower of Babel:

> The meaning of history! How, in what way, can the pen cope with this aggregation of races, tongues, creeds: with the vegetative—nay, zoological—pace of the crumbling-down of the tower of Babel, at the end of which one fine day, among the teeming ruins, an individual catches himself gazing in terror and alienation at his own hand or at his procreative organ, not in Wittgensteinian fashion but possessed, rather, by a sensation that these things don't belong to him at all, that they are but components of some do-it-yourself toy set: details, shards in a kaleidoscope through which it is not the cause that peers at the effect but blind chance squinting at the daylight. ("Flight," 426)

Contemporaneity is envisioned here as an "after-history" space, where incoherence and loss of causality prevail, and an individual is left not with a sense of "family resemblance" (the reference to Wittgenstein) but a sense of total alienation, absurdity of existence, and loss of meaning.[42] The apocalyptic vision is paralleled with the author's Dantean descent, when the author, now stuck in traffic in the middle of a political demonstration in contemporary Athens, imagines the final inferno:

> In the evening, when I went out looking for a place to have supper, I found myself in the thick of a highly excited throng shouting something unintelligible. As far as I can make out, elections are imminent. I was shuffling along some endless main street blocked by people and vehicles, with car horns wailing in my ears, not understanding a word, and it suddenly dawned on me that this, essentially, is the afterlife—that life had ended but movement was still continuing; that this is what eternity is all about. ("Flight," 412)

The representation of touristic displacement, expressed through a linguistic disorientation of chaotic sounds and noise, reinforces the apocalyptic vision of contemporaneity as "after history"; time has run out and all that is left is the despotism of space, the "linear principle"—or tourism, an activity that the author ascribes to the "linear principle" at the beginning of his essay, in a self-reflective moment: "Any movement along a plane surface which is not dictated by physical necessity is a spatial form of self-assertion, be it empire-building or tourism. In this sense, my reason for going to Istanbul differed only slightly from Constantine's" ("Flight," 398). Eventually, the author's conception of history produces a position given to fatalism, something he is quick to acknowledge himself:

> Civilizations move along meridians; nomads (including our modern warriors, since war is an echo of the nomadic instinct) along latitudes. This seems to be another version of the cross Constantine saw. Both movements possess a natural (vegetable or animal) logic, considering which one easily finds oneself in the position of not being able to reproach anyone for anything. In the state known as melancholy—or, more exactly, fatalism. It can be blamed on age, or on the influence of the East, or, with an effort of the imagination, on Christian humility. ("Flight," 445)

Brodsky's traveler blames all three: Christian humility, since "it is . . . always achieved at the expense of the mute helplessness of the victims of history, past, present, and future"; the influence of the East, whose negative "human potential" the essay is designed to reveal; and age, which has left the individual with only one option for responding to the former two, and that is a "smile of contempt," with which Brodsky's traveler leaves Istanbul, observing the Third Rome's aircraft carriers passing the Second on their way to the First.

To conclude the discussion of Brodsky's oriental journey as a polemic: the sweeping generalizations, the deliberate and nondeliberate distortion of historical facts, disregard of cultural and ethnic diversity, and overall dismissive attitude to "otherness"—all of which the text construes—conform to the cultural essences the author proclaims he has discovered.[43] In this respect, the author's geographical and historical imagination draws on intellectual operations similar to the nationalist and messianic formations with which the author forcefully polemicizes. Moreover, the naturalized conceptions of culturally conditioned phenomena and historical contingencies that Brodsky's historical and geographical imagination produces, draw on an essentialism similar to the one underlying the metaphysics of the Orientalist myth.

The Metaphysics of the Orientalist Myth

Before going to Istanbul, Brodsky's author of "Flight from Byzantium" goes to Greece, the emblem of Western cultural origins. In his third chapter, just when the stage seems to be set for the reader to get some information about the actual trip to Istanbul, he sets out to describe not his arrival or stay there but his departure. Instead of Istanbul, he describes his current whereabouts at a hotel in Sounion in Greece, the site of Poseidon's temple:

> I arrived in Istanbul, and left it, by air, having thus isolated it in my mind like some virus under a microscope. If one considers the infectious nature of any culture, the comparison does not seem irresponsible. Writing this note in the Hotel Aegean in the little place called Sounion—at the southeast corner of Attica, forty miles from Athens, where I landed four hours ago—I feel like the carrier of a specific infection, despite constant inoculations of the "classical rose" of the late Vladislav Khodasevich, to which I have subjected myself for the greater part of my life. ("Flight," 395–96)

The encounter with the "East" has made the author sick, and the cure is a dose of the "West," represented by his geographical location in Sounion, at one of the most famous sites of Greek antiquity. By referring to Khodasevich's "classical rose,"[44] and his own poetic affiliation with it, he introduces the idea of Petersburg representing Western heritage within Russia, which is developed further by the dream sequence, where the author imagines himself having a conversation at the Leningrad University with D. E. Maksimov, the Petersburg specialist on Silver Age poetry. This anticipates the topic of classical poetry, and more specifically Roman elegiac poetry and the Alexandrian tradition, a topic that takes up two chapters in both the English and Russian versions. The author eulogizes the Roman elegiac poets, "disciples of the Alexandrian school of poetry": "The Alexandrian tradition was a Grecian tradition: one of order (the cosmos), of proportion, of harmony, of the tautology of cause and effect (the Oedipus cycle)—a tradition of symmetry and the closed circle, *of return to the origin*" ("Flight," 401–2). Lyric poetry and the circular principle it manifests is opposed to epic poetry and its "linear movement," represented by Virgil's poetic culture, "dictated by the expansion of the Empire" (ibid., 402). The Alexandrian elegists' concept of poetry was that of a "personal, private art" as opposed to "something civic, as a form of state propaganda" (ibid., 399). This contrast between lyric and epic poetry is delivered as a presentiment of the thought that the author develops throughout the essay; the lyric principle is the principle of individualism incarnated by the "West" and opposed to the collectivity and the "linear" expansionism of imperialism, monotheism, utopianism, despotism, and, the anti-individualism of the "East." The italicized "return to the origin" discloses a metatextual meaning, which points two ways: first, it is a comment on Brodsky's own literary journey as a return, not to the Soviet Union, but to the origins of its despotism, the "Byzantine soil," from where he returns to the West, and second, more specifically to Greece, the origins of the poetic and aesthetic practices he is personally affiliated with.[45]

When the author finally encounters the "East," it is signaled by a stark change in narrative mode away from the eulogy of Greek and Roman poetry presented in his previous chapters. The postponing of the encounter constitutes the parodic character of Brodsky's Oriental journey, but when the encounter takes place there seems to be very little parody left. The impressions that relate to the author's stay in Istanbul, "the primeval *kishlak*," as he pejoratively calls the city—*kishlak* being a Turkic word used in Russian for a "village in Central Asia" ("selenie v Srednei Azii")—constitute an expression of sheer disgust:

> The delirium and horror of the East. The dusty catastrophe of Asia. Green only on the banner of the Prophet. Nothing grows here except mustaches. A black-eyed, overgrown-with-stubble-before-supper part of the world. Bonfire embers doused with urine. That smell! A mixture of foul tobacco and sweaty soap and the underthings wrapped around loins like another turban. Racism? But isn't it only a form of misanthropy? And that ubiquitous grit flying in your muzzle . . . and yet one feels grateful even for that. ("Flight," 403)

The author's disgust with his environment is represented through a cluster of motifs persistent in attitudes toward the Orient: barren ("Nothing grows here"), unhygienic ("embers doused with urine"), bad-smelling ("mixture of foul tobacco and sweaty soap"), fanatically religious ("Green only in the banner of the Prophet"), offers itself to sexual metaphorics ("underthings wrapped around loins like another turban"). In other words, it is threatening and offensive to the point of being comparable only to a sickness or a disease, an attitude anticipated in the medical metaphors of his chapter 3. Another stereotype, which is especially enduring in Russian perceptions of the East, and which Brodsky's author reverts to repeatedly, is the perception of violence inherent in Eastern (*vostochnyi, aziatskii, kavkaszkii*) cultures. In Russian, he evokes images of stereotypical oriental violence imitating Caucasian pronunciation of the verb "rezat'" (to cut, slaughter) by replacing in print the "e" with "e oborotnoe."[46] In the English essay the verb is translated as massacre: "I massacre, therefore I exist" ("Flight," 429); this is the Eastern version of the Cartesian slogan as imagined by Brodsky, supported by the author's recounting of the history of Ottoman sultans' violence:

> Oh, all these countless Osmans, Muhammads, Murads, Bajazets, Ibrahims, Selims, and Suleimans slaughtering their predecessors, rivals, brothers, parents, and offspring—in the case of Murad II, or III (who cares?), eighteen brothers in a row—with the regularity of a man shaving in front of a mirror. Oh, all these endless, uninterrupted wars: against the infidel, against their own but Shiite Muslims, to extend the Empire, to avenge a wrong, for no reason at all, and in self-defense. ("Flight," 428)

The inherence of violence in the East is also represented through the image of castration, highlighted in the essay in such a manner that, as Katherine Tiernan O'Connor writes, it "suggests Brodsky sees it as an iconic act of Eastern violence and savagery."[47]

At the end of the essay the chaotic and unorganized Istanbul is, again, contrasted with the pastoral idyll of Sounion, where the author has arrived after the Kafkaesque way out of Istanbul:

> Forty miles from Athens, in Sounion, at the top of a cliff plummeting to the sea, stands a temple to Poseidon, built almost simultaneously—a difference of some fifty years—with the Parthenon in Athens. It has stood here for two and a half thousand years. It is ten times smaller than the Parthenon. How many times more beautiful it is would be hard to say; it is not clear what should be considered the unit of perfection. It has no roof. There is not a soul about. Sounion is a fishing village with a couple of modern hotels now, and lies far below. There, on the crest of the dark cliff, the shrine looks from a distance as if it had been gently lowered from heaven rather than been erected on earth. Marble has more in common with the clouds than with the ground. Fifteen white

> columns connected by a white marble base stand evenly spaced. Between them and the earth, . . . and the blue sky of Hellas, there is no one and nothing. ("Flight," 442)

Apart from this contrast between the celestial Sounion and the infernal Istanbul, the dichotomy between East and West is imagined through yet another conceptual opposition, that of time and space, developed in a passage inspired by the author's visit to Hagia Sophia, the negative counterpart of Poseidon's temple in Sounion. First, the mosque "with her minarets and with her Christian-Muslim decor" provided the author with a "sensation, instilled by both history and the Arabic lace, that everything in this life intertwines—that everything is, in a sense, but a pattern in a carpet" ("Flight," 432–33). In the chapters that follow, he contradicts, however, this idea of cultural synchrony, using the image of Arabic lace to elaborate on his perception of the fundamental difference between East and West. The basic "unit of Eastern ornament is the sentence, the word, the letter," and this "decorative use of sentences, words, letters" is a proof of "a literally spatial—because conveyed by distinctly spatial means—perception of any sacred locution." The basic unit of Western ornamentation, on the other hand, is "the notch, the tally, recording the passage of days. Such ornament, in other words, is temporal. Hence its rhythm, its tendency toward symmetry, its essentially abstract character, subordinating graphic expression to a rhythmic sense." In other words, Eastern cultures are oriented toward space, and Western toward time, the latter being on the top of this metaphysical hierarchy, since "the natty little bordure on a Grecian urn is superior to a pattern in a carpet" (ibid., 434).[48] Brodsky then moves on to tie up the idea of temporal and spatial orientation with the idea of individualism: "let us nastify our conclusion somewhat," he writes, "and add that an awareness of time is a profoundly individualistic experience . . . these notches are a profoundly solitary activity, isolating the individual and forcing him toward an understanding, if not of his uniqueness, then at least of autonomy of his existence in the world. That is what the basis of our civilization is, and that is what Constantine walked away from to the East" (ibid., 435). The "East" is presented, once again, as an antithesis to individualism, which, in turn, is associated with the "West" and now tied up with Brodsky's conception of individual and artistic freedom, "notches" being a metaphor for writing.[49]

The opposition between time and space was an integral part of Brodsky's poetic imagination, but in the context of re-imagining East and West, it conforms to one of the reoccurring motifs of the Orientalist myth. The temporal and spatial opposition underscores Western and Russian discourses of the Orient, where, to quote Monika Greenleaf's Saidian formulation, adapted to the nineteenth-century Russian Oriental poem, the East equals a perception of "time reverting to space," whereas in representations of the West "space [is] incorporated into European 'destiny,' historical meaning."[50] A remarkable example of how this binary opposition has worked in the Russian imagination is Chaadaev's *Philosophical Letters* and *Apology of a Madman*. Here, Chaadaev, equaling in uncompromising severity Rudyard Kipling's later (in)famous formulation, presents his view of the essential difference between the "two natural forces" of East and West, creating a narrative of how the two emerged:[51]

> The world has from all time been divided into two spheres, the East and the West. This is not a geographical division; it is an order of things which develops from the very nature of intelligent being. East and West are two principles which correspond to two dynamic natural forces, two ideas which encompass the whole economy of mankind. In the East the spirit of man found its power in self-concentration, in meditation, in shutting itself up within the sphere of its own activity; in the West it developed by spreading outward, by radiating in all directions, by struggling with all obstacles. Society was naturally set up on the basis of this primitive data. In the East the intellect retired within itself, took refuge in repose, hid in the desert, and allowed the power of social position to become master of all goods of the earth; in the West the intellect spread out in all directions, embraced all the needs of men, aspired to all goods, based power on the principle of law. Still, in both these realms life was strong and fruitful; in neither was human intelligence lacking in high inspiration, profound ideas, sublime creations.[52]

Chaadaev's narrative, connecting natural and cultural history through organic imagery typical of Romantic thought, is characterized by a set of conceptual oppositions, which are a commonplace in European imaginings of the Orient: the East represents passiveness, inwardness, overt spirituality and rigid hierarchies, whereas the West is characterized through its activity, outwardness, rationality, equality and legality.[53] This dichotomy becomes even clearer when Chaadaev moves on to elaborate on the final victory of the West over the East:

> The East came first and poured over the earth a flood of light from the depths of its silent meditation. Then came the West with its immense activity, its eager word took hold of its labors, completed what the East had begun, and finally enveloped it in its vast embrace. But in the East, the intellect, docile, kneeling before the authority of time, exhausted itself in the years of the world by its exercise of absolute submission, and one day it stopped motionless and silent, unaware of the new destiny prepared for it; while in the West it walked proud and free, bowing only before the authority of reason or of Heaven, stopping only before the unknown, its gaze ever fixed on the boundless future.[54]

The West's supremacy over the East is completed by the image of the "docile" East becoming "motionless and silent" and yielding to the West's "authority of time"; the West represents dynamism and personifies the future, while the East stands for stagnation representing a thing of the past—in other words, the West equals time and the East equals space. Finally, the passive and stagnated East represents for Chaadaev "only some dust left for us to look at."[55]

Drawing from a cluster of literary and philosophical models, Brodsky appropriates and refashions popular and highbrow mythologies of East and West with equal vigor; his conjectures of East and West are equally textual, equally imaginative. But the power of his historical and geographical imagination works to the West's advantage, leaving the East distorted, undesired and rejected; just as for Chaadaev, for Brodsky, too, "dust" (*pyl*) constitutes "the very essence" of the East and its formlessness ("Flight," 405). When set in the context of the conception of history Brodsky's author advances, "East" and "West" emerge as "structures," with order, harmony, legality, democracy, rationality, individualism, dynamism, and temporality constituting the "essence" of the "West," and chaos, formlessness, violence, despotism, indifference, irrationality, hierarchic stagnation, and spatial orientation being the "essence" of the "East." Such is the "order of things" as imagined by the author of Brodsky's oriental journey.

Within the context of the late Soviet period the typology of cultures Brodsky creates in "Flight from Byzantium" both parallels and contrasts with Olzhas Suleimenov's linguistic hypotheses, put forward in 1975 in the controversial *Az i IA*. In this book, Olzhas Suleimenov, a native of Kazakhstan and a successful Soviet poet, attempts to show how the influence of Turkic languages on *The Tale of Igor's Campaign*, a seminal text of medieval Russian literature, was overlooked by Soviet scholars, while he also proposes that there exists an ancestral link between Sumerian and Turkic cultures.[56] For Suleimenov, Turkic languages and cultures represent spatial orientation, while Indo-European languages are temporally oriented. The value judgments that underlie Suleimenov's linguistic operations reverse, however, the traditional hierarchy that the binary opposition implies. Suleimenov aimed at debunking the Indo-European orientation of Soviet linguistics and the ethnic and cultural hierarchies it produced; his project was directed toward reversing the hierarchies of Western, and Soviet/Russian, Orientalist discourse, whereas Brodsky, writing from the ideological vantage point of Russian metropolitan imagination, reinforces the discourses' common stance by placing the temporal (Western) orientation on top of the spatial (Eastern). Written in exile, but from the viewpoint of his Leningradian Eurocentrism, Brodsky's essay occupied, within the dissenting voices of the late Soviet era, a position diametrically opposed to that of someone like Suleimenov, who, writing inside the Soviet Union, attempted to assert a Central Asian view of the Soviet empire.

Oriental Identity as a Discursive Strategy

One of the most striking discursive conflicts in Brodsky's travelogue is the conflict between the polemic and the confessional modes. These two modes are played against each other in a way that highlights the conflict's role as a specific strategy in his writing. Near the beginning of the essay, in chapter 9, in which the author launches his belligerent characterization of the East—"The delirium and horror of the East. The dusty catastrophe of Asia. Green only on the banner of the Prophet. Nothing grows here except mustaches"—the uncompromising authorial voice is instantly undermined by his anticipation of the reader response: "Racism?" and then as an afterthought, "But isn't it only a form of misanthropy?" This prepares for the confessional mode at the end of the passage where the author reflects on his own attitude and on its sources:

> Misanthropy? Despair? Yet what else could be expected from one who has outlived the apotheosis of the linear principle? From a man who has nowhere to go back to? From a great turdologist, sacrophage, and the possible author of *Sadomachia*? ("Flight," 403)

In claiming to have "outlived the . . . linear principle," the author refers to the Soviet regime's totalitarian rule and to the fact that he survived it. Meanwhile, his identification as a "turdologist, sacrophage, and the possible author of *Sadomachia*" continue to weave the myth of an infamous poet with a controversial reputation, familiar from Brodsky's late 1960s poems and the self-depreciating and self-ironic mode in which this self-fashioning is performed challenges the author's discursive authority once again. The confessional undermines the polemic, and with that the author seeks redemption for his expressions of "racism" and "misanthropy." As if knowing that he has gone too far in his negative attitude toward Istanbul and Turkey, the author pleads for his Soviet (that is, Eastern) origins and for his exilic condition.

The author's origins are most at stake in the confessional passages of Brodsky's essay. At the end of the essay, after having exhausted his imaginative and intellectual powers to condemn all that he perceives as Eastern, the author questions his own identity and ponders whether he really *is* from the East himself: "Who knows," he writes. "Perhaps my attitude toward people has in its own right a whiff of the East about it, too. When it comes down to it, where am I from? Still, at a certain age a man gets tired of his own kind" ("Flight," 443). In the passage that follows, he represents himself as a victim of something similar to Chaadaev's *fait geographique* as Russia emerges in his historical narrative: "I'm not a historian, or a journalist, or an ethnographer. At best, I'm a traveler, a victim of geography. Not of history, be it noted, but of geography. This is what still links me with the country where it was my fate to be born, with our famed Third Rome" (ibid., 443–44). By identifying himself as "a traveler," the author seeks to evade the epistemological responsibility his generalizations and statements would carry if they were based on historical, ethnographic, or linguistic expertise and articulated within scholarly discourse. Not having this expertise, and not aspiring to have any, he is free to articulate his opinions about the East as subjectively as he desires, especially since, and this is his final strategy in seeking redemption for his "racism" and "misanthropy," he is partially "Eastern" himself, and even more than that, "a victim" of the East. The liminality of the author's identity is referred to in an earlier passage, where it is imagined through the culturally loaded parallel between Istanbul and Leningrad/St. Petersburg:

> The quality of reality always leads to a search for a culprit—more accurately, for a scapegoat. Whose flocks graze in the mental fields of history. Yet, a son of a geographer, I believe that Urania is older than Clio; among Mnemosyne's daughters, I think, she is the oldest. So, born by the Baltic, in the place regarded as a window on Europe, I always felt

> something like a vested interest in this window on Asia with which we shared a meridian. On grounds perhaps less than sufficient, we regarded ourselves as Europeans. By the same token, I thought of the dwellers of Constantinople as Asians. Of these two assumptions, it's only the first that proved to be arguable. I should also admit, perhaps, that East and West vaguely corresponded in my mind to the past and the future. ("Flight," 440)

The acknowledgment of the uneasy location of Petersburg/Leningrad and Constantinople/Istanbul on the boundary between East and West serves as a metatextual commentary on the writing of "Flight from Byzantium": the travelogue is a fragmentary autobiography, a study of the author's own identity and its origins projected on the larger cultural paradigm of the East and West, and that paradigm's Russian appropriations. Constantine, the historical figure Brodsky mentions many times in the course of the essay, plays an important role in this process of self-fashioning. Constantine's expansionist movement is presented as a similar crossing of the border as the author's trip to Turkey (ibid., 398), while Constantine's life-story presents a case of displacement and liminality similar to the author's.[57]

To return to the discursive conflict between the polemic and the confessional, do the confessional mode and the author's admission of his own partial "Easternness" really undermine his authority as a polemicist? Does not the emotional engagement function as a strategy to make the reader sympathize with the author's cause? Is it not, according to the author's own implicit reasoning, his own "Easternness," after all, that provides him with the experience and authority to articulate his polemic against the East? Throughout the essay, the author presents himself as someone in a position to advise his readers about the "East." Here I am reminded of Brodsky's poem titled "Nazidanie," or "An Admonition," as it appears in his *Collected Works,* and "Advice to a Traveler," as it appeared in the first published version in English.[58] The poem was published four years after Brodsky's trip to Turkey, but despite its first line, "Puteshestvuia v Azii," which literally means "Traveling in Asia," the poem does not seem to draw from that trip as much as it draws from the travel experience Brodsky gathered much earlier in life; the poem re-evokes his participation on expeditions and trips to Soviet Central Asia:

> Путешествуя в Азии, ночуя в чужих домах,
> в избах, банях, лабазах—в бревенчатых теремах,

чьи копченые стекла держат простор в узде,
укрывайся тулупом и норови везде
лечь головою в угол, ибо в углу трудней
взмахнуть—притом в темноте—топором над ней,
отяжелевшей от давеча выпитого, и аккурат
зарубить тебя насмерть. Вписывай круг в квадрат.
(4:13)

Trekking in Asia, spending nights in odd dwellings, in
granaries, cabins, shacks—timber abodes whose thin
squinted windowpanes harness the world—sleep dressed,
wrapped in your sheepskin, and do your best
always to tuck your head into the corner, as
in the corner it's harder—and in darkness at that—to swing an ax
over your heavy, booze-laden gourd
and to chop it off nicely. Square the circle, in short.
(*CP*, 356)

In the following stanzas the speaker gives advice as to where to hide the money, how to move in the mountains, and how to cross rivers in Asia, and he warns against "broad cheekbones" and "brown eyes," against strangers, against halting in the desert, and against "cring[ing]" when "they rip a cur's throat"—in the Russian original "cut" is the same verb, "rezat'," that also appears in "Flight" when Brodsky evokes imagery of stereotypical oriental violence (cf. p. 139). But what gradually emerges from these images of "Asia" is what the reader suspects to be the Soviet Union, and when the speaker advises, "Try not to stand out—either in profile or / full face," the sardonic admonition invokes the idea of collectivity seminal to a Soviet education, which Brodsky recalls, for instance, in the first chapter of the autobiographical essay "Less Than One." Apart from referring to the actual travel experience, the "trekking in Asia" grows into a metaphor for "living in the Soviet Union." In the penultimate stanza the image of writing a letter that "can be intercepted"—an unambiguous reference to Soviet *byt*—refers simultaneously to the censorship of letters sent within the Soviet Union as well as from there; it recalls the speaker's Soviet past, while it also evokes his current exilic condition:

В письмах из этих мест не сообщай о том,
с чем столкнулся в пути. Но, шелестя листом,

повествуй о себе, о чувствах и проч.—письмо
могут перехватить. И вообще само
перемещенье пера вдоль по бумаге есть
увеличенье разрыва с теми, с кем больше сесть
или лечь не удастся, с кем—вопреки письму—
ты уже не увидишься. Все равно, почему.
(4:15)

In your letters from these parts don't divulge whom and
what you've seen on your way. If anything should be penned,
use your varying feelings, musings, regrets, et al.:
a letter can be intercepted. And after all,
the movement of a pen across paper is,
in itself, the worsening of the break between you and those
with whom you won't any longer sit or lie down—with whom,
unlike the letter, you won't share—who cares why—a home.
(*CP*, 358)

Apart from the concrete experience of Soviet Central Asia, and of Soviet reality in general, and apart from the violent and desolate imaginary Asia that Brodsky creates in the poem, the image of Asia also has a metaphysical dimension; it becomes a metaphor for the world at large, and more specifically, it becomes a metaphor for that against which the speaker defines his own being-in-the-world:

Когда ты стоишь один на пустом плоскогорьи, под
бездонным куполом Азии, в чьей синеве пилот
или ангел разводит изредка свой крахмал;
когда ты невольно вздрагиваешь, чувствуя, как ты мал,
помни: пространство, которому, кажется, ничего
не нужно, на самом деле нуждается сильно во
взгляде со стороны, в критерии пустоты.
И сослужить эту службу способен только ты.
(4:15)

When you stand on an empty stony plateau alone
under the fathomless dome of Asia in whose blueness an airplane
or an angel sometimes whips up its starch or star—

when you shudder at how infinitesimally small you are,
remember: space that appears to need nothing does
crave, as a matter of fact, an outside gaze,
a criterion of emptiness—of its depth and scope.
And it's only you who can do the job.
(*CP*, 358–59)

The final stanza reads like the speaker's acknowledgment of the lessons learned in Asia. An "outside gaze" equals a poet's vision, and the speaker's poetic vision was initially formulated in the Soviet Union against its realities. But more than that, the speaker articulates here the ethos of his poetic calling in general: writing poetry is an "outside gaze," and this implies not only regaining the Russian language from the Soviet idiom through poetic diction, but it implies measuring the "depth and scope" of emptiness by means of poetry, structuring it by means of language. To conclude: in "An Admonition," "Asia" or its metaphysical counterpart "space" stands for the "imperfection of reality" that poetry must "resist," quoting Brodsky's essay written as a foreword for a collection of Thomas Venclova's poetry.[59] Asia, in short, is a metaphor for the realities of life.

To return to the travelogue from Turkey, it is the life-story, experience, and knowledge of Asia, as exhibited in "The Admonition," that inform the authoritative voice of "Flight" and its condemnation of the East. Brodsky's author conjures up the liminality of Russia on the border of East and West not to *undermine* his discursive authority but to *underline* it. By recalling the liminality of Leningrad/Petersburg and by questioning the ideological makeup of his own identity construction on the East-West axis, Brodsky points to the fact that Russia challenges the fundamental division between East and West. To put it in the terms of Said's critical apparatus, and quoting Nathaniel Knight, the author of a scrupulous historical case study of Russian Orientalism: "The stark dichotomy between Orient and Occident around which Said's analysis hinges transforms in the Russian context into an awkward triptych: the west, Russia, the east."[60] Aware of this, Brodsky's author presents his Russianness to the reader as a birthright to knowledge about the East. The adoption of the partly Oriental identity emerges, then, as a discursive strategy by means of which the author seeks not to further question the dichotomy but, rather, to insist on it. The author adopts a liminal identity not to deconstruct the East-West dichotomy but to argue that for the West's sake it should be maintained.[61]

Reviewed in the context of contemporary travel writing and its critique, the narrative voice in which Brodsky's author self-ironically reflects on his Eastern identity, while he launches a forceful polemic against all that he perceives as Eastern, brings to mind Holland and Huggan's observation that the self-irony seminal to contemporary travelogues "affords a useful strategy of self-protection—as if the writer, in revealing his/her faults, might be relieved of social responsibilities."[62] The question of whether the self-ironic toying with the liminality of Russian identity, together with the mask of an "accidental, inexpert observer" (Venclova's phrase), relieves Brodsky of "social responsibility" in regard to his negative stereotyping of Istanbul and Turkey is a question that each reader will answer. In this reader's opinion, the essay does demonstrate, and for its part also reinforces Holland and Huggan's claim, that "behind its [travel writing's] apparent innocuousness and its charmingly anecdotal observations lies a series of powerful distorting myths" (*TWT*, 8).

When it comes to describing Istanbul, the author of Brodsky's essay is primarily interested, as is the case with many contemporary travel writers, in the "imaginative texture of place—the process by which places and their inhabitants are shaped and reshaped by (literary) myth" (ibid.), and his writing produces "powerful distorting myths" of what the author perceives as the "East" and the "Eastern" type. Myths are not necessarily value categories, as Venclova reminds us in his reading of Brodsky's travelogue ("Journey," 145), but Brodsky uses myths exactly to that end; he invests them with meanings loaded with hierarchical and categorical judgments: in short, he turns them into value categories.[63] Moreover, while Brodsky's mythopoetics, his use of "Urania" and "Clio" to represent his historical and geographical imagination, undermines authorial credibility from the viewpoint of a strictly scholarly discourse, it also provides a strategy for asserting discursive authority by reinforcing the author's affiliation with Western canonical learning. Here, Brodsky is in Istanbul not as "Said's arrogant Westerner," as David Bethea reminds us; rather, he has come there as the "chastened man fleeing from the 'obedient' and 'despotic' East . . . to the 'law-abiding' West,"[64] and yet the textual attitude his author exhibits is equal to that of many an "arrogant Westerner." It informs his search for, as he declares, "an atmosphere that at present seems to have totally vanished everywhere else" ("Flight," 394), or, as he further asserts: "I came to Istanbul to look at the past, not the future—since the latter doesn't exist here" (ibid., 444). Even if the double-edged "past" signifies not only Turkey's past but the author's own Soviet past, Brodsky, again, reverts to another seminal aspect of the Orientalist myth, the perception of the East as a thing of the past, a space to be conquered by means of literary tourism.

Orhan Pamuk, a Turkish writer born and raised in Istanbul, and now a Nobel Prize winner too, places Brodsky's essay in the context of literary tourism to Turkey, when he reflects in *Istanbul: Memories of a City* on the thoughts that the reading of Brodsky's essay provoked in him:

> As trains and steamships brought Istanbul closer to the West, there were suddenly more Western travelers wandering the streets, and this led many to speculate indulgently about what had brought them to this terrible place. Ignorance embroidered their pretensions and creative presumptions prompted them to say exactly what they thought; and so even 'cultivated' writers like André Gide saw no need to bother with cultural differences, the meaning of local rituals and traditions, or the social structures that underpinned them. . . . Having nothing of interest to say about the city, he [Gide] and his ilk are confident enough to blame their boring, featureless subject, and they make little effort to hide their military and economic chauvinism from more 'critical' Western intellectuals: for them the west sets the standard for all humankind. These writers came to Istanbul at a time when it had ceased to be exotic, due to Westernisation and the prohibitions of the Atatürk era—the banishing of the Sultan, the shutting of the harem and the dervish lodges, the tearing down of the wooden houses and other tourist attractions, the replacement of the Ottoman Empire with the little, imitative Republic of Turkey.

In the passage that immediately follows this, Pamuk identifies Brodsky as one of the belated representatives of Gide's "ilk":

> After a long period when no one of consequence came to Istanbul, and local journalists interviewed any foreigner who turned up at the Hilton Hotel, the Russian-American poet Joseph Brodsky published a long piece entitled "Flight from Byzantium" in the *New Yorker*. . . . At the time I was living a long way from the city and wanted to read only good things about it, so his mockery was crushing, and yet I was glad when Brodsky wrote, "How dated everything is here! Not old, ancient, antique, or even old-fashioned, but dated!" He was right. When the

> Empire fell, the new republic while certain of its purpose was unsure of its identity; the only way forward, its founders thought, was to foster a new concept of Turkishness, and this meant a certain cordon sanitaire from the rest of the world. It was an end of the grand polyglot, multicultural Istanbul of the imperial age; the city stagnated, emptied itself out, and became a monotonous, monolingual town in black and white.[65]

Pamuk puts Brodsky in his place with the other twentieth-century practitioners of literary tourism. Meanwhile, he also suggests a parallel between his own nostalgia for the "multicultural Istanbul of the imperial age" and Brodsky's longing for Leningrad's imperial past in "A Guide to a Renamed City," one of the Leningrad essays in *Less Than One*, the collection in which "Flight from Byzantium" was included. Moreover, Pamuk evokes a parallel between the "monotonous, monolingual town in black and white," as Istanbul emerged after Kemal's reforms, and Brodsky's exilic visions of his contemporary Soviet Leningrad. In doing this, Pamuk comes to point to the common biographical ground between Brodsky's vision and Pamuk's own of his native city.

Whether intended as a counterargument to Said or not, Brodsky's imaginative geographies and histories in "Flight from Byzantium" end up reinforcing the point Said's *Orientalism* sought to make. Brodsky uses Istanbul as a contrasting image to define his own Westernized position in opposition to the East and in opposition to that which he perceived as the East in his native Russia. Returning the ticket of Russia's Orientalization to the English-language audience, Brodsky was writing back from a position not unlike that of a postcolonial subject—a hyphenated Oriental subject at that—but at the same time, his anti-Islamic and anti-Turkish remarks, when articulated in English and published through the leading North American publishers (in the fourth printing of *Less Than One*, these opinions were repeated with the authority of the Nobel Prize for Literature, as the cover of the edition proclaims), contributed to what Said referred to as the "latest phase" of the Orientalist discourse in North American academic and popular culture practices.[66]

6

Staging Cultural Differences

Venice

In a book-length essay on Venice titled *Against Venice* (*Contre Venise*) and published some years after Brodsky's *Watermark*, the French writer and philosopher Régis Debray attacks Venice as an icon of Western cultural values promoted by a narrow privileged elite, while he also writes against the touristic Venice, the "culture boutique" of popular consciousness—not that the two are entirely unrelated.[1] Rather than being directed against the city itself, Debray's polemic is directed against the canonized perception of it: "Constructed more by writers than masons, more by painters than architects, more of words than of bricks," he writes, Venice epitomizes the "well-established rule . . . that discourse about things becomes an integral part of the things themselves."[2] The fact that one cannot "improvise before the palimpsest of polychrome marbles" annoys Debray, and for him the *veduta* leave two choices: "recitation or graffiti." Instead of Venice, he urges his reader to go somewhere "still unsullied by a metaphor, through which Musset, D'Annunzio and Henri de Régnier have had the good grace never to have passed" (*Against Venice*, 31). But despite his polemic stance against the discourse on Venice, Debray is nostalgic toward a Eurocentric past, disclosed in his anticipation of Venice being a "mirror of a future that is plausible," of "the insular Europe of tomorrow reduced to its most picturesque . . . a Europe oblivious to outer space research, to the planet and to its century" (ibid., 44).

Unlike Debray's quest, Brodsky's in *Watermark* is a quest not for the popular or common perception of Venice, but for private meanings.[3] Brodsky's essay is an intimate account of the author's "Venice sickness," something

Debray claims he has never suffered from—"the way homesick patriots say they suffer from 'France sickness'" (ibid., 3). The private meanings Brodsky invests in Venice, however, point to collective significances. From the vantage point of a Parisian intellectual, Debray challenges the significance of the "textbook town" he "learned to venerate in class," whereas Brodsky, from his vantage point of a Soviet emigrant, does not challenge but preserves the meanings Venice had for him and for the Leningrad aesthetic practices, with which he affiliated, and for the Petersburg cultural mythologies that he rearticulated in many instances.[4] In *Watermark* Brodsky affectionately preserves the cultural significance of Venice for those formations, which, in his understanding, carried on the Russian cultural heritage through the Soviet years. *Watermark* is an apotheosis of the city's *genius loci* and an appeal for the preservation of the last outpost of European civilization (as understood by Brodsky).

The writing of Brodsky's essay on Venice was initiated by a request from the *Venice Water Authority—Consorzio Venezia Nuova*, the local authority fighting the ecological crisis threatening the environment of the Veneto region and the foundations of Venice.[5] It is reasonable to assume that the officials of *Venezia Nuova* turned to Brodsky, who was known to visit the city regularly and who had established a circle of friends there, in the hope that his Nobel fame and authority would attract international attention to the preservation of Venice. Among Brodsky's recollections of his frequent trips there are passages in *Watermark* that reflect this initial motivation for the writing of the essay:

> I think it was Hazlitt who said that the only thing that could beat this city of water could be a city built in the air. That was a Calvinoesque idea, and who knows, as an upshot of space travel, that may yet come to pass. As it is, apart from the moon landing, this century may be best remembered by leaving this place intact, just by letting it be. I, for one, would advise even against gentle interference. . . . Yet I would argue that the idea of turning Venice into a museum is as absurd as the urge to revitalize it with new blood. For one thing, what passes for new blood is always in the end plain old urine. And secondly, this city doesn't qualify to be a museum, being itself a work of art, the greatest masterpiece our species produced. You don't revive a painting, let alone a statue. You leave them alone, you guard them against vandals whose hordes may include yourself. (*W*, 115–16)[6]

This passage is typical of Brodsky's idiosyncratic prose style with its quirky oscillation from one idiom to another, resulting in a certain discursive disorientation. The stylistic device of combining the colloquial with the formal, the casual with the outmoded and high-sounding, produces an ironic effect but leaves the reader wondering at what or whom the irony is directed. When read against the confessional urgency that underlies most of the essay, however, the authorial position remains unambiguous. Writing *Watermark* is celebrating the city.

Brodsky's perception of Venice in *Watermark* draws from the discourse on Venice that evolved at the end of the nineteenth century, when the idea of Venice as the "world's inheritance" gained currency among European, American, and Russian elites. John Pemble has located the origins of this discourse in the 1880s, when a group of British art historians and critics launched a campaign to preserve St. Mark's basilica, and approached several leading American and European writers and artists to join them. Ivan Turgenev was asked to promote the campaign in Russia, and the critic Vladimir Stasov reported of it in the Petersburg newspapers. As Pemble shows, it was this moment that marked a change in European perceptions of Venice. Once thought of as an odd ruin and an exotic wreck accessible only to a few by the inconvenient waterway, Venice had turned into a place that the cultivated tourist could reach conveniently by train in order to participate in the admiring, lamenting, and preserving of the city's "shattered majesty." Venice had become "our city," as Henry James called it in his *Italian Hours*; it had become a site of the "world's inheritance," whose preservation concerned not only the Italians but all cultured Europeans and Americans. As Pemble concludes:

> In the early 1800s Venice had been generally regarded as an odd and rather depressing wreck which could qualify to be beautiful only when seen at a distance or by moonlight. By the end of the century the most fastidious sensibility was not only able but eager to contemplate the detail of its ruin. A transfiguring myth had developed, rooted in esoteric cults of art and literature; and as those cults became obsolete, the metabolism occurred that converts yesterday's highbrow conceit into today's middlebrow cliché. The myth lived on, providing a language and an iconography for advertising, journalism, and mass entertainment.[7]

The change in the way Venice was perceived had to do with the growth of tourism. The turning point was 1846, when Venice was connected to the mainland by a viaduct; in 1857 a railway opened, and after 1871, when Monte Cenis, the first railroad tunnel through the Alps, opened, the "hordes of tourists" in Venice became a commonly repeated phrase in travel journalism. By the early 1880s Lido had been turned into a beach resort.[8] This "Disneyfication" of Venice, "stripping its myth of contemporary political relevance," to quote another recent scholar on Venice, was a precondition for ascribing Venice to its role as "the world's cultural heritage," removed beyond the social realities or political turmoil that eventually led to the European conflicts of the first half of the century.[9]

Russian late nineteenth- and early twentieth-century intellectual opinion also adopted the new way of looking at Venice as common cultural heritage.[10] Vasilii Rozanov, shocked by the news that the Campanile di San Marco, the famous twelfth-century bell tower, had unexpectedly collapsed on July 14, 1902, reflected this in an article published in the Petersburg newspaper *Novoe Vremia* ten days after the incident. Rozanov's "Zolotistaia Venetsiia" ("Golden Venice"), included later in his *Ital'ianskie vpechatleniia* (*Italian Impressions*), discloses a sense of both personal and collective loss. Venice and the Campanile were symbols of European civilization comparable to the monuments of Greek Antiquity:

> The collapse of St. Mark's bell tower in Venice has destroyed my dream to see the city once more. . . . If St. Basil's is moved to London or especially to New York, it not only is ruined itself but it ruins the square on which it is re-erected. The same can be said about the tower. What was ruined with the collapse of the tower was a singularly most beautiful, significant, and memorable place on the face of the earth, that is, St. Mark's Square. It is not the disappearance of the tower that is so painful, but the fact that this square suddenly lost its thousand-year-old look. The re-erection of the tower is a matter of absolute urgency. To lose St. Mark's Square is the same for European civilization as for Athens to loose Propylaea or Athena Promachos on the Acropolis. It is quite possible to imagine that there will be a universal petition for the re-erection of the tower, according to the old dimensions, of course, a full copy of the ancient original.[11]

At the time the Campanile collapsed, Venice had become a fashionable tourist attraction for many Russians traveling to Italy. Rozanov himself had made a trip there the previous year, and he was among the many artists and writers, later recognized as the elite of Russian modernism, who visited Venice at the turn of the century. The painter Mikhail Vrubel' went there to copy Byzantine mosaics in 1884; the poet Innokentii Annenskii visited in 1890; Chekhov took a trip to Venice in 1891 and spent some time with Dmitrii Merezhkovskii and Zinaida Gippius, leading figures of the Russian symbolist movement. In a letter to his brother, Chekhov wrote: "Merezhkovskii, whom I met here, is out of his mind with delight. For a Russian, humbled and poor, it is not difficult to go out of his mind in this world of beauty, exuberance, and freedom."[12] The art and literary critic Petr Pertsov visited Venice for the first time in 1894. His popular articles on Venetian art and architecture were published as a book called *Venetsiia* (*Venice*) in 1905.[13] Aleksandr Benois, the *primus motor* of the *World of Art* movement, was there for the first time on his wedding trip in 1894 and many times thereafter. Sergei Diagilev started visiting Venice in the 1890s, and it was in Venice that he died in 1929. Leading Russian poets, too, were among the increasing number of Russian tourists to Venice. Mikhail Kuzmin was in Venice in 1897. Valerii Briusov was there in 1902 and 1908, Aleksandr Blok in 1909, Andrei Belyi in 1910; Vladislav Khodasevich worked as a tourist guide in Venice in 1911, Anna Akhmatova and Nikolai Gumilev visited Venice on their wedding trip in 1912, the young Boris Pasternak went there from Germany in 1912 and wrote about the trip later in his memoir *Okhrannaia gramota* (*Safe Conduct*), and even Marina Tsvetaeva visited Venice hastily on her honeymoon with Sergei Efron.[14]

All these visits and trips contributed to a vast number of Venetian reflections in Russian arts and writing. These reflections were built on a staple of poems and lyrics about Venice, which had first been introduced to Russian readers a generation before by nineteenth-century writers. Apart from Pushkin—who never traveled to Venice but who had his Evgenii Onegin dream of the Brenta shores by the Neva in St. Petersburg—the Russian nineteenth-century canon of Venice includes such writers as Prince Viazemsky, who wrote some forty poems related to his two stays in Venice in the 1850s and 1860s, Karolina Pavlova, Fedor Tiutchev, Apollon Grigor'ev, Aleksei Apukhtin, and Ivan Kozlov, who, although he never visited the city, captured the core of the Russian Romantic Venice with Byronic references and nocturnal images *luna, gondoly, barkaroly, Torkvata oktavy* (the moon, gondolas, barcaroles, Torquato Tasso's octaves) in the 1825 "Venetsianskaia noch'" ("Venetian Night"). This last was also known as a romance composed by Mikhail Glinka and imitated in numerous Russian poems about Venice.[15]

Ivan Turgenev had Insarov, the hero of *Nakanune* (*On the Eve*), die in Venice, thus anticipating the fin-de-siècle fascination with death and Venice. Such late nineteenth-century literary responses to Venice as Kuzmin's play *Venetsianskie bezumtsy* (*Venetian Madmen*), Blok's poetic cycle "Venetsiia," and Briusov's poems drew from these earlier imaginings and followed the literary and artistic conventions constituting the Romantic myth of the esoteric and erotic city of desire. A more sober sensibility in regard to Venice is exhibited by Gumilev's 1912 poem "Venetsiia," where Gumilev entered into an Acmeist polemic with the symbolist Blok by sinking Blok's otherworldly Venice in the canal through parodic allusions to the older poet's Venetian cycle.[16] Anna Akhmatova's 1912 poem, also titled "Venetsiia," offers dispassionate reflections on the touristic Venice. Khodasevich, too, turns to the Russian Venetian canon with a cool eye; in the 1920 "Brenta" the speaker wonders how the narrow and insignificant river has attracted so much poetic attention—the object of his irony was above all Pushkin's line "Adriaticheskie volny! O, Brenta!" (Adriatic waves! Oh, Brenta!) in *Eugene Onegin*. Khodasevich distances himself from his predecessors by focusing on the mundane details of Venetian street life rather than the textualized landscape of gondolas and full moons as, for instance, in the poem "Net nichego prekrasnei i privol'nei" ("There is nothing more splendid and free").[17]

At the beginning of the twentieth century Venice haunted the Russian poetic imagination, but it was Pavel Muratov's 1911 *Obrazy Italii* (*Images of Italy*) that became a huge success among the reading public and the quintessential prerevolutionary travel book to Italy. It both reflected and reformed Russian views and opinions of Italy.[18] Venice was the first and final stop on Muratov's itinerary. Following his British literary models Walter Pater and John Addington Symonds—Symonds in particular was one of the most influential Victorian Venetophiles—Muratov introduced his Russian readers to Venetian art and architecture, while also inviting his readers to look for the picturesque vistas of what he called the *drugaia Venetsiia* (other Venice), the Venice of the ruin and the back canals. Apart from these travel notes and poetry about Venice, the city also occupied a place in the turn-of-the-century Petersburg imagination through the historical parallel between Petersburg and Venice, which, as V. N. Toporov has shown, had turned into a "'cultural' cliché" by the beginning of the twentieth century. The parallel drew on the imagery of "doom, sunset, 'catalycity,' and death," acquiring an eschatological emphasis, most hauntingly, perhaps, in Mandelstam's collection *Tristia*, where apocalyptic visions of the dying "Petropolis," the classical Pushkinian

Petersburg, correspond with Mandelstam's melancholy fantasy of the dying Venice in the 1922 poem "Venetsianskaia zhizn'" ("Venetian life"). Mandelstam's Venice, belated but perhaps the most powerful manifestation of the fin-de-siécle Venice in Russian letters, was envisioned from a distance through biblical references and Renaissance art—his ekphrasis relates as much to Venice as to a painting by the Venetian Tintoretto: *Susanna and the Elders.* "In the 1920s," as Toporov records Akhmatova saying, "Mandelstam saw Petersburg as half-Venice, half-theater."[19]

This Russian Venetian canon came to Brodsky, as he indicated in *Watermark,* through literature (Kuzmin's translations of Henri Régnier) and memorabilia (postcards and souvenirs). Although written in English, the cultural positionality imbedded in *Watermark* is that of a Soviet Russian-language poet. Russian cultural knowledge is established in the text through numerous references and allusions to Russian encounters with Venice. The beginning of the essay evokes Pasternak's arrival in the city in *Safe Conduct,* and Pasternak's poem about Venice is referred to later in the essay ("Pasternak compared it [Venice on the map] to a swollen croissant" [*W,* 45]). While the chronology of the author's frequent visits to Venice forms a narrative in which he arrives in Venice from Europe or North America—the first trip, he recalls, took off from Detroit—his authorial position is construed as if he approached the city from the opposite geographical direction through Muratov's "golden gates of Venice." The author lives in the West and works in American academia, but his impressions of Venice are conveyed through the prism of his "previous incarnation," as he refers to his life in the Soviet Union.

This disjunctive temporality informs the peculiar chronotope, the multilayered nostalgia of Brodsky's Venice. The dream to travel out of the Soviet Union to Europe is re-evoked in *Watermark* through Brodsky's recollection of the author reading an issue of *Life* magazine with a "stunning color photo of San Marco." In the 1960s and 1970s Aleksandr Kushner, Brodsky's fellow poet from the Leningrad years, wrote a series of poems about Venice, in which the city is imagined as a distant dream woven of Pushkin, Canaletto, Henry James, Thomas Mann, and Blok, and which illustrate the longing Venice signified for Brodsky and the Leningrad poets he affiliated with.[20] It signified the longing to travel to Europe, on the one hand, and the culturally conditioned longing for Europe's cultural heritage, which also encompasses the Petersburg heritage, on the other. This is nostalgically evoked in Brodsky's "Spoils of War" (1986), an English-language essay describing the author's first encounters with Western consumer goods, among them a set of postcards of fin-de-siècle Venice given to him as a present in Leningrad in the 1960s:

> The texture and the melancholy it conveyed, because so familiar to me in my hometown, made these pictures more comprehensible, more real. It was almost like reading relatives' letters. And I read them and reread them. And the more I read them, the more apparent it became that this was what the word "West" meant to me: a perfect city by the winter sea, columns, arcades, narrow passages, cold marble staircases, peeling stucco exposing the red-brick flesh, putti, cherubs with their dust-covered eye-balls: civilization that braced itself for the cold times. (*GR*, 15)

As this nostalgic re-evocation of the initial nostalgia shows, in the 1960s Leningrad counterculture with which Brodsky associated himself, imagining, talking, writing, and longing for Venice was part of the cultural practices through which young intellectuals, such as Brodsky, negotiated their relation with the Soviet reality and the Russian past. Venice was among those "texts" to which David Bethea refers in mapping out the makings of Brodsky's "creation of exile," when he observes how in the Soviet-Russian context the Saidian-Foucauldian understanding of the relation between culture and power was turned curiously on its head.[21] Brodsky's case—that is, his gradual transformation from a Russian dissident poet into an American public intellectual—reinforces the accuracy of Said's model when applied to a Western situation. As a poet, particularly as a non-English-language poet, Brodsky was and perhaps remained a *marginal* writer in the American literary scene, but he was not a *marginalized* writer. In the United States the cultural institutions sanctioned him as poet laureate. The adherence to the Western canon that left Brodsky outside the official culture in the Soviet Union gained him the stature of a Nobel Prize winner in the West. At the same time, Brodsky's lyric poetry and critical writing reflect a sense of disillusion and discomfort in the role of a public intellectual. He often expressed his disdain for his contemporary intellectual environment in openly polemic terms: "Flight from Byzantium" (discussed in chap. 5) is just one instance.

In the context of Russian culture Brodsky's case presents, then, an interesting reversal. The Acmeist formula of *longing for world culture* was transformed into a *longing for Leningrad culture*. The self-reflective reaching from the peripheral Russia to the centers of Western culture made a full circle and turned into a longing, from the popularized, decanonized, and deconstructed West for an ideal Russia of (Western) canons, hierarchies, and fixed identities. Venice became a central site of this longing. Brodsky's recollections of his youthful fantasies about Venice in *Watermark,* his memories of Venice imagined and dreamed in 1960s Leningrad, reveal a longing for the initial state of longing.

The souvenir plays an important role in Brodsky's Venetian imaginings and produces multilayered meanings of nostalgia. The postcards Brodsky nostalgically recalls receiving from a female friend in Leningrad in the 1960s in "Spoils of War" reappear in *Watermark* together with a photograph in *Life* and other memorabilia of Venice:

> One day another friend, who is still alive, brought me a disheveled issue of *Life* magazine with a stunning color photo of San Marco covered with snow. Then a bit later a girl whom I was courting at the time made me a birthday present of an accordion set of sepia postcards her grandmother had brought from a pre-revolutionary honeymoon in Venice, and I pored over it with my magnifying glass. Then my mother produced from God knows where a small square piece of cheap tapestry, a rag really, depicting the Palazzo Ducale, and it covered the bolster on my Turkish sofa—thus contracting the history of the republic under my frame. And throw into the bargain a little copper gondola brought by my father from his tour of duty in China, which my parents kept in their dressing tables, filling it with loose buttons, needles, postage stamps, and—increasingly—pills and ampoules. (*W,* 39)

The significance of the souvenir for its owner is always nostalgic. "The souvenir speaks to a context of origin through a language of longing," as Susan Stewart writes, "for it is not an object arising out of need or use value; it is an object arising out of the necessarily insatiable demands of nostalgia."[22] The set of Venetian postcards in Brodsky's writing present a specific case of the souvenir in that the nostalgia they signify does not arouse from a personal connection with the signified: Brodsky had them in his possession before he had ever been to Venice. But despite that, or perhaps because of that, the nostalgic meanings Brodsky invests in the postcards function simultaneously on two temporal axis and refer to multiple objects—his youth in Leningrad, his home there, his parents, friends—and the nostalgia experienced toward Western culture in Leningrad as a young man. The object of this cultural nostalgia, the

West, represented for him the authentic origin of culture, the opposite of the "kafkaesque cosmos" of the Soviet reality. As Susan Stewart asserts:

> The double function of the souvenir is to authenticate a past or otherwise remote experience and, at the same time, to discredit the present. The present is either too impersonal, too looming, or too alienating compared to the intimate and direct experience of contact which the souvenir has as its reference. This referent is authenticity. . . . The location of authenticity becomes whatever is distant to the present time and space; hence we can see the souvenir as attached to the antique and the exotic. (Stewart, *On Longing*, 139–40)

Brodsky's *Watermark* is a showcase of how the "location of authenticity" signified by the souvenir may alter. The nostalgic meanings Brodsky invests in the postcards, and the experience of authenticity these meanings convey, function on two temporal axis: viewed from the Soviet Union, authenticity was located in the West, which Venice emblematically signified for the owner of the set of postcards, while at the time of writing *Watermark* authenticity was located in the 1960s Leningrad, which turns into the place of the author's original and now lost innocence. The longing for authenticity, the search for it, and the experiencing of it always implies a utopia. Authenticity, as Stewart writes, is "placed beyond the horizon of present lived experience, the beyond in which the antique, the pastoral, the exotic, and other fictive domains are articulated" (ibid., 133). The referent of Brodsky's initial longing was, then, the utopia of the West and Europe, as the longing for Europe, in Brodsky's youth, also signaled a longing for a Petersburg past as perceived through the cultural and literary heritage associated with it.

In this sense, to return to the parallel between Brodsky and Régis Debray, Brodsky's position is not entirely different from Debray's. Even if Brodsky and Debray came at it from opposite ends of Cold War Europe, both writers' essays about Venice communicate nostalgia for an imaginary Eurocentric past. Venice, as the ultimate ruin, narrates the history of the West, as Judith Seaboyer sums it up:

> The material traces of the order of meaning by which the West has constructed itself are preserved here [in Venice] in a kind of a time warp, and as edge cities and malls seem to sprawl out of control, flattening before them both history and landscape which once defined the boundary

> between city and country, Venice, its feminized body exposed to the world's gaze, promises a meaningful story of the past.[23]

This is, as Seaboyer asserts, "only one view," but it is the one that poignantly elaborates on Brodsky's fascination with Venice. The Venetian lagoon creates a "semiotic cut," to quote Debray, and by transgressing this semiotic border we submit ourselves to

> the essentially intransitive experience: trans-shipment, change of vehicle and tempo, obligatory slowing down of vital rhythms. Here we are, somewhere else, a dismounted pedestrian or a cork on water; no doubt about it: we have indeed passed over to the other side of the mirror. (*Against Venice*, 10)

Here Debray comes to answer his own provocative question, "Why does Venice turn the head of the French academician?" The answer extends its relevance beyond the scope of the question, pointing to Debray's own fascination with the city, as well as to the fact that Venice is a paradigmatic tourist city. For a sensibility that regrets the loss of the referent, the historicity of Venice offers itself to be read as the haven of the original. The Venetian semiosis with its mirrorings, reflections, masks, doubles, and duplicates presents an endless play of the sign, with the referent never escaping but always in sight. The transgression of the semiotic border with the change of the tempo allows the transgressor to indulge in this play, and to transgress the semiotic border in the winter—Brodsky's season to visit Venice—minimizes the chance of encountering other transgressors, whose presence cancels out the authenticity of the experience.

Venice as a *Third Space*

Apart from *Watermark*, Brodsky wrote several poems about Venice. In his Russian collected works there are seven poems that relate to the city: "Lagoon" (1973), "San Pietro" (1977), "Venetian Stanzas 1" and "Venetian Stanzas 2" (1982), "In Italy" (1985), "Venice: Lido" (1991), "Homage to Girolamo Marcello" (1991), and "In Front of Casa Marcello" (1995).[24] Even if not intended to be read as a poetic cycle, these texts nevertheless create a unique sequence in Brodsky's poetic works. The seven poems, reflecting Brodsky's sustained interest in Venice and his regular visits there, generate a chronology of texts, which disclose his life-story imbedded in his appropriation of Venice as a cultural and textual space by means of lyric poetry. By recording the twenty-three years of "chronic tourism," his Russian poems of Venice from "Lagoon," which he began to write on a trip to Venice some six months after his emigration in 1972, to "In Front of Casa Marcello," written just months before his death in January 1996, narrate his transition from the exiled Leningrad poet and Soviet tourist into an internationally acknowledged Russian poet and American essayist with a cosmopolitan network of friends and professional alliances.[25]

Transitional realities are always translational phenomena, as such critics of postcolonial postmodernity as Homi Bhabha remind us, and Brodsky, too, performed his transculturation by way of translation. The Russian-language poems record his gradual transition from the marginal position of a Russian-language poet into his desired center of English-language literary community, a process recalled in *Watermark*, where the transition is translated into a singular text-event, now in his adopted English. This translational performance takes place in *Watermark* on many levels. Brodsky literally translates poetic images from his earlier Russian poems into his English-language prose; the most fascinating instances are those where he reworks these images into a new cultural context of subtexts and allusions interwoven with autobiographical fragments of people and events, real and imaginary. Meanwhile, he also reuses and often expands on the autobiographical materials introduced in the Russian poems; for instance, the opening passages of *Watermark*, which nostalgically recall the author's first visit to Venice, present an elaborate commentary on the first two stanzas of "Lagoon."

Valentina Polukhina has discussed the relation of Brodsky's poetry and prose in *Watermark*, pointing to the way Brodsky "transfers whole chunks of his poetry into prose" to "poetize his prose," as she argues, concluding that "by writing his Venetian *poema* in prose Brodsky demonstrates that the polarity of poetry and prose has been transcended."[26] The focus of my discussion of the relation between Brodsky's Russian Venetian poems and the English essay is elsewhere. I am interested in the way Brodsky's self-translations foreground the question of cultural difference in the sense that Homi Bhabha defines the term when he writes that "cultural difference is the process of the *enunciation* of culture as 'knowledge*able*,' authoritative, adequate to the construction of systems of cultural identification."[27] The genre difference between poetry and prose, which Polukhina highlights, was in Brodsky's case connected with "cultural identification" in a fatal fashion, something that the writing of *Watermark* demonstrates; *Watermark* does not, in my view, manifest as much an effort to *transcend* as to *reckon with* a cultural difference between the Russian- and English-language literary and poetic practices, which had both fertilized Brodsky's poetic talent and presented some of the greatest challenges to it.[28] *Watermark*, then, presents a remarkable case of what David Bethea has referred to as Brodsky's "cultural triangulation," by which he means the triangular vision characteristic of the mature Brodsky's works, where Russian and Western sources merge with Brodsky's own earlier writings as the third source.[29]

Brodsky's position as a poet, bound to the formal achievements of Russian classicism and its modernist heritage, "dramatized" in an unprecedented way, to use Bhabha's vocabulary, the "activity of culture's untranslatability."[30] Cultural untranslatability was a topic Brodsky himself frequently addressed, even if approaching it from the opposite direction, regarding it not so much an arena for newness and reinvention as a deplorable fact of cultural loss. In "In the Shadow of Dante," Brodsky's essay on the Italian poet Eugenio Montale, Brodsky expresses this approach by asserting that "a poem is the closest possible interplay between ethics and aesthetics. This interplay, lamentably, is precisely what tends to vanish in translation."[31] Nevertheless, Brodsky's English poetry, including his translations of his own poems as well as his English-language prose, not to say anything of his polemic articulations of what translation should be, everything that formed a major part of his writing career in emigration, elucidated his position on the cultural borderline, constantly negotiating cultural translation. Brodsky's *Watermark* can be understood in terms of just such translation, revealing "the performative nature of cultural communication. It is language *in actu* (enunciation, positionality) rather than language *in situ* (*énoncé*, or propositionality). And the sign of translation continually tells, or 'tolls' the different times and spaces between cultural authority and its performative practices."[32] Bhabha's theoretization is inspired by Walter Benjamin's insights into the assimilation in modern metropolitan life, and more specifically, Benjamin's discussion in *Illuminations* of the subject of cultural difference as the "irresolution, or liminality, of 'translation,' the *element of resistance* in the process of transformation, 'that element in a translation that does not lend itself to translation.'"[33]

In other words, translation "stages" rather than transcends or conceals cultural differences, while the liminality of the translational subject foregrounds the conflict between the Ovidian exile, who believes that "migration only changes the surface of the soul, preserving identity under its protean form," and the Lucretian exile, for whom, as Bhabha continues, the "crossing of cultural frontiers permits freedom from the essence of the self."

From this theoretical viewpoint, Brodsky's Venice in *Watermark* emerges as the space in between, a "third space," a site of rediscovery and reinvention where a fixed identity is transformed into a hybrid and more fluid subjectivity.[34] The liminality that Barry Curtis and Claire Pajaczkowska detect in Venice is an ideal cultural space for this transformation:

> Venice has always been regarded as intermediate. . . . In Western eyes, Venice was always a renowned meeting place for different cultures and its own forms of cultural expression were hybrid and exotic. It was frequently presented as indeterminate in its relation to the East—partaking of some of the characteristics attributed to the Orient, whilst representing Italian and European culture. Venice was the bulwark of Christianity against the territorial and trading ambitions of the Muslim, although it maintained highly ambivalent relations with Byzantium. . . . The city simultaneously embodied Orient and Occident in binarised and superimposed associations of oligarchy and democracy, timelessness and modernity, obscurity and visibility.[35]

Venice, and more specifically the Venetophile discourse, offered the "ambivalent space of enunciation," to adopt Bhabha's idiolect, where Brodsky's cultural translation was performed. In this sense, the act of writing *Watermark*, its very being in the world, challenges the claims to origins and inherent cultural essences underlying "Flight from Byzantium"; *Watermark* narrates the author's diasporic identity as a borderline hybridity, while it dramatizes the conflict of the in-between existence of cultural displacement. This conflict creates the tension of the text, which its author, the metropolitan ironist, aspires to come to terms with by narrating in English his entry and belonging to the English language cultural knowledge. Brodsky's Russian poems of Venice, on the other hand, articulate the narrative of his hyphenated identity from the other side, in his native diction, that of Russian lyric poetry.

In what follows, Brodsky's Venetian poems are discussed with the focus on the images, allusions, and autobiographical recollections informing the textual attitude that shapes the cultural knowledge and authorial positionality of *Watermark*'s arresting and troublesome translation, the translation of the Ovidian exilic poet, articulated by means of Russian lyric poetry, into the

Lucretian exilic tourist, the postmodern subjectivity freed from, though nostalgically longing for, the essence of the self.

"Lagoon," Ezra Pound, and the Tear

"Lagoon," Brodsky's first poetic text on Venice, is now among the most anthologized of his poems, which most likely has to do with the fact that it deploys three popular themes: it is written in Venice, relates to Christmas, and expresses a powerful anti-Soviet sentiment.[36] "Lagoon" is an expression of exilic anxiety where the lyric subject fluctuates between anger at the Soviet regime and recognition of his own displacement and insignificance. The "absolute nobody, a man in a raincoat" (translated in the authorized English version as "a nameless lodger, a nobody"), who has lost his "memory, homeland, and son," raises his arm in the ninth stanza to show the "hammer-and-sickle sign / with which to salute our era and bestow / a mute up-yours-even-unto-the-elbow / upon the nightmares of our time" (*CP*, 80–81). In Brodsky's original Russian the allusion to the relationship between the devil and the witch Soloha in Gogol's *Night before Christmas* creates a double entendre, emphasizing the brutal necessity of the gesture of defiance: "zhest poluchim, pokhozhii na / molot v serpe—i kak chort Solokhe, / khrabro pokazhem ego epokhe, / priniavshei obraz durnogo sna" (3:45–46) (literally, "we get a gesture, resembling / a hammer in a sickle—and like the devil to Solokha, / we bravely show it to the age, / which has taken the form of a bad dream").

The meanings Brodsky invests in Venice in "Lagoon" have to do with individualism and ideological freedom; he presents Venice as a symbol of these, for him, Western ideals and as the antipode of the Soviet Union. This is expressed in the unambiguous imagery of the eighth stanza, where the sound a gondola makes when it "knocks against its moorings" cancels out the sounds of the "derzhava" (literally, "power," translated in the English version as "nation"), where, in the Russian version, "hands are raised as pinewood forests" and the "spit freezes in the mouth":

> Гондолы бьет о гнилые сваи.
> Звук отрицает себя, слова и
> слух; а также державу ту,
> где руки тянутся хвойным лесом
> перед мелким, но хищным бесом
> и слюну леденит во рту.
> (3:45)

The gondola knocks against its moorings. Sound
cancels itself, hearing and words are drowned,
as is that nation where among
forests of hands the tyrant of the State
is voted in, its only candidate,
and spit goes ice-cold on the tongue.
(*CP*, 80)

The images of the pinewood forest and freezing spit symbolize totalitarianism, while they also invoke the idea of the North, or a northern (Soviet) "power," juxtaposed with the "gondola" symbolizing the West and the Mediterranean South. In the previous stanza—where Brodsky recapitulates the culturally important association of Petersburg with Venice by comparing the sphinxes common in the Petersburg topography with the emblem of Venice, St. Marks' Lion—North and South are not juxtaposed in the way they are in the stanza referring to the Soviet power. The comparison between Petersburg sphinxes and Venetian lions has a culturally affirmative function in that it encloses the poet's native landscape in the Venetian environment: "winged lion, which can read and write, / southern kin of northern sphinxes of renown, / won't drop his book and holler, but calmly drown / in splinters of mirror, splashing light" (*CP*, 80). On the other hand, the contrast between "holler" (in the original Russian the more militant "ratui," literally, "fight"), and the peaceful and bookish Venetian lion anticipates the symbols of northern totalitarianism juxtaposed with the cultured South, which, in turn, invokes the cultural commonplace in which the positive significations related to the ancient Mediterranean culture are opposed to the negative ones associated with the barbaric North.

The anti-Soviet sentiment, on the one hand, and the references to the Petersburg and Venetian myths, on the other, exhibit the speaker's awareness of his own position in Venice and the city's significance for an exiled Russian writer.[37] In the "drowning city" at "Christmas without snow, tinsel, or tree," he is settling with his present and future life:

Так и будем жить, заливая мертвой
водой стеклянной графина мокрый
пламень граппы, кромсая леща, а не
птицу-гуся, чтобы нас насытил

предок хордовый Твой, Спаситель,
зимней ночью в сырой стране.
(3:45)

So this is how we cope, putting out the heat
of grappa with nightstand water, carving the meat
of flounder instead of Christmas roast,
so that Thy earliest backboned ancestor
might feed and nourish us, O Saviour,
this winter night on a damp coast.
(*CP*, 80)

The image of the "wet/moist eye," suggesting a tear, in the seventh stanza of "Lagoon"—"A drowning city, where suddenly the dry / light of reason dissolves in the moisture of the eye"—points the way to Brodsky's later Venetian imaginings: a tear is also suggested in "In Italy" and in "Venetian Stanzas 2." In "In Italy" it occurs in the lines that make up the enjambment between the third and fourth stanzas, and which combine quotes from two poems by Anna Akhmatova, "Venetsiia" ("Venice") and "Letnii sad" ("Summer Gardens"), creating an image in which Venice and Petersburg merge: "And the world's best lagoon with its golden pigeon // coop gleams sharply enough to make the pupil run" (*CP*, 340).[38] The image suggesting a tear in "Venetian Stanzas 2" echoes the one in "In Italy":

Стынет кофе. Плещет лагуна, сотней
мелких бликов тусклый зрачок казня
за стремленье запомнить пейзаж, способный
обойтись без меня.
(3:240)

And the coffee grows cold. And the blinding lagoon is lapping
at the shore as the dim human pupil's bright penalty
for its wish to arrest a landscape quite happy
here without me.
(*CP*, 308)

By rhyming "(zrachok) kaznia," that is, "punishing the pupil," with "menia," the objective form of the personal pronoun "I," Brodsky creates a rhyming pair, the semantics of which suggest pain and blindness, even self-mutilation (*kaznit'* means to execute, to put to death, to punish). Blindness is suggested also in "In Italy," where the rhyming pair "slepia" / "sebia," ending the first two lines of the second quatrain, forms a double rhyming pair with "(zrachok) slezia" / "nelz'ia" (wetting the pupil / cannot), ending the first two lines of the fourth and last quatrain. The two rhyming pairs create a semantic field, pointing to the speaker's ambivalence toward emotions, such as exilic nostalgia, which intervene with his ironic and rational assessment of life, threatening to shatter the pose of a stoic seminal to "In Italy" (see "'In Italy' and the Question of Self-Translation," pp. 197–201).

In *Watermark* the tear is a reoccurring image but less obviously related to exilic nostalgia. In the final passage of the essay, the author sums up his sentiments on beauty and Venice in the following terms:

> By rubbing water, this city improves time's looks, beautifies the future. That's what the role of this city in the universe is. Because the city is static while we are moving. The tear is a proof of that. Because we go and beauty stays. Because we are headed for the future, while beauty is the eternal present. The tear is an attempt to remain, to stay behind, to merge with the city. But that's against the rules. The tear is a throwback, a tribute of the future to the past. Or else it is the result of subtracting the greater from the lesser: beauty from man. The same goes for love, because one's love, too, is greater than oneself. (*W*, 134)

This passage, which is placed after an intimate and affectionate recollection of W. H. Auden, ends the essay, and the final aphoristic thought, "because one's love is greater than oneself," can be understood as the author's confession of professional and filial affection toward Auden. And yet, in the textual space of *Watermark* the image of the tear and the topic of beauty also invoke Ezra Pound, the literary modernist who, while not as paramount a figure for Brodsky as Auden, was, however, a well-known "Venetophile." One of the longer passages in the otherwise fragmented *Watermark* is Brodsky's description of his visit with Pound's widow, Olga Rudge, in the company of Susan Sontag, which prompts Brodsky to review Pound's work and controversial position after World War II:

> Well, to begin with, in my line of work Ezra Pound is a big deal, practically an industry. Many an American graphomaniac has found in Ezra

> Pound both a master and a martyr. As a young man, I had translated quite a bit of him into Russian. The translations were trash, but came very close to being published. . . . I liked the original for its sophomoric freshness and taut verse, for its thematic and stylistic diversity, for its voluminous cultural references, then out of my reach. I also liked his "make it new" dictumliked it, that is, until I grasped that the true reason for making it new was that "it" was fairly old; that we were, after all, in a body shop. As for his plight in St. Elizabeth's, in Russian eyes, that was nothing to rave about and, anyhow, better than the nine grams of lead that his wartime radio spiels might have earned him elsewhere. . . . A fair thing to do, I thought, would be to publish both his poems and his speeches in one volume, without any learned introduction, and see what happens. Of all people, a poet should have known that time knows no difference between Rapallo and Lithuania. . . . He was still big with some of my friends, and now I was to see his old woman. (*W*, 69–70)

This assessment of Pound's life and works disclose the author's narrative of his own graduation from a poetic apprenticeship to creative maturity and critical authority, while it also narrates his cultural transition from a young Leningrad poet (whose "plight" at the hands of Soviet psychiatry gave him the confidence to talk about Pound's) into a New York–based writer. Once reaching, through the practice of poetic translation, toward the imaginary centers of English-language literature, he is now befriended by his contemporary cosmopolitan intellectuals with access to the immediacy of the distant idols of his youth.

The differences between Brodsky's and Pound's positions are obvious, not the least of them being the fact that Brodsky was the son of a Jewish navy officer, for whom the Soviet anti-Jewish actions denied rank after the war, while Pound was associated during the war with fascist ideologues. The passage preceding the one on Pound in *Watermark* is Brodsky's description of a photograph of a wartime execution of three Lithuanians by German soldiers, which anticipates the topic of anti-Semitism central to the passage on Pound—from here the juxtaposition of Lithuania and the Italian Rapallo, where Pound resided during the war. But despite the differences, there was also a striking similarity in Brodsky's and Pound's cultural position and aesthetic stance, foregrounded by their fascination with Venice. Though a latecomer to the English-language literature of the latter half of the twentieth century, Brodsky occupied a position in regard to Europe not unlike the one the American Pound did in the first half of the century; both Pound, the American ex-patriot from Indiana, and Brodsky, the Americanized Russian émigré writer from Leningrad, exhibited a desire to assimilate to European traditions and cultural achievements through their fascination with Italy, and especially with Venice, which they both perceived as a central site of these achievements.[39] Pound lived in Venice in various stages of his life and died there in 1972; his first book of poetry was collected and published there, and included a number of poems about the city; and Venice is also seminal to the later *Cantos,* especially 17 and 14–16, and the autobiographical essay "Indiscretions." Though the nostalgia so incessant in Brodsky's *Watermark* is alien to Pound's family chronology in "Indiscretions," there is a similarly self-ironic acknowledgement of the author's cultural position in regard to Venice in both, as Pound ironically states: "Venice is an excellent place to come from Crawfordsville, Indiana."[40] Viewed from this perspective, the passage on Pound in *Watermark* comes across as an astonishing case of anxiety of influence, and with Brodsky's recollections of his youthful translations of Pound in mind, it is not unconceivable that the image of the tear, so central to *Watermark,* and suggested in several of Brodsky's Venetian poems, owes something to Pound's first poem on Venice, "Night Litany":[41]

> O, Dieu, purifiez nos coeurs!
>   purifiez nos coeurs!
>
> Yea the lines hast thou laid unto me
>   in pleasant places,
> And the beauty of this thy Venice
>   hast thou shown unto me
> Until is its loveliness become unto me
>   a thing of tears . . .
>
> O God of waters,
>   make clean our hearts within us
> And our lips to show forth thy praise,
>   for I have seen the
> shadow of this thy Venice
> floating upon waters . . .[42]

"Night Litany," typical of Pound's juvenilia, is an epiphanic monologue, where the tear is triggered by the encounter with the city, an encounter resembling a religious revelation. The speaker is overwhelmed by the city's beauty, and the tear is a token of this emotion: it is a token of awe, as well as fulfillment and presence, much the same way as the "moisture of the eye" is at the sight of the "drowning city" in "Lagoon"—though the exilic recollection of the "northern sphinxes," which immediately follows, probably also induces the moistening of the eye, the same way as the sight of the Akhmatovian "golden pigeon coop" in "In Italy" does. In "Venetian Stanzas" and *Watermark* the tear appears when parting with the city, triggered not only by an encounter but also by the anticipation of a departure. In *Watermark* the tear is a token of unfulfillment, incapacity, and loss: "Because we go and beauty stays." The tear shed in *Watermark* has been read as a tear of gratitude and healing nostalgia, but it also implies negation and melancholia, in "Venetian Stanzas" even self-abasement, suggested by the semantic potential of the rhyming pair "kaznia" / "menia" (see above).[43] Brodsky's descriptions of his frequent pilgrimages to Venice in *Watermark* speak of a repeatedly enacted loss, where parting with the city appears more fulfilling than the reunion with it. Brodsky's tear, then, signifies an encounter not so much with the beautiful as with the sublime, to use Edmund Burke's classic distinction, according to which the sublime is always "individual and painful," whereas the beautiful is "social and pleasant."[44] In "In Front of Casa Marcello," the last poem Brodsky wrote about Venice, all these tears, engendered by the encounter with Venice, are summoned in the lines that establish the significance of Venice for the lyric subject: "Here, where plenty / of saliva, rapturous tears, and even / seed has been shed, in a nook of the earthly Eden, / I stand in the evening . . ." (*CP*, 435).

The encounter with the Venetian sublime is one of the topics that Brodsky ironically toys with in *Watermark*. The passage where he recalls his first impressions of the city on the first morning of his first visit evokes the book of Genesis, but apart from the playful biblical reference Pound's epiphanic vision too is implied:

> The city came into focus. "And the earth was without form, and void; and darkness was upon the face of the deep. And the Spirit of God moved upon the face of the waters," to quote an author who visited here before. Then there was the next morning. It was Sunday, and all the bells were chiming. (*W*, 42)

In the next passage Brodsky follows up the biblical image of "the Spirit of God moved upon the face of waters" (Pound's "God of Waters") and develops it into a poetic contemplation on the mythology of metaphysics seminal to his creative imagination. Repeating his central poetic metaphor of water being the image of time, he concludes: "It is as though space, cognizant here more than anyplace else of its inferiority to time, answers it with the only property time doesn't possess: with beauty" (*W*, 44). This relates, later in the essay, to a similar passage, which consists of a prose translation of "Doklad dlia simpoziuma" ("A Lecture for a Symposium"), a poem Brodsky wrote in Russian at about the same time as he was working on *Watermark* in English. The poem is a mock-treatise on the concept of beauty; its parody is targeted at the convention of a philosophical treatise and the speaker's own claim to authorship of such a treatise, while the treatise's topics, beauty and aesthetic value, were concepts that Brodsky revered in earnest. Beauty as a concept is, in fact, one of the main objects of Brodsky's aphoristic inquiry in *Watermark*. In the passage on Pound quoted above, one of the points of Brodsky's critique of Pound has to do with the concept of beauty: "*The Cantos* too left me cold," he writes. "The main error was an old one: questing after beauty. For someone with such a long record of residence in Italy, it was odd that he hadn't realized that beauty can't be targeted, that it is always a by-product of other, often very ordinary pursuits" (*W*, 70). Brodsky's critique of Pound "questing for beauty" sounds peculiar, especially coming from an author who, when appointed poet laureate of the United States, declared in his inaugural speech at the Library of Congress that "the purpose of evolution, believe it or not, is beauty" (*GR*, 207).

Tony Tanner, the literary historian on Venice, writes about Pound, beauty, and Venice: "Pound prefaced his essay on 'Religio' with the assertion, 'To replace the marble goddess on her pedestal at Terracina is worth more than any metaphysical argument,' and clearly Pound's sense of the sacred, or the numinous, had a strong inclination to the plastic—granite, marble, ivory; sapphire, jade, emerald, diamond: crystal. And—'this thy Venice.'"[45] Marble statues frequently function in Brodsky's poetry as an impetus for metaphysical explorations (a marble statue is a seminal image in such poems as "Torso," "Roman Elegies," "The Bust of Tiberius," and the play *Marbles*), and he certainly located in the "marble stasis" of Venice, which he contrasts with the "mobility" of human anatomy in *Watermark*, a sense of the sacred. Marble was a central image to Brodsky's poetic imagination as "the material of art and piety; of civic beauty," just as it was for Pound.[46] Brodsky does not elaborate on the image of marble in his Venetian poems the way Pound does in the

Cantos, where the "white forest of marble" is the leading metaphor of the city, but in the two instances when marble does appear in "Venetian Stanzas," Pound's lines on Venice in the *Cantos* are instantly evoked. In "Venetian Stanzas 1," nocturnal Venice is first given in images of silence and music (stanza 1), as in the oxymoron of "napeless gondolas, fiddling numbly / the out-of-sync silence, sway." Then the nocturnal city is imagined (stanza 2) as a "marble aquarium," after which the fish imagery is further developed as the city is likened to an underwater world (stanza 6):

> Так меркнут люстры в опере; так на убыль
> к ночи идут в объеме медузами купола.
> Так сужается улица, вьющаяся как угорь,
> и площадь—как камбала.
> Так подбирает гребни, выпавшие из женских
> взбитых причесок, для дочерей Нерей,
> оставляя нетронутым желтый бесплатный жемчуг
> уличных фонарей.
> (3:236)

> That's how chandeliers dim at the opera; that's how cupolas
> shrink, like medusas, in volume, the tighter night hugs the place;
> that's how streets coil and dwindle, like eels; that's how
> just-as-populous
> squares mimic plaice.
> That's how, treating his daughters, Nereus nears us,
> pinching the combs from ladies' wind-ravaged curls,
> leaving untouched the quays' yellow, nervous,
> cheap electrical pearls.
> (*CP*, 304)

The image of the marble aquarium and the reference to the Greek sea-divinity Nereus' underwater realm in a poem set in the silent and nocturnal Venice evoke Pound's Canto 17, where Venice is depicted as an underwater world of "trees growing in water, / Marble trunks out of stillness, . . . The light now, not of the sun":

> Between them,
> Cave of Nerea,

> she like a great shell curved,
> And the boat drawn without sound,
> Without odour of ship-work,
> Nor bird-cry, nor any noise of wave moving,
> Nor splash of porpoise, nor any noise of wave moving,
> Within her cave, Nerea,
> she like a great shell curved
> In the suavity of the rock.[47]

Brodsky's Nereus returns the comb, so to speak, to Pound's Nerea or Nereid, one of the daughters of Nereus and, in Greek mythology, a sea nymph. Nereids also appear in "San Pietro," Brodsky's earlier poem about Venice (see below).

A Pound subtext reoccurs again in stanza 2 of "Venetian Stanzas 2," where Venice is depicted as a female figure, the "cold, naked, pallid marble / thighs" of which are being photographed voyeuristically by the "new elders," presumably tourists (specified as "Japanese" tourists when Brodsky reuses the image in *Watermark*). Brodsky here recapitulates Mandelstam's ekphrasis of Tintoretto's *Susannah and the Elders* in the 1922 poem "Venetsianskaia zhizn'" ("Venetian life"). The lines in stanza 2 anticipate the Botticelli-like rising of Venice from the waves in stanza 7:

> Так выходят из вод, ошеломляя гладью
> кожи бугристый берег, с цветком в руке,
> забывая про платье, предоставляя платью
> всплескивать вдалеке.
> Так обдают вас брызгами. Те, кто бессмертен, пахнут,
> водорослями . . .
> (3:239)

> That's how some rise from the waters, their smooth skin stunning
> the knobbly shore—while a flower may sway
> in the hand—leaving the slipped dress scanning
> the dry land from far away.
> That's how they wash you in spray, for the immortals' ardent
> perfume of kelp is what marks them from us . . .
> (*CP*, 307)

The image of the rising Venus/Aphrodite is a seminal image in Pound's *Cantos*, where goddesses repeatedly appear from the sea and are associated with Venice in numerous ways, as in Canto 17: "And Aletha, by bend of the shore, / with her eyes seaward, / and in her hands sea-wrack / Salt-bright with the foam." Pound's "sea-wrack" evokes the same marine vegetation as the "kelp" in Brodsky's poem; Brodsky makes much out of it in *Watermark*, where the smell of seaweed triggers off the author's reminiscences of the past. Brodsky adds to this image a northern dimension: it is not the smell of seaweed, but of "freezing" seaweed that is a synonym of "happiness" for the author, "partly because of onomatopoeic aspects of the very conjunction (in Russian, a wonderful *vodorosli*), partly due to a slight incongruity and a hidden underwater drama in this notion" (*W*, 5). As for comparing Venice with a female beauty rising from the water, both Pound and Brodsky had Byron's anthologized model to refashion: "She looks a sea Cybele, fresh from ocean, / Rising with her tiara of proud towers / At airy distance, with majestic motion," as the Venetian canto in *Childe Harold's Pilgrimage* depicts the spectacle of Venice.

It would be a poetic conjecture on the critic's part to positively assert—based on the above—that the literary source for the tear in Brodsky's Venetian imaginings from "Lagoon" to *Watermark* was the one shed in Pound's "Night Litany." Neither the tear as a signifier of an encounter with the sublime, nor the book of Genesis as a subtext for expressing such an encounter, especially in the watery Venice, strike one with their originality to an extent that it would rule out the possibility of a simple poetic coincidence between Pound and Brodsky. It is entirely possible to read Brodsky's Russian poems about Venice without their evoking any associations with Pound, regardless of the poetic origins of the tear, the marble aquarium, Nereus, or Venus/Venice (in Pound's treatment this, too, was a well-worked-out simile originating with Byron). Moreover, the meanings Brodsky invests in the image of a tear in *Watermark* point at his perception of artistic autonomy and individuality seminal to his understanding of a writer's place in the world: "Aesthetics' main tool, the eye, is absolutely autonomous. In its autonomy, it is inferior only to a tear" (*W*, 109). It is through his understanding of the "absolute autonomy" of the aesthetic sense that he comes to the following conclusion, expressed here in *Watermark*, and echoed his Nobel Prize speech: "Aesthetic sense is the twin of one's instinct for self-preservation and is more reliable than ethics" (ibid.). This is a position shaped by experiences in a totalitarian system, where Brodsky's "aesthetic isolation," a phrase he uses in the

Mandelstam essay (*LTO*, 134), equaled his aesthetic integrity and individual freedom.[48] Pound with his Rapallo speeches, on the other hand, was associated in Brodsky's worldview with those who threatened this autonomy.

With all these reservations considered, it remains that Pound is a towering figure in *Watermark*, while the significance of Venice for the two writers was not entirely dissimilar. Venice, Pound's "thing of tears," was certainly a thing of tears for Brodsky, too, while it also became a "pleasant place" for him, perhaps the most pleasant of all places. Venice is as paradisiacal a landscape in Pound's overtly intertextual and sometimes obscure visions in the *Cantos* as it is in Brodsky's *Watermark*, even if their stylistic strategies in representing this idea differed from one another. Brodsky did, after all, come to his paradisiacal landscape seventy years after Pound on an entirely different aesthetic key informed by an entirely different historical moment. For him the notion of paradise could only be advanced with irony. But, again, Pound was one of the cosmopolitan modernists, and part of the reference set that informed the evolution of Brodsky's aesthetic practices. The anecdotal meeting with Olga Rudge in *Watermark* gave Brodsky an opportunity to reckon with the Venetian shadow of Ezra Pound. And more than that, Brodsky's Venetian dialogue with Pound calls attention to Brodsky's position on the cultural borderline; the fact that Pound is a towering figure in the English Venetian canon but entirely absent in the Russian literary tradition of Venice dramatizes the activity of cultural untranslatability, which Brodsky's encounters with Venice highlight.

"San Pietro," Auden, and the Fog

The encounter with the Venetian sublime has invoked a paradigm of responses in literary tradition. There is the Poundian yielding to an aesthetic experience, where the aesthetic turns into the religious, and beauty merges with divinity, while there is also the skeptic's approach, expressed at its most sober by the murderous understatement opening Mary McCarthy's *Venice Observed*: "The rationalist mind has always had its doubts about Venice."[49] McCarthy's phrase captures acutely the mode in which Aleksander Hertzen wrote about Venice during his visit to the city at the time of the first carnival after the withdrawal of Austrian troops in 1867. The chapter on Venice in Hertzen's autobiography *My Past and Thoughts* starts with him noting that "a more magnificent absurdity than Venice does not exist."[50] Farther on he expresses some admiration for the beauty of the city but does not abandon his skepticism: "To build a city there, where a city cannot be built, is in itself madness;

but to build that way one of the most elegant and grandiose cities is the madness of genius" (ibid.). Brodsky captures this duality in the lines of "Lagoon" quoted above with "reason dissolv[ing] in the moisture of the eye," and in *Watermark* the ebb and flow of the author's ecstasy and skepticism is rendered through a self-ironic love analogy, his "one-way love affair" with the city.

The exiled Hertzen must have felt the similarity between the urban space of Venice and the capital of the Russian Empire, St. Petersburg, just as Brodsky, the native of the most "premeditated" of all cities, did a century later.[51] Venice, like Petersburg, is "eccentric," to adopt Yuri Lotman's terminology coined with regard to Petersburg, in that it is located on the border of two natural elements (sea/land), as well as of two cultural entities (East/West), and the collision of artifice and nature gives birth to substratial conditions, which, in V. N. Toporov's reading of the symbolic landscape of Petersburg, produce such semiotically charged phenomena as reflections, mirror images, and doubles, frequently deployed in literary representations of the city in the "Petersburg text."[52]

"San Pietro" captures the phenomenological peculiarity of the two cities by way of negation. The poem deploys what Bożena Shallcross has called Brodsky's "strategies of disappearance" and depicts the Venetian cityscape during *nebbia*, the Venetian fog, which as a natural phenomenon is a reversal of reflections and mirror images, canceling out their semiotic potential.[53] As Brodsky writes in *Watermark*:

> The local fog, the famous *nebbia*, renders this place more extemporal than any palace's inner sanctum, by obliterating not only reflections but everything that has a shape: buildings, people, colonnades, bridges, statues. . . . The fog is thick, blinding, and immobile. (*W*, 58–59)

The poetic structure of "San Pietro" supports the idea of the obliteration of form. It is written in *verse libre*, it is unrhymed, and the stanzaic patterns differ from the classical structures favoured by Brodsky. There are three sections in the poem, each with a diverse stanzaic pattern. The first and the second have three stanzas each, but the number of the lines per stanza vary. The first section is composed of stanzas with eleven, thirteen, and seventeen lines; the second section of stanzas with twenty-seven, fourteen, and twenty-seven lines. The third section has two stanzas with twenty and thirteen lines. This type of formal irregularity is uncharacteristic of Brodsky's poetics; in "San Pietro" the classical structure is disregarded in order to create one that supports the thematic level of the poem, the formlessness and shapelessness, a landscape stripped of all elements organizing and structuring the space. The first line of the poem depicts a city wrapped in a thick fog:

> Третью неделю туман не слезает с белой
> колокольни коричневого, захолустного городка,
> затерявшегося в глухонемом углу
> Северной Адриатики . . .
> (3:156)

> Three weeks now and the fog still clings to the white
> bell tower of this dull brown quarter
> stuck in a deaf-and-dumb corner
> of the northern Adriatic . . .
> (*CP*, 158)

The townscape turns into a static space, while the fog seems concretely to prevent the passing of time:

> Туго спеленутые клочковатой
> марлей стрелки на городских часах
> отстают от меркнущего вдалеке
> рассеянного дневного света.
> (3:157)

> Tightly swaddled in tattered gauze,
> the hands of the town clock
> lag behind the scattered daylight
> fading in the distance.
> (*CP*, 159)

In the stagnant, formless landscape the fog limits the vision and hearing, which process is emphasized by repeating the phrase "no wind, stillness":

> . . . ничего не видишь,
> кроме хлопьев тумана. Безветрие, тишина.
> Направленье потеряно . . .
> (3:157)

> . . . you can't see a thing
> Except scraps of fog. No wind; only stillness.
> Indirection . . .
> (*CP*, 159)

> Безветрие; и тишина как ржанье
> никогда не сбивающейся с пути
> чугунной кобылы Виктора-Эммануила.
> (3:157)

> No wind.
> And stillness like the whinny of Victor
> Emmanuel's never faltering cast-iron mare.
> (*CP*, 159)

> Смеркается; безветрие, тишина.
> (3:159)

> Twilight. No wind. The stillness.
> (*CP*, 161)

The architectural and topographic features of Venice together with the landscape dissolve in the fog: "columns guttering like stearin," "a canal bridge . . . keeps the hazy bank . . . from breaking away and drifting seaward," "colorless air / condenses into a pigeon or a sea gull, / but quickly dissipates." The landscape acquires a more illusory and abstract character, in which the reference to a solitary equestrian statue, "Victor / Emmanuel's never faltering cast-iron mare," evokes an allusion to St. Petersburg and its literary representations; the foggy city seems to disappear and all that is left, as in Dostoevsky's well-known image, is the swamp and the Bronze Horseman.

The poem's title discloses the poem's double signification. "San Pietro," St. Peter, is an allusion to the name of St. Petersburg. The play with the foggy ambiguity of Venetian landscape as well as the mythological potential of the name "San Pietro" forms the crux of writing "San Pietro." The image of Petersburg emerges in the first lines of the poem, when the speaker describes the "dull brown quarter / stuck in a deaf-and-dumb corner / of the northern Adriatic." This is a quotation from a poem by Umberto Saba, which starts with the line "in the depth of the wild Adriatic." Venice is located "in the corner" of the Adriatic, Leningrad/Petersburg "in the corner" of the Baltic Sea.

The subject of Saba's autobiographical poem is, in fact, not Venice but his native Trieste, and this reveals the function of the intertext: Brodsky's "San Pietro" is as much about his native Petersburg as it is about Venice. The autobiographical reference to Leningrad/Petersburg has a further significance, since Brodsky had translated Saba's poem into Russian not long before his emigration, something he remembers in *Watermark*.[54] In Saba's poem the childhood memories of the port and ships in Trieste resemble the episodes of Brodsky's childhood in Petersburg in his autobiographical essays. There are several references to childhood in "San Pietro." With the speaker's vision limited by the fog the eye turns to the past; the thicker the fog, the closer Petersburg:

> Так, дохнув на стекло, выводят инициалы
> тех, с чьим отсутствием не смириться;
> и подтек превращает заветный вензель
> в хвост морского конька. Вбирай же красной
> губкой лёгких плотный молочный пар,
> выдыхаемый всплывшею Амфитритой
> и ее нереидами! Протяни
> руку—и кончики пальцев коснутся торса,
> покрытого мелкими пузырьками
> и пахнущего, как в детстве, йодом.
> (3:158)

> So then, on breath-coated glass, one can trace the initials
> of those whose absence is hard to swallow;
> and a cherished monogram trickles down
> as the tail of a sea horse. Apply that red
> sponge of your lungs and soak up the thick milky
> mist—the breath of Amphitrite and her Nereids!
> Stretch out a hand—and your fingertips
> will touch a torso that's flecked with tiny
> bubbles and scented with the iodine of childhood.
> (*CP*, 160)

Apart from evoking the scene in Pushkin's *Eugene Onegin* in which Tatiana draws Onegin's initials on a window—"zavetnyi vensel'" (cherished monogram) is a direct quotation from Pushkin's prose poem—these lines are imbued with allusions to Osip Mandelstam's poetry. The emphasis on breathing, the enumerating of objects, the heightened awareness of small details, the physicality and the emphasis on touching, the creating of a certain sensuality, and the context of Greek mythology are all central features of Mandelstam's poetry. Furthermore, there is an illusion to Mandelstam with the last two lines' "iodine of childhood" recalling Mandelstam's Leningrad poem "I've come back to my city" with its imagery of childhood illness: "I've come back to my city. These are my own old tears, / my own little veins, the swollen glands of my childhood."[55]

But apart from Petersburg, the title of the poem also designates a concrete place in Venice, San Pietro di Castello, a small island with an old basilica (mentioned in the poem twice: "the white bell tower" in lines 1–2 and "the rusty brick of the old basilica" in lines 63–64), which used to serve as the main cathedral of Venice before the building of San Marco. In an interview with Peter Vail', Brodsky commented on the area depicted in the poem in the following terms: "San Pietro is not the most fascinating place in Venice, on the contrary. From the Arsenal towards the island of San Michele, there is an area where a tourist's foot does not trod: all kinds of small dock yards."[56] Brodsky's description of San Pietro resembles a passage from John Ruskin's *The Stones of Venice*, where he too is describing the area:

> The present church is among the least interesting in Venice; a wooden bridge, something like that of [London's] Battersea on a small scale, connects its islands, now almost deserted, with a wretched suburb of the city behind the arsenal; and a blank level of lifeless grass, rotted away in places rather than trodden, is extended before its mildewed and solitary tower.[57]

Ruskin's two-volume *The Stones of Venice*, originally published in 1851–53, was immensely influential on how Venice was perceived in European literature, and many writers of the Russian Silver Age were influenced by Ruskin's work.[58] In "San Pietro" Brodsky continues the Ruskinian tradition passed on to him by the Silver Age writers in that his exploring of Venice is directed to what can be described by the Italian term *Venezia non turistica*, or the Russian *drugaia Venetsiia* (other Venice), for whose search the major part of *Watermark* is dedicated, too. Even for the skeptic Régis Debray, San Pietro reveals the authentic Venice by not having "any local color":

> I don't deny that in certain peripheral quarters off to the north of the railroad station, for example . . . or at the other end of the island, east of the Arsenal—not the picturesque disused part which is all for show, but the small functioning naval workshops—at twilight around the San Pietro Canal, the aesthete can finally feel disoriented, anonymous, lost in pallid desolation *à la* Chirico, a no man's land without any local color. (*Against Venice*, 5–6)

Brodsky was not the first Russian poet writing Venice through the Petersburg lens: one of his predecessors was Prince Viazemsky, who set off on his first journey to Venice the same year as the third volume of Ruskin's *The Stones of Venice* was published (1853). Although Viazemsky in the following extract of his diary from August 1853 does not describe the Venetian fog but the famous floods—yet another mythologically charged substratial element typical of both cities—it exhibits the same Russian/Petersburg view of Venice as Brodsky's poem:

> We are no longer in Venice but in Petersburg. It is the third day since the metamorphosis happened. Day after day the weather has been changing radically. Today the water rose from the canals to the pavement, exactly as in Chernaia rechka. Venice is not a pleasant sight in ugly weather.[59]

To go back to Brodsky, he returned to the Venetian *nebbia* in the final passages of *Watermark*. The essay ends with Brodsky describing a winter night at the Piazza di San Marco:

> Fog began to engulf the piazza. It was a quiet invasion, but an invasion nonetheless. I saw its spears and lances moving silently but very fast, from the direction of the *laguna*, like foot soldiers preceding their heavy cavalry. "Silently, and very fast," I said to myself. Any time now you could anticipate their king, King Fog, appearing from around the corner in all his cumulus glory. "Silently, and very fast," I repeated to myself. Now, that was Auden's last line from his "Fall of Rome," and it was this place that was "altogether elsewhere." (*W*, 132)

The last stanza of Auden's "The Fall of Rome," from which Brodsky quotes, reads in full:

Altogether elsewhere, vast
Herds of reindeer move across
Miles and miles of golden moss,
Silently and very fast.[60]

In Brodsky's text the phrase "altogether elsewhere" refers to the illusory, miragelike cityscape, to the feeling of otherness that the sight of the foggy Venetian townscape can arouse. Auden's image, on the other hand, refers to a northern landscape with "herds of reindeer" and "moss," the otherness of which is due to its being distant and unknown. The "altogether elsewhere" in Auden's poem is placed in the mythological north, a place that in the context of "The Fall of Rome" poem appears as a certain idyll in opposition to the corrupted urban civilization. In relation to Brodsky's "San Pietro," the "altogether elsewhere" acquires a different meaning; it refers to the northern foggy landscape of Leningrad.

But there is another poem by Auden that seems to have informed the writing of "San Pietro": "Thank You, Fog," the title poem of Auden's last collection, which he prepared for publication shortly before his death in 1973.[61] Brodsky's long and detailed study on the foggy landscape can be read as an elaborate exploitation of Auden's short and effective line "Outdoors a shapeless silence," starting the third stanza of "Thank You, Fog." Both poems deal with emigration, Auden's directly and Brodsky's in a more implied fashion through the evocation of the native landscape. Auden had returned from the United States to his native England a year before writing the poem, which is filled with joyous emotions and a feeling of gratitude. The fog is associated with, and becomes a symbol of, all that the speaker perceives as native:

Grown used to New York weather,
all too familiar with Smog,
You, Her unsullied Sister,
I'd quite forgotten and what
You bring to British winters:
now native knowledge returns.[62]

Brodsky's "San Pietro" was written in circumstances that were the reverse of Auden's. At the time of writing the poem he had been living in exile for six years, and there was no realistic chance of returning to Russia; the autobiographical background is not the return of a poet to his native country but the realization of the impossibility of such return. This explains the stoic resignation, expressed in the lines, highlighted by the use of an imperative, while the speaker of the poem turns to himself.

> . . . Помни:
> любое движенье, по сути, есть
> перенесение тяжести тела в другое место.
> Помни, что прошлому не уложиться
> без остатка в памяти, что ему
> необходимо будущее. Твердо помни:
> только вода, и она одна,
> всегда и везде остается верной
> себе—нечувствительной к метаморфозам, плоской,
> находящейся там, где сухой земли
> больше нет. И патетика жизни с ее началом,
> серединой, редеющим календарем, концом
> и т.д. стушёвывается в виду
> вечной, мелкой, бесцветной ряби.
> (3:159)

> . . . Remember:
> any movement is basically
> a shift of body weight from one location
> to another. Remember: the past won't fit
> into memory without something left over;
> it must have a future. And remember carefully:
> only water, and it alone,
> everywhere and always stays true to it-
> self, unsusceptible to metamorphoses, level,
> present wherever dry land
> is gone. And the inflation of living—
> with its beginning, middle, thinning calendar,
> end, et cetera—shrinks before
> colorless, shallow, eternal ripples.
> (*CP*, 161)

This impersonal tone of voice with the aspiration toward the universal and existential is typical of Brodsky, and as David Bethea suggests, an attitude he adopted mainly from Auden.[63] It is the "anti-heroic posture" Brodsky admiringly refers to when discussing Auden's poetry in "To Please a Shadow" (*LTO*, 367). But despite the speaker's stoic posture, "San Pietro" is underlined by a nostalgic tone, evoked by the use of literary allusions and subtexts. The Venetian fog invoked his "native knowledge," which "returned" by way of the intertextual allusions and references.

Brodsky literally translated into English some of the images of the Russian version of "San Pietro" when writing *Watermark* ten years later, as the passage with the description of "the famous *nebbia*" shows. But in the passage that ends *Watermark*, he returns to the image of fog and gives it now new meanings. In the Russian poem, the description of fog, with the title's reference to Petersburg, conveys meanings that associate the poem with the speaker's native Leningrad and the significations fog has in the "Petersburg text," to quote Toporov's term. The fog functions as a signifier of nostalgia, as it does again in *Watermark*, but there the signified has been changed. The passage continues after the quote from Auden's "The Fall of Rome" with the author evoking an imaginary scene, which he then presents as a recollection told to him by Auden's friend Stephen Spender. Brodsky affectionately recalls Auden, while he evokes a scene that communicates his nostalgic attitude toward Anglo-American modernism at large:

> All of a sudden I felt he was behind me, and I turned as fast as I could. A tall, smooth window of Florian's that was reasonably well lit and not covered with a board gleamed through the patches of fog. I walked toward it and looked inside. Inside, it was 195?. On the red plush divans, around a small marbled table with a kremlin of drinks and teapots on it, sat Wystan Auden, with his great love, Chester Kallman, Cecil Day Lewis and his wife, Stephen Spender and his. Wystan was telling some funny story and everybody was laughing. In the middle of the story, a well-built sailor passed by the window; Chester got up and, without so much as a "See you later," went in hot pursuit. "I looked at Wystan," Stephen told me years later. "He kept laughing, but a tear ran down his cheek." At this point, for me, the window had gone dark. King Fog rode into the piazza, reined in his stallion, and started to unfurl his white turban. (*W*, 132–33)

A parallel reading of this intimate and partially fictional memory of Auden in *Watermark* with "San Pietro" illustrates how Brodsky negotiated between his two sets of cultural knowledge in the discursive space of Venice. In the Russian poem, the title of which evokes a parallel between St. Petersburg and Venice, he re-appropriates the Russian myth of Petersburg and one of its central motifs, the city's affinity with Venice, which, as Toporov has pointed out, had turned into a "cultural cliché" among the Petersburg intelligentsia by the beginning of the twentieth century.[64] Meanwhile, the Russian poem also incorporates Brodsky's knowledge of non-Russian culture through its use of Auden as a subtext. When writing in English about Venice ten years later, he returned to Auden and the image of fog, translating the poem's subtext into an affectionate recollection of Auden. The object of nostalgia is not Leningrad but Auden, not the Petersburg mythology but the mythologies of Anglo-American modernist cosmopolitanism. All this stages the cultural differences that Brodsky negotiated in *Watermark* and exposes the processes of the enunciation, to use Bhabha's terminology, of Brodsky's transnational subject. The way Brodsky transposed the image of fog from a textual play with a Russian myth onto his personal memories of Auden dramatizes the activity of culture's untranslatability. This activity is performed in *Watermark* through the author's touching narrative of his own transculturation.

"Venetian Stanzas" and Shakespeare's Moor

It is hardly an exaggeration to claim that the encyclopedic frenzy and the formal inventiveness of Brodsky's "Venetian Stanzas 1 and 2" revived the Russian literary experience of Venice, an experience that more or less stopped developing in the 1920s and remained outside the mainstream of Soviet Russian literature.[65] Here the city is not fantasized from a distance as, for instance, in Aleksandr Kushner's poems of the 1960s and 1970s, but it is mapped out with the lyric subject inserted into its topography in the fashion of Blok, Gumilev, and Khodasevich.[66] The poems, written in dactyls and anapests with the first four dactylic lines creating a metrical reverse of the last four anapestic lines of each stanza, and the eight-line stanzas mirroring the structure of the eight-stanza poems, renew this tradition by depicting Venice through a series of *veduta*, which enclose a twenty-four-hour cycle of the speaker touring Venice in the morning, daytime, evening, and night. In *Watermark* Brodsky explicated this artistic method now applied to English-language prose: "Scanning this city's face for seventeen winters, I should by now be capable of pulling a credible Poussin-like job: of painting this place's likeness, if not at four seasons, then at four times a day" (*W*, 21).

Brodsky's "Venetian Stanzas" highlight the Venetian textuality through the wealth of literary and cultural references anticipated by the title with its dual reference to Mandelstam's "Peterburgskie strofy" ("Petersburg Stanzas") and Goethe's *Venezianische Epigramme* (*Venetian Epigrams*). Goethe's *Römische Elegien* (*Roman Elegies*), written the same year as the *Venetian Epigrams,* come into play, too, through the image of Brodsky's poet-tourist who "flop[s] to the bed" next to the "soft bone's hot mirror from whose amalgam no finger will scratch him off" after "jettisoning his lines to the page's edge"; the conceit of creative powers and erotic inspiration articulated on a backdrop of a historical city evokes Goethe's lyric pose in *Roman Elegies.* Meanwhile, the diptych presents a metapoetic history of the myth of Venice, both Russian and Western, with allusions and references to Goethe, Shakespeare, the Romantic poets (Pushkin, Lermontov, Byron), Italian Decadence (D'Annunzio evoked through Eleonora Duse), *World of Art* (Diagilev), the Acmeists (Mandelstam), and Ezra Pound.[67] It is into this literary landscape that Brodsky inserts his lyric subject.

The two poems form a diptych, with the elegiac "Stanzas 1" deploying the myth of the drowning city and the odic "Stanzas 2" capturing the city's splendor and magnificence. The nocturnal "Stanzas 1" is saturated with musical metaphors; Brodsky reworks the image of the silent and dying Venice that stretches back to Byron's *Childe Harold's Pilgrimage*—"In Venice Tasso's echoes are no more, / And silent rows the songless gondolier; / Her palaces are crumbling to the shore, / And music meets not always now the ear," recaptured numerous times before Brodsky by Russian poets, with Pushkin's Onegin imagining the distant Venice as their prototype: "But sweeter 'mid the pastimes of the night / is the strain of Torquato's octaves."[68]

Here is how Brodsky addresses the most frequent conceit of Venice, death in Venice and the dying of Venice, through musical metaphors, while referring at the same time to the commonplace literary association of Venice and homosexuality, suggested by the image of Diagilev, "Perm's citizen":

Так смолкают оркестры. Город сродни попытке
воздуха удержать ноту от тишины,
и дворцы стоят, как сдвинутые пюпитры,
плохо освещены.
Только фальцет звезды меж телеграфных линий—
там, где глубоким сном спит гражданин Перми.

Но вода аплодирует, и набережная—как иней,
осевший на до-ре-ми.
(3:236–37)

That's how orchestras fade. The city, while words are at it,
is akin to attempts to salvage notes from the silent beat,
and the palazzi, like music stands, stand scattered,
hoarded and poorly lit.
Only up where Perm's citizen sleeps his lasting sleep, a falsetto
star is vibrating through telegraph wires, reaches a minor key.
But the water applauds, and the quay is a hoarfrost settled
down on a do-re-mi.
(*CP*, 304)

This nocturnal Venice of "Stanzas 1" is juxtaposed to the Venice of "Stanzas 2," conveyed through images and metaphors that refer to painting and visual arts and engage all the senses, not just hearing:

I
Смятое за ночь облако расправляет мучнистый парус.
От пощечины булочника матовая щека
приобретает румянец . . .
. . . Как прутьями по ограде
школьники на бегу, утренние лучи
перебирают колонны, аркады, пряди
водорослей, кирпичи.
(3:238)

A sleep-crumpled cloud unfurls mealy mizzens.
Slapped by the baker, matte cheeks acquire
a glow . . .
. . . Like lengthy, supple
sticks run by hot-footed schoolboys along iron gates,
the morning rays strum colonnades, red-brick chimneys, sample
curled seaweed, invade arcades.
(*CP*, 306)

II
Долго светает. Голый, холодный мрамор
бедер новой Сусанны сопровождаем при
погружении под воду стректотом кинокамера
новых старцев . . .
(3:238)

Dawn takes its time. Cold, naked, pallid marble
thighs of the new Susannah wade waves, being watched with glee
by new elders whose lenses squint, whirr, and gargle
at this bathing . . .
(*CP*, 306)

IV
Свет разжимает ваш глаз, как раковину . . .
(3:238)

Light pries your eye—like a shell . . .
(*CP*, 306)

V
День. Невесомая масса взятой в квадрат лазури,
оставляя весь мир—всю синеву! . . .
(3:239)

Leaving all of the world, all its blue, in the rearguard,
the azure—squared to a weightless mass—
(*CP*, 307)

VIII
. . . Плещет лагуна.
(3:240)

. . . And the blinding lagoon is lapping.
(*CP*, 308)

Brodsky reworks the Byronic paradigm of the Venetian spectacle, where the vanishing Venice, the magnificent ruin of Western civilization in decline, co-exists with the eternal Venice of triumphant and glorious beauty, which rises "fresh from ocean" while "gems in sparkling showers" are "poured in her lap" to quote *Childe Harold's* Canto 4. In Brodsky's diptych this is reinterpreted through a juxtaposing of time and space: "Venetian Stanzas 1" shows how time works on space, while "Venetian Stanzas 2" functions as a poetic manifestation of the idea found in *Watermark*: "It is as though space, cognizant here [in Venice] more than anyplace else of its inferiority to time, answers it with the only property time doesn't possess: with beauty" (*W*, 44).

Brodsky updates the Byronic paradigm with mundane scenes of the Venetian everyday, the tourist experience, and the cross-cultural references of the dedications that frame the diptych. "Venetian Stanzas 1" is dedicated to the American writer Susan Sontag, the namesake of the beauty that is evoked through a reference to Mandelstam in "Venetian Stanzas 2"; while "Venetian Stanzas 2" is dedicated to Gennadii Shmakov, a critic, translator, author of a biography of Mikhail Baryshnikov, and Brodsky's Leningrad friend, who died of AIDS in New York in 1988 and was, as Brodsky describes him in an interview, a "a great fan of Diagilev," who is buried in the Venetian graveyard of San Michele, a fact Brodsky refers to in "Venetian Stanzas 1" through the image of Perm's citizen. In *Watermark* Brodsky reused the autobiographical materials that these intertexts disclose; Susan Sontag's role in Brodsky's Venice was discussed in the previous chapter in the connection with Ezra Pound, and Gennadii Shmakov was the "friend" who gave Brodsky Mikhail Kuzmin's translations of Henri de Régnier's Venetian stories in Leningrad in the 1960s. It is to the reading of de Régnier's stories that he ascribes, apart from the poetic model learned from water, the associative and fragmentary poetics of his own prose piece (*W*, 36–38).[69]

Apart from these intertexts, there are three cultural figures that contribute to the construction of the lyric identity in "Venetian Stanzas." The speaker associates himself with the historical, mythological, and literary figures of Claude Lorraine, St. George, and Shakespeare's "Moor." Referring to the lyric subject as the "pupil of Lorraine" in "Stanzas I" establishes Claude Lorraine—the seventeenth-century French painter, known in art history as the representative of ideal landscapes, a neoclassical genre made popular by Loraine and Nicolas Poussin—as the speaker's aesthetic model for picturing Venice at different times of the day. The reference to Lorraine also evokes a reminiscence of Leningrad, where Brodsky must have seen Lorraine's landscapes for the first time in the Hermitage Museum. The significance of St. George and the "Moor" points elsewhere. Relating the lyric subject to St. George draws on the convention of the saint being depicted with a sword, and by comparing his speaker to the saint, Brodsky makes use of the creative and sexual connotations of the image. The "Moor," on the other hand, highlights, again, Brodsky's position on the cultural borderline. The "Moor" ("mavr") appears in the first stanza of "Venetian Stanzas 1":

> Мокрая коновязь пристани. Понурая ездовая
> машет в сумерках гривой, сопротивляясь сну.
> Скрипичные грифы гондол покачиваются, издавая
> вразнобой тишину.
> Чем доверчивей мавр, тем чернее от слов бумага,
> и рука, дотянуться до горлышка коротка,
> прижимает к лицу кружева смятого в пальцах Яго
> каменного платка.
> (3:235)
>
> The wet hitching post of the quay: a sulky hackney
> fights off sleep in the twilight, twitching the iron bay
> of her mane; napeless gondolas, fiddling numbly
> the out-of-sync silence, sway.
> As the Moor grows more trusting, words turn the paper darker,
> and a hand, short of snapping a neck, though keen on the gothic lace
> of a stone kerchief crushed in the palm of Iago,
> presses it to its face.
> (*CP*, 303)

The last four lines capture a moment of the lyric subject's writing a poem in Venice. The proper name of the Moor is not mentioned, but Shakespeare's play *Othello, the Moor of Venice* is identified by the mention of Iago, its other main character. Othello is one of the characters whom Edward Said recognizes as belonging to the canon of Western literary inventions in which "the Orient and Islam are always represented as outsiders having a special role to play *inside* Europe."[70] By identifying the lyric subject with Othello, then, Brodsky creates an image of the speaker as an outsider and stranger in Venice: he is the Oriental other in the West.[71]

Brodsky is not the first Russian writer to use Venice as a discursive place for reflecting on the liminality of Russian identity. A brief historical overview of Russian intellectual approaches to Venice shows how, for many Russian writers, artists, and philosophers, the Russian discourse on Venice has provided a textual space where Russian self-definitions vis-à-vis Europe have been negotiated. In nineteenth-century European imaginings, to contrast Russian approaches with European perceptions of the city, Venice was the "domestic Orient," as recently argued.[72] Venice was often the last stop on British, French, and North European tours of Italian cities, and even if these visitors came to Italy to see only Venice, they approached the city from the West; Venice was one of the last outposts of Europe before the exotic and unknown East. Mme de Staël was one of the first to capture these Oriental and exotic associations of Venice in her 1807 *Corinne*:

> The Piazza San Marco, all encircled with blue tents sheltering throngs of Turks, Greeks, and Armenians, is closed at one end by a church whose facade looks more like a mosque than a Christian temple. This square gives an idea of the indolent life of Orientals who spend their days in cafés drinking sherbet and smoking perfumes. Occasionally, Turks and Armenians are seen drifting by, nonchalantly lying in open boats, with pots of flowers at their feet.[73]

The emblem of Venice, St. Mark's Basilica, reminded Mme de Staël of an Oriental building, while the depiction of Turks and Armenians complies with the representation of the "Oriental" or "Asiatic" type common in European literature of the time.[74]

For the Russians, who approached Venice from the opposite direction, the Oriental quality of Venice was perceived in an altogether different way. This is conveyed in Prince Viazemsky's 1863 poem "Marii Maksimilianovne, printsesse Badenskoi" ("For Maria Maksimilianovna, the Princess of Baden"). The poem depicts a meeting between the speaker and the princess, who, despite her German title, was born in Petersburg and related to both Russian and French imperial families. The meeting takes place in Venice in winter. The winter is described as native and familiar, "the cold familiar to us, / And native snow and winter's veil." In the second stanza, where the viewpoint is ascribed to the Petersburg princess, Venice reminds her of the "ancient beauty of Moscow," while the gondolas slide on the ice like the "sleighs riding at trot on the Neva." The unusual exotic beauty of winter in Venice is projected onto the scenes familiar from the speakers' and princess' native Russia:

Вас, с хладной полночи красавица младая,
По-русски встретила Венеция и мы:
И теплые сердца, и стужа нам родная,
И снег родной, фата прабабушки зимы.

Сан-Марко с площадью под инеем и снегом
Вам древней красотой напоминал о Москве,
А гондола, скользя меж льдин поспешным бегом,
Как в санках на рысях катались по Неве.

Меняясь звуками и складом русской речи,
Вы дни минувшие одушевили вновь;
И все в один привет слилось для вашей встречи:
И русская зима, и русская любовь.[75]

[You, young beauty, with the cool of midnight / were greeted in Russian by Venice and us: / by warm hearts, and by the cold familiar to us, / and by native snow and winter's veil. // St. Mark's and the piazza white with frost and snow / reminded you of Moscow's ancient beauty, / and the gondolas sliding smoothly on the ice / were like sleighs riding at a trot on the Neva. // Exchanging sounds and rhymes of Russian speech, / you enlivened the past days anew; / and all flowed into one greeting to meet you: / both Russian winter and Russian love.]

Viazemsky's view of Venice, which he assigns to the Petersburg princess, projects what he perceives as "Russian" on Venice. He assumes a Western viewpoint toward both Russia and Venice, and the "ancient beauty" of Moscow together with the historical parallel between Petersburg and Venice Orientalize both Russia and Venice. Viazemsky's view of Venice is not unlike Mme de Staël's, with the difference that in the "Oriental" Viazemsky recognizes what is "native" to him. This liminality of Venice, and the role its intermediate position between East and West has played in Russian self-definitions, was commented on some fifty years after Viazemsky by Vasilii Rozanov:

Despite the almost generally accepted observation that "St. Mark's is ours, Byzantine, almost Russian," I can't agree with it and allow myself to preserve the originality of my opinion. Let them bring the horses to

> the Uspensky Cathedral, copy the bathing Susanna, and have three fourths of the paintings depict Genesis, and I will agree. But now all they need is to see that the "beard and hands" of some saints are represented as in Greek medieval paintings, and they scream: "It's ours!" There is very little that this cathedral does not have: it even has columns taken away from a mosque, but because of that one should not conclude that "the cathedral is somewhat Muslim." The spirit of castration separated once and for all everything Byzantine, and all that originates from Byzantium, from everything West European.[76]

Rozanov dissociates himself from the Russian opinion according to which the Byzantine influence on Venetian art and architecture affiliates Venice with Russia. For Rozanov, the "spirit of eunuchs" marks off "everything Byzantine and all that it engendered" from "everything West European," including Venice, which for Rozanov remains emblematically European. Pavel Muratov captured the Russian perception of Venice as an emblem of the "West European" in *Images of Italy*, where his study on Giovanni Bellini's "Allegoria Sacra" ends with him contracting the Russian "Venice sickness":

> For us, Northern people, who enter Italy through the golden gates of Venice, the waters of the lagoon become, in fact, Lethe's waters. In the hours we spent watching old paintings which decorate the Venetian churches, or gliding on a gondola, or getting lost in silent laneways. . . . We drink the sweet wine of forgetting. All that is left behind, all past life becomes a light burden. . . . Italy is waiting for us—Italy, so close, beyond the space of the lagoon![77]

Starting their journey on the *venskii poezd*, the train to Vienna, Russian tourists often arrived in Venice first and continued their Italian sojourn from there, "entering Italy through the golden gates of Venice," as Muratov writes. Venice was their first encounter with Italian, that is, Western, art, but at the same time, it also reminded them of what was left behind in Russia. As Muratov's book manifests, many Russians felt like Rozanov; despite the Byzantine influences on Venetian arts, history, and religion, Venice and Venetian art equaled Europe and European art. This equation was not, however, always to Europe's advantage. In *The Brothers Karamazov* there is a scene where Ivan declares his wish to travel to Europe. "And yet I know," he says to Alyosha, "that I am only going to a graveyard," and when Fyodor Karamazov later in the novel throws the wish back at Ivan—"Where are you going now—to Venice? Your Venice will keep another two days"—the graveyard is associated with Venice; Venice is associated with Europe, but with a Europe that is dead.[78] Meanwhile, however, for those Russians who emphasized Russia's affiliation with Europe, as many leading figures of the Petersburg art scene did, Venice became a major point of cultural reference invested with affirmative meanings. For many Petersburg intellectuals at the turn of the century, the equation of Petersburg with Venice entailed an equation of Petersburg with Europe. And yet, the Oriental aspects of Venice continued to inform Russian perceptions of the city.

It is this Russian discourse on Venice that Brodsky's lyric identification with Othello draws from. Brodsky assumes a Western perspective for himself, Orientalizing his lyric subject—here the term, in its Saidian sense, can of course be used only metaphorically. But does the "Moor" really represent for Brodsky the non-Western other in the Saidian sense? Othello represents a marginal identity, and by referring to himself as the "Moor," Brodsky stages his own "otherness" as a Russian-language Jewish poet within the realm of canonical Western culture. From the Russian viewpoint, however, the "Moor," a Shakespearean literary invention, represents Western canonical culture, which Brodsky idealized and monumentalized throughout his writing career. In other words, the cultural referent of the lyric identification, and the significations the referent produces, are entirely Western and canonical. Othello offered a canonized identity for Brodsky to relate to in the Venetian literary space; he sees himself as the other, but a Western canonical other.

"Othello," then, represents for Brodsky the "West" rather than its antipode, the non-West. And, most significantly, from the viewpoint of Russian canonical culture, Othello's African origins also conveniently evoke another canonical figure, the figure of Alexander Pushkin. Viewed from the Russian perspective, Brodsky's identification with the "Moor of Venice" writes him into a literary canon rather than marginalizes him within it. Finally, the "Moor" does not reappear in *Watermark*, unlike Claude Lorraine and St. George, both of whom are mentioned in the English-language essay, and this highlights again the untranslatability of Brodsky's position on the cultural borderline. Referring to oneself as the "Moor" in English-language travel prose relating to Venice does not insinuate one's cultural positionality the way it does in Russian poetry, where Shakespeare represents Western canonical culture, and Othello's ethnic marginality is associated with the mythic figure of Pushkin.

"In Italy" and the Question of Self-Translation

At the beginning of Brodsky's essay about Constantine Cavafy, he makes an ironic but unambiguously critical comment on those Western approaches in twentieth-century literary criticism that challenged the dominance of biographical studies, when he observes that the "uneventfulness" of Cavafy's life "would have made the strictest of New Critics happy" (*LTO*, 53). After this he ventures on to turn Cavafy's "uneventful" life into a myth and a legend. Brodsky weaves this myth about Cavafy and his works around the city of Alexandria, which, according to Brodsky, became a metaphor of life in Cavafy's poetry. It is difficult not to see the parallel between Cavafy's Alexandria as discussed by Brodsky and the way Brodsky writes about his relation with his own hometown. The Cavafy essay is followed in the collection *Less Than One* by "A Guide to a Renamed City," Brodsky's retrospective travel guide to Leningrad (see chap. 2). In the essay Brodsky introduces to the Western reader an interpretation of Russian cultural history informed by his Leningradian nostalgia for the historical Petersburg, and he establishes a Russian literary canon that he affiliated himself with. The meanings Brodsky invests in Leningrad in this essay as well as in the title essay "Less Than One," a more directly autobiographical text about Brodsky's childhood and youth, point to a similar understanding of the significance of a writer's hometown for the writer's life, as Brodsky's views of Cavafy's life and works express. The city the writer grows up in forms and defines his artistic sensibility as well as his sense of history, time, and space.

"In Italy," a poem Brodsky wrote in 1985, is a showcase of how Brodsky puts into poetic practice the ideals of the Petersburgian neoclassical aesthetics, which he traced from the urban space of the city in the essays about Leningrad and the Petersburg culture. The lyric voice of "In Italy," with its intense autobiographical tone, is the voice of a man coming to terms with tragic events and personal losses. The poem recalls the death of Brodsky's parents. At the same time, the artful use of classical poetics and cultural referents points to an author aware, and self-assured, of his place in the Russian cultural tradition. Through the appropriation of the ideals of neoclassical aesthetics and through the evocation of images of Russian Silver Age mythologies, Brodsky presents a poetic endorsement of the cultural and poetic genealogies, which he advanced in the Petersburgian narratives created in his prose texts.

The poetic structure of "In Italy" draws from the classical principles of harmony, symmetry, and perspective. It is composed of four stanzas, each stanza of four lines. This symmetry is further emphasized by the rhyming scheme: the rhyme pair ending the first two lines is masculine, the pair ending the latter two feminine—the scheme *aabb* is the same in all four stanzas. Brodsky did not, as a rule, use alternating masculine and feminine rhymes, which further emphasizes the significance of the rhyming scheme in this particular poem: the symmetric division of each stanza into two suggests the division of the poetic text into two sections.[79] In the first two stanzas the speaker describes a city, which belongs to the past reconstructed through his memory (there-then), and in the last two stanzas he describes a city related to his immediate surrounding (here-now). The two cities are paralleled throughout the poem; this parallel is achieved by the conjunction "i," literally, "also" or "and," opening the poem. The symmetric structure of the poem creates a poetic space where the two cities become each other's mirror images reflected in one another in the speaker's memory; the idea of reflection is suggested by locating the lyric plot by a lagoon, where the sun's reflection makes the speaker's "pupil run," initiating the recollecting process captured by the poem. The coherence of the symmetric structure is further supported by the rhyme pairs, which bind the first and the third stanzas (the exclamations "rastli! rastli!" // "gad! uidi!" ["they raped! they raped" // "scumbag! go away!"]), as well as the second and the fourth stanzas (the gerunds "slepia" // "slezia" ["blinding" // "moistening (with a tear)"]).[80]

Apart from symmetry and reflection, the poem also evokes the classical principle of perspective. The final image advances a view of human life according to which life is not worth living at the point when we realize that we are either unworthy of another person's love or that there is no one who will show love (parental affection) to us. This is the point when one is hidden in the "perspective," when one accepts one's own insignificance and finality; the image of perspective, then, is associated with dying. Brodsky linked the idea of dying with the image of perspective in an earlier poem, "Pokhorony Bobò" ("The Funeral of Bobò"), where the image is brought up through the mention of the Rossi street ("ulitsa Rossi"), famous for the perfectly harmonious perspective at a specific location on the Petersburg map; the street ends in the back of the main body of the Aleksander Theater, which was designed by Carlo Rossi in the early 1830s. Rossi's buildings, in turn, are regarded as one of the last neoclassical ensembles of the Golden Age of Petersburg architecture.[81] The idea of a perspective is also suggested in the first stanza of "In Italy" in the image of an "endless embankment" ("beskonechnaia naberezhnaia"), anticipated by the continuous flow of the syntax. This recalls the nostalgic sentiment in "A Guide to a Renamed City": "to walk under this sky, along the brown granite embankments of this immense gray river, is itself an extension of life and a school of farsightedness" ("Guide," 89). In the poem, the "school of farsightedness" is acted out by introducing the idea of life's temporal limitation in the same line with the "endless embankment," which "makes life" seem "short." The final word of the first stanza, "short," anticipates, in turn, the change in the syntactic flow after a series of enjambments; the first line of the second stanza ends in a full syntactic closure: "Now the sun sets there blinding the caryatids." The syntactic shortness anticipates the theme of not seeing, or blindness, suggested by the image of the caryatids; in other words, seeing far is turned into not seeing at all, and not seeing refers to not seeing the past, in other words, the difficulty of remembering.

As these observations of the poetic structure of "In Italy" indicate, the "perfect order" of the neoclassical architectonics, which organizes its poetics, is constantly undermined by the poem's semantic level. The view of human life the poem introduces is not that of harmony, order, or grandeur but of physical degradation (blindness), intellectual instability (the image of the "local philosopher"), inadequacy of memory (compared to dogs sniffing leftovers), personal conflicts (recalled in the familiarity of the foreign exclamation "scumbag!"), resignation, and death (the final image of hiding in perspective). This discrepancy between the structural and semantic levels is highlighted by the last stanza, where the symmetry and controlled geometrical regularity, suggested in the image of perspective, is challenged by the image of the uncontrollable flow of time; the point of resignation is the point when, in a literal translation, one gives up "swimming against the furious current" ("brezguia plyt' protivu" / "beshenogo techen'ia"). The attribute "furious" ("beshenoe") reinforces the unpredictable and obdurate force that time has over humans; in Brodskian terms, dying means being overcome by time. This calls up the image of the dogs (sniffing leftovers of memories) in the second stanza: unlike "beshenoe techen'e" ("furious/mad flow"), the combination "beshenaia sobaka" ("furious/mad dog") is a conventional one, connoting a dog with rabies. The association of time with the image of a rabid dog further emphasizes the idea of life's unpredictability and absurdity. It highlights the poetics of incongruity, the contradiction between the poem's ordered classical structure, and the meanings the poem's imagery conveys. It reinforces the symmetric structure by binding an image introduced in the second stanza with an image introduced in the fourth, while it also reinforces the semantics of disorder, despair, and absurdity by associating the flow of time with the image of crazed dogs. And finally, the poetics of incongruity is supported by the imagery indicating the spatial orientation of the poem: the upward movement of the first two lines with the "statues growing on buildings" is contradicted in the second stanza with image of the setting sun, after which the descending movement of the sunset takes over the poem's elegiac mode.

While the attitude toward the speaker's personal fate, and life in general, induced by the poem's imagery, is that of resignation and desperation, the attitude toward the cultural products the poem exhibits is entirely the opposite. By reverting to the neoclassical ideals and the Petersburgian aesthetics of "perfect order" that he popularized in his essays, Brodsky makes a poetic statement, which is affirmative and honorific in relation to the cultural models he promoted and appropriated. The symmetric composition functions as a pastiche and a commentary, presented in terms of poetic practice, of eighteenth- and nineteenth-century classical poetry, its symmetric compositions, and their relation with Petersburgian architecture. The intertextual play, through which the poem's two cities are represented, endorses this authorial attitude. The central image of the poem establishing its imaginary location in Venice—"the world's best lagoon with a golden pigeon coop"—is introduced in a line that binds two of Akhmatova's poems: "the world's best lagoon" refers to Akhamatova's Petersburg poem "Summer Garden," with the line "where there is the world's best fence"; and "golden pigeon coop" is the image opening Akhmatova's 1912 poem on Venice: "Golden pigeon coop by the water." Apart from the citation from Akhmatova's canonical Petersburg poem ("Summer Garden"), turn-of-the-century Petersburg is also evoked in the image of the "local philosopher," whom Brodsky identified as Vasilii Rozanov.[82] This image conveys the twice-felt nostalgia typical of Brodsky's émigré imaginings of Leningrad and the historical Petersburg. It is the city, imagined initially in the 1960s Leningrad through the collective cultural nostalgia for Silver Age Petersburg, which, in turn, is reimagined through the 1980s exilic longing.

The intertextual play through which Brodsky evokes turn-of-the century Petersburg and parallels Venice with it draws on the fact that the two cities are thoroughly textualized and mythologized in the Petersburgian tradition Brodsky ascribes to: comparing Petersburg to Venice has been a common topos in representing Petersburg since the foundation of the city, and by the turn of the century it had turned into a standard cultural cliché. This comparison was inseparably intertwined with the imperial ideology informing the beginnings of the myth of St. Petersburg: in the eighteenth-century panegyric visions the city was represented not only as "Northern Palmyra" but also as "Northern Venice"; this allegory was reintroduced to the Russian discourse of Petersburg at the turn of the century by Mikhail Kuzmin and other artists and writers close to the *World of Art* movement.[83] The title of Brodsky's poem, "In Italy," maps out the cultural space in which the poem is situated, after which it is sufficient to give the reader just a few metonymic hints of the cities in question. The images of the two cities are literary constructions to such a point that it hardly comes as a surprise to find out that the poem was not written in Venice but inspired by Milan; its "Venetian ambience" was conceived, according to Brodsky, during a visit to the home of Milan-based Italian writer Roberto Calasso, to whom, along with his wife, the poem is dedicated.[84]

The poem is the first of the Venetian poems that was translated into English by Brodsky himself. The translation of the Russian "In Italy" presents an attempt to carry the cultural knowledge imbedded in the Russian poem over to the English audience by means of careful structural imitation of the original. Brodsky sustained the symmetric mirrorlike structure of the poem in his English version with its stanzaic pattern, rhyme scheme, and the placing of the key word "memory" in the third stanza before the caesura dividing the line. By rendering the neoclassical aesthetics of his poetic craftsmanship into English poetic diction, Brodsky performed not only a linguistic translation but a cultural translation of his poetic credo and cultural knowledge. Few readers of the English text, however, can detect the Akhmatova citations. What disappears in the translation is, then, the homage Brodsky paid to Akhmatova and to the Silver Age heritage, the authorities of his aesthetic dissent and freedom. It is this type of disappearance that Brodsky most likely had in mind when he lamented, in his essay on Eugenio Montale, that it is the "interplay between ethics and aesthetics" that "tends to vanish in translation" (*LTO*, 99). Meanwhile, as this parallel reading of the Russian-language "V Italii" and the English-language "In Italy" shows, the process of self-translation stages cultural differences rather than transcends them: Brodsky's self-translations dramatize, to return to Bhabhas' idiolect, the activity of culture's untranslatability, while from the viewpoint of the English-language poetry and its readership, they present a case of newness entering the world.

An Aging Male Writer: "Venice: Lido"

When a Russian poet such as Brodsky—highly conscious of his poetic calling, firm in his belief in the significance of logos, martyrized by the Soviet authority, and obsessed with his own death since his early poetic output—successfully reinvents himself as a Russian-American writer and then dies to be buried in Venice, the city he idealized in writing, the myth of not only a writer's death but a writer's death in Venice is played out in a powerful and perplexing manner. Brodsky's literary career, his untimely death of a heart condition, his fascination with Venice together with his burial place on a Venetian cemetery next to Diagilev and Stravinsky, and the honorific reception of his legacy in Russia—all these issues at once invoke and challenge one of the pivotal metaphors of twentieth-century literary criticism, pinned down by Roland Barthes's book titled *The Death of the Author.*

To be more precise, Brodsky's literary personality highlights the argument put forward by Svetlana Boym about the *inapplicability* of the Foucauldian or Barthesian conception to the Russian context. As Boym argues, "Behind Foucault's erasure of life, the Mallarméan *blanc,* there is an assumed normative middle-class, eventless life and an assumed historical context that makes it possible. . . . In other contexts—such as, for instance, the Russian one—there is a different conception of what Eikhenbaum calls 'the writer's fate,' that is, a sense of the extreme importance of the writer's civic and spiritual mission, which cannot be erased from Russian or Soviet collective cultural consciousness."[85] Throughout the 1990s post-Soviet cultural debates in Russia, however, one of the burning issues was the demise of the writer, the weakening of the writer's traditional role as a cultural and moral leader.[86] Even if Russian critical opinion, as Boym's writing implies, and the Russian collective consciousness, as she explicitly claims, was not ready to accept the idea of the subjectivity and voice of an author being dissolved into discourses and reader-generated text-production, the debates about the writer's role did manifest the need to reconsider the social significance of the author's voice and the myths surrounding it. The "death of the author" in this peculiar Russian sense was in vogue particularly when Russian literary postmodernism was discussed.[87] While the reception of Brodsky in Russia shows that Boym's argument about the writer's cultural significance in Russia is still relevant, there are signs of an emergence of a different kind of sensibility, too.[88] The opinion articulated by a Russian reviewer of *Venetsianskie tetradi: Iosif Brodskii i drugie/Quaderni veneziani: Joseph Brodsky and Others,* an anthology of Brodsky's Venetian essay and poems, implies a less conventional approach: "It would seem that there is nothing more banal for a reader than the theme of 'Brodsky and Venice.' His poems about the city are well-known as is the fact that he is buried there."[89] Even if the reviewer's attitude to the book and its contents turns more affirmative after the polemic beginning, his tone reveals a sense of exhaustion. His response to Brodsky and the association with Venice implies that the Russian myth of a poet, the Romantic image preserved in literary practices and reader expectations for generations after its initial emergence, has lost some of its cultural authority. Brodsky's *biograficheskaia legenda* (biographic legend), and the poet's *sud'ba* (fate), were, perhaps, the final culmination of this myth. From this viewpoint, then, Brodsky's death would signal the death of the Russian myth of the poet in Romantic and modernist configurations as perceived at least by some constituencies of the Russian readership. This said, there is a large number of responses to Brodsky and Venice, which manifest exactly the opposite, supporting Boym's argument.[90] Brodsky's Venetian poems and prose are extensively represented in the anthology *Znamenitye russkie v Venetsii* (*Famous Russians in Venice*), and the author, Aleksei Kara-Murza, also includes photographs of specific Brodsky sites: hotels Brodsky stayed in, restaurants he allegedly preferred, the cemetery he was buried in, and the Venetian palace where, according to the author, "Joseph Brodsky's funeral banquet was organized after his burial in Venice at Lord Byron's former apartment."[91] Brodsky's Venice has become a Russian tourist attraction, while Brodsky and Venice have become inseparably associated with each other in the Russian creative mind.[92]

In his last three poems about Venice titled "Venice: Lido," "Homage to Girolamo Marcello," and "In Front of Casa Marcello" (all three were written in Russian and the latter two later rewritten in, or translated into, English by Brodsky himself), Brodsky continued to weave his biographic legend by inserting it into the literary space of Venice. These poems together with the revised versions of *Watermark* make up the texts in which Brodsky worked on the theme of Venice in his last years, deploying the myth of a privileged aging male aesthete in Venice. The pose of the aging writer in Venice was established as a modernist topos by Thomas Mann in *Death in Venice*. One of the later transfigurations of Mann's Aschenbach, without the homoerotic connotations, was Hemingway's Colonel Cantwell in *Across the River and Into the Trees*. Brodsky does not mention or explicitly refer to Hemingway's ill-reputed Venetian novel in his poems or essay, but it is reasonable to presume that he knew it and perhaps read it in his youth: the novel was included in Hemingway's Russian collected works, which came out in 1968, signaling Hemingway's popularity among the 1960s Thaw and post-Thaw Soviet readership.[93] Hemingway's Cantwell was not a writer, but the fact that he dictates his memoirs in Venice, creating an autobiography while having an affair with a young Italian woman, renders the novel a metaphor of waning male creativity and vitality. As for Mann's novel, Brodsky mentions it dismissively in *Watermark* when remembering nostalgically the ways Venice was imagined in 1960s Leningrad. Indeed, Brodsky's perception of Venice as the emblematic Western city can be interpreted as a polemic response to Mann's vision of the city as corrupting, destructive, and Oriental.[94] Brodsky makes an equally dismissive gesture at Luchino Visconti's popular filmization of Mann's novel, but acknowledges his own fascination with its arresting opening scene:

> Then the friend who gave me Régnier's novels and who died a year ago [Gennadii Shmakov] took me to a semiofficial screening of the smuggled, and for that reason black-and-white, copy of Visconti's *Death in Venice* with Dirk Bogarde. Alas, the movie wasn't much to speak of; besides, I never liked the novel much, either. Still, the long opening sequence with Mr. Bogarde in a deck chair aboard a steamer made me forget about the interfering credits and regret that I was not mortally ill; even today I am still capable of feeling that regret. (*W*, 39–40)

Whether Brodsky had in mind the opening scene with Visconti's Aschenbach, played by the English actor Dirk Bogarde, arriving in Venice on a steamboat, when he penned the first lines to the "Homage to Girolamo Marcello"—"Once in winter I, too, sailed in / here from Egypt"—remains a moot point. In an interview with Petr Vail', Brodsky implies that the poem was inspired by the sight of a passenger ship approaching Venice, which he observed from the wharf in Le Zattere, while being reminded that the relics of St. Mark, the patron saint of Venice, were brought to the city from Egypt—thus, the particle "too."[95] The opening lines of the poem, nevertheless, invoke the opening of Visconti's film, while they also evoke an earlier poem by Brodsky, the 1968 "Elegy" with the opening line "Once this southern small town" (I discuss this poem in more detail below). But before turning to "Homage to Girolamo Marcello," a few words must be said about "Venice: Lido," where the pose of an aging writer in Venice is not articulated through retrospective recollections in the first person, as is the case in the other two late Venetian poems, but where it is constructed by means of asserting a subject position and discursive authority over what is being depicted.

"Lido"—the English title has "Venice" added to it to locate it on the tourist map of Italy—stands out among Brodsky's Venetian poems, as well as among the Russian literary *vedutas* of Venice, in that it presents scenes, not of canals, bridges, *fondamente*, or *piazzette*, as both "Venetian Stanzas" do, and not even of "non-touristic" back canals, as "San Pietro" does, but, instead, of something entirely other and unexpected in relation to Venice. "Venice: Lido" presents a scene on a run-down Romanian vessel anchored off shore by Lido and observed by the speaker on shore. Brodsky debunks the high-cultural expectations associated with the Venetian Lido, such as the holidaying fin de-siècle bourgeoisie à la Mann/Visconti or the Byronic horse-riding sessions, and conjures up a desolate scene of a dingy tanker and its shabby crew:

> Ржавый румынский танкер, барахтающийся в лазури,
> как стоптанный полуботинок, который, вздохнув, разули.
>
> Команда в одном исподнем—бабники, онанюги—
> загорает на палубе, поскольку они на юге.
> (4:108)
>
> A rusty Romanian tanker, wallowing out in the azure
> like a down-at-heel shoe discarded with sighing pleasure.
>
> The crew, stripped to their pants—womanizers and wankers—
> now that they're in the south, sun themselves by the anchors.
> (*CP*, 386)

The Mediterranean "azure," a seminal symbol of the maritime sublime and the cultured European south since Romantic poetry, is contrasted here with a prosaic scene from the contemporary postcommunist reality. The speaker, who first observes the tanker from land, moves closer and imagines the scene onboard, where the crew, "womanizers and wankers . . . without a coin in their pockets," long to get ashore to see the oasis-like town looming in distance:

> О, Средиземное море! после твоей пустыни
> ногу тянет запутаться в уличной паутине.
>
> Палубные надстройки и прогнивший базис
> разглядывают в бинокль порт, как верблюд—оазис.

Ах, лишь истлев в песке, растеряв наколки,
можно, видать, пройти сквозь ушко иголки,

чтоб сесть там за круглый столик с какой-нибудь ненаглядной
местных кровей под цветной гирляндой.
(4:108)

Ah, the Mediterranean! After your voids, a humble
limb craves a labyrinth, a topographic tangle!

A camel-like superstructure, on its decaying basis,
through binoculars scans the promenade's oasis.

Only by biting the sand, though, all tattoos faded,
can the eye of the needle truly be negotiated

to land at some white table, with a swarthy darling
of local stock, under a floral garland.
(*CP*, 386)

As the poem's viewpoint unfolds, it becomes more obvious that imagining the penniless Romanian sailors has a dual significance for the speaker. For all their financial and material plight, the Romanian sailors represent, for the speaker, an ideal community of male comradeship and freedom. The representation is ironic, with the clichéd "smell of sweaty armpits, guitars idly plucking," but nevertheless, it conveys an ideal masculine existence with the obligatory erotic fantasies familiar from popular films and adventure readings for young men represented by the dream of the "swarthy darling" ("nenagliadnaia"). And since the speaker articulates all this in Russian—it, too, a language spoken on the totalitarian side of the Iron Curtain (though about to collapse at the time the poem was written)—his own position in regard to the oasis-like city emerges not unlike the one he imposes on the Romanian sailors. The exclamation "Ah, the Mediterranean!," the adoration of the south and the city that "resembles a distant pretty / postcard pinned to the sunset," and, especially, the desire "to land at some white table, with a swarthy darling / of local stock, under a floral garland" all convey autobiographical meanings and point to Brodsky's Soviet past, to the time when Venice was still a distant dream. The speaker puts himself in the place of the seamen and observes the city from outside, and the *tsarstvo bozhie*, the kingdom of God, where, according to the biblical saying that Brodsky paraphrases in the poem, it is easier for a camel to go through the eye of a needle than it is for a rich man to enter (Matt. 19:24), always remains for him a distant dream. The distant miragelike image of Venice, which Brodsky fantasizes on behalf of the Romanian seamen, comes across in its unreachable distance not unlike the Venice dreamed in Leningrad and retrospectively captured in *Watermark*. The idea of Venice as an unattainable erotic fantasy is something Brodsky toys with in *Watermark* through many variations; one of them is the self-consciously literary *Veneziana*, the female personification of the city and object of the author's erotic desire, expressed finally in the playful confession of the author having "never slept, let alone sinned, in a cast-iron family bed."[96] Despite these images, the speaker of the poem is, nevertheless, someone whose poetic competence and discursive authority allows him to establish authorial power and express patronizing sympathy to the post-Ceausescu Romanians. With his viewpoint firmly fixed on the terra firma of Lido, and his "tattoos faded," to quote the English poem, he is much closer to the oasis than the sailors of his poem. He is, after all, at least financially closer to the possibility to "do the city," to quote the colloquial double entendre of the English poem, than are the Romanian sailors his poetic imagination conjures up.

A Venetian Past: "Homage to Girolamo Marcello"

"Homage to Girolamo Marcello," which Brodsky dated "1988" in *Peizazh s navodneniem* (*Landscape with Flood*), but which in his Russian collected works has the date "1991," signaled a break from his earlier poems about Venice in terms of the speaker's attitude to the city and his relation with it.[97] This is the first of the Venetian poems where he looks back nostalgically at the history of his own tourism in much the same way as he does in *Watermark*. The poem does not present the same type of formal play with classical poetics as "Venetian Stanzas" or "In Italy" do. Rather, its nonmetrical prosody and unrhymed lines structured by enjambments resemble *Watermark*'s memoiristic prose:

> Однажды я тоже зимою приплыл сюда
> из Египта, считая, что буду встречен
> на запруженной набережной женой в меховом манто
> и в шляпке с вуалью. Однако встречать меня
> пришла не она, а две старенькие болонки
> с золотыми зубами. Хозяин-американец

объяснял мне потом, что если его ограбят,
болонки позволят ему свести
на первое время концы с концами.
Я поддакивал и смеялся.

Набережная выглядела бесконечной
и безлюдной. Зимний, потусторонний
свет превращал дворцы в фарфоровую посуду
и население—в тех, кто к ней
не решается прикоснуться.
Ни о какой вуали, ни о какой манто
речи не было. Единственную прозрачной
вещью был воздух и розовая, кружевная
занавеска в гостинице «Мелеагр и Аталанта»,
где уже тогда, одиннадцать лет назад . . .
(4:111)

Once in winter I, too, sailed in
here from Egypt, believing that I'd be greeted
on the crowded quay by my wife in resplendent furs
and a tiny veiled hat. Yet I was greeted
not by her but by two small, decrepit
Pekinese with gold teeth. Their German owner
told me later that, should he be
robbed, the Pekinese might help him
to make ends meet; well, at least initially.
I was nodding and laughing.

The quay was infinite and completely
vacant. The otherworldly
winter light was turning palazzi into porcelain crockery
and the populace into those who won't
dare to touch it.
Neither veil nor, for that matter, furs
were at issue. The sole transparent
thing was the air and the pinkish laced
curtain in the hotel "Meleager and Atalanta,"
where, as far back as then, eleven years ago . . .
(*CP*, 397)

Through this recollection of a past visit to Venice, which opens the poem, including a reminiscence of the hotel "Meleager and Atalanta" of "eleven years ago," the speaker sets up a dialogue between his present and past selves. Even if the visit recollected in the poem must refer to a visit later than the 1972 stay at "the *pension* Accademia" in "Lagoon" (which would have been almost twenty years earlier), "Homage to Girolamo Marcello" can be read as the mature poet's response to the younger poet's effort to reckon with his fate in his first Venetian poem. In "Lagoon" the speaker imagines himself, literally translated, as the "raincoated figure" who is "settling into place," where "the only tense that is / is present." Now, in the later poem, reflecting on his "own maxims," no longer "imitating [the hotel room's] furniture"—an image that evokes the detailed interior of the hotel room in "Lagoon"—he realizes that "I could have surmised, I gather, / that the future already / had arrived," since, "when a man's alone, / he's in the future." If the thought of dying of grief passed through his mind then, it is now a futile thought, since "now to die of grief / would mean . . . to die belatedly."

The pose of an aging writer is construed through a retrospective glance at an earlier visit to Venice, the absence of the sole witness of that visit (the "amerikanets" of the Russian poem and the "German" of the English), and the image of the "youngsters chattering in Arabic" so that the "quay swarms." This pose culminates in the idea that ends the poem: "What seems to have survived / is but water and me, since water also / has no past." Water signified the passing of time in "Lagoon," where,

> створку моллюска пустив ко дну
> пряча лицо, но спиной пленяя,
> Время выходит из волн, меняя
> стрелку на башне—ее одну.
> (3:45)

> Having scuttled and sunk its scallop shell,
> concealing its face while flaunting its backside,
> Time rises from the goddess's frothy tide,
> yet changes nothing but clock hand and bell.
> (*CP*, 80)

But now, in "Homage to Girolamo Marcello," water has acquired another, more personal significance. From a poetic image, which symbolizes the passing of time, it has been transformed into an image through which the speaker conveys his perception of his life and *sud'ba* (fate). This personal significance is felt already in "San Pietro," the "maxims" of which the speaker may well have in mind, too—if "Homage to Girolamo Marcello" was written in 1988, and not 1991, then it was indeed exactly eleven years after the visit to which the 1977 "San Pietro" relates. There the thought that "the past won't fit / into memory without something left over; / it must have a future" is followed by an aphorism of water: "only water, and it alone, / everywhere and always stays true to it— / self, unsusceptible to metamorphoses, level, / present wherever dry land / is gone" (*CP*, 161). This ties water with the lyric subject's position; just as water does, the lyric subject's exilic stoicism implies "staying true to oneself," that is to the Ovidian essence of self—to recall Homi Bhabha's paradigm of Ovidian and Lucretian exile. The idea of water being "unsusceptible to metamorphoses" appears anomalous, but it seems to refer to water's stable presence "wherever dry land is gone." It is here that the poetic thought of "Homage to Girolamo Marcello" picks up from and imagines water in its stable presence, in its impersonal immutability, as something that "has no past," just as the lyric subject does not have one, either; he only has the future, which has merged with presence, since the future, where "man is alone" and "unhappy," has already arrived.

It is, however, peculiar that the sentiment "I have no past" ends a poem that begins with a line that, by all accounts, states exactly the opposite: "Once in winter I, too, sailed in / here from Egypt." The anecdotal arrival in Venice that follows the opening establishes a Venetian past for the speaker, a past on which to build an entire biographical legend. Moreover, the opening line refers not only to a biographical fact of past visits to Venice, but evokes a set of poems written in the past, which Brodsky in *Watermark* calls his "previous incarnation," that is, in his life in the Soviet Union. "Once in winter I, too, sailed" recalls "Once this southern town," an elegy titled simply "Elegy" and dated "1968(?) Yalta" in Brodsky's Russian collected works. The 1968 "Elegy" is one of the Black Sea poems Brodsky wrote in the late 1960s. These poems form a textual precedent to, and a poetic presentiment of, his later Venetian works. Apart from "Elegy," they include the 1967 "Morskie manevry" ("Nautical maneuvers"), the 1969 "Zimnim vecherom v Ialte" ("On a Winter Evening in Yalta"), the 1969 "S vidom na more" ("With a view to the sea"), the 1969 detective story in verse called "Posviashchaetsia Yalte" ("Homage to Yalta"), the 1968(?) "Pered pamiatnikom A. S. Pushkinu v Odesse" ("In front of A. S. Pushkin's statue in Odessa"), and the 1970s poems

"Science Fiction," "Sonet" ("Sonnet") (dedicated to Evgenii Rein), and "Vtoroe Rozhdestvo na beregy" ("A second Christmas by the shore"). The poems on Yalta present the same chronotope as the later Venetian poems: an exotic southern tourist resort by the sea around New Year's, with the lyric subject by himself in a desolate setting, often at a café with a drink in front of him.[98] The images and even the lexicon anticipate the later Venetian landscapes; consider, for instance, this stanza from "On a Winter Evening in Yalta":

Январь в Крыму. На черноморский брег
зима приходит как бы для забавы.
Не в состоянье удержаться снег
на лезвиях и остриях агавы.
Пустуют ресторации. Дымят
ихтиозавры грязные на рейде.
И прелых листьев слышен аромат.
«Налить вам этой мерзости?» «Налейте».
(2:291)

Crimean January. Winter comes
As though to romp along the Black Sea shore.
The snow loses its grip on the thin-tipped
and spiny-margined leaves of agave plants.
The restaurants are nearly empty now.
Ichthyosaurs belch their black smoke and soil
the roadstead. Rotting laurel permeates
the air. "And will you drink this vile stuff?" "Yes."[99]

The last stanza of "Venetian Stanzas 2" depicts a similar scene with the lyric subject "outdoors, in winter, / on a white iron chair, in my shirtsleeves, a little drunk," while the marine creatures (ichthyosaurs) and smells (rotten leaves) anticipate "chordate," "ichthus," and the "smell of the frozen seaweed" in *Watermark*. This not to say that these images appear exclusively in Brodsky's Venetian texts; in fact, the rotten marine odors function as something of a Proustian madeleine in Brodsky's elegiac imagination, as, for instance, in the last line with "rank seaweed" ("gnil'e otliva") from the 1989 elegy "Darling, I stepped out today late at night" indicates.[100] But the marine creatures and seaweed do not appear simultaneously elsewhere. The "ichthyosaurs" already appear in the first of the Black Sea poems, "Nautical maneuvers": "The attack of pterodactyls on the herd of ichthyosaurs" (2:192). Moreover, in "With a view to the sea," written in Koktebel in 1969, the speaker, drinking his "first coffee on the quay," not as in "Venetian Stanzas," in "mere jacket" (literally) or "shirtsleeves" (in the English version), but rather "half-dressed," comments directly on his touristic habit of avoiding the high season at a seaside resort:

Поехать к морю в несезон,
помимо матерьяльных выгод,
имеет еще тот резон,
что—это временный, но выход
за скобки года, из ворот
тюрьмы. Посмеиваясь криво,
пусть Время взяток не берет—
Пространство, вдруг, сребролюбиво!
(2:308)

[To go to the sea out of season, / apart from material advantages, / is based also on the reasoning that it is, even if temporal, still an exit / beyond the brackets of the year, the gates of / the prison. With a wry smile / let Time not take bribes— / Space, it turns out, is money-grubbing!]

The Time-Space opposition is there, anticipating the aphoristic thought in *Watermark* about time's superiority in regard to space and space's relation with beauty. In the last stanza of "With a view to the sea," the speaker's mundane approach turns more elegiac and seeks reasoning for his seaside vacations from the soothing presence of the seascape:

Когда так много позади
всего, в особенности—горя,
поддержки чьей-нибудь не жди,
сядь в поезд, высадись у моря.
оно обширнее. Оно
и глубже. Это превосходство—
не слишком радостное. Но
уж если чувствовать сиротство,

то лучше в тех местах, чей вид
волнует, нежели язвит.
(2:310)

[When so much of all is / behind, especially of sorrow, / do not expect support of any kind, / but board a train and get off by the sea. / It is broader. It is / deeper, too. This superiority / is not too joyous. But / if one is to experience orphanage, / it is better to do it in places the sight of which / makes you anxious rather than wounds.]

If not "orphanage," as it is expressed in this poem, then at least extreme solitude, even if self-inflected, is what the lyric subject experiences in the "Elegy" written a year earlier at Yalta. The poem is one of Brodsky's recapitulations of the Pushkinian "Vnov' ia posetil" (Again I visited), and it is the one recalled in "Homage to Girolamo Marcello." The poem reconstructs a plot of a friendship and its end, and it is the site of this friendship that the poet revisits:

Однажды этот южный городок
был местом моего свиданья с другом;
мы оба были молоды и встречу
назначили друг другу на молу
сооруженном с древностью; из книг
мы знали о его существовании.
Немало волн разбилось с той поры.
Мой друг на суше захлебнулся мелкой,
но горькой ложью собственной; а я
пустился в странствия.
И вот я снова
стою здесь нынче вечером. Никто
меня не встретил. Да и самому
мне некому сказать уже: приди
туда-то и тогда-то.
(2:251)

[Once this southern town / was the place of my meeting with a friend; / we were both young and had the meeting / on a pier / built in ancient times; from books / we knew of its existence. / Many waves have broken [on the shore] since then. / My friend on dry land choked of his own petty / but bitter lie; and I / set out to wander. / And now again I / stand here in the evening. Nobody / came to meet me. And as far as I'm concerned, well, I do not have anyone to tell: come / to such and such a place at such and such a time.]

Apart from the parallel first lines with the opening "once" ("odnazhdy"), the 1968 "Elegy" and "Homage to Girolamo Marcello" share the same lyric situation, a place revisited, a "southern town," an expectation of a meeting, and a betrayal, which is an outspoken theme in the earlier poem indicated by the friend's "petty but bitter lie" and an implied theme in the latter with the "wife's" failure to meet the speaker.[101] The final thought of the 1968 "Elegy" sums up the lyric thought seminal for the later poem, too:

Видимо, земля
воистину кругла, раз ты приходишь
туда, где нету ничего, помимо
воспоминаний.
(2:251)

[It seems that the earth / indeed is round, since you come back / here, where there is nothing apart from / memories.]

In the Yalta "Elegy" Brodsky refashions the elegiac identity of Pushkin's southern exile with its Ovidian undertones, reworked into the Russian modernist discourse of exile by Mandelstam's *Tristia*. "Homage to Girolamo Marcello" transfers this topos to another, yet similar, location. Much like Yalta by the Black Sea, Venice by the Adriatic is southern, exotic, and associated in high cultural formations with watery imagery and literary exile. And in addition, Brodsky's last three Venetian poems appropriate yet another feature that Venice and the Black Sea resorts share: the two locales as erotic spaces.

As this parallel reading of Brodsky's pre-1972 poems about the Black Sea with his Russian and English versions of "Homage to Girolamo Marcello" indicates, Brodsky transposed the poetic experience of his Russian Black Sea poems on his Venetian imaginings. This foregrounds the self-conscious construction of Brodsky's lyric persona as the Russian Ovid before his actual exile. The reinvention of this Ovidian position in actual exile exposes the nostalgia imbedded in this "translation" of the self, performed also as a linguistic translation. "Homage to Girolamo Marcello," and *Watermark* even more so, exhibits the translation of the Ovidian exilic poet into what Bhabha calls the Lucretian postmodern subjectivity, which is freed from, though nostalgically longs for, the essence of the self. The autobiographical motif that Brodsky introduced in the title of this poem foregrounds the significance of the reinvention: his acquaintance with the Venetian Girolamo Marcello, a descendant of an old Venetian family of doges and admirals—woven into Brodsky's biographical legend again in the poem "In Front of Casa Marcello," which he wrote some years after the one at hand—functions as a sign of the speaker's reinvention, his new status in Venice, and the world at large.[102]

The Sunset: "In Front of Casa Marcello"

> Venice, phantom of past greatness, magic place of beauty and decay, where Time seems to have a stop and sunsets assume an ultimate character, sinking city of marble liquefied and water petrified, appealed—as we have seen—to the (predominately northern) romantic imagination as a powerful elegiac symbol, part of its death-in-life mythology made up of beauty and terror.
>
> —WERNER VON KOPPENFELS, "Sunset City—City of the Dead: Venice and the Nineteenth-Century Apocalyptic Imagination"

Tony Tanner's broad survey of literary responses to Venice in *Venice Desired* shows how the city has inspired a range of writers of different periods, and how these responses reveal a "paradigmatic doubleness" the city seems to incorporate. The writers Tanner discusses include Byron, John Ruskin, Herman Melville, Henry James, Hugo von Hoffmansthal, Marcel Proust, Ezra Pound, Thomas Mann, and Jean-Paul Sartre. As a conclusion, Tanner quotes the early twentieth-century sociologist and *Kulturphilosoph* Georg Simmel, for whom the Venetian duality embodied Schopenhauer's idea of "absolute ambiguity." For Simmel, Venice was a facade, "a soulless theatrical set, the false beauty of the mask . . . all action seems to represent a foreground which has no background. . . . The nature of all Venetian rhythms denies us the shakings and batterings which we require for a sense of complete reality, bringing us closer to dreams where we are surrounded by the appearance of things without the things themselves." This leads to the idea of Venetian ambiguity, demonstrated by its palaces and squares, and the city as a whole: "Ambiguous, too, is the double-life of the city, at once a maze of alleyways and a maze of canals, so that the city belongs to neither land nor water." Simmel ends up presenting Venice as a metaphor of life: "The fact that our life represents merely the foreground, with death standing behind it as the only certainty—this is the final reason, as Schopenhauer says, for the 'absolute ambiguity' of life." This Schopenhauerian double meaning, which Simmel located in Venice, manifests itself, as Tanner argues, in one form or another in all these writer's responses to Venice:

> For Melville, it [Venice] was a triumph of the art of Pan, which proved to have a Basilisk glance; for Byron, the greenest island of his imagination turned into a sea-Sodom; for Ruskin it was the Hesperid Aegle with a Medusa face; for James, it was brilliantly Veronesean but also darkly venereal; for Hofmannsthal it offered ecstasy and effected dissolution; for Proust, the promise of all but unbearable beauty turned into vacancy; for Pound, it always retained some miraculous beauty, but, somehow, at some time, fraud and corruption had entered the city; for Rilke, it was voluptuous but weary, radiant and fatal; for Mann, this most supreme of cities disclosed the sickness of art . . . and for Sartre, was it the place of "le vrai" or "le vide"? Venice is, indeed, the site of "absolute ambiguity."[103]

This Venetian paradigm underscores Brodsky's Venice too, especially the 1995 "In Front of Casa Marcello," the poem that was to be his last on Venice. It brings into focus the issues of death, myth, and literary personality in an astonishingly direct way. What astonishes most in the poem is the way Brodsky continues to fabricate, no matter how ironically, his biographical legend and the conventional myth of the poet, feeding the reader's expectations with images of an elderly, resigned poet writing his likely-to-be-last lines in Venice. It is as if he were trying to dictate his own literary fate. To convey all this—and this is no less astonishing—Brodsky uses the utterly worked-out conceit of sexual activity as a metaphor of creativity, even if he debunks the conventionality of the conceit by using an image of copulating pigeons to contrast their "quest for timing" with his own for "rhyming," to quote the last lines of the English version of the poem. The scene Brodsky imagines in the poem is one of the most thoroughly worked-out topoi associated with Venice. The images of waning physical and creative powers of a male poet/writer/artist/tourist/exile conveyed against the backdrop of the Venetian cityscape at sunset evoke numerous representations of a similar "death in Venice," made popular in cinema, theater, novels, poems, opera librettos, and tourist guides:[104]

Солнце садится, и бар на углу закрылся.

Фонари загораются, точно глаза актриса
окаймляет лиловой краской для красоты и жути.

И головная боль опускается на парашюте
в затылок врага в мостовой шинели.

И голуби на фронтоне дворца Минелли
е.утся в последних лучах заката,

не обращая внимания, как когда-то
наши предки угрюмые в допотопных
обстоятельствах, на себе подобных.

Удары колокола с колокольни,
пустившей в венецианском небе корни,

точно падающие, не достигая
почвы, плоды. Если есть другая

жизнь, кто-то в ней занят сбором
этих вещей. Полагаю, в скором

времени я это выясню.
(4:200)

The sun's setting, and the corner bar bangs its shutters.
Lampposts flare up, as though an actress

paints her eyelids dark violet, looking both rum and scary.
And the headache is parachuting squarely

behind enemy wrinkles. While five enormous
pigeons on the Palazzo Minelli's cornice

are copulating in the last rays of sunset,
paying no heed, as our Stone Age ancest-

ors did, no doubt, to their scruffy neighbors,
already asleep or a little nervous.

The booming bells of the slant bell tower
rooted in the ultramarine sky over

this town are like fruits keen on falling rather
than hitting the ground. If there is another

life, someone picks them up there. Well, pretty
soon we'll find out . . .
(*CP*, 435)

The apocalyptic imagination exhibited by the poem shows how Brodsky deflates the high-cultural expectations associated with the Venetian sunset by imagining pigeons, compared to "our ancestors in antediluvian circumstances" (in a literal translation of the Russian), copulating on a pediment of a palace, while he simultaneously reinforces some of these expectations by toying with the concept of Venetian theatricality to create a scene of a personal apocalypse. The images of a sunset and a closing bar, and the reference to an actress's mask prepare the stage for the lights to come on ("Lampposts flare up") and for the sound effects to begin ("The booming bells of the slant bell tower") and, finally, for the speaker to enter in person:

Здесь, где столько
пролито семени, слез восторга

и вина, в переулке земного рая
вечером я стою, вбирая

сильно скукожившейся резиной
легких чистый, осенне-зимний,

розовый от черепичных кровель
местный воздух, которым вдоволь

не надышаться, особенно—напоследок!
пахнущий освобожденьем клеток

от времени.
(4:201)

Here, where plenty

of saliva, rapturous tears, and even
seed has been shed, in a nook of the earthly Eden,

I stand in the evening, absorbing slowly
with the dirty sponge of my lungs the lovely,

transparent, autumn-*cum*-winter, lucent
local oxygen, pink with loosened

tiles and a windowsill's carnation,
and giving the scent of cell's liberation

from time . . .
(*CP*, 435–36)

All this sets up an expectation of a grand finale, a final scene of "beauty and terror" ("krasota i zhut'")—the "rum and scary" of Brodsky's translation does not capture the same ominous contrast as the original Russian does.

The English title, "In Front of Casa Marcello," underlines the perception of Venice as a theater set by drawing attention to Venetian buildings and their peculiarity, which Barry Curtis and Claire Pajazckowska analyze in the following way:

> The sense of theatricality which was managed by the state and is now a component of the tourist experience extends to the buildings in a number of ways. They rivaled and exceeded those of other major cities in terms of scale and grandeur and had to be constructed in ways which took into account the insubstantial land on which they were built. The facades can be likened to masquerades, concealing the fragility of the foundations, contributing to the perception of Venice as a theatrical set.[105]

Brodsky deploys this phenomenological peculiarity of Venice in two ways: by setting his lyric subject in front of a Venetian building—in the Russian version the reader has to reconstruct this setting from the lyric situation, but in the English version it is established explicitly by the title—and by zooming in the speaker's and the reader's view to the pigeons on the facade of another building, the Palazzo Minelli. Theatricality foregrounds representation, something that the poem's Russian title "S natury" directly draws attention to: *s natury* (from life) refers to the convention of visual representation as in to paint from life (*risovat', pisat' s natury*).

There are two things that the poet depicts "from life": the poet himself in the landscape and the pigeons on the cornice. The pigeons are the poem's central image, indicated by the fact that Brodsky called the English version "The Pigeons" before he changed the title to "In Front of Casa Marcello" for the poem's initial publication in the *New Republic*.[106] The significance of the pigeon image is highlighted by the poem's structure. The poem is made up of forty lines. The initial line, "The sun's setting, and the corner bar bangs its shutters," is spaced typographically apart from the next line to stand out by itself. The following nine lines are arranged in three two-line stanzas (2–7) followed by a three-line stanza (8–10). The image of the pigeons is conveyed in a syntactic unit taking up lines 6–10. After the pigeon image the poem's rhymes, which in the first seven lines break up the stanzaic pattern, are arranged in rhyming pairs forming the fifteen couplets that the poem's remaining thirty lines are made up of. The English version, in comparison, has thirty-six lines, all of which are arranged in couplets. The extensive use of couplets is associated with Venice in Brodsky's last Russian collection *Landscape with Flood*. There are only two other poems written in couplets in the collection; "Pesnia o krasnom svitere" ("Song about a Red Sweater") belongs to the cycle of poems written in the 1970s and published first in this collection, but "Venice: Lido," written in the early 1990s, pairs off with "In Front of Casa Marcello" in terms of the period, form, and subject matter—that is, Venice. But to return to the image of the pigeons, it is emphasized in structural terms by an enjambment in the English text, while in the Russian text it is emphasized by the partially omitted verb in the seventh line, introducing the image. The verb, which connotes the coital act in the Russian poem, is used in vulgar or colloquial language, but in Russian poetic diction the use of the verb is unconventional.[107] The English version gives a more detailed picture of the carnal scene but leaves out the English equivalent of the Russian colloquialism and replaces it by the more neutral "copulate": "While five enormous / pigeons on the Palazzo Minelli's cornice // are copulating in the last rays of sunset" (435). The pigeons are re-evoked at the end of the poem in a syntactically complex sentence, which stretches over the last seven couplets of the poem (lines 27–40):

Мятая точно деньги,
волна облизывает ступеньки

дворца своей голубой купюрой,
получая в качестве сдачи бурый

кирпич, подверженный дерматиту,
и ненадежную кариатиду,

водрузившую орган речи
с его сигаретой себе на плечи

и погруженную в созерцанье птичьей,
освободившейся от приличий

вывернутой наизнанку спальни,
выглядящей то как слепок с пальмы,

то—обезумевшей римской
цифрой, то—рукописной строчкой с рифмой.
(4:201)

The money-like, crumpled water
of the canal, buying off the palazzo's outer

riches, ends up with a somewhat shady,
peeling-off deal that includes a shaky

caryatid shouldering still the organ
of speech, with its cigarette, and ogling

the scenes, breathtaking for their oblivion
of propriety, happening in the avian

bedroom, exposed to a passing party,
and resembling now a windswept palm tree,

now a jumble of numerals insane with their quest for timing,
now a line scrawled in haste and rhyming.
(*CP*, 436)

Due to the excessive use of participles in the Russian, the syntactic structure is somewhat ambiguous, but in essence it conveys the following situation: the caryatid on the facade of a water-beaten palace is observing the copulating birds, who resemble three things at once—a plaster mold of a palm tree, an unrecognizable (or unintelligible) Roman number, and two rhyming lines in a manuscript.

Apart from the caryatid it is, of course, the speaker himself who is observing the pigeons. Their coital act, as a symbol of vitality, is contrasted with his own frail physical state. The headache of the first lines is matched with the images of "skukozhivshaiasia rezina legkikh," literally, "shrunk rubber of the lungs," and "buryi kirpich podverzhennyi dermatitu," again, literally, "brown brick susceptible to dermatitis." Dermatitis, a type of skin inflamation, refers to the red brick on the wall exposed by erosion, an image that reoccurs in Brodsky's poetry, and that metaphorically connotes an infection, especially that of the heart, as, for instance, in the 1989 poem "Fin de Siècle":

Век скоро кончится, но раньше кончусь я.
Это, боюсь, не вопрос чутья.
Скорее—влияние небытия

на бытие; охотника, так сказать, на дичь,—
будь то сердечная мышца или кирпич.
(4:73)

The century will soon be over, but sooner it will be me.

That's not the message, though, of a trembling knee.
Rather, the influence of not-to-be

on to-be. Of the hunter upon—so to speak—his fowl,
be that one's heart valve or a red brick wall.
(*CP*, 387)

It is difficult not to read "In Front of Casa Marcello," with its intimate account of the lyric subject's physical condition played against the Venetian landscape, as a poetic testament. The almost uncanny anticipation of the author's nearing death, which the speaker invokes with a typically Brodskian juxtaposition of stylistic registers, shifting from the biblical references, such as "antediluvian," "falling fruit," and "earthly paradise," to the colloquial understatement of: "If there is another // life, someone picks them up there. Well, pretty / soon we'll find out." Venice, his "earthly paradise," or "Eden" in the English version, the place where once "plenty // of saliva, rapturous tears, and even / seed has been shed," is now a place where he senses a nearing end.

In the same testamental vein, the poem cultivates extensively two signature devices of Brodsky's poetics: inventive rhymes and complex syntactic structure. The long and winding syntax of the lines, which present the lyric situation, unfolding from line 17 on with the lyric subject's assertion "Here . . . I stand," is jagged with enjambments and packed with adjectival attributes and subordinate clauses, and interrupted by a full syntactic closure only in line 27, which marks the beginning of another syntactically complex structure, packed with participles and gerunds and taking up the poem's remaining thirteen lines. This syntactic complexity is juxtaposed with the regularity of the rhyming couplets. These two structural elements, the complex syntactic structure and the regular couplets, create the effect of the speaker reading the poem in a voice out of breath (the syntax) and with heartbeats faintly audible (the rhymes). The rhymes in the Russian text are typically Brodskian in their inventive ungrammaticality, and even if not the poem's most unexpected rhyme, one can only imagine what it meant for Brodsky to end the Russian text in a couplet with "rimskoi" / "rifmoi" (the adjective "Roman" corresponds phonetically with the genitive form of the noun "rhyme") as its final rhyme. It is through these breathtaking couplets that Brodsky projects his aging lyric subject onto the Venetian waters, with images of life and death that render Venice a metaphor of life's "absolute ambiguity."

Conclusion

There is a curious moment in Prince Viazemsky's notes describing the first days of his visit to Venice in 1853. After mentioning that "since my arrival I have been to St. Mark's basilica almost every day," he goes on to name the other famous tourist sites he has seen—the Doge's Palace, the Public Gardens, Ponte Rialto, and Lido. He then stops to describe his visit to the Armenian Convent on San Lazzaro. A large Egyptian mummy and some rare manuscripts, which Viazemsky mentions as worthy of a visitor's attention, are followed by an attraction of a different kind: "The table at which Byron learned the Armenian language. With Father Aucher, who is now very old and defeated by paralysis." After recording the brief conversation he had with Father Aucher, Viazemsky concludes his tour of the convent by remarking on the price of the book he purchased partly as a souvenir: "The typography is well organized. I bought there an Armenian-Russian grammar. . . . Quite expensive: the grammar costs 10 francs, and the multilingual edition 15."[1] It is curious to read Viazemsky's dispassionate account of his visit to one of the Byronic shrines in Venice. It displays no particular excitement over the opportunity, even if belated, to see the convent or to meet Byron's famous tutor. On the contrary, Viazemsky, once a leading propagator of Russian *baironizm*, ends his notes by recording laconically the mundane details of what he bought and how much it cost. His hastily jotted observations and their matter-of-fact tone reveal the aging Viazemsky's detachment from his past: "*We all looked up to* Napoleons and Byrons and many of us pretended to be them quite successfully" (21), as he writes ironically later in the same journal.

Viazemsky's notes reflect not only the changes in his own life-history between 1819, when he first read Byron, and 1853, when he first visited Venice, but they also reflect the transformation the Byron cult as well as European travel culture had gone through by the mid-nineteenth century. Viazemsky was not the first visitor to the Armenian Convent. In the early 1830s John Murray III, the future author of popular travel books, wrote from Venice, after a visit to the convent, that Father Aucher "is I fancy very much pestered with visits from English people."[2] Murray's comment refers to the fact that during the two decades after the publication of *Childe Harold's Pilgrimage*, Byron's itinerary in Europe had come to define many British travelers' Continental tour. The gradual democratization of the European travel scene began in the post-Napoleonic years and continued in the following decades. Travel books and guides were a vital part of the thriving tourist industry. The English authors of these travel books appropriated Byron's travel verse and revised it by omitting the political content to foreground the emotive and aesthetic aspects. By 1855 an Englishman standing on the Bridge of Sighs and citing the opening lines of *Childe Harold*'s Canto 4 had become an object of popular satire.[3] Venice had become a major tourist city and Byron one of its major tourist attractions. This was also reflected in Russian satirical literature. I. P. Miatlev's celebrated travel parody in verse, *Sensatsii i zamechaniia gospozhi Kurdiukovoi za granitseiu, dan l'etranzhe* (*Sensations and observations of Mrs Kurdiukova abroad, dan l'etranzhe*), was based on the author's trips to Europe in 1836–38. In the passage on Venice, Miatlev has the diarist-narrator, Mrs. Kurdiukova, Miatlev's caricature of a Russian provincial gentlewoman, reflecting on Byron and *Childe Harold*:

> *Мусье* Байрон, *ле* поэт,
> Тут трагедии сюжет
> Отыскал, любовь прибавил,
> И событие прославил,
> И приплел тут свой роман.[4]

> [*Monsieur* Byron, *le* poet, / here the plot of a tragedy / found, added some love, / praised the events, / and plaited in his romance.]

Venice is the quintessential tourist city in Europe. At the same time, the city's representations in Western canonized literature are linked with narratives and identities traditionally seen as antithetical to the collective experience suggested by tourism. In the literary high-art formations Venice is the city of artistic displacements and literary exiles, with Byron as the Romantic prototype. And yet again, all these artists and exiles, Byron included, came to Venice as visitors and experienced Venice as tourists. Gustav Aschenbach, Mann's modernist interpretation of artistic displacement and death in Venice, was not only a German writer but also a North European tourist, staying at the Excelsior, the first luxury hotel on the then fashionable beaches of Lido.

On the topography of contemporary global mass tourism, Venice is associated with Euro-American cultural travel and the material means related to it. Literary and artistic models play an important role in the high-cultural touristic discourses. Joseph Brodsky's *Watermark*, as well as his other travel texts in poetry and prose, exhibit the author's nostalgia for the modernist male traveler, shaped by the Byronic myth and those Romantic formations, in which the imperial myth of the gentleman-colonizer, another and related authorial model Brodsky appropriated, also originated. Apart from exilic nostalgia, Brodsky's travel writing exhibits imperial nostalgia, the makings of which are illuminated by his inventive re-appropriation of Russian imperial mythologies in "A Guide to a Renamed City." The geopolitical scope of Brodsky's imperial nostalgia is expanded in his textual encounters with Mexico and Brazil. In "Mexican Divertimento" and "After a Journey, or Homage to Vertebrae" his imperial nostalgia encompasses an ironic longing for the aesthetic practices and the authentic travel and adventure of Europe's colonial past. Among the exilic and imperial, Brodsky's travel writing also exhibits expressions of touristic nostalgia; the phenomenology of tourism Brodsky writes in *Watermark*, discloses his continuous search for an authentic Venice, the intimate, the private, the nontouristic, while Venice also represents for him the historically authentic, the genuine ruin. Moreover, the narrative of repeated returns and partings discloses the author's nostalgia for the mythical homecoming of antiquity, his nostalgia for the authenticity of the Odysseus narrative.

Apart from a dialogue with contemporary literary tourism, this book's project has concerned itself with putting Joseph Brodsky's travel poetry and prose in a dialogue with some of the leading representatives of postcolonial and postmodern theories. It is only through this twofold dialogue that we can begin to see how Brodsky's engagement with his contemporary cultural practices in the West—incorporated in his poetry and prose in terms of both subject matter and representational strategies—contributed to these texts' status as exceptional and unique literary events within postwar Russian cultural practices. Applying theories, initially developed to critique Euro-imperial knowledge, power, and cultural practices, to a poet for whom these practices were an object of nostalgia is a challenge to the critic and the critical apparatus. But engaging Brodsky's works in a dialogue with these theories exposes the complexity of his multilayered nostalgia and uncovers the imperial makings of his historical and geographical imagination.

Brodsky's traveling author is constantly negotiating between two forms of displacement, exilic and touristic, while he is also negotiating his dissenting position toward what he perceived as the Soviet "empire" and a nostalgic position toward Russia's and Europe's imperial past. Brodsky came from a place where the "age of empire," to quote Eric Hobsbawm's phrase, had been followed by another age of another empire, an empire with whose ideological premises or imperial/ist policies Brodsky could not agree. In his rejection of the *inauthentic* imperial culture of the Soviet Union, he embraced what emerges in his travel writing as the *authentic* imperial culture of Europe's and Russia's past. In doing this, Brodsky projected a world view, which many of his contemporaries among European and North American intellectuals perceived as an expression of the attitudes and cultural practices of the era of "high" or "classical" imperialism that still exerted immense influence—despite the arrival of the nominally "postimperial" era—on the cultural sphere of the metropolitan West.[5] Because of the incompatibility between imperial experience in the West and that in the Soviet Union—displayed in the meanings that Western intellectual formations, on the one hand, and dissenting Soviet intellectuals, on the other, invested in the concept of empire—the dialogue between Brodsky and the theories of postcoloniality demands that the critic constantly re-review and readjust the critical position. Reading Brodsky's "Flight from Byzantium," as a polemic against Western perceptions of the East, Edward Said's *Orientalism* included, shows how Brodsky's authorial position at once questions and supports the fundaments that Said seeks to critique but which his critical apparatus also presupposes. The way Brodsky addresses the construction of his own authorial identity highlights the fact that Russia's historical and geopolitical position challenges the East-West dichotomy on which Said grounds his argumentation. At the same time, Brodsky's appropriation of the Orientalist myth supports that dichotomy and reinforces Said's point: Brodsky used Istanbul and Turkish culture as a contrasting image to define his own Westernized position in opposition to the East and in opposition to that which he perceived as the East in Russia and, especially, in the Soviet Union.

Finally, the analyses of Brodsky's travel texts point the way to further investigations into the significance of the concept of empire in the geographical and historical imaginings of the post-Stalin generation of Russian intellectuals. They lead to further examination of how the non-Russian territories within Soviet imperial space and the nonmetropolitan world at large were represented by the metropolitan intellectuals of the late Soviet period. These geopolitical imaginings, at least in Brodsky's case, often seem to coincide with a nostalgic attitude toward Russia's and Europe's common cultural heritage of imperial myths.

Notes

Introduction

1. Joseph Brodsky in *Joseph Brodsky: A Maddening Space,* directed by Lawrence Ritkethly, produced by Public Broadcasting Service and Channel 4.

2. Svetlana Boym, *The Future of Nostalgia* (New York: Basic Books, 2001), 307. "Penelope of a city" is a quotation from Brodsky's *Watermark* (New York: Farrar, Straus and Giroux).

3. Brodsky's use of a group of modernist cosmopolitans as his "reference set," to quote a term Patrick Colm Hogan has conjured in his discussion of canonical literature and its use in the identity-construction of such postcolonial writers as Derek Walcott, is illustrated at the beginning of the essay "To Please a Shadow." There the author, reflecting on his motivations to write in English, rejects the model set by such bilingual literary modernists as Conrad, Nabokov, and Beckett, who resorted to "a language other than [their] mother tongue" out of "necessity," "burning ambition," and "for the sake of greater estrangement." His own goal, the author asserts, is to "find myself in closer proximity to the man whom I considered the greatest mind of the twentieth-century: Wystan Hugh Auden" (*LTO,* 357). While rejecting these canonical modernists' motifs as a model for his own adoption of the English language, he inadvertently foregrounds their importance as a point of cultural reference for his identity construction, not to say anything of the affectionate affiliation with Auden, the modernist and cosmopolitan model for Brodsky's self-fashioning. For Hogan's discussion of Walcott, see Patrick Colm Hogan, *Empire and Poetic Voice: Cognitive and Cultural Studies of Literary Tradition and Colonialism* (Albany: State University of New York Press, 2004), 157–96.

4. Dean MacCannel points to the link between tourism and postmodernity when he states in the introduction to the 1989 edition of *The Tourist* (1976), his now classic

study on tourism, that much of the phenomenon examined by him as "the process by which modernity, modernization, modern *culture* was establishing its empire on a global basis" has since then been ascribed not to modernity but to postmodernity. MacCannel rejects the proclamations of "dead subjects, dead epochs, dead values" voiced by the major critics of the postmodern: for him they present "unrealized mourning" and "expressions of an anticreative ethos, nostalgia for the bourgeois or Cartesian subject, and a Eurocentric past—the very institutions and concepts which the critics seek to deconstruct." Nevertheless, MacCannel wonders whether his tourist "was really an early postmodern figure, alienated but seeking fulfilment in his own alienation—nomadic, placeless, a kind of subjectivity without spirit, a 'dead subject.'" See Dean MacCannel, *The Tourist* (Berkeley: University of California Press, 1999), xv–xviii.

5. I will introduce the names of Brodsky's poems and essays in the language of the original with the English or Russian translation in parentheses. After this first reference I will only use the English titles.

6. "After a Journey" (included in *Grief and Reason*) and "Flight from Byzantium" (included in *Less Than One*) were written originally in Russian but co-translated into English by Brodsky and Aleksandr Sumerkin, and Brodsky and Alan Myers, respectively. The other three essays Brodsky wrote in English. The Leningrad essay, included in *Less Than One*, appeared originally in *Vogue* (September 1979), titled "Leningrad: A City of Mystery"; it was translated into Russian by Lev Loseff and published in the journal *Chast' rechi* (no. 1, 1980). "A Place as Good as Any," included in *Grief and Reason*, was translated into Russian by Elena Kasatkina, and the first Russian publication was in a special issue of *Zvezda* (no. 1, 1997) dedicated to Brodsky. *Watermark* was first published in a limited Italian edition titled *Fondamenta incurabili*, which is also the title of the Russian version, "Naberezhnaia neistselimykh," translated by Grigorii Dashevskii.

7. The term transculturation originates in ethnography, more precisely in the work of Cuban sociologist Fernando Ortiz. Mary Louise Pratt's definition of the term captures the meanings relevant to my discussion: according to Pratt the term is used to describe "how subordinated or marginal groups select and invent from materials transmitted to them by a dominant or metropolitan culture." See Mary Louise Pratt, *Imperial Eyes: Studies in Travel Writing and Transculturation* (London: Routledge, 1992), 6.

8. Peter Hulme and Tim Youngs, introduction to *The Cambridge Companion to Travel Writing*, ed. Hulme and Youngs (Cambridge: Cambridge University Press, 2002), 1–13. The elusiveness of the genre is indicated by the variety of terms used in reference to travel writing. In English there are, among others, the terms literature of travel, travel literature, travel genre, travelogue, travel account, travel notes, travel narrative, travel tale, and travel poetry. In Russian at least the following are used: *literatura puteshestviia, zhanr puteshestviia, travelog, putevye zametki, putevye ocherki,* and *putevoditel' v stikhakh.* Some of these terms can be viewed as subgenres with specific features (most readers probably associate travelogue, for instance, with a longer narrative than a travel account), but they all represent discursive practices that can be described as travel writing.

9. Edward Said, *The World, the Text, and the Critic* (Cambridge, Mass.: Harvard University Press, 1983), 4. Said's theoretical point of departure is a critique of a structuralist understanding of the text as a "hermetic textual cosmos . . . whose significant dimension of meaning is . . . a wholly inward or intellectual one" (35). He opposes this by asserting that "texts have ways of existing that even in their most rarefied forms are always enmeshed in circumstance, time, place, and society—in short, they are in the world, and hence worldly" (ibid.), and he proposes dealing with a text "as significant form, in which . . . worldliness, circumstantiality, the text's status as an event having sensuous particularity as well as historical contingency, are considered as being incorporated in the text, an infrangible part of its capacity for conveying and producing meaning" (39).

10. This historical outline follows Andreas Schönle's study *Authenticity and Fiction in the Russian Literary Journey, 1790–1840* (Cambridge, Mass.: Harvard University Press, 2000), esp. 1–16. See also Sara Dickinson's *Breaking Ground: Travel and National Culture in Russia from Peter I to the Era of Pushkin* (Amsterdam: Rodopi, 2006); T. Roboli, "The Literature of Travel," in *Russian Prose*, ed. B. M. Eikhenbaum and Yury Tynianov, trans. and ed. Rey Parrot (Ann Arbor, Mich.: Ardis, 1985); Reuel K. Wilson, *The Literary Travelogue. A Comparative Study with Special Relevance to Russian Literature from Fonvizin to Pushkin* (The Hague: Martinus Nijhoff, 1973); and Derek Offord, *Journeys to a Graveyard: Perceptions of Europe in Classical Russian Travel Writing* (Dordrecht: Springer, 2005).

11. See Susan Layton, *Russian Literature and Empire: Conquest of the Caucasus from Pushkin to Tolstoi* (Cambridge: Cambridge University Press, 1994), esp. 54–70; Monika Greenleaf, *Pushkin and Romantic Fashion: Fragment, Elegy, Orient, Irony* (Stanford, Calif.: Stanford University Press, 1994), 8–55, esp. 144–45.

12. Julie Buckler, *Mapping St. Petersburg: Imperial Text and Cityshape* (Princeton, N.J.: Princeton University Press, 2005), 89–115.

13. See, for instance, Blok's "Molnii iskusstva" ("Lightning of Art"), Belyi's *Putevye zametki* (*Travel Notes*), Gumilev's *Mik. Afrikanskaia Poema* (*Mik. African Poem*) and *Shater* (*Tent*), Pasternak's *Okhrannaia gramota* (*Safe Conduct*), Mandelstam's *Puteshestvie v Armeniu* (*Journey to Armenia*), and Mayakovsky's "Stikhi o Parizhe" ("Poems about Paris") and *Moe otkrytie Ameriki* (*My Discovery of America*).

14. On the Russian modernist perception of Africa, see Gwen Walker, "Silver-Age Writers on the 'Black' Continent: Russia, Africa and the Celebration of Distance" (PhD diss., University of Wisconsin–Madison, 2003).

15. See Carol Avins, *Border Crossings: The West and Russian Identity in Soviet Literature 1917–1934* (Berkeley: University of California Press, 1983), 139; 150.

16. There is a recent English translation of Il'f and Petrov's travelogue under the title *Ilf and Petrov's American Road Trip: 1935 Travelogue of Two Soviet Writers*, ed. Erika Wolf, trans. Anne O. Fischer (Princeton, N.J.: Princeton Architectural Press, 2007). The negative reviews Mandelstam's essay received by his contemporary Soviet critics anticipated the stiffening of Stalinist cultural institutions; see Osip Mandelstam, *Sochineniia*, vol. 2 (Moscow: Khudozhestvennaia literatura, 1990), 420–23.

17. See Anne E. Gorsuch, "'There Is No Place Like Home': Soviet Tourism in Late Stalinism," *Slavic Review* 4 (2003): 760–85.

18. Travel abroad was still, however, strictly controlled by the state. See Marina Balina's description of literary travel abroad in official Soviet literary practices in "A Prescribed Journey: Russian Travel Literature from the 1960s to the 1980s," *Slavic and East European Journal* 38 (1994): 261–70.

19. For the significance of travel *romantika* for the *shestidesiatniki*, see Petr Vail' and Aleksandr Genis, *60-e: Mir sovetskogo cheloveka* (Ann Arbor, Mich.: Ardis, 1988), 93–135.

20. Hulme and Youngs, *Cambridge Companion to Travel Writing*, 1.

21. Apart from *The Cambridge Companion to Travel Writing*, the studies on travel and travel writing I have found useful are Mary Louise Pratt, *Imperial Eyes*; Alison Russell, *Crossing Boundaries: Postmodern Travel Literature* (New York: Palgrave, 2000); Maria Alzira Seixo, ed., *Travel Writing and Cultural Memory* (Amsterdam: Rodopi, 2000); Steve Clark, ed., *Travel Writing and Empire: Postcolonial Theory in Transit* (New York: St. Martin's Press, 1999); Dennis Potter, *Haunted Journeys: Desire and Transgression in European Travel Writing* (Princeton, N.J.: Princeton University Press, 1992); and Patrick Holland and Graham Huggan, *Tourists with Typewriters: Critical Reflections on Contemporary Travel Writing* (Ann Arbor, Mich.: University of Michigan Press, 1998). On travel in theoretical formations, see Caren Kaplan, *Questions of Travel: Postmodern Discourses of Displacement* (Durham, N.C.: Duke University Press, 1996).

22. From the viewpoint of history studies and social sciences the concept of empire is an ambiguous term to define. Mark R. Beissinger points this out in his discussion of the term's applicability to Soviet history: "The more one examines the variety of meanings attached to empire across history, the more one is tempted to conclude that the notion has always contained some metaphorical element, even in its original Roman usages." Empire "with its large arrays of referents," Bessinger continues, persists as a tool of political analysis as well as political practice, and is "applied to multiple sets of objects—even in a world in which empires formally no longer exist." In the late 1980s and early 1990s referring to the Soviet Union as an empire became "a 'banal' fact" and "a common frame through which the Soviet state and its collapse [were] analyzed, with regard both to the relationship between the Soviet state and its multicultural population and to Soviet control over eastern Europe" (*Slavic Review* 2 [2006]: 294–303). Apart from above, the discussion of the concept of empire in Brodsky's works in this book draws on the fact that the perception of the Soviet Union as an empire was common in Soviet Russian unofficial intellectual discourses even before its collapse, something such Brodsky 1960s poems as "Anno domini" (1968) and "Post aetatem nostrum" (1970), for instance, indicate. In "Kolybel'naia treskovogo mysa" ("Lullaby of Cape Cod") (1975) Brodsky uses the term "empire" in reference to both the Soviet Union and United States. For the use of "empire" in reference to the Soviet Union in the 1960s, see also Vail' and Genis, *60-e*, 250–66.

23. By "imperial knowledge" I refer to a textual tradition, the formation of which Edward Said has described in *Orientalism*. Said writes about the function of travel

narratives in the production of knowledge, pointing out that travel narratives are often underscored by textual attitude—the reliance on a previous text in representing an encounter with the unknown, and when legitimized by the authority of "academics, institutions, and governments," as Said argues, these types of texts "*create* not only knowledge but the very reality they appear to describe. In time such knowledge and reality produce a tradition, or what Michel Foucault calls a discourse, whose material presence or weight, not the originality of a given author, is really responsible for the texts produced out of it" (Edward Said, *Orientalism* [1978; repr., New York: Vintage Books, 1994], 94–95).

24. Derek Offord's study of Russian travel writing in the eighteenth and nineteenth centuries offers some ideas of how the Eurocentric conceit has functioned in the construction of Russian national identity vis-à-vis Europe; see Offord, *Journeys to a Graveyard*, 7–13.

25. Holland and Huggan, *Tourists with Typewriters*, 22–23.

26. Fredric Jameson made the connection between the new, postmodernist aesthetic practices and the postimperial, or neocolonial, period of late capitalism, in his now classic "Postmodernism and Consumer Society," recognizing the 1960s as a transitional period, in which "the new international order (neo-colonialism, the Green Revolution, computerization and electronic information) is . . . set in place and is swept and shaken by its own internal contradictions and by external resistance." See Fredric Jameson, "Postmodernism and Consumer Society," in *The Anti-Aesthetic: Essays on Postmodern Culture*, ed. Hal Foster (New York: New Press, 1998), 113.

27. For understanding empire as a discursive practice, see Edward W. Said, *Culture and Imperialism* (New York: Vintage Books, 1993), 12–13. See also n. 22, this chapter.

28. Linda Hutcheon, "Irony, Nostalgia, and the Postmodern," 1998, http://www.library.utoronto.ca/ute/criticism/hutchinp.html (accessed April 10, 2008).

29. Susan Stewart, *On Longing: Narratives of the Miniature, the Gigantic, the Souvenir, the Collection* (Durham, N.C.: Duke University Press, 1993), 135.

30. For the first position, see Andrei Ranchin, *Na piru mnemoziny: Interteksty Iosifa Brodskogo* (Moscow: NLO, 2001), 12; for the latter, see Mikhail Epstein and Aleksandr Genis's article in *Russian Postmodernism: New Perspectives on Post-Soviet Culture*, ed. Mikhail Epstein, Alexander Genis, and Slobodanka Vladyi-Glover (New York: Berghahn Books, 1999), 473.

31. Thomas Epstein in Epstein, Genis, and Vladyi-Glover, *Russian Postmodernism*, vii.

32. "Postmodern condition," now a commonplace in the discourse on the postmodern, originates in Jean-François Lyotard's discussion of the "crisis of narratives," and especially the "grand narrative," which he introduced in relation to his ideas of how knowledge is produced, controlled, and legitimized in the West in *The Postmodern Condition: A Report on Knowledge* (1978; English translation, 1984). See Bill Readings, *Introduction to Lyotard: Art and Politics* (London: Routledge, 1991), esp. 63.

33. Pratt, *Imperial Eyes*, 10.

34. Pratt uses the term "contact zone" to denote the "space of colonial encounters," and even though Brodsky's "Flight" is not strictly speaking a testimony of such an

encounter, the imaginative space his text creates represents Istanbul as a "space in which peoples geographically and historically separate come into contact with each other and establish ongoing relations, usually involving conditions of coercion, radical inequality, and intractable conflict," as Pratt further defines the term (*Imperial Eyes*, 6).

35. On "third space" see Homi K. Bhabha, *The Location of Culture* (London: Routledge, 1995), 36–39, 216–19; see also 263n34 in this book.

Chapter 1. Exile, Tourist, Traveler

1. I refer here to the following reviews on Brodsky's travel poetry and prose: George L. Kline, "Variations on the Theme of Exile," in *Brodsky's Poetics and Aesthetics*, ed. Lev Loseff and Valentina Polukhina (London: Macmillan, 1990), 56–88; Lev Loseff, "Home and Abroad in the Works of Brodskii," in *Under Eastern Eyes: The West as Reflected in Recent Russian Émigré Writing*, ed. Arnold McMillin (London: Macmillan, 1992), 25–41; Gerald Stanton Smith, "England in Russian Émigré Poetry: Iosif Brodskii's 'V Anglii,'" in McMillin, *Under Eastern Eyes*, 17–24; Petr Vail', "Prostranstvo kak metafora vremeni: stikhi Iosifa Brodskogo v zhanre puteshestviia," *Russian Literature* 37 (1995): 405–16; Valentina Polukhina, "Landshaft liricheskoj lichnosti v poezii Iosifa Brodskogo," in *Literary Tradition and Practice in Russian Culture*, ed. Valentina Polukhina, Joe Andrew, and Robert Reid (Amsterdam: Rodopi, 1993), 229–45. See also Viktor Kulle's essay "Iosif Brodskii: novaia Odisseia" in the first volume of *Sochineniia Iosifa Brodskogo*, 7 vols. (St. Petersburg: Pushkinskii fond, 1999), 1:283–97. The first part of chapter 1 of my work first appeared in print as "Poet kak odinokii turist: Brodskii, Venetsiia i putevye zametki," *Novoe literaturnoe obozrenie* 67 (2004): 162–80.

2. Vail', "Prostranstvo kak metafora vremeni," 413.

3. Kline distinguishes three groups of "poems of exile" in Brodsky's works: the first group includes the poems written by Brodsky during his internment in 1964–65 in Norenskaia; the second includes poems written in 1972 "in anticipation of permanent exile"; and the third group consists of poems written after the emigration in the United States, England, and Italy "with the special emphasis on the periods of 1974–77 and 1980" (Kline, "Variations on the Theme of Exile," 56–57).

4. Kline, "Variations on the Theme of Exile," 70–71. (I have quoted Kline as printed in the source. He does not indicate clearly the direct quotation from Loseff.)

5. Smith, "England in Russian Émigré Poetry," 20.

6. David Bethea, *Joseph Brodsky and the Creation of Exile* (Princeton, N.J.: Princeton University Press, 1994), 52 (hereafter *Creation of Exile*). Mikhail Kreps, the author of the first monograph on Brodsky, is one of the few critics who assigns Brodsky's travel poems to a "tourist" experience. Mikhail Kreps, *Poetika Brodskogo* (Ann Arbor, Mich.: Ardis, 1984).

7. Malcolm Bradbury, "The Cities of Modernism," in *Modernism: 1890–1930*, ed. Malcolm Bradbury and James McFarlane (Atlantic Highlands: Humanities Press, 1978), 101.

8. Julia Kristeva, *Strangers to Ourselves*, trans. Len S. Roudiez (New York: Harvester Wheatsheat, 1991), 5–8.

9. Joseph Brodsky, "Says Poet Brodsky, ex of the Soviet Union: 'A writer is a lonely traveler and no one is his helper,'" trans. Carl Proffer, *New York Times Magazine*, October 1, 1972, 11, 78–79, 82–84, 86–87. The letter, translated from Russian into English by Carl Proffer, was, together with a short review, "Zametka o Solov'eve" ("A Note on Solov'iev"), in *Russian Literature Triquarterly* 4 (1972), Brodsky's first prose text to appear in an American publication, but the feature in the *New York Times* Sunday supplement was his initial introduction to wider American audiences. This is the original Russian extract: "Я приехал в Америку и буду здесь жить. Надеюсь, что смогу заниматься своим делом, то есть сочинительством, как и прежде. Я увидел новую землю, но не новое небо. Разумеется, будущее внушает большие опасения, чем когда бы то не было. Ибо если прежде я не мог писать, это объяснялось обстоятельствами скорее внутренними, чем внешними. . . . Но я предвижу и другие поводы для паралича: наличие иной языковой среды. . . . Для того, чтобы писать на языке хорошо, надо слышать его—в пивных, в трамваях, в гастрономе. Как с этим бороться, я еще не придумал. Но надеюсь, язык путешествует вместе с человеком. . . . Перефразируя одного немецкого писателя, оказавшегося тридцать пять лет назад в похожей ситуации: 'Die Russische Dichtung ist da wo ich bin.'" The original Russian text was published in the journal *Zvezda* 5 (2000): 3–9, and in the seventh volume of Brodsky's collected works under the title "Pisatel'—odinokii puteshestvennik" (*Sochineniia Iosifa Brodskogo*, 7:62–71).

10. Thomas Mann's often quoted words were recorded first by the *New York Times* upon Mann's arrival in the United States in February 1937: "Where I am, there is Germany. I carry my German culture with me. I have contact with the world and I do not consider myself fallen." See Donald Prater, *Thomas Mann: A Life* (Oxford: Oxford University Press, 1995), 275.

11. Edward W. Said, *Reflections on Exile and Other Essays* (Cambridge, Mass.: Harvard University Press, 2000), 174.

12. Brodsky, *On Grief and Reason*, 22–23.

13. David Bethea has commented on the difference between Said's and Brodsky's approach in the following way: "Just as Said is trying to give voice to the Eastern exile too often neglected in our Western tradition, Brodsky will not let us forget the Western heritage that had been selectively distorted and exiled from the 'Eastern' discourse, authoritarian to the core, of his Soviet schooling" (Bethea, *Creation of Exile*, 45).

14. For a discussion of how influential the idea of exile as aesthetic gain has been in Euro-American modernisms, see Kaplan, *Questions of Travel*, 227–40. See especially Kaplan's discussion of exile, travel, and tourism in the chapter "'This Question of Moving': Modernist Exile/Postmodern Tourism." Kaplan's focus is mainly on Anglo-American and French criticism, and her discussion does not cover Russian literature or literary criticism.

15. Jameson, "Postmodernism and Consumer Society," 124.

16. For a discussion of the hierarchies of displacement in Euro-American high-cultural formations, see Kaplan, *Questions of Travel*, 1–64.

17. William Wordsworth, *Poems*, vol. 1 (New Haven, Conn.: Yale University Press, 1981), 402.

18. George Sand, *Oeuvres autobiographiques*, vol. 2 (Paris: Gallimard, 1971), 900–901.

19. P. A. Viazemsky, *Polnoe sobranie sochinenii kniazia P. A. Viazemskogo*, vol. 10, 1853–1878 (St. Petersburg: Tipografiia M. M. Stasiulevitsa, 1886), 83.

20. Quoted in V. V. Bronguleev, ed., *Posredine stranstviia zemnogo: Dokumental'naia povest' o zhizni i tvorchestve Nikolaia Gumileva; Gody 1886–1913* (Moscow: Mysl', 1995), 287.

21. Helen Carr, "Modernism and Travel (1880–1940)," in Hulme and Youngs, *Cambridge Companion to Travel Writing*, 79.

22. Gorsuch, "'There Is No Place Like Home,'" 761. See also Irina Sandomirskaia, "Proletarian Tourism: Incorporated History and Incorporated Rhetoric," in *Soviet Civilization between Past and Present*, ed. Mette Bryld and Erik Kulavig, Odense University Slavic Studies 10 (Odense: Odense University Press, 1998), 39–52.

23. Vas. Lebedev-Kumach, *Pesni* (Moscow: Moskovskii rabochii, 1947), 202–4.

24. Quoted in Vail' and Genis, *60-e: Mir sovetskogo cheloveka*, 115.

25. MacCannel, *Tourist*, 5.

26. Daniel, J. Boorstin, *The Image; or, What Happened to the American Dream* (New York: Atheneum, 1961).

27. Umberto Eco, *Travels in Hyperreality: Essays* (San Diego: Harcourt Brace Jovanovich, 1986), 6. See also John Urry, *The Tourist Gaze: Leisure and Travel in Contemporary Societies* (London: Sage, 1990), 7.

28. Paul Fussell, *Abroad* (Oxford: Oxford University Press, 1980), 41.

29. Jonathan Culler, "Semiotics of Tourism," *American Journal of Tourism* 1, nos. 1–2 (1981): 128–30.

30. Kaplan, *Questions of Travel*, 27.

31. Cf. 233n26 in this book.

32. Kaplan, *Questions of Travel*, 28.

33. Jameson's visions confirm MacCannel's views in the introduction of the 1989 edition of *The Tourist*, where MacCannel wonders whether the tourist as characterized by him was a postmodern figure, marking the end of individualism. Cf. n. 4 in introduction.

34. David Patterson argues that the "motif of exile" has been one of the "distinguishing features of Russian thought over the last century and a half." According to him, "for the Russian, exile is not only a social problem or a form of punishment for political crimes. Beyond these categories, it is an expression of that Russian condition that most of all announces the homelessness of the modern human condition in its existential and metaphysical aspects" (ix). Patterson uses exile as a key metaphor in his exploration of Russian thought, and whether one agrees with Patterson's conclusions as a whole or not, the significance of *izgnanie* and *ssylka* for Russian culture is hard to deny. David Patterson, *Exile: The Sense of Alienation in Modern Russian Letters* (Lexington: University Press of Kentucky, 1995).

35. Lev Loseff writes: "The fact is that from the very beginning in Brodskii's poetry a motif was visibly present that Tsiavlovskii called, applying it to the work of Pushkin,

'abroadsickness.' . . . Much of early Brodskii is imbued with this Pushkinian mood" (Loseff, "Home and Abroad in the Works of Brodskii," 26). Petr Vail' writes about Brodsky's "Pushkinian complex" ("pushkinskii kompleks"), defining it as a "desire to travel and non-desire to leave for good, which the facts of Brodsky's biography confirm" in "Prostranstvo kak metafora vremeni" (Vail', "Prostranstvo kak metafora vremeni," 406). See also Oleg Lekmanov's analysis of necrologies on Brodsky's death in Moscow newspapers and journals, in which the comparison between Brodsky and Pushkin is made time after time. Oleg Lekmanov, "'Chto zhe pishut v gazetakh?' (Smert' Iosifa Brodskogo v zerkale moskovskoi pressy)," *Novoe literaturnoe obozrenie* 3 (2004): 233–34.

36. Vail' and Genis, *60-e*, 105–7.

37. Quoted in Josephine Woll, *Real Images: Soviet Cinema and the Thaw* (London: I. B. Tauris, 2000), 133.

38. See Gorsuch, "'There Is No Place Like Home,'" 769–70; Irina H. Corten, *Vocabulary of Soviet Society and Culture: A Selected Guide to Russian Words, Idioms, and Expressions of the Post-Stalinist Era, 1953–1991* (Durham, N.C.: Duke University Press, 1992), 41, 148.

39. Anatolii Naiman, "Hava Nagila—A Memoir," *Commentary*, July 1997, 34. The Finnish sociologist Anna Rotkirch has analyzed the Soviet south as a space for sexual encounters (see Anna Rotkirch, "Traveling Maidens and Men with Parallel Lives—Journeys as Private Space During Late Socialism," in *Beyond the Limits: The Concept of Space in Russian History and Culture*, ed. Jeremy Smith [Helsinki: Suomen historiallinen seura, 1999], 131–49). Anatolii Naiman's memoir contributes to this data by recounting Brodsky's nocturnal activities on a ship from Yalta to Feodosia, while it also contributes to the post-Pushkinian mythology of escape across the Black Sea: "Brodsky woke me twice. The first time was to ask whether I thought we were far from Turkey, or close enough to swim there. I said it was 200 miles once you reached neutral waters. He left, but then returned to ask how far it was to neutral waters. In general he was quite busy through the night, as became clear in the early morning when we transferred from the ship to the Feodosia cutter and a woman's hand waved farewell from the upper deck" (Naiman, "Hava Nagila," 38).

40. Compare this to the more official literature of travel in the Soviet Union as described by Balina, "A Prescribed Journey."

41. See Thomas Venclova's commentary on Brodsky's 1964 "Otryvok" written as reflections of a *Koster*-assigned *kommandirovka* to Pilnau in "'Keningsbergskii tekst' russkoi literatury i keningsbergskie stikhi Iosifa Brodskogo," in *Brodski w analizach i interpretacjach*, ed. Pitora Fatsa and Joanny Madloch (Katowice: Śląsk, 2000), 14–15. For Brodsky's participation in geological expeditions, see Polukhina's chronology ("Khronologiia zhizni i tvorchestva Brodskogo," in *Opyt literaturnoi biografii*, by Lev Loseff [Moscow: Molodaia gvardiia, 2006], 323–424) and Liudmila Shtern's memoir *Brodskii: Osia, Iosif, Joseph* (St. Petersburg: Retro, 2005), 54.

42. I refer to the following poems: "Proshchai," "Pamiati E. A. Baratynskogo," "Vitezslav Nezval," "Uezzhai, uezzhai, uezzhai," "Liubi proezdom rodinu druzei" (from

"Iul'skoe intermetstso"), "Ia kak Uliss," "Uzhe tri mesiatsa podriad," "Instruktsiia opechalennym," "Estonskie derev'ia ozabochenno," "Utrenniaia pochta dlia A. A. Akhmatovoi iz goroda Sestroretska," "Vot ia vnov' prinimaiu parad," "Voron'ia pesnia," "Pesni shchastlivoi zimy," "Proshchal'naia oda," and the 1962 "Otryvok" and "Einem Alten Architekten in Rom," the two last written in Norenskaia but related to Brodsky's 1963 visit to the Kaliningrad region on the *kommandirovka* from *Koster*. The poem related to Pskov, "Pskovskii reestr (dlia M. B.)," was written in Norenskaia, too, but obviously includes reminiscences of an earlier visit to Pskov. The biographical data gathered by Valentina Polukhina in the chronology of Brodsky's life, included in Lev Loseff's *Opyt literaturnoi biografii* (Moscow: Molodaia gvardiia, 2006), shows that Brodsky traveled in the Soviet Union far more extensively than the poems in his Russian *Works* allow one to understand. There are a number of poems, excluded from the Russian *Works* but initially published in the 1965 collection of Brodsky's poems (Iosif Brodskii, *Stikhotvoreniia i poemy* [Washington, D.C.: Inter-Language Literary Associates], 1965), that capture Brodsky's expedition experience and many trips to Moscow.

43. See Brodskii, *Stikhotvoreniia i poemy*, 36, 70.

44. Ibid., 74–75.

45. "Doroga," Vail' and Genis's reminiscence, was "the key word" of the time and signified illusion. They read Brodsky's 1958 "Pilgrimy" ("Pilgrims") and 1961 "Shestvie" ("Procession") as "characteristic of the epoch of movement" (Vail' and Genis, *60-e: Mir sovetskogo cheloveka*, 108).

46. The symbol // indicates a stanza break.

47. The poem's addressee, "O. B.," is most likely Olga Brodovich, then a student and later a specialist in the English language. I owe this observation to the Petersburg poet Sergei Zavialov. The other subtext invoked by the title, James Joyce's *Ulysses*, was widely discussed in Leningrad literary circles, as David MacFadyen's interviews with Brodsky's contemporaries testify, but it was available in Russian translation mostly in Leningrad university and college libraries, which were out of Brodsky's reach (see Lev Loseff in David MacFadyen, *Joseph Brodsky and the Soviet Muse* [Montreal: McGill-Queen's University Press, 2000], 279), and by 1961, when he was starting to learn English, the English original could scarcely have been in his mind.

48. Alfred Tennyson, *Collected Poems* (London: Longman, Green and Co. Ltd, 1969), 561–66.

49. This quotation is from a text published on the Internet at http://imwerden.de/pdf/brodsky_pismo_tomaschewskoi.pdf (accessed April 10, 2009). The original Russian reads: "Ia zhival po-raznomu i poetomu vsem proisshedshem ne ochen' obeskurazhen. O prichinakh ia i vovse ne dumaiu. Po-moemu, nikto ne v chem ne vinovat. Vidimo, slishkom veliko bylo moe *autsaiderstvo*." On the influence of Western cultural practices, such as French existentialism, on Leningrad's unofficial culture, see Stanislav Savitskii, *Andergraund: Istoriia i mify leningradskoi neofitsial'noi literatury* (Moscow: NLO, 2002).

50. Brodsky's fascination with Dos Passos is reflected in an unpublished poem, "Romans o mertvom Parizhe" ("Zhenshchiny Dos Passosa v Parizhe mertvy"),

mentioned in Polukhina's chronology (329) and in Brodsky's own recollections of the exchange his mother and father would have about him: "'Are you reading your Dos Passos again?' she would remark, setting the table. 'Who is going to read Turgenev?' 'What do you expect from him?' my father would echo, folding the paper. 'Loafer is the word'" (*LTO*, 456). For the significance of the Anglo-American modernist canon, especially the restless urban modernism of Dos Passos, and Brodsky's generation of Leningrad writers, see MacFadyen, *Brodsky and the Soviet Muse*, 30–54. For Hemingway, Dos Passos, and other English-language writers seminal to the modernist travel canon, see Fussell's *Abroad*.

51. For T. S. Eliot and modernist travel, see Carr, "Modernism and Travel," 81.

52. On these films' significance for the Thaw period, see Woll, *Real Images*, 142–50, 158–60.

53. See in Greenleaf, *Pushkin and Romantic Fashion*, 208.

54. Brodsky re-evoked this poem in a later autobiographical prose fragment, where he remembers how "one day, when I was fifteen or sixteen, I sat in a courtyard of a huge apartment complex" located "in some grimy industrial outskirt of Leningrad, Russia." Planning to join a geological expedition to the Soviet Far East, he suddenly heard from an open window "A-Tisket, A-Tasket," a jazz tune sung by Ella Fitzgerald (*GR*, 12–13).

55. MacFadyen pairs this poem with an unpublished verse, the first line of which is "Ia—syn predmest'ia, syn predmest'ia, syn predmest'ia" (I am a son of suburb, son of suburb, son of suburb). MacFadyen states that the two poems "form a well-defined poetic stance of 1962"; see MacFadyen, *Brodsky and the Soviet Muse*, 82.

56. For recollections of jazz and its influence on Brodsky's circle of friends and their generation, see Evgenii Rein and Anatolii Naiman in MacFadyen, *Brodsky and the Soviet Muse*, 17–20.

57. Bethea, *Creation of Exile*, 32.

58. MacFadyen, *Brodsky and the Soviet Muse*, 6–7.

59. Valentina Polukhina, *Joseph Brodsky: A Poet for Our Time* (Cambridge: Cambridge University Press, 1989), 237; Kaplan, *Questions of Travel*, 41.

60. See what Vail' and Genis write about Brodsky as the poet who articulated the late 1960s intelligentsia's perception of the Soviet Union as an empire and their sense of imperial despair, chaos, and entropy, in Vail' and Genis, *60-e: Mir sovetskogo cheloveka*, 260–62.

61. For Thomas Venclova on Brodsky's poems about Lithuania, which, apart from the ones written while in the Soviet Union, also include "Litovskii noktiurn: Tomasu Venclova" ("Lithuanian Nocturne"), written in 1973 in emigration, see Venclova's essays in "'Litovskii divertisment' Iosifa Brodskogo," in *The Third Wave: Russian Literature in Emigration*, ed. Olga Matich and Michael Heim (Ann Arbor, Mich.: Ardis, 1984), 191–201, and *Neustoichivoe ravnovesie: Vosem russkikh poeticheskikh tekstov* (New Haven, Conn.: Yale Center for International and Area Studies, 1986), 165–78, and "O stikhotvorenii Iosifa Brodskogo 'Litovskii noktiurn: Tomasu Venclovu,'" *Novoe Literaturnoe Obazrenie* 33, no. 5 (1998): 205–22. The Soviet imperial aspirations were

also ironically expressed in the 1966 poem "Osvoenie kosmosa" ("Invasion of Space"), which addresses not the areas covered by "a sixth of the globe" but the Cold War aspirations to conquer the *kosmos.*

62. According to Polukhina's chronology (in Loseff, *Opyt literaturnoi biografii,* 344), the first trip was related to Brodsky's work on a war film located in Sevastopol.

63. For an English translation of this poem by Glyn Maxwell, see Joseph Brodsky, *Nativity Poems* (New York: Farrar, Straus, and Giroux, 2001), 11.

64. Lidiia Ginzburg, *O lirike* (Moscow: Sovetskii pisatel', 1964), 163.

65. Kaplan, *Questions of Travel,* 28.

66. See, for instance, Yuri Druzhnikov's Pushkin biography, *Prisoner of Russia: Alexander Pushkin and the Political uses of Nationalism,* trans. Thomas Moore and Ilya Druzhnikov (New Brunswick, N.J.: Transaction Publishers, 1999), 119–207.

67. In this respect I disagree with Andrei Ranchin's reading of the poem, in which he sees Brodsky following in Pushkin's steps. See Ranchin's reading in "'Ia rodilsia i vyros v baltiiskikh bolotakh, podle . . .': poeziia Iosifa Brodskogo i 'Mednyi vsadnik' Pushkina," *Novoe literaturnoe obozrenie* 45 (2000): 166–80; esp. 178.

68. Kaplan, *Questions of Travel,* 53.

69. See John Givens's enlightening reading of Brodsky's "Kvintet/Sextet" against Mark Strand's poetry in "The Anxiety of a Dedication: Joseph Brodsky's 'Kvintet/Sextet' and Mark Strand," *Russian Literature* 37 (1995): 203–26.

70. See, for instance, Monica Greenleaf's discussion of Pushkin and the Oriental poem in Greenleaf, *Pushkin and Romantic Fashion,* 108–55.

71. Elizabeth Bishop, *The Complete Poems 1927–1979* (London: The Hogarth Press, 1984), 93–94.

72. Mandelstam's preoccupation with naturalists and biological evolution in the travel essay "Journey to Armenia" and the poem "Lamark" ("Lamarck") come to mind; see more on this in chap. 5 on Brodsky and Orientalism.

73. See also the poem "Pamiati ottsa: Avstraliia" ("In memory of my father: Australia").

74. See Readings, *Introduction to Lyotard,* 63–85.

75. Holland and Huggan, *Tourists with Typewriters,* 23.

76. Claude Lévi-Strauss, *Tristes Tropiques,* trans. John and Doreen Wieghtman (London: Pan Books, 1989).

77. Fussell, *Abroad,* 38.

78. For a concise discussion of the Platonic idea of a copy in relation to Baudrillard and Deleuze, see John Frow, "Tourism and the Semiotics of Nostalgia," *October* 57 (1991): 126–27.

79. Brodsky's self-conscious nostalgia resembles the "reflective" nostalgia that Svetlana Boym assigns to one end of the paradigm of nostalgia she launches in *Future of Nostalgia,* with the other being "restorative" nostalgia. The latter, she argues, is the force underscoring nationalist movements "reconstructing emblems and rituals of home and homeland in an attempt to conquer and spatialize time," whereas "reflective nostalgia cherishes shattered fragments of memory and temporalizes space. Restorative

nostalgia takes itself dead seriously. Reflective nostalgia, on the other hand, can be ironic and humorous. . . . [It] does not pretend to rebuild the mythical place called home. . . . [Its] nostalgic narrative is ironic, inconclusive, and fragmentary." Boym relates this paradigm to Freud's dichotomy of grief and melancholy: "Reflective nostalgia has elements of both mourning and melancholia. While its loss is never completely recalled, it has some connection to the loss of collective frameworks of memory. Reflective nostalgia is a form of deep mourning that performs a labor of grief both through pondering pain and through play that points to the future" (Boym, *The Future of Nostalgia*, 49–50, 55).

80. Kaplan, *Questions of Travel*, 50.

81. Layton, *Russian Literature and Empire*, 24.

82. W. H. Auden and Louis MacNeice, *Letters from Iceland* (New York: Random House, 1969), esp. 21, 23–24.

83. Solomon Volkov, *Conversations with Joseph Brodsky: A Poet's Journey through the Twentieth Century* (New York: Free Press, 1998), 129.

Chapter 2. A Travel Guide to Imperial Mythologies

1. There are many scholarly analyses of Brodsky's use of empire as a metaphysical concept; see, for instance, Dan Ungurianu, "The Wandering Greek: Images of Antiquity in Joseph Brodsky" in *Russian Literature and the Classics*, ed. Peter I. Barta, David H. J. Larmour, Paul Allen Miller (Amsterdam: Hardwood Academic Publishers, 1996). Ungurianu, echoing many other scholars, captures the metaphysical significations the concept of empire has in Brodsky's works: "The concept of empire is not purely political, but rather philosophical; it is an existential category based on his [Brodsky's] view of time, space, and death" (166). Rather than the transcendent, the focus of my discussion is, however, on the worldly significations of the imperial theme in Brodsky's works. For the significance of "empire" in post-Stalin unofficial discourses, on the one hand, and for the ambiguity of "empire" as an analytical tool on the other, see introduction (p. 13), 232n22, and 233n27 in this book.

2. For the Russian text, see *Sochineniia* 7, 223–79, and for the English, Joseph Brodsky, *Marbles* (New York: Farrar, Straus and Giroux, 1989).

3. Valentina Polukhina approaches empire in Brodsky's works as one of his "principal conceptual metaphors." She analyzes a number of Brodsky's poems and points out how he uses empire mostly as a "metaphor for a system of government which is inimical to the human personality," and then moves on to discuss the theme of empire in Brodsky's play *Mramor* to show how Brodsky, through his metaphysical contemplation of "Empire," ends up condemning it. See Valentina Polukhina, *Joseph Brodsky: A Poet for Our Time* (Cambridge: Cambridge University Press, 1989), 195–210. For another enlightening commentary on the metaphysics of empire in Brodsky's play, see Petr Vail' and Aleksandr Genis, "Ot mira—k Rimu," in *Poetika Brodskogo*, ed. Lev Losev (Tenafly: Ermitazh, 1986), 198–206.

4. Brodsky evokes this paradigm in the play also by referring to the turn-of-the-century debate about the Scythians through a quotation from an Anna Akhmatova

poem. On this in more detail, see George Nivat, "An Ironic Journey into Antiquity," in *Brodsky's Poetics and Aethetics*, ed. Lev Loseff and Valentina Polukhina (Houndmills: Macmillan, 1990), 92.

5. See Vail' and Genis, *60-e*, 262.

6. Brodsky's identification with Propertius not only reflected his nonofficial status in terms of the official Soviet cultural politics but also disclosed a marginalization of a different kind. In "Anno Domini" (1968) the allusions to Propertius convey an image of a poet whose role as a social outcast in the intellectual circles was generated by his literary, as well as his amatory, behavior. The lyric plot takes place in an imaginary Roman province transposed on the geographical hierarchies of the Soviet empire; the contemporary counterpart of the historical Roman province is Soviet Lithuania, identified at the end of the poem through the dating, "January 1968, Palanga." The lyric subject is paralleled first with a governor-general ("namestnik"), fallen out of Caesar's grace, and eventually the speaker comes forth as relating himself to Propertius, (in)famous among his contemporaries for provoking a scandalous image of a lyric subject and his relations with the unreciprocating Cynthia, as Propertius calls the addressee of his love elegies and as Brodsky calls the spouse/mistress of his lyric subject, cf. chap. 1, p. 40, in this book.

7. On Michelina and her real-life model, see Vail's interview with Brodsky in Iosif Brodskii, *Peresechennaia mestnost'*, ed. Petr Vail' (Moscow: Nezavisimaia gazeta, 1995), 177.

8. Here follows C. E. Bennett's English translation of those lines in Horace's Ode that are particularly relevant to Brodsky's essay: "Not for ever do the showers fall from the clouds on the sodden fields, nor the rough blasts always fret the Caspian waves, nor on Armenian borders, friend Valgius, does the lifeless ice linger through every month, nor are Garganus' oak-groves always lashed by the blasts of the North and the ash-trees reft of their leaves. . . . Cease at length thy weak laments, and let us rather sing of the new trophies of Augustus Caesar, ice-bound Niphates and the river of the Medes rolling in smaller eddies, now 'tis added to the list of vanquished nations, and the Geloni riding now within bounds prescribed over their narrowed plains" (Horace, *The Odes and Epodes* [Cambridge, Mass.: Harvard University Press, 1968], 129).

9. Hyperborea was the name of the land in the north in Greek and Roman geographies and mythologies.

10. *Niphates* refers to a range of mountains in Armenia, and *Geloni* to a Scythian people.

11. Patrick Colm Hogan's term "reference set," in discussing Walcott's appropriation of Western literary tradition, points to the affinity between the strategies of identity-creation between Walcott and Brodsky, even if the English-language culture was the colonizer's culture for Walcott, and the desired adopted culture for Brodsky (cf. 229n3 in this book). In Hogan's definition reference sets are "of central importance to cultural and literary self-evaluation and thus to cultural and literary identity. . . . Reference sets enter into the creation of individual works by establishing models, standards of comparison (which guide an author at each stage of composition), and

so on" (159). Clearly, John Donne and W. H. Auden, for instance, offered for Brodsky exactly this kind of reference set.

12. Brodsky's fascination with imperial pomp and power and its aesthetic articulations is implied in Daniel Weissbort's recollection of Brodsky's first visit to London, recorded in an essay about Brodsky's funeral in Venice: "I recalled Joseph's adoration of England, the land of John Donne. . . . London, in fact, is where I met him shortly after his expulsion from the Soviet Union, when Auden brought him to Poetry International, for his first reading in the West. Jan Morris has pointed out that 'Everywhere in Venice there are still reminders of her political prime, like India Offices in Whitehall,' and I'm reminded also of an amble through Whitehall with Joseph, on that first visit. We paused before the Foreign Office, Joseph remarking that it was a pity Great Britain had given up its Empire, to which I could not help responding that perhaps it had not been entirely voluntary. Evidently we came at this from different places" (Daniel Weissbort, *Times Literary Supplement*, July 7, 2000, 15).

13. See M. Yu. Lotman and B. A. Uspenski, "Rol' dual'nykh modelei v dinamike russkoi kul'tury," in *Istoriia i tipologiia russkoi kul'tury* (St. Petersburg: Iskusstvo-SPB, 2002), 106. In English, see "The Role of Dual Models in the Dynamics of Russian Culture (Up to the End of the Eighteenth Century)," in *The Semiotics of Russian Culture*, ed. Ann Shukman (Ann Arbor: Dept. of Slavic Languages and Literatures, Univeristy of Michigan, 1984), 26.

14. See Chaadaev's first letter in P. Ya. Chaadaev, *Philosophical Letters and Apology of a Madman*, trans. Mary-Barbara Zeldin (Knoxville: University of Tennessee Press, 1969), 33–51, esp. 40.

15. On the uses of the Kafkaesque perception of the Soviet empire among the *shestidesiatniki*, see Vail' and Genis, *60-e*, 260.

16. As Harsha Ram observes: "The task of representing and propagating a discourse of empire under Peter devolved primarily onto two realms, the visual arts, architecture, and spectacle, on the one hand, and panegyric prose, on the other. . . . Panegyric oratory . . . became a powerful tool for the festive propagation of Petrine ideology, and a significant precursor to the victory ode" (Harsha Ram, *The Imperial Sublime: A Russian Poetics of Empire* [Madison: University of Wisconsin Press, 2003], 31–32).

17. Buckler, *Mapping St. Petersburg*, 89–90.

18. Ibid., 35–36, 108–12. By "preservationists" Buckler refers to Katerina Clark's discussion of the movement in her *Petersburg, Crucible of Cultural Revolution* (Cambridge, Mass.: Harvard University Press, 1995), 54–73.

19. In the case of Lotman, consider, for instance, his perception of the "antithesis between water and stone" as the "realization of the struggle between nature and culture," seminal to his reading of the Petersburg myth in the article "Simvolika Peterburga i semiotika goroda," which echoes Antsiferov's observation of the city as an "antithesis to its natural environment." Furthermore, Antsiferov's approach to the literary space of the city points the way to the view that there exists a coded way of reading the cityscape of Petersburg, an idea that V. N. Toporov developed into the scholarly concept of "peterburgskii tekst" ("Petersburg text"). Yuri M. Lotman's and

Toporov's writings on the topic were initially published in *Semiotika goroda i gorodskoi kul'tury*, in *Tartu riikliku ülikooli toimetised*, Vihik 664 (Tartu: University of Tartu Press, 1984). Toporov's series of articles on the concept of the "peterburgskii tekst" have been republished as one book in V. N. Toporov, *Peterburgskii tekst russkoi literatury: Izbrannye trudy* (Iskusstvo: Petersburg, 2003), 7–108. For an English-language article on Lotman's and Toporov's approaches, see Pekka Pesonen, "Semiotics of a City: The Myth of St. Petersburg in Andrey Bely's Novel *Petersburg*," in *Teksty zhizni i iskusstva: Texts of Life and Art* (Helsinki: Department of Slavonic and Baltic Languages and Literatures, 1997), 129–45. These scholarly approaches to Petersburg have also inspired an investigation of Brodsky's poems about Leningrad/Petersburg; see Maija Könönen, *Four Ways of Writing a City: St. Petersburg-Leningrad as a Metaphor in the Poetry of Joseph Brodsky* (Helsinki: Department of Slavonic and Baltic Languages and Literatures, 2003), esp. 17–91. See also Andrew Reynolds, "Returning the Ticket: Joseph Brodsky's 'August' and the End of the Petersburg Text?" *Slavic Review* 64, no. 2 (2005): 307–32.

20. On uses of antiquity in imperial aesthetics, see Greenleaf, *Pushkin and the Romantic Fashion*, 57.

21. On eclecticism and Petersburg acrhitecture, see Buckler, *Mapping St. Petersburg*, 27–60.

22. Quoted in Efim Etkind, "Oligarkhicheskaia estetika," in *Peterburg—okno v Evropu*, Studia Slavica Finlandensia 13, ed. Natalia Baschmakoff (Helsinki: Institute for Russian and East European Studies, 1996), 58.

23. Buckler, *Mapping St. Petersburg*, 35. Buckler observes the tendency to imagine the architectural Petersburg as "frozen" in the classical Pushkinian era in the works of some leading twentieth-century intellectuals: she specifically refers to Yuri Lotman's evocations of the city in "Simvolika Peterburga i semiotika goroda" and to Brodsky's in "A Guide to a Renamed City." The retrospective glance superimposes the Pushkinian Petersburg onto the contemporary perception of the city—this characterizes Efim Etkind's authorial views of Petersburg, too, in his discussion of the *stroinost'* of the Petersburgian aesthetics; see Etkind, "Oligarkhicheskaia estetika."

24. K. Clark, *Petersburg*, 54–73.

25. Aleksandr Benois, "Zhivopisnyi Peterburg," *Mir iskusstva* 1 (1902): 1–5.

26. Benois' works were removed from the cultural scene with the rise of the Stalinist culture (Benois himself emigrated in 1926 and died in Paris in 1960), but they re-entered the Russian intellectual scene in the 1960s. His rehabilitation was signalled by the publication of two books. In 1965 there was the lavish edition of Benois' life and works by Mark Etkind, which still bore the Soviet bias to Benois' significance, but had extracts of "Zhivopisnyi Peterburg" ("Painterly Petersburg"). The 1968 *Aleksandr Benua razmyshliaet* (*Thoughts by Aleksandr Benois*) sought to overturn the bias and restore Benois' place among Russian artists and art critics by focusing on his post-1917 writings. See *Aleksandr Nikolaevitsh Benua, 1870–1960*, ed. Mark Etkind (Leningrad-Moscow: Izdatel'stvo Iskusstvo, 1965); I. S. Zil'bershtein and A. N. Savinov, eds., *Aleksandr Benua razmyshliaet. . . .* (Moscow: Sovetskii Khudozhnik, 1968).

27. Nikolai Antsiferov, *Dusha Peterburga* (Paris: YMCA-Press, 1978 [1922]). On the significance of the publication of the reprint from an émigré perspective, see Dmitrii Bobyshev's article "Dusha Peterburga v nebesnom i zemnom voploshcheniiakh," in *Moi Peterburg* (Moscow: Elle/Vargius, 2003), 102–9.

28. Ibid., 33–34.

29. Benois, "Zhivopisnyi Peterburg," 3.

30. For the uses of the myth of the "one sixth" in Soviet cinema see Emma Widdis, *Visions of the New Land: Soviet Film from the Revolution to the Second World War* (New Haven, Conn: Yale University Press, 2003). In the essay Brodsky does not, in my view, refer to the myth of the "one-sixth" in order to subvert Soviet rhetoric by embracing its mythologies, a device he appropriated, for instance, in "The End of Beautiful Era," where he refers to the world outside the Soviet Union as "piaterka shestykh ostaiushchikhsia v mire chastei" (2:312) ("five-sixths of remaining landmass" [39]).

31. In the narrative of his life-story that Brodsky created in his autobiographical poems and essays, he associated his own interest in geography with his father, who "held two degrees: in geography, from Leningrad University, and in journalism, from the School of Red Journalism" (*LTO*, 461). See also the poem "Pamiati ottsa: Avstraliia" ("In memory of my father: Australia").

32. K. Clark, *Petersburg*, 9.

33. David MacFadyen, *Joseph Brodsky and the Baroque* (Montreal: McGill-Queen's University Press, 1998), 173.

34. The panegyric vision of the North provided seminal symbolic imagery for Russian imperial discourse: Catherine II was referred to as "Semiramis severa" (Semiramis of the North), Lomonosov was known as "Severnyi Pindar" (the Northern Pindar), and Petersburg as "Severnaia Palmira" (Northern Palmyra), "Severnyi Rim" (Northern Rome), or simply, "Severa stolitsa" (the capital of the North).

35. See Otto Boele, *The North in Russian Romantic Literature* (Rodopi: Amsterdam, 1996), 26, 30–31.

36. See Vail' and Genis, *60-e*, 69–75. On the Russian expansion eastward, see J. L. Black, "Opening up Siberia: Russia's 'Window on the East,'" in *The History of Siberia: From Russian Conquest to Revolution*, ed. Alan Wood (Routledge: London, 1991), 57–68.

37. Joost van Baak makes this observation in "'Northern Cultures' What Could This Mean? About the North as a Cultural Concept," *Tijdschrift voor Skandinavistiek* 16, no. 2 (1995): 25–26.

38. On the concept of the north in Brodsky's poetry, see Joost van Baak, "Brodsky and the North," in *Neo-Formalist Papers: Contributions to the Silver Jubilee Conference to Mark 25 Years of the Neo-Formalist Circle*, ed. Joe Andrews and Robert Reid (Rodopi: Amsterdam, 1998), 242–68.

39. G. P. Fedotov, *Sud'ba i grekhi Rossii: izbrannye stat'i po filosofii istorii i kul'tury v dvukh tomakh*, vol. 1 (St. Petersburg: Izdatel'stvo Sofiia, 1991), 51. I owe this observation to Denis Akhapkin.

40. Osip Mandelstam, "Pushkin and Scriabin," in *The Complete Critical Prose and Letters* (Ann Arbor, Mich.: Ardis, 1979), 91, 94–95. On Mandelstam and the ideal of

Greek harmony, see B. M. Gasparov, "Russkaia Gretsiia, russkii Rim," in *Christianity and the Eastern Slavs*, vol. 2, *Russian Culture and Modern Times*, ed. Robert P. Hughes and Irina Paperno (Berkeley: University of California Press, 1994), 278–79.

41. M. Gasparov, "Poeziia Goratsiia," in *Kvint Goratsii Flakk: Ody, epody, satiry, poslaniia* (Moscow: Khudozhestvennaia literature, 1970). Quoted here from the website http://www.philology.ru/literature3/gasparov-70.htm (accessed April 10, 2008).

42. Quoted in Greenleaf, *Pushkin and the Romantic Fashion*, 365n18.

Chapter 3. A Postcolonial Elegy

1. For the circumstances of Brodsky's visit to Mexico, see Brodsky's own account in an interview with Petr Vail' in Brodskii, *Peresechennaia mestnost'*, 158–59. Octavio Paz recalls his acquaintance with Brodsky in an interview with Michael Ignateff in *Iosif Brodskii: trudy i dni*, ed. Lev Loseff and Petr Vail' (Moscow: Nezavisimaia gazeta, 1998), 256–58. For the details of Mayakovsky's trip to the Americas, see Charles A. Moser, "Mayakovsky's Unsentimental Journeys," *American Slavic and East European Review* 19, no. 1 (1960): 85–100; Edward J. Brown, *Mayakovsky: A Poet in the Revolution* (Princeton, N.J.: Princeton University Press, 1973), 261–64.

2. Lev Loseff has observed that Brodsky, in such poems as "Speech on Spilt Milk," "Letter to General Z," and "The End of a Beautiful Era," anticipated "the rhetoric of the anti-*zastoi* (stagnation) which gained currency in Soviet society some twenty years later." See Lev Loseff, "Politics/Poetics," in *Brodsky's Poetics and Aesthetics*, ed. Lev Loseff and Valentina Polukhina (London: Macmillan, 1990), 51. As for Brodsky's concern over Leningrad intellectuals' suppression: in 1975 Brodsky was trying to draw Western public attention to Vladimir Maramzin's case by writing letters to the *New York Review of Books* and *Le Monde*. Maramzin, who had gathered Brodsky's poetry into a four-volume *samizdat* collection, was arrested in 1974. Mikhail Kheifets, the author of the *samizdat* article "Joseph Brodsky and His Generation," was also arrested, and apart from being occupied by these incidents, Brodsky was actively participating in the Russian émigré scene in the States and in Europe by becoming, for instance, a member of the editorial board of *Kontinent*, founded in Paris in 1975 (see Polukhina's chronology of Brodsky's life in Valentina Polukhina, "Khronologiia zhizni i tvorchestva Brodskogo," in *Opyt literaturnoi biografii*, ed. Lev Loseff (Moscow: Molodaia gvardiia, 2006), 364.

3. V. V. Mayakovsky, *Sobranie sochinenii v vos'mi tomakh*, vol. 4 (Moscow: Izdatel'stvo Pravda, 1968), 343. All quotations of Mayakovsky's poems are from this edition, and the translations are mine.

4. Mayakovsky had visited Latvia three years before his visit to Mexico and reflected on his impressions in a poem titled "How a Democratic Republic Works," in which Latvia is presented as an example of bourgeois unfreedom. On Mayakovsky and Latvia, see Moser, "Mayakovsky's Unsentimental Journeys," 87.

5. For early Soviet perceptions of Latin America, see Russell H. Bartley's "Introduction," in *Soviet Historians on Latin America: Recent Scholarly Contributions*, ed. Russell H. Bartley (Madison: University of Wisconsin Press, 1978), 3–29. Russian preoccupation

with Latin American affairs goes much farther than the early Soviet interest; for a historic overview, see L. A. Shur, *Rossiia i Latinskaia Amerika* (Moscow: Izdatel'stvo sotsial'no-ekonomicheskoi literatury "Mysl'," 1964). Shur's "Conclusions" is itself an expression of post-Stalin interest in Latin America inspired by the Cuban revolution (153).

6. This passage is from an interview with Petr Vail' (Brodskii, *Peresechennaia mestnost'. Puteshestviia s kommentariami*, 158). Vail' himself made the parallel between a Latin American country and a Soviet Central Asian republic with his cowriter Aleksandr Genis, when, recalling the reception of the Cuban revolution in the 1960s Soviet Union, they place Cuba on their imaginative map shaped by a Soviet metropolitan perspective: "The Soviet Union could have fitted Cuba in the Tajik Soviet Socialist Republic" (Vail' and Genis, *60-e*, 41).

7. The statue on top of the column called *El Ángel de la Independencia* is, in fact, a statue of a winged goddess of victory.

8. Mikhail Kreps draws a similar conclusion in his reading of "Encyclopedia Entry" in Kreps, *Poetika Brodskogo*, 244–45.

9. Susan Layton (*Russian Literature and Empire*) shows how central and how well-popularized the argument of imperialism's "civilizing mission" in Russia became in the course of the nineteenth century—often in relation to the Caucasus.

10. For Said the concept of "textual attitude" is seminal to the production of imperial knowledge and to how that knowledge is established as a "discourse" in the Foucauldian sense, and travel writing has an important role to play in these processes; see Said, *Orientalism*, 92–94. Cf. also n. 23 in the introduction to this book.

11. Both James Fenimore Cooper's and Mayne Reid's novels were important in popularizing the Euroimperial viewpoint of the New World, and their Russian translations, as Mayakovsky's poem attests, shaped the knowledge about Latin America of the generation of leading modernists. Nabokov writes in *Speak, Memory* that "The Wild West fiction of Captain Mayne Reid (1818–83), translated and simplified, was tremendously popular with Russian children at the beginning of this century, long after his American fame had faded," and a page later Nabokov, too, recalls his own childhood games inspired by Mayne Reid. See Vladimir Nabokov, *Speak, Memory* (London: Weidenfeld and Nicolson, 1967), 195–97.

12. David Rigsbee, the author of a monograph focusing on the elegiac aspects of Brodsky's poetry, excludes it, too, from the poetic corpus he examines. See Rigsbee, *Styles of Ruin*.

13. L. G. Frizman, *Zhizn' liricheskogo zhanra: russkaia elegiia ot Sumarokova do Nekrasova* (Moscow: Izdatel' tsvo Nauka, 1973), 12–13.

14. Bethea, *Creation of Exile*, 120–21.

15. While Mexican themes appear in Russian poetry before Brodsky (Mayakovsky's cycle is a powerful example), I have not been able to detect a Russian-language poem about Mexico that could be ascribed to the elegiac tradition, which Brodsky's "Cuernavaca" draws from. For Mexican themes in Russian modernist poetry, see Roman Timenchik's article, "'1867,'" in *Joseph Brodsky: The Art of a Poem*, ed. Lev Loseff and Valentina Polukhina (Houndmills: Palgrave, 1999), 63–66.

16. This summary is based on *The Course of Mexican History*, ed. Michael C. Meyer and William L. Sherman (Oxford: Oxford University Press, 1983), 385–401. See also Henry Bamford Parkes, *A History of Mexico* (1938; repr., Boston: Houghton Mifflin, 1969). I have used Parkes's book as one of my sources, since it is a classic textbook of Mexican history and appeared in Russian translation in the postwar Soviet Union, and was thus a book Brodsky possibly knew. For a more contemporary biography of Maximilian, see Jasper Ridley, *Maximilian and Juárez* (London: Constable, 1993).

17. About this extravagance Henry Parkes writes: "During his [Maximilian's] first six months in Mexico he gave seventy lunches, twenty banquets, sixteen balls, and twelve receptions, and his wine bill during his first year exceeded one hundred thousand pesos" (Parkes, *History of Mexico*, 264).

18. See ibid., 265.

19. According to Parkes, Maximilian, when surrounded by Juárez's republican troops, sent one of his trusted men to acquire more men and money, and "for Maximilian—books and piano music and a supply of burgundy" (ibid., 272).

20. In the English version the Russian "mulatka" is translated into the ethnically unmarked "gorgeous."

21. http://www.bobak.ru/story_jarhmark.shtml (accessed April 20, 2008). Here follows the lyric of Beethoven's "Marmotte": "Ich komme schon durch manches Land / Avec que la marmotte / Und immer was zu essen fand / Avec que la marmotte / Avec que sí / Avec que là /Avec que la marmotte" ("Through many a land have I passed / with the marmot / Always finding something to eat / with the marmot / Here with the marmot, there with the marmot / Everywhere, with the marmot") (http://www.recmusic.org/lieder/get_text.html?TextId=6287 [accessed April 10, 2008]).

22. On the myth see Ram, *Imperial Sublime*, 205–6.

23. Mikhail Gasparov, *Sovremennyi russkii stikh: metrika i ritmika* (Moscow: Izdatel'stvo Nauka, 1974), 8.

24. Mikhail Gasparov, *Ocherk istorii russkogo stikha: metrika, ritmika, rifma, strofika* (Moscow: Izdatel'stvo Nauka, 1984), 115–17.

25. See Roman Timenchik's fine commentary on this in Timenchik, "'1867,'" 59–67.

26. Greenleaf, *Pushkin and the Romantic Fashion*, 89.

27. Jahan Ramazani, *Poetry of Mourning: the Modern Elegy from Hardy to Heaney* (Chicago: University of Chicago Press, 1994), 8.

28. I have in mind Fredric Jameson's definition of pastiche: "Pastiche is, like parody, the imitation of a peculiar or unique style, the wearing of a stylistic mask, speech in dead language: but it is a neutral practice of such mimicry, without parody's ulterior motive, without the satirical impulse, without laughter, without that still latent feeling that there exists something *normal* compared to which what is being imitated is rather comic" (Jameson, "Postmodernism and Consumer Society," 114).

29. Ram, *Imperial Sublime*, 211.

30. In the context of Western cultural practices, within which Brodsky's Russian cycle was articulated and into which it was integrated through translation, the elegiac pastiche in "Cuernavaca" resembles the aesthetic mode of expression which Renato

Rosaldo in another context has termed as "imperialist nostalgia." Rosaldo's postcolonial critique was prompted by a group of British, American, and South African popular films of the 1980s where the collapse of white colonial societies was portrayed in an "elegiac mode of perception." Brodsky represents Mexico's colonial past in the same elegiacally stylized manner as the films discussed by Rosaldo. See Renato Rosaldo, *Culture and Truth: the Remaking of Social Analysis* (Boston: Beacon Press, 1984), 68–70. See also Holland and Huggan's discussion of imperialist nostalgia in English-language travel writing (*Tourists with Typewriters*, 29–30).

31. Joseph Brodsky, *A Part of Speech* (Oxford: Oxford University Press, 1980), 151.

32. Timenchik's detailed analysis of the intertexts Brodsky uses in the poem shows how all cultural references in the poem are, in fact, European and Russian representations of Latin America, even if Timenchik does not point this out. See Timenchik, "'1867.'"

Chapter 4. The Metropolitan Man and the Third World

1. See Holland and Huggan, *Tourists with Typewriters*, 27–65

2. See Layton, *Russian Literature and Empire*, esp. 175–91.

3. The highly ironic "imperial imposture" that Holland and Huggan (*Tourists with Typewriters*, 44–45) have detected in V. S. Naipaul's appropriation of the English gentleman traveler reminds one of Brodsky's elegiac identity in "Cuernavaca."

4. Bitov's *Uroki Armenii* (*Lessons of Armenia*) and *Gruzinskii al'bom* (*Georgian Album*) are abundant with examples of the "gentleman-colonizer's" authoritative gaze, of which the author is painfully aware, but does not want to, or makes the appearance of not being able to, rid himself of. In English see Andrei Bitov, *A Captive of the Caucasus*, trans. Susan Brownsberger (New York: Farrar, Straus and Giroux, 1992).

5. Bethea's discussion refers to the following theses in Said's *The World, the Text and the Critic*: "Culture is used to designate not merely something to which one belongs but something one possesses and, along with that proprietary process, culture also designates a boundary by which the concepts of what is extrinsic and intrinsic to the culture come into forceful play. . . . This means that culture is a system of discriminations and evaluations . . . for a particular class in the State able to identify with it; and it also means that culture is a system of exclusions legislated from above but enacted throughout its polity, by which such things as anarchy, disorder, irrationality, inferiority, bad taste, and immorality are identified, then deposited outside the culture and kept there by the power of the State and its institutions" (quoted in Bethea, *Creation of Exile*, 44, 45).

6. Pratt, *Imperial Eyes*, 201–27, esp. 204–5, 217.

7. I have not been able to establish why this poem is not included in the English cycle. According to Alan Myers, who co-translated the cycle with Brodsky, "In the Hotel 'Continental'" was not included in the materials he received from Brodsky (personal correspondence, Alan Myers to ST).

8. Patrick Holland and Graham Huggan have pointed out that the cultural voyeurism of travel writers takes many forms and often eroticizes their work, even when an erotic encounter is not the subject (*Tourists with Typewriters*, 18).

9. For the "discourse of negation" and the "theme of historical lack" in colonial discourse see David Spurr, *The Rhetoric of Empire: Colonial Discourse in Journalism, Travel Writing and Imperial Administration* (Durham, N.C.: Duke University Press, 1993), 92–108, esp. 98–102.

10. Urania, the muse of astronomy in Greek mythology, was a central image for Brodsky's poetic imagination. He used it extensively as a metaphor for space and geography. It appears in the title of his 1987 Russian collection, and his second English collection of poetry.

11. Pratt, *Imperial Eyes*, 219.

12. Ibid., 218.

13. Consider the long tradition of European Orientalization of Russia. One of the most influential texts in forming European opinion about Russian has been the Marquise de Custine's travelogue of 1839, *La Russie en 1839* (published in English under such titles as *Empire of the Czar: A Journey through the Eternal Russia* and *Letters from Russia*), with its characterization of Russians as "Orientals," "Tartars," and "bears." For a discussion of the European Orientalization of Russia and its impact on Russian self-definitions and intellectual formations, see Layton, *Russian Literature and Empire*, 79–81.

14. Pratt, *Imperial Eyes*, 220.

15. Mogadishu is the capital of Somalia, which, in the 1970s, was a socialist state and an ally of the Soviet Union. Why Brodsky uses Ivory Coast as the other generalizing example of an African country in this context is unclear to me; Ivory Coast was not one of the African countries included in the Soviet bloc.

16. Holland and Huggan, *Tourists with Typewriters*, 25.

Chapter 5. Time, Space, and Orientalism

1. The English translation, which appeared in the *New Yorker* in 1985, was made by Alan Myers on Brodsky's initiative, but the title was Brodsky's. The changes to the English translation printed later in *Less Than One* were made by Brodsky (personal correspondence, Alan Myers to ST). My reading of Brodsky's essay is based on the version Brodsky edited for *Less Than One*.

2. The Russian text was reprinted in the journal *Petropol'* (3 [1991]: 33–66), the anthology *Gorod i mir* (Leningrad, 1991), and a 1990 Estonian publication of Brodsky's selected works with commentaries (*Iosif Brodskii: razmerom podlinnika* [Tallin, 1990]), and more recently in the second edition of Brodsky's Russian *Works* in Iosif Brodskii, *Sochineniia Iosifa Brodskogo*, vol. 5, 281–314. For the Italian and German translations, see *Fuga da Bisanzio* (Milan: Adelphi, 1987), and *Flucht aus Byzanz* (Munich: Hanser Verlag, 1988).

3. For Russian responses to Brodsky's essay, see, for instance, the Petersburg scholar Igor Sukhikh's commentary; Sukhikh points to the "strangeness" of Brodsky's text, which has to do with the fact that it is constructed on the "associative laws of verse." See Igor' Sukhikh, "Puteshestvie v Stambul (o poetike prozy I. Brodskogo)," in *Iosif Brodskii: tvorchestvo, lichnost', sud'ba* (St. Petersburg: Zhurnal Zvezda, 1998),

232–36. Valentina Polukhina seeks to make a similar point in "The Prose of Joseph Brodsky: A Continuation of Poetry by Other Means," when she quotes a passage on ornamentation from "Flight from Byzantium" to present it as a "key to an understanding of the poetic structure of Brodsky's prose" (claiming erroneously that Brodsky is writing about Eastern ornamentation, when the sentences she cites in fact refer to Brodsky's notions of Western ornaments; see *Russian Literature* 41 [1997]: 223–40, esp. 226). What catches Katherine Tiernan O'Connor's attention in the same passage, on the other hand, is the way Brodsky establishes a cultural dichotomy to exhibit his preference for the West over the East; see Katherine Tiernan O'Connor, "From Kabul to Byzantium and Back," in "A Forum on Politics in Poetry," *Russian Review* 61, no. 2 (2002): 201–11, esp. 210. O'Connor is one of the contributors to the roundtable discussion of Brodsky's poem "On the Talks in Kabul" published in the *Russian Review*, with many of the participants setting the poem against the background of "Flight from Byzantium." The other contributors included David Bethea, Catherine Ciepiela, Sarah Pratt, Stephanie Sandler, G. S. Smith (the term "sustained jeremiad" belongs to him), and Michael Wachtel. On Bethea's comments on "Flight from Byzantium," see also Bethea, *Creation of Exile*, 51–52, 209–11. The Lithuanian poet Thomas Venclova, writing from the viewpoint of Russian-language culture, starts his discussion of Brodsky's essay by pointing to its "strangeness" and "idiosyncrasy" in much the same way as Sukhikh does. Venclova focuses on stylistic questions but discusses also what he calls Brodsky's "fundamental, but controversial, philosophy of history," which, as Venclova acknowledges, has "shocked some critics" (Thomas Venclova, "Journey from Leningrad to Istanbul," in Losef and Polukhina, *Brodsky's Aesthetics and Poetics*, 135–49).

4. Since Edward Said's influential *Orientalism* (1978), it has become nearly impossible to use the term in reference to "Oriental" languages and cultures without invoking Said's views. In Said's conception the "Orient" is a metaphor; it is the "other" against which Western identity is constructed, while "Orientalism" refers to the discursive power imbedded in the system of knowledge about the "Orient." "Orientalism," as Said writes, "is a system of representations framed by a whole set of forces that brought the Orient into Western learning, Western consciousness, and later, Western empire" (Said, *Orientalism*, 202–3). Applying Said's critique to Russian attitudes towards Russia's "Orients" has confirmed, in some critics' minds, the view that Russian imperial attitudes to the Caucasus and Central Asia were comparable with European attitudes to its colonies. For thoughtful adaptation of Said from this viewpoint into the study of Russian nineteenth-century literature, see Layton, *Russian Literature and Empire*, and Greenleaf, *Pushkin and the Romantic Fashion*, esp. 108–55; see also Sara Dickinson, "Russia's First 'Orient': Characterizing the Crimea in 1787," *Kritika* 3, no. 1 (2002): 3–25. Meanwhile, some historians have raised questions about the applicability of Said's model to the Russian situation, drawing attention to the specifics of the relation between power and knowledge in imperial Russia; Nathaniel Knight takes this viewpoint in the scrupulous case study "Grigor'ev in Orienburg, 1851–1862: Russian Orientalism in Service of Empire?" *Slavic Review* 59, no. 1 (2000): 74–100. For more on the topic of Russia and "Orientalism," see Kalpana Sahni, *Crucifying the Orient*

(Bangkok: White Orchid Press, 1997); Vera Tolz, *Inventing the Nation: Russia* (London: Arnold, 2001), 132–51; David Schimmenpenninck van der Oye, "Orientalizm—delo tonkoe," *Ab Imperio* 1 (2002): 249–64; Aleksander Etkind, "Bremia britogo cheloveka, ili vnutrenniaia kolonizatsiia Rossii," *Ab Imperio* 1 (2002): 264–98.

5. Venclova, "Journey from Leningrad," 137.

6. Schönle, *Authenticity and Fiction*, 1–16. Schönle situates in the Sternian space of irony such Russian travel texts as Pushkin's "Journey to Arzrum" and "Journey from Moscow to Petersburg," Gogol's "Journey from Lausanne to Vevey. Letter to M. P. Balabina," and a series of other post-Sentimentalist nineteenth-century travelogues such as A. F. Vel'tman's *The Wanderer* and O. I. Senkovskii's *The Fantastic Journeys of Baron Brambeus*. See also Roboli, "The Literature of Prose," 45–66. On Sterne's influence on Karamzin's *The Letters of a Russian Traveler*, see also Offord, *Journeys to a Graveyard*, 80, 86, 88. One notable instance of Russian *sternizm* is Viktor Shklovski's fascination with Sterne, exhibited in Shkolvskii's theoretical works and in the title of his 1923 memoir *Sentimental'noe puteshestvie* (*Sentimental Journey*).

7. Laurence Sterne, *A Sentimental Journey through France and Italy* (London: Oxford University Press, 1928), 13–15. The parallel between Sterne's and Brodsky's "journeys" needs two qualifications: the "literaturization" of the author's personality, as Roboli calls the Sternian device of creating a sense of the author as a literary character (Sterne/Yorrick), is absent in Brodsky's text; and furthermore, while Sterne's irony was his way of responding to his contemporary sentimentalism and Locke's epistemology, Brodsky's irony has other uses related to his contemporary anxieties and subject positions.

8. Holland and Huggan, *Tourists with Typewriters*, 10. See also Stacy Burton's discussion of postmodern travel literature in the light of Mikhail Bakhtin's concept of "heteroglossia" in Stacy Burton, "Difference and Convention: Bakhtin and the Practice of Travel Literature," in *Carnivalizing Difference: Bakhtin and the Other*, ed. Peter I. Barta, Allen Miller, Charles Platter, and David Shepherd (London: Routledge, 2001), 225–45.

9. Rob Nixon, *London Calling: V. S. Naipaul's Postcolonial Mandarin* (Oxford: Oxford University Press, 1992), 15.

10. See Bethea, *Creation of Exile*, 51–52, for Bethea's comment on the "third textual space" that Brodsky's commentary on his earlier works in "Flight" creates.

11. See Greenleaf, *Pushkin and the Romantic Fashion*, 144–52, esp. 147; also Layton, *Russian Literature and Empire*, 62–65.

12. Philip Mansel's book title captures the religious and military claims shaping the history of the city in *Constantinople: City of the World's Desire, 1453–1924* (New York: St. Martin's Press, 1996).

13. John Gross, *New York Times*, May 6, 1986.

14. In his discussion of "Flight from Byzantium" David Bethea discusses the opposite positions Said and Brodsky occupied in the American intellectual life in the following terms: "if someone like Edward Said has attempted to demonstrate in *Orientalism* and other works that we in the West have made people into mysterious and inarticulate

others only to better subjugate and colonize them, then Brodsky, coming from a heritage that has historically swallowed up the individual within its 'community' and *kosnost'*, argues why the Western tradition is so crucial for the survival of Russian culture and of any Russia worth saving" (Bethea, *Creation of Exile*, 209).

15. The Marquise de Custine's travelogue of 1839 *La Russie en 1839* (published in English under such titles as *Empire of the Czar: A Journey through the Eternal Russia* and *Letters from Russia*) has been among the most influential texts in forming European opinions of Russia, with its characterization of Russians as "Orientals," "Tartars," and "bears." For a discussion of the European Orientalization of Russia and its impact on Russian self-definitions in nineteenth-century Romantic thought, seminal to Russian intellectual formations, see Layton, *Russian Literature and Empire*, 79–81.

16. The idea that Russians, subjugated to the "East" through their Byzantine heritage, are more susceptible to questions of evil than Westerners is implied throughout the essay Brodsky wrote as a response to the Czech writer Milan Kundera at about the same time he was working on "Flight from Byzantium." In an open letter, "Why Milan Kundera Is Wrong about Dostoyevsky," published in the *New York Times Literary Supplement*, Kundera emerges as a representative of Western metaphysical naivety, unable to comprehend the susceptibility to the questions of good and evil, which create the crux of Dostoevsky's works: "for where he [Kundera] sees universes of feelings or of reason, his Russian predecessor [Dostoevsky] sees the human propensity to evil." See Joseph Brodsky, "Why Milan Kundera Is Wrong about Dostoyevsky," *New York Times Literary Supplement*, February 15, 1985. Brodsky's views of Dostoevsky's and Russians' superior sensitivity on questions of good and evil, especially in terms of the ability to explore them through individuals' actions, echo many Russian religious thinkers' insistence on Russians' distinguished sensibility on moral questions. Nikolai Berdyaev's assertion that "Russia's moral values are defined by an attitude towards man, and not towards abstract principles of property or of the State, nor towards good in the abstract" comes to mind; see Nicolas Berdyaev, *The Russian Idea* (London: Geoffrey Bles, 1947), 253. As for Brodsky's preoccupation with questions of good and evil in general, Lev Loseff suggests Pavel Florenskii as a source; his "Iconostasis" circulated in *samizdat* and was, Loseff claims, "perhaps the most influential text in which the concept of evil was explained for Brodsky's generation" (Loseff, "Politics/Poetics," 54). In my view, there is also a Shestovian subtext here. When suggesting that the "East" is actually the "metaphysical center of all humankind," since Christianity and all other belief systems "came from there," the author of Brodsky's essay pleads for the reader to understand the "West" for its "lack of this sort of inventiveness, for which it has paid quite heavily, that pay including the *reproaches of excessive rationality one hears to this day*" ("Flight," 408; emphasis added). This is a reference to Lev Shestov's critique of Western "autocracy of reason," which he developed mostly in *Sola Fidé*. For the development of Shestov's criticism of Greek thought, see Brian Horowitz, "The Tension of Athens and Jerusalem in the Philosophy of Lev Shestov," *SEEJ* 43, no. 1 (1999): 156–73.

17. An anonymous letter from a reader published in *Kontinent* reflects the controversy Brodsky's travelogue caused in the émigré community. The author of the letter

expressed support for Vladimir Maksimov, the founder and editor in chief of *Kontinent*, for his decision to publish writers like Brodsky, whose "meditations on eastern Christianity clearly differ from the views held by a majority of the authors who appear in *Kontinent* and Maksimov himself." The reader then anticipates an attack from the "group of Russian Orthodox Christians," who critiqued the journal for printing Brodsky's poems in the past (*Kontinent* 50 [1985]: 378). If there were protests about Brodsky's negative stereotyping of Turkish, Ottoman, and Islamic cultures in readers' letters to *Kontinent*, the journal did not publish them.

18. This formulation of Constantinople and especially Hagia Sophia is Paul Valliere's; see Paul Valliere, *Modern Russian Theology: Bukharev, Soloviev, Bulgakov* (Grand Rapids, Mich.: Eerdman, 2000), 283.

19. On "Moscow, the Third Rome," see, for instance, David M. Goldfrank's encyclopedic definition: "A formula designating the doctrine that Russia succeeded Byzantium as the heir to Rome and is the final center of Orthodox Christianity. The Third Rome doctrine had a complex origin, became an integral part of Muscovite religious self-consciousness, fell out of official favor and then had a strange fate" (Goldfrank, *The Modern Encyclopedia of Russian and Soviet History*, ed. Joseph L. Wieczynski [Gulf Breeze, Fla.: Academic International Press, 1981], 118). The idea circulated initially in three works, the most well-known of them today being the Pskovian monk Filofei's missive, which includes this classic formulation: "All the Christian monarchies, according to the books of the prophets, have come to an end and have been gathered into the single monarchy of our sovereign, that is to say, the Russian monarchy. The two Romes have fallen; the third stands still; and the fourth shall not be" (quoted in *Modern Encyclopedia*, 118). One of the appropriations of the doctrine occurred in the nineteenth century, when "the underlying notion of the Third Rome doctrine, the idea of an exclusive 'Holy Russia' (a term found in the *Tale of the White Cowl* [one of the original sixteenth-century versions of the idea]), experienced a revival at the hands of the Slavophiles and their nationalistic successors in the nineteenth century" (ibid., 120). See also Yuri Lotman's analysis of the idea in the Petrine period in "Otzvuki kontseptsii 'Moskva—tretii Rim' v ideologii Petra Pervogo," 349–61, esp. 352–53.

20. According to Vail' and Genis, among Soviet intellectuals in the 1960s "there existed the strange concept of 'third Rome,' which nominated Russia as the successor of the most famous of all empires, the Roman Empire" (*60-e*, 261). As an example of this they quote the Estonian poet Jaan Kaplinski, who appropriated this parallel to subversive ends through "pompous Roman rhetoric" in a poem that became the "genuine national hymn of Estonia." Recognizing Kaplinski's dissident views on disassociating Estonia from the Soviet empire, Vail' and Genis note that "it was possible to take Red Square for the Forum only when looking at it from Tallinn," since "in the Russian [*rossiiskoi*] 'Roman Empire' Rome itself was absent" and "the entire empire consisted only of outskirts," which, in turn, as they claim, caused the fact that "in the new Russian [*rossiiskoi*] culture there was no Virgil, but there was an Ovid—Joseph Brodsky" (*60-e*, 261–62). For commentary on Brodsky's "To a Friend: In Memoriam," see Rigsbee, *Styles of Ruin*, 108. There is a reference to "Moscow, the Third Rome" also in Brodsky's "Ekloga 5-ia. Letniaia" ("Eclogue V: Summer").

21. Venclova's observation that the "three empires [Roman, Ottoman, and Soviet] are semiotically isomorphic [in Brodsky's essay]: regardless of difference in culture and religion, each is a logical continuation of its predecessor" seems to me to overlook the ideological emphases of Brodsky's historical narrative and the hierarchy of empires it produces.

22. I refer to the lines "kalendar Moskvy zarazhen Koranom" and "T'fu-t'fy, my vyrosli ne v Islame" in "Rech' o prolitom moloke," and "polumesiats plyvet v zapylennom okonnom stekle / nad krestami Moskvy, kak lykhaia pobeda Islama" in "Vremia Goda—zima" (2:179). See also David Bethea's commentary on "Vremia goda—zima" in Bethea, *Creation of Exile*, 208–11.

23. Brodsky quotes Leontiev's "putrid, prophetic exclamation," "'Russia must rule shamelessly,'" as an example of Eastern expansionism, which he traces to "Bajazet, Tamerlane, Selim, Muhammad" ("Flight," 438). On Leontiev's Byzantinism, see Andrzej Walicki, *A History of Russian Thought: from the Enlightenment to Marxism* (Oxford: Clarendon Press, 1980), 300–308. M. Suslov is Mikhail Aleksandrovich Suslov (1902–82), one of the major Stalinist politicians, the "gray emissary" of Brezhnev's era; Pavel Mikhailovich Miliukov (1859–1943), a Russian historian and later the leader of the White Movement, supported the conquest of Constantinople in 1916. In literary history he is known as being the man whom Vladimir Nabokov's father shielded during an assassination attempt, resulting in the older Nabokov's death.

24. Nikolai Ustrialov was the leading theoretician and propagator of Russian nationalism among the Bolsheviks.

25. Georgii Fedotov, "Rossiia i svoboda," in *Sud'ba i grekhi Rossii: izbrannye stat'i* (Moscow: Dar', 2005), 390, 416, 435. Fedotov's essay was originally published in the New York–based émigré journal *Novyi Zhurnal,* to which Fedotov contributed after having emigrated to the United States. Apart from *Novyi Zhurnal,* Brodsky may have encountered Fedotov's essay when it was reprinted in New York in 1981 in a collection of Fedotov's writings in *Rossiia i svoboda: sbornik statei*, ed. M. A. Meerson (New York: 1981).

26. Ibid., 416.

27. Ibid., 435.

28. Nikolai Berdyaev detected a similar despotic impetus in the Third Rome ideology, narrating its transformation from Muscovy to Bolshevik rule: "The spiritual pit into which the idea of Moscow the Third Rome falls is due precisely to the fact that the Third Rome presented itself to their minds as a manifestation of sovereign power, as the might of the State. It was taken as expressed in the Tsardom of Moscow and then in the Empire and in the end as the Third International" (Berdyaev, *Russian Idea*, 9). David Goldfrank's analysis of the transformation of "Moscow, the Third Rome" seems to me to enclose Fedotov's, as well as Berdyaev's, stance, formed within Orthodox thought, and also the stance Brodsky represents, formed, of course, outside Orthodoxy and formulated after Goldfrank's analysis: "Later critics of Russian nationalism and of Bolshevism used 'Moscow, the Third Rome' as a buzz word to designate the combination of xenophobia and messianism that they claimed to see in these movements and

among the Great Russian people. Analysis of this sort continues in various quarters to the present and is explained by Moscow's central and often guiding role in the Communist movements throughout the world since 1917" (Goldfrank, *Modern Encyclopedia*, 120).

29. Chaadaev, *Philosophical Letters*, 42.

30. Ibid., 171.

31. Ibid., 178.

32. A. S. Pushkin, "O vtorom tome 'Istorii russkogo naroda' Polevogo," in *Polnoe sobranie sochinenii*, vol. 2 (Moscow: Akademii nauk, 1937–58), 127; A. I. Hertzen, *Sobranie sochinenii v 30-h tomah*, vol. 7 (Moscow: Akademiia nauk, 1956), 16.

33. Brodsky, *Less Than One*, 130. See Mandelstam's essay "Petr Chaadayev," the second chapter of which starts with Mandelstam's echo of Chaadaev's thought in the exclamation, "In the West there is unity!" in Osip Mandelstam, *Complete Critical Prose*, 84.

34. M. O. Gershenzon's bilingual editions *Sochineniia i pis'ma P. Ia. Chaadaeva* (Moscow, 1913–14) were the first publications of Chaadaev's works in Russia since the scandalous publication of the *First Letter* in the *Telescope* in 1836. Gershenzon's editions included *Four Letters* and the *Apology*, all of which were initially written in French.

35. Mandelstam, *Complete Critical Prose*, 84.

36. "In the thirty-first year after the birth of the century / I returned, no—read: I was forcibly / returned to Buddhist Moscow, / But before that I did, after all, see / Ararat as rich as a Biblical table-cloth / and spent two hundred days in the land of Sabbaths / that is called Armenia" (Osip Mandelstam, *Sobranie sochinenii*, vol. 3 [Moscow: Art-Biznes-Tsentr, 1994], 56).

37. Ibid., 38.

38. Another crucial difference between Brodsky's and Mandelstam's "journeys" is highlighted by the circumstances in which they were written. Mandelstam embraced Christian Armenia at a time when such an embrace, not to say anything of his "poetic extravagance" (Andrew Wachtel's term), was becoming more and more difficult, while Brodsky was able to articulate his rejection of Islamic Turkey and publish it with great success through leading Western publishers. On the circumstances of Mandelstam's trip and on the negative reception of the essay, see Osip Mandelstam, *Sochineniia*, vol. 2, 420–23. For a discussion of the essay in the context of the Soviet travelogue, see Avins, *Border Crossings*, 150–51; Andrew Wachtel, "Voyages of Escape, Voyages of Discovery: Transformations of the Travelogue," in *Cultural Mythologies of Russian Modernism: From the Golden Age to the Silver Age*, ed. Boris Gasparov, Robert P. Hughes, and Irina Paperno (Berkeley: University of California Press, 1992), 128–49.

39. Compare this to Mandelstam's: "'Head in Armeanian is *glukh'e* with a soft *l* and a short aspiration after the *kh*. It contains the same root as the Russian word for 'head' [*golova, glava*]. . . . But would you like a Japhetic novella? If you please: 'To see, to hear, to understand'—all these meanings coalesced at once into a single semantic bundle. At the very deepest levels of language there were no concepts, just directions, fears,

longings, needs and apprehensions. The concept of 'head' was sculpted over a dozen millenia out of a bundle of foggy meanings, and its symbol became 'deafness' [*glukhota*]" (Mandelstam, *Complete Critical Prose*, 350).

40. See Boris Gasparov's enlightening reading of Mandelstam's poem "Lamarck" and *Journey to Armenia* in "Tridtsatye gody—zheleznyi vek (k analizu motivov stoletnego vozvrashcheniia u Mandel'shtama)," in *Cultural Mythologies of Russian Modernism*, 150–79; in English, "The Iron Age of the 1930s: The Centennial Return to Mandelstam," in *Rereading Russian Poetry*, ed. Stephanie Sandler (New Haven, Conn.: Yale University Press, 1999), 78–103.

41. See G. S. Smith's remarks on the "merciless reductivism" of Brodsky's "On the Talks in Kabul" in the *Russian Review* roundtable; see n. 3 in this chapter.

42. Wittgenstein compiled his first major philosophical work, *Tractatus Logico-Philosophicus*, while serving in the Austrian army. Brodsky's reference to this fact reflects the fascination with the figure of Wittgenstein exhibited in a number of novels, plays, poetry books and films since the 1960s, all of which contributed to the "growing body of Wittgensteiniana" as discussed by Marjorie Perloff in *Wittgenstein's Ladder: Poetic Language and the Strangeness of the Ordinary* (Chicago: University of Chicago Press, 1996), 23.

43. Referring to Naipaul's India and Cristopher Iyer's Japan, Holland and Huggan note that their observations "miraculously conform to a cultural 'essence' each writer believes he has discovered. In this sense, there is something Socratic about the inquiries made by many travel writers: they seek after 'truths' they imagine they already have in their possession" (*TWT*, 11).

44. The Khodasevich quote is from the last stanza of the 1926 "Peterburg" included in his last collection of poetry, *Evropeiskaia noch'* (*European Night*). The opening poem of the cycle relates to the speaker's pre-exilic life in Soviet Russia: "i kazhdyi stikh gonia skvoz' prozu, / vyvikhivaia kazhduiu strochku, / privil-taki klassicheskuiu rozu / k sovetskomu dichku" ("and driving every verse through prose / and every line pulling out of joint, / I still managed to graft the classical rose / to the Soviet wilding"). See Vladislav Khodasevich, *Stikhotvoreniia* (Leningrad: Sovetskii pisatel', 1989), 155. The English translation is from David Bethea, *Khodasevich: His Life and Art* (Princeton, N.J.: Princeton University Press, 1983), 278.

45. Istanbul and Athens come thus to symbolize the dichotomy between the East and West, and here Brodsky's polemic turns to concern Lev Shestov (cf. n. 16), a thinker he would often praise, as numerous interviews record. See Volkov, *Conversations with Joseph Brodsky*, 178–79; Cynthia L. Haven, ed., *Joseph Brodsky: Conversations* (Jackson: University Press of Missisippi, 2002), 124–25. See also Octavio Paz's recollection of his conversation with Brodsky about Shestov in *Iosif Brodskii: trudy i dni*, ed. Lev Loseff and Petr Vail' (Moscow: Nezavisimaia gazeta, 1998), 257. Shestovian topics permeate Brodsky's works, but unlike such poems as "Isaak i Avraam" ("Isaac and Abraham") and "Razgovor s nebozhitelem" ("Conversation with a Celestial Being"), which appear as poetic affirmations of Shestov's recognition of the "horrors of life," religious individualism, and existential faith, "Flight from Byzantium" brings to fore the

culturo-philosophical dimension of Shestov's last book, *Afiny i Ierusalim* (*Athens and Jerusalem*), even if Brodsky replaces Jerusalem with Constantinople/Istanbul, a symbolic center of not Christianity and Judaism but Christianity and Islam. Shestov invokes the juxtaposition between religion and philosophy in the introduction to *Athens and Jerusalem* (Shestov, "Athens or Jerusalem, religion or philosophy?" 7), and provides a reply that seeks to amalgamate both: "religion together with rational thought (philosophy)." Brodsky's essay with its pronounced preference of Athens, i.e., philosophy, rationality and arts, and repudiation of Constantinople/Istanbul, comes across as a rejection of religion. This rejection, however, has a Shestovian undercurrent in that Brodsky proclaims disdain for religion as an institutionalized belief system, not as an expression of individual faith, a distinction that underscored all of Shestov's works and that he maintained in *Athens and Jerusalem*, too (Lev Shestov, *Afiny i Ierusalim* [Paris: YMCA-Press, 1951], 317).

46. Instead of "режу," Brodsky writes "рэжу" (5:304).

47. O'Connor, "From Kabul to Byzantium and Back," 209.

48. Thomas Venclova traces Brodsky's "historico-philosophical system" to Oswald Spengler's morphology and its opposition between "Apollonian" and "magic" cultures in *Decline of the West* (Venclova, "Journey," 146). Spengler's *Decline of the West* reentered the Russian intellectual horizon when the émigré philosopher Sergei Averintsev wrote about it *Religiia i literatura* (Ann Arbor, Mich.: Hermitage, 1981). Brodsky knew Averintsev's book, since he quotes it almost word-for-word elsewhere in "Flight"; see Venclova, "Journey from Leningrad to Istanbul," 146n19.

49. David Bethea extracts from Brodsky's essay another dichotomy represented through the time-space opposition, that is, poetry and empire: "If the travelogue is read against Yeats, Mandelstam, and especially Brodsky, the following formula emerges: poetry is the temporalization (or dematerialization) of space, while empire, including social utopias and applied Christianity (e.g., Marxism), is the spatialization of time" (Bethea, *Creation of Exile*, 52).

50. Greenleaf, *Pushkin and the Romantic Fashion*, 113.

51. Rudyard Kipling's 1889 poem "The Ballad of East and West" starts with the memorable lines: "Oh, East is East, and West is West, and never the twain shall meet, / Till Earth and Sky stand presently at God's great Judgment Seat" (Rudyard Kipling, *Rudyard Kipling's Verse* [London: Hodder and Stoughton, 1973], 234).

52. Chaadaev, *Philosophical Letters*, 169.

53. It is instructive to compare Chaadaev's way of imagining the East to what Said writes about the representations of the Orient in European Romantic thought; see Said, *Orientalism*, esp. 113–97.

54. Chaadaev, *Philosophical Letters*, 169–70.

55. Ibid., 120.

56. See Olzhas Suleimenov, *Az i IA.* (1975; repr., Alma Ata: Zhalyn, 1989). Suleimenov's book was withdrawn from circulation soon after its publication, but in the post-Soviet period it has been reprinted many times. On Suleimenov's book

and the controversy it caused, see Harsha Ram, "Imagining Eurasia: The Poetics and Ideology of Olzhas Suleimenov's *Az i IA*," *Slavic Review* 60, no. 2 (2001): 289–311.

57. Here Brodsky's travelogue illustrates Yuri Lotman's argument that the question of Russian identity, as formulated on the East-West, or Europe-Asia, axis, is especially crucial to Petersburgian self-definitions. The heightened awareness of an outsider's gaze, recognized either as a European or Russian (Muscovite) gaze, shapes Petersburgian subjectivity, while this subjectivity is also shaped by a heightened awareness of its own viewpoint on Europe or Russia. Petersburg has traditionally been invested with two contradictory ideological meanings of either "Asia in Europe" or "Europe in Asia," and consequently, the ideological viewpoints shaping the construction of the Petersburg identity include an awareness of being both an object of European Orientalization and an active subject of casting an Orientalizing gaze at Russia, to adopt Said's terms to Lotman's thought. See Yuri Lotman, "Simvolika Peterburga i semiotika goroda," in *Semiotika goroda i gorodskoi kul'tury*, 37.

58. The *Times Literary Supplement* (London), May 12–18, 1989. Brodsky translated the poem with George L. Kline. I am grateful to Tatyana Filimonova for pointing this poem out to me.

59. "Poetry as a Form of Resistance to Reality" was initially published in the Polish-language collection of Thomas Venclova's poetry. The English version, translated and adapted by Alexander Sumerkin and Jamey Gambrell, was published in *PMLA* 107 (March 1992): 220–25.

60. Knight, "Grigor'ev in Orienburg, 1851–1862," 77. Knight's article concerns the historical period of Russia's imperialist expansion. He questions the applicability of Said's ideas to the Russian context, maintaining that Orientalism did not have the same kind of disciplinary power in nineteenth-century Russia as it did in the West (ibid., 97–99).

61. In *Narrating Post/Communism: Colonial Discourse and Europe's Borderline Civilizations* (London: Routledge, 2008), Nataša Kovačević makes the claim that the native expertise, which Eastern European and Russian exiles and dissidents from Vladimir Nabokov to Milan Kundera and Joseph Brodsky established in their literary narratives, reinforced the process of re-orientalizing Russia and Eastern European societies during the Cold War period.

62. Holland and Huggan, *Tourists with Typewriters*, 7.

63. According to Venclova, "one ought to always keep in mind the mythopoetic nature of this essay, and also that in it Turkey and Islam serve as metaphor (or metonymy) for other (broader) cultural-historical phenomena" ("Journey," 142). This is exactly what makes Brodsky's writing "Orientalist" from a Saidian perspective: Brodsky uses Istanbul to project on it his metaphysical ramifications and the undesirable end of his "poetic typology of culture" (Venclova's term).

64. Bethea, *Creation of Exile*, 211.

65. Orhan Pamuk, *Istanbul: Memories of a City* (London: Faber and Faber, 2005), 214–15.

66. See Said, *Orientalism*, 284–328.

Chapter 6. Staging Cultural Differences

1. Debray advances his critique from his position as the *enfant terrible* of the French literati, and criticizes what he knows best: the French intellectuals of his own educational background and social status. Debray's translator Philip Wohlstetter characterizes Debray in the following terms: "child of privilege, son of prosperous right-wing lawyers in Paris, stellar philosophy student at *École Normale*, protégé of Althusser, friend of Castro, theorist of revolution, 'French Red,'" who in the 1960s fought with Che Guevara and in the 1980s worked as President Francois Mitterand's advisor. See Philip Wohstetter, "Introduction," in *Against Venice*, by Régis Debray (Berkeley: North Atlantic Books, 1999), ix–xiv.

2. Debray, *Against Venice*, 30–31.

3. David MacFadyen looks at Venice as a space that matched Brodsky's aesthetics of "nomadism" and "politics of independence"; see MacFadyen, *Joseph Brodsky and the Baroque*, 164–90.

4. In an article titled "Brodskij 'protiv' Venecii" ("Brodsky against Venice") the Italian scholar Gian Pietro Piretto quotes Debray's essay, suggesting a similarity in the writers' approaches to the city. See Gian Pietro Piretto, "Brodskij 'protiv' Venecii," *Russian Literature* 41–44 (1997): 519–32. My parallel reading of Brodsky's and Debray's essays will insist on a similarity, too, but on different grounds than Piretto. The first stages of the arguments presented in this chapter were put forward in an essay on Brodsky's *Watermark*; see Sanna Turoma, "Joseph Brodsky's *Watermark*: Preserving the Venetophile Discourse," *Russian Literature* 52 (2003): 485–502.

5. Brodsky in a press conference in Helsinki (August 23, 1995).

6. Brodsky refers to William Hazlitt's (1778–1830) *Notes of a Journey through France and Italy* (1826): "A city built in the air would be something still more wonderful; but any other must yield the palm to this for singularity and imposing effect" (quoted in *English Writers and Venice 1350–1950/Scrittori inglesi e Venezia 1350–1950*, ed. Marilla Battilana [Venice: Stamperia di Venezia, 1981], 140). The "Calvinoesque idea" refers to Italo Calvino's novel *Invisible Cities* with its fantasies of imaginary cities.

7. John Pemble, *Venice Rediscovered* (Oxford: Oxford University Press, 1995), 1, 140–65.

8. Ibid., 15.

9. The nineteenth-century European discourse on Venice was not entirely free of political undertones; even if Venice itself no longer played a politically important role on the map of Europe, its historical power still had symbolic meaning. The comparison of contemporary Britain with Venice, once a ruling maritime power, functioned as a moral warning in some Victorian views: the fin-de-siècle British Empire was destined to perish the same way the once great Venetian Republic had perished (Pemble, *Venice Rediscovered*, 100–109). Meanwhile, in Italy Gabriele D'Annunzio made *Venezia la bella*, as he would refer to Venice, one of the cornerstones of his nostalgic Decadent aesthetics; he opposed the building of a bridge for road traffic from the mainland and campaigned against any restoration that disguised the erosion of time. His epic drama *La Nave* (*The Ship*, 1907) was a celebration of the foundation of Venice, and it was

from Venice that he made his nationalist speeches during the First World War. As a response to D'Annunzio and others' aestheticization of Venice, on the other hand, Filippo Tommaso Marinetti, campaigning against the old Italy with its cities, museums and masters, provocatively proposed that the Venetian *palazzi* should be demolished and the masonry used for filling up the canals (*Venice Rediscovered*, 158–65).

10. For this change in the Russian perception and its intertwining with the European discourse on Venice, and for the involvement of such cultural figures as Ivan Turgenev and Vladimir Stasov in it, see Turoma, *Watermark*, 2003. Despite the increase of scholarly interest, there is no equivalent to Pemble's thorough historiographical study on the perception of Venice in the context of Russian culture. There are two relatively recent books on the theme of Venice in Russian literature: N. E. Mednis, *Venetsiia v russkoi literature* (Novosibirsk: Izdatel'stvo novosibirskogo universiteta, 1999), and Paul Hinrichs, *In Search of Another St. Petersburg: Venice in Russian Poetry* (Munich: Otto Sagner, 1997). The bibliography of Russian writers on Venice, compiled by Hinrichs, is invaluable for anyone interested in the topic, while Mednis's book offers some interesting readings of individual texts.

11. Rozanov's article, published first in 1902 in the July 24 issue of *Novoe Vremia*, was later included in his *Ital'ianskie vpechatleniia*, in V. V. Rozanov, *Sobranie sochinenii*, vol. 1, *Sredi khudozhnikov: Ital'ianskie vpechatleniia*, ed. A. N. Nikoliukin (Moscow: Izdatel'stvo Respublika, 1994), 115–22. See also Rozanov's "K padeniiu bashni sv. Marka," written at about the same time and republished in *Sredi khudozhnikov*, 122–24.

12. A. P. Chekhov, *Polnoe sobranie sochinenii*, vol. 12, *Pis'ma* (Moscow: Nauka, 1976), 202.

13. P. Pertsov, *Venetsiia* (St. Petersburg: Gerol'd, 1905).

14. I have used the following books for this overview: Hinrichs, *In Search of Another St. Petersburg*; Aleksei Kara-Murza, *Znamenityi russkie v Venetsii* (Moscow: Nezavisimaia Gazeta, 2001); Zinaida Gippius, *Zhivye litsa*, vol. 2, *Vospominaniia* (Tbilisi: Merani, 1991); Justin Doherty, "Acmeist Perceptions of Italy," in *Literary Tradition and Practice in Russian Culture*, ed. Valentina Polukhina, Joe Andrew, and Robert Reid (Amsterdam: Rodopi, 1993), 106–21.

15. On the Russian Romantic canon of Venice, see Lev Loseff, "Real'nost' Zazerkal'ia: Venetsiia Iosifa Brodskogo," *Inostrannaia literatura* 5 (1996): 226; Hinrichs, *In Search of Another St. Petersburg*, 20–41. On Venice in European Romanticism, see Carlo Pellegrini, ed., *Venezia nelle letterature moderne* (Venice: Instituto per la collaborazione culturale, 1955) and Franco Meregalli, "Venice in Romantic Literature," *arcadia* 18, no. 3 (1975): 225–39. On Byron and Venice, see Tony Tanner, *Venice Desired* (Cambridge, Mass.: Harvard University Press, 1992), 17–66.

16. This poetic dialogue has been discussed by Georges Nivat, "l'Italie de Blok et celle de Gumilev," *Revue des Études Slaves* 4 (1982): 697–709; Samuil Schwarzband, "Aleksandr Blok and Nikolaj Gumilev," *Slavic and East European Journal* 33, no. 3 (1988): 373–86; see also Doherty, "Acmeist Perceptions of Italy"; and Aleksandar Flaker, "Venetsianskie literaturnye veduty," *Russian Literature* 43 (1998): 149–58. See also Anna Lisa Crone, "Blok's 'Venecija' and *Molnii iskusstva* as Inspiration to Mandelstam:

Parallels in Italian Materials," in *Aleksandr Blok Centennial Conference*, ed. Walter N. Vickery (Columbus, Ohio: Slavica Publishers, 1984), 73–88.

17. Khodasevich, *Stikhotvoreniia*, 97, 299.

18. On Muratov's *Obrazy Italii* see Patrizia Deotto, "Impressioni, dipinti, visioni: l'Italia nell'immaginario russo," *Europe Orientalis* 15, no. 2 (1996): 51–76.

19. V. N. Toporov, "Italiia v Peterburge," in *Italiia i slavianskii mir: Sovetsko-ital'ianskii simpozium in honorem Professore Ettore Lo Gatto* (Moscow: Akademiia nauk SSSR, Institut Slavianovedeniia i Balkanistiki: Moskva, 1990), 49–81.

20. See Kushner's poems "Venetsiia," "Progulka," and "Urok geografii" in the 1986 *Stikhotvoreniia*; "Nichto k smerti nas ne priblizhaet" in *Nochnaia muzyka* (Leningrad: Lenizdat, 1991), 93–94; and "1974 god" in *Literaturnaia gazeta*, August 22, 1990.

21. Bethea, *Creation of Exile*, 45; cf. pp. 106–7 in this book.

22. Stewart, *On Longing*, 135.

23. Judith Seaboyer, "Robert Coover's *Pinocchio in Venice*: An Anatomy of a Talking Book," in *Venetian Views, Venetian Blinds: English Fantasies of Venice*, ed. Manfred Pfister and Barbara Schaff (Amsterdam: Rodopi, 1999), 239.

24. These are the English titles of these poems as they appear in Brodsky's *Collected Poems in English*. "Lagoon" was translated by Anthony Hecht, "San Pietro" by Barry Rubin, "Venetian Stanzas" co-translated by Jane Ann Miller and Brodsky; "In Italy" is Brodsky's own translation, "Venice: Lido" was translated by Alan Myers; "Homage to Girolamo Marcello" and "In Front of Casa Marcello" are both Brodsky's own translations. "Lagoon" and "San Pietro" appeared first in the collection *Chast' rechi* (*A Part of Speech*) and "Venetian Stanzas" and "In Italy" were included in *Uraniia* (*Urania*); the Russian "Lido" was included in the 1993 Russian collection *Kappadokiia*, while in English it appeared together with "Homage to Girolamo Marcello" and "In Front of Casa Marcello" in Brodsky's last English collection, *So Forth*; and the Russian versions of the last three were included in Brodsky's last Russian collection, *Peizazh s navodneniem* (*Landscape with Flood*). Apart from these poems, there is at least one poem, "Ostrov Prochida," which in Brodsky's Russian collected works is dated "November, 1994, Venice" and which may indicate that the poem was written in Venice, even if the title refers to Isla Procida on the Bay of Naples. "Zamershii kisel'nyi bereg" ("With riverbanks of frozen chocolate"), dated "December 1985," evokes the Venetian landscape familiar from Brodsky's Russian poems and *Watermark*, but there is no specific reference to Venetian *realia*, and the poem may relate to some other townscape.

25. "Chronic tourism" is from John Updike's review of *Watermark* published in the *New Yorker* and quoted on the cover of the 1996 Noonday Press edition of Brodsky's essay. For Updike, *Watermark* is among other things "an attempt . . . to fashion of one's personal chronic tourism a crystal whose facets reflect an entire life, with exile and ill health glinting at the edges of planes whose direct glare is sheer beauty." For Brodsky's recollection of writing "Laguna," see Brodskii, *Peresechennaia mestnost'*, 170.

26. Valentina Polukhina, "The Prose of Joseph Brodsky: A Continuation of Poetry by Other Means," *Russian Literature* 41 (1997): 223–40. Brodsky reuses the poetic images of his Venetian poems extensively, especially "Venetian Stanzas," in *Watermark*,

and these prosaic renderings of his poems have inspired some of the most negative reviews of his English prose; see n. 28 below. I do not itemize these translations but point at them when it is relevant to my discussion. For a more or less full list, see Polukhina's "The Prose of Joseph Brodsky."

27. Bhabha, *Location of Culture*, 34.

28. For an insightful assessment of Brodsky's bilingualism, see, for instance, Givens, "The Anxiety of a Dedication," and David Bethea, "Brodsky's and Nabokov's Bilingualism(s): Translation, American Poetry, and the *Muttersprache*," *Russian Literature* 37 (1995): 157–84. See also Michael Molnar's assessment of Brodsky's self-translation of the 1985 elegy ""Proshlo chto-to okolo goda" ("About a year has passed"), in *Russian Literature* 37 (1995): 333–37. Beyond these approaches, Brodsky's complicated entry into English-language poetry has been a topic of many controversial reviews and discussions. I want to point out briefly that in some of the negative reviews of Brodsky's English poetry and prose written by critics with native competence in an English-language culture, there has been little tolerance of Brodsky's linguistic idiosyncrasy or little desire to review his achievement in English from the viewpoint of "how newness enters the world," to quote the subtitle of one of Bhabha's essays in *Location of Culture* (see esp. 227–28). One example of this is the crushing review of *Watermark* by the British travel writer, historian, and expert on Venice, John Julius Norwich. In support of his opinion that Brodsky's English is far from the level of Nabokov's or Conrad's, Norwich picks on passages that are almost literal translations of Brodsky's Russian poems, something Norwich apparently is unaware of. See John Julius Norwich, "Did This Man Really Win the Nobel Prize?" *Literary Review*, June 1992, 12–13.

29. Bethea, *Creation of Exile*, 48–52.

30. Bhabha, *Location of Culture*, 224.

31. Brodsky, *Less Than One*, 99.

32. Bhabha, *Location of Culture*, 228.

33. This is how Bhabha's describes the "liminality of migrant experience" in his reading of Salman Rushdie's *Satanic Verses*, 224.

34. On the concept of the "third space" in Fredric Jameson and its elaborations by Bhabha, see Bhabha, *Location of Culture*, 36–39, 216–19. The most relevant passage of Bhabha's sophisticated theoretical articulations is the following: "It is only when we understand that all cultural statements and systems are constructed in this contradictory and ambivalent space of enunciation, that we begin to understand why hierarchical claims to the inherent originality or 'purity' of cultures are untenable, even before we resort to empirical historical instances that demonstrate their hybridity. . . . It is that Third Space, though unrepresentable in itself, which constitutes the discursive conditions of enunciation that ensure that the meaning and symbols of culture have no primordial unity or fixity; that even the same signs can be appropriated, translated, rehistoricized and read anew" (ibid., 37).

35. Barry Curtis and Claire Pajaczkowska, "Venice: Masking the Real," in *Hieroglyphics of Space: Reading and Experiencing the Modern Metropolis*, ed. Neil Leach (London: Routledge, 2002), 157.

36. Apart from *A Part of Speech* and Brodsky's collected works, the poem is included, for instance, in the multilingual anthology *Venetsianskie tetradi: Iosif Brodskii i drugie/Quaderni veneziani: Joseph Brodsky and Others*, ed. Ekatarina Margolis (Moscow: OGI, 2002) and the posthumous English collection of Brodsky's poems with the theme of Christmas titled *Nativity Poems*. Brodsky recalls the anti-Soviet underpinnings of the poem and their alleged impact on his readers in an interview with Petr Vail' in Brodskii, *Peresechennaia mestnost'*, 170.

37. For an analysis of how Italian and Russian themes are juxtaposed in "Laguna" and intertwined with exilic nostalgia, see Kreps, *Poetika Brodskogo*, 62–67.

38. Brodsky's line combines the first line of Akhmatova's "Summer Gardens" ("Where the best of gardens") and the first line of her "Venice" ("Golden pigeon coop by water"). For the Russian originals, see Anna Akhmatova, *Sochineniia v dvukh tomakh*, vol. 1 (Moscow: Tsitadel', 1997), 70, 286.

39. Pound's contemporary compatriot John Gould Fletcher's remark on Pound is illustrative in this respect. For him, Pound represented those Americans "who had come abroad before the European War, bent on submitting their own rude and untaught native impulses to the task of assimilating and, if possible, surpassing the traditional achievements of Europe" (quoted in Tanner, *Venice Desired*, 271).

40. Ezra Pound, *Pavannes and Divagations* (Norfolk, Conn.: New Directions, 1958), 5. For Pound and Venice, see Tanner, *Venice Desired*, 268–348.

41. See also Solomon Volkov's interviews with Brodsky, where Brodsky recalls "how I once almost met up with Pound" in Volkov, *Conversations with Joseph Brodsky*, 193–97. As for the translations Brodsky mentions in *Watermark*, unfortunately I have not been able to trace them.

42. Pound, *Pavannes and Divagations*, 60.

43. See Boym, *Future of Nostalgia*, 302–7.

44. On the concept of the sublime, see Stewart, *On Longing*, 74–78.

45. Tanner, *Venice Desired*, 280.

46. Ibid., 306. For the significance of marble statues in Brodsky's poetics, see George Nivat, "An Ironic Journey into Antiquity," in *Brodsky's Poetics and Aesthetics*, ed. Lev Loseff and Valentina Polukhina (London: Macmillan, 1990), 89–97; and Dan Ungurianu, "The Wandering Greek," 161–91. Viktor Yukht, too, touches on the subject in "K probleme genezisa statuarnogo mifa v poezii Iosifa Brodskogo (1965–1971 gg.)," *Russian Literature* 44 (1998): 409–32.

47. Ezra Pound, *The Cantos of Ezra Pound* (London: Faber and Faber, 1957), 81.

48. On Brodsky from this viewpoint, see Richard Martin, "The Autonomous Eye of Joseph Brodsky," in *Ethics and Aesthetics: The Moral Turn of Postmodernism*, ed. Gerhard Hoffman and Alfred Hornung (Heidelberg: Universitätsverlag C. Winter, 1996), 243–53.

49. Mary McCarthy, *Venice Observed* (Lausanne: R. Bernier, 1957), 6.

50. The chapter on Venice is titled "Venezia la bella" after a romantic cycle of poems, popular in their day, by Apollon Grigor'ev. See A. I Hertzen, *Byloe i dumy, vol. 6–8* (Moscow: Khudozhestvennaia literatura, 1982), 375.

51. Hertzen's approach to the city as a "living organism" greatly influenced P. N. Antsiferov's approach to the urban space of St. Petersburg in *Dusha Peterburga*, 16–18.

52. Lotman, "Simvolika Peterburga i semiotika goroda," 30–45; Toporov, *Peterburgskii tekst russkoi literatury*, 7–118. See also Lev Loseff, "Real'nost' Zazerkal'ia," for a discussion of Brodsky's Venice and his concept of "dramatic order," which echoes Lotman's "eccentric city." For Brodsky's Venice and the concept of the "Petersburg text," see Piretto, "Brodskij 'protiv' Venecii," 520.

53. Bożena Shallcross, *Through the Poet's Eye: The Travels of Zagajewski, Herbert, and Brodsky* (Evanston, Ill.: Northwestern University Press, 2002), esp. 103–22.

54. For the full translation and a short description of the circumstances of its initial publication in the Soviet Union, see Margolis, *Venetsianskie tetradi*, 195–97.

55. Osip Mandelstam, *Selected Poems*, trans. Clarence Brown and W. S. Merwin (Harmondsworth: Penguin, 1977), 84.

56. Brodskii, *Peresechennaia mestnost'*, 171.

57. John Ruskin, *The Stones of Venice*, vol. 1, *The Foundation* (New York: Garland Publishing, 1979), 351.

58. On Ruskin's influence, see Tanner, *Venice Desired*, 67–156. For Ruskin in Russia, see Deotto, "Impressioni, dipinti, visioni," 51–76.

59. Viazemsky, *Polnoe sobranie sochinenii*, 10:31.

60. W. H. Auden, *Selected Poems* (London: Faber and Faber, 1979), 184.

61. See Edward Mendelson, *Later Auden* (New York: Farrar, Straus and Giroux, 1999), 499, 508.

62. W. H. Auden, *Thank You, Fog* (London: Faber and Faber, 1974), 13.

63. Bethea, *Creation of Exile*, 137.

64. Toporov, "Italiia v Peterburge," 49–81.

65. There are some traces of Venice in the Soviet literary canon, as, for instance, Nikolai Zabolotskii's 1957 poem "Venetsiia"; for Zabolotskii's and others' reflections of Venice in Soviet and Russian émigré poetry, see Hinrichs, *In Search of Another St. Petersburg*, 54–58. The émigré writers and scholars Yuri Ivask and Vladimir Veidle function as interesting predecessors to Brodsky. There is a curious moment of Soviet Cold War politics in the lyric poet Evgenii Dolmatovksii's 1963 poem "Venetsiia," which reflects the speaker's disappointment in the "fairytale of childhood" where "the cruiser 'Garibaldi' with a rocket launcher" makes the speaker imagine how "Venice sinks to the bottom of the lagoon like Kitezh-grad"; see Hinrichs, *In Search of Another St. Petersburg*, 57.

66. See Hinrichs, *In Search of Another St. Petersburg*, 47–48; Nivat, "l'Italie de Blok et celle de Gumilev," 697–709; Schwarzband, "Aleksandr Blok and Nikolaj Gumilev," 373–86; and Doherty, "Acmeist Perceptions of Italy," 106–21. See also Flaker, "Venetsianskie literaturnye veduty," 149–58.

67. See Natalia Galatskaia's informative reading of the poem's intertexts in Natalia Galatskaia, "Venetsianskie strofy (1)—smert' v Venetsii?" in *Meddelanden från slaviska institutionen Nr 34/1. Föredrag hållna vid Fjortonde nordiska slavistmötet i Helsingfors, augusti 1997*, vol. 1 (Stockholm: Universitet Stockholm, 1997), 33–44.

68. See n. 15. The English translation of Pushkin's lines is from Aleksandr Pushkin, *Eugene Onegin: A Novel in Verse*, vol. 1, trans. Vladimir Nabokov (Princeton, N.J.: Princeton University Press, 1975), 116.

69. On the significance of Sontag and Gennadii Shmakov for Brodsky in his own words, see Brodsky in an interview with Vail' in Brodskii, *Peresechennaia mestnost'*, 172.

70. Said, *Orientalism*, 71.

71. An earlier version of this reading was put forward in Sanna Turoma, "Joseph Brodsky and Orientalism: A Russian Moor in Venice?" *Ulbandus, the Slavic Review of Columbia University* 7 (2003): 143–54.

72. Manfred Pfister, "*The Passion* from Winterson to Coryate," in Pfister, *Venetian Views, Venetian Blinds*, 16.

73. Mme de Staël, *Corinne, or Italy*, trans. Avriel H. Goldberger (New Bruswick, N.J.: Rutgers University Press, 1987), 297–98.

74. In "British and French estimation," as John Pemble writes, "Venice was more Oriental than much of the Orient" (Pemble, *Venice Rediscovered*, 118–20). The English writer/traveler William Beckford had commented on Venice in much the same terms in 1782; for him, too, St. Mark's was a "mosque," while "the perfume of coffee, the shade of awnings, and the sight of Greeks and Asiatics sitting cross-legged under them made me think myself in the bazaars of Constantinople" (quoted in Pemble, *Venice Rediscovered*, 118). On Beckford and Venice as "Liminal City," see Elinor Shaffer, "William Beckford in Venice, Liminal City: The Pavilion and the Interminable Staircase," in Pfister, *Venetian Views, Venetian Blinds*, 73–88.

75. Viazemsky, *Polnoe sobranie sochinenii*, 12:44.

76. Rozanov, *Sobranie sochinenii*, 227.

77. Pavel Muratov, *Obrazy Italii*, ed. V. N. Grashchenkov (Moscow: Galart, 1993), 35.

78. Fyodor Dostoevsky, *The Brothers Karamazov*, trans. Constance Garnett (New York: Random House, 1950), 275, 329. On the image of Europe, and Venice, as a graveyard in Russian writing, see Offord, *Journeys to a Graveyard*, 250–51.

79. For a detailed study of Brodsky's rhymes, see Barry Scherr, "Beginning at the End: Rhyme and Enjambment in Brodsky's Poetry," in *Brodsky's Poetics and Aesthetics*, ed. Lev Loseff and Valentina Polukhina (Houndsmill: Macmillan, 1990), esp. 180, 184.

80. In this chapter all the translations of "In Italy" are mine.

81. See Buckler, *Mapping St. Petersburg*, 36.

82. According to Evgenii Rein, Brodsky had written Rozanov's name in the margins of the poem in the Russian copy of *Uraniia* (the collection where the poem first appeared) that he gave to Rein. See Evgenii Rein, "Moi ekzempliar 'Uranii,'" in *Iosif Brodskii: trudy i dni*, ed. Lev Loseff and Petr Vail' (Moscow: Nezavisimaia gazeta, 1998), 150. See also Polukhina's reading of this poem in Valentina Polukhina, "Akhmatova i Brodskii (k probleme pritiazhenii i ottalkivanii)," in *Akhmatovskii sbornik*, vol. 1, ed. S. Dediulin and G. Superfin (Paris: Institut d'études slaves, 1989), 143–53.

83. Paintings, illustrations, and stage sets made by artists affiliated with the movement manifest the interest in eighteenth-century Venice and its aesthetics of carnival.

Brodsky points to Kuzmin's fascination with Venice in *Watermark* by recalling Kuzmin's translation of Henri de Régnier's Venetian prose and how Brodsky got hold of them in Leningrad in the 1960s (*W*, 36–38).

84. See Brodskii, *Peresechennaia mestnost'*, 173.

85. Svetlana Boym, *Death in Quotation Marks* (Cambridge, Mass.: Harvard University Press, 1991), 24–25. Boym's discussion is an effort to review the Russian Formalists, mainly Yuri Tynianov, within the context of the critique of subjectivity, author, and biography in contemporary literary criticism, informed by such, mainly French, critics' texts as Maurice Blanchot's "Death of the Last Writer," Roland Barthes's "The Death of the Author," Michel Foucault's "What Is an Author?" and Paul de Man's "Autobiography as De-Facement."

86. Viktor Erofeev's critique of the Soviet legacy of this Russian tradition launched the debate over Russian literary postmodernism; see "Pominki po sovetskoi literature," *Literaturnaia Gazeta*, July 4, 1990. For an English translation of Erofeev's article, see *Re-Entering the Sign: Articulating New Russian Culture*, ed. Ellen E. Berry and Anessa Miller-Pogacar (Ann Arbor, Mich.: University of Michigan Press, 1996), 147–54.

87. See, for instance, Viktor Krivulin, "Pisatel' posle istorii ili Antigona-dva (K voprosu o roli pisatelia v situatsii postmoderna)," in *Modernizm i postmodernizm v russkoi literature i kul'ture*, Studia Russica Helsingiensia et Tartuensia 5 (Helsinki: Department of Baltic and Slavonic Languages and Literatures, University of Helsinki, 1996), 67–72.

88. One example of a hagiographic approach to Brodsky was the exhibit "Iosif Brodskii: Uraniia—Venetsiia—N'iu Iork" (Joseph Brodsky: Urania, Venice, New York) in the Anna Akhmatova museum during the St. Petersburg tercentenary celebrations in the summer of 2003. It displayed a number of previously unseen archival materials, as well as a reconstruction of Brodsky's study in the South Hadley house in Massachusetts. The archival materials, such as photographs, letters, manuscripts, and other documents relating to Brodsky's life both in the Soviet Union and the United States, were placed in large built-in drawers on two walls. One wall was covered by an enlarged photograph of Dom Muruzi, Brodsky's apartment building in Leningrad; the other was covered by a similar photograph of the townhouse in which he lived in Greenwich Village in New York City. In order to see the exhibited objects, the visitor had to look inside Brodsky's two homes, which, apart from a certain sense of voyeurism, created an illusion of the visitor participating in the reconstruction of the narrative of Brodsky's private life and memories. There were a number of photos of Brodsky in various locations on his numerous trips, and these touristic snapshots created a narrative with Petersburg as the initial, and Venice as the terminal, point of Brodsky's life—for a viewer with knowledge of the Russian parallel between the two cities, the exhibit produced a circular narrative of Brodsky's life.

89. See Dmitrii Apollonov's review in *Russkii Zhurnal*, January 9, 2002.

90. See, for instance, Valentina Polukhina's commentary, where she analyzes Brodsky's contemporaries' contribution to the making of the myth of Brodsky, while her own writing exhibits just as powerful myth-making as the materials she analyzes (Valentina

Polukhina, "The Myth of the Poet and the Poet of the Myth: Joseph Brodsky," in *Russian Writers on Russian Writers*, ed. Faith Wigzell [Oxford: Berg Publishers, 1994], 139–59). See also Oleg Lekmanov's analysis of Necrologies on Brodsky in the Moscow press and the use of the attributes *velikiii* (great) and *genial'nyi* (genius) in them (Lekmanov, "'Chto zhe pishut v gazetakh?'" 233–34).

91. Kara-Murza, *Znamenityi russkie v Venetsii*, 231.

92. Consider, for instance, the bulk of poetic responses to Brodsky and Venice, ranging from Brodsky's contemporaries and associates, such as Aleksandr Kushner and Lev Loseff, to the younger generation, such as the Moscow poet Maria Stepanova. The Petersburg scholar Maria Levchenko gave an interesting talk on the perception of Brodsky's Venice in Russia at the conference "The Intelligentsias of Russia and Poland" at Lund University, Sweden, August 22–25, 2002.

93. For the reception of Hemingway in the Soviet Union from the late 1920s to the late 1970s, see Raisa Orlov, *Heminguei v Rossii* (Ann Arbor, Mich.: Ardis, 1985). For Hemingway's significance to the literary circles Brodsky affiliated with, see MacFadyen, *Joseph Brodsky and the Soviet Muse*, 30–54.

94. On Mann's Venice, see Tanner, *Venice Desired*, 353–60.

95. Brodsky recalled the writing of this poem in the following terms: "Sometime in 1989 in Venice, I was standing on Calle del Venti, in Zattere, watching how an enormous ship approached the city, and I remembered how I once arrived here in a steamboat. It was a ferry which sails on the route Alexandria—Piraeus—Venice, very cheap to travel. As a matter of fact I arrived not in winter nor from Egypt, but from Greece, from Piraeus. Why should I tell the truth all the time? I liked the beginning, and I also remembered that the relics of St. Mark were brought here from Egypt" (Brodskii, *Peresechennaia mestnost'*, 173).

96. Virginia Richter has a thoughtful passage on Brodsky's *Watermark* and the fantasy of the unattainable Venice it evokes in an article where she looks at Daphne du Maurier's and Ian McEwan's Venice from the viewpoint of tourism. Analyzing the significance of the Venetian "bric-a-brac" for Brodsky's text, she writes that "these battered objects, having crossed the border from a hermetically sealed-off world, seem to carry with them, both metaphorically and metonymically, the fantasmatic kernel of Venetian associations: decay, desire, death. But the main point of Brodsky's retrospective account is not so much its imaginative content, but the evocation of Venice as a space of fantasy, a 'not-real,' unattainable city" (Virginia Richter, "Tourist Lost in Venice: Daphne du Maurier's *Don't Look Now* and Ian McEwan's *The Comfort of Strangers*," in Pfister, *Venetian Views, Venetian Blinds*, 181).

97. Iosif Brodskii, *Peizazh s navodneniem* (Dana Point, Calif.: Ardis, 1996), 61–62.

98. For similar setting, see also Brodsky's 1960s poems, which relate to the Lithuanian resort Palanga, the 1967 "V Palange" ("In Palanga"), and the 1968 "Elegia" ("Elegy") with the first line "Podruga milaia, kabak vse tot zhe" (Darling, the restaurant is still the same) (2:249).

99. Brodsky, *Selected Poems*, 96.

100. "Dorogaya, ia vyshel segodnia iz domy pozdno vecherom" ("Dear, I ventured out of the house late this evening, merely") is the last of the elegies to M. B.—the title of the English translation, "Brise Marine," evokes not Proust but Mallarmé, whose "sea-wind" (the title of a Mallarmé poem) Brodsky's lyric subject steps out to breathe, only to realize that the wind carries with it "rank seaweed" (*CP*, 364) as he translates the "gnil'e otliva" (4:64).

101. The elegy is dedicated to Anatoli Naiman and may refer to the trip Brodsky made with Naiman in 1967, which Naiman writes about in his short memoir "Hava Nagila." There is a thematic correspondence that links the Palanga and the Yalta "Elegies" of the same year with each other; the Palanga one is dedicated to M. B., and its main theme is betrayal—"Zachem lgala ty?" ("Why did you lie?")—while the Yalta elegy, which also deals with betrayal, is dedicated to Anatolii Naiman, a poet and Brodsky's friend of the time.

102. Daniel Weissbort gives a quick journalistic sketch of the real-life Girolamo Marcello in Weissbort, "Letter from Venice," *Times Literary Supplement*, July 7, 2000.

103. Tanner, *Venice Desired*, 366.

104. It is surprising to discover how many contemporary evocations of Venice deploy this Mannian topos; see Judith Seaboyer, "Robert Coover's *Pinocchio in Venice*: An Anatomy of a Talking Book," in Pfister, *Venetian Views, Venetian Blinds*, 237–55.

105. Curtis and Pajaczkowska, "Venice: Masking the Real," 156.

106. The original manuscript with the title "The Pigeons" was displayed in a Brodsky exhibit at the Anna Akhmatova Museum in 2003. The exhibition catalogue lists the manuscript by the title of the published English version; see *Iosif Brodskii: Urania; Leningrad-Venetsiia-N'iu-Iork* (St. Petersburg: Zvezda, 2003), 58. The typed manuscript belongs to Joseph Brodsky Memorial Fellowship Fund. I'm grateful to Ann Kjellberg, Brodsky's personal assistant and editor of the *Collected Poems*, who informed me in correspondence that the revision of the title, which ended up in the later reprints of the poem, was made before the publication in the *New Republic*.

107. The line in Russian reads: "I golubi na frontone dvortsa Minelli / e.utsa v poslednikh luchakh zakata." The verb referring to the coital act is partially omitted and renders the written form to something equivalent of the English "f*cking." The omitted version appears in print in Brodsky's Russian collected works, as well as in the 1995 Ardis collection of Brodsky's poems titled *Peizazh s navodneniem*. I have not been able to confirm whether this is an editorial decision or Brodsky's own spelling.

Conclusion

1. P.A. Viazemsky, *Polnoe sobranie sochinenii*, 10:6.

2. Quoted in James Buzard, "The Uses of Romanticism: Byron and the Victorian Continental Tour," *Victorian Studies* 35, no. 1 (1991): 41.

3. Ibid., 29–30.

4. I. P. Miatlev, *Sensatsii i zamechania gospozhi Kurdiukovoi* (Leningrad: Sovetskii pisatel', 1969), 465.

5. See Said, *Culture and Imperialism*, 7.

Bibliography

Brodsky's Works

Brodskii, Iosif. *Peizazh s navodneniem*. Dana Point, Calif.: Ardis, 1996.

———. *Peresechennaia mestnost': Puteshestviia s kommentariami*. Edited by Petr Vail'. Moscow: Nezavisimaia gazeta, 1995.

———. *Sochineniia Iosifa Brodskogo*. 7 vols. St. Petersburg: Pushkinskii fond, 1997–2001.

———. *Stikhotvoreniia i poemy*. Washington, D.C.: Inter-Language Literary Associates, 1965.

Brodsky, Joseph. *Collected Poems in English*. New York: Farrar, Straus and Giroux, 2000.

———. *Less Than One*. New York: Farrar, Straus and Giroux, 1986.

———. *Marbles*. New York: Farrar, Straus and Giroux, 1989.

———. *Nativity Poems*. New York: Farrar, Straus and Giroux, 2001.

———. *On Grief and Reason*. New York: Farrar, Straus and Giroux, 1995.

———. *A Part of Speech*. Oxford: Oxford University Press, 1980.

———. *Selected Poems*. Translated by George L. Kline. New York: Harper and Row, 1973.

———. *Watermark*. New York: Farrar, Straus and Giroux, 1992.

———. "Why Milan Kundera Is Wrong about Dostoyevsky." *New York Times Literary Supplement*, February 15, 1985.

Other Sources

Akhmatova, Anna *Sochineniia v dvukh tomakh*. Vol. 1. Moscow: Tsitadel', 1997.

Antsiferov, Nikolai. *Dusha Peterburga*. 1922. Reprint, Paris: YMCA-PRESS, 1978.

Auden, W. H. *Selected Poems*. London: Faber and Faber, 1979.

———. *Thank You, Fog*. London: Faber and Faber, 1974.

Auden, W. H., and Louis MacNeice. *Letters from Iceland*. New York: Random House, 1969.

Averintsev, Sergei. *Religiia i literatura*. Ann Arbor, Mich.: Hermitage, 1981.

Avins, Carol. *Border Crossings: The West and Russian Identity in Soviet Literature 1917–1934*. Berkeley: University of California Press, 1983.

Balina, Marina. "A Prescribed Journey: Russian Travel Literature from the 1960s to the 1980s." *Slavic and East European Journal* 38 (1994): 261–70.

Bartley, Russell H. Introduction to *Soviet Historians on Latin America: Recent Scholarly Contributions*, edited by Russell H. Bartley, 3–29. Madison: University of Wisconsin Press, 1978.

Battilana, Marilla, ed. *English Writers and Venice 1350–1950/Scrittori inglesi e Venezia 1350–1950*. Venice: Stamperia di Venezia, 1981.

Baudrillard, Jean. *Simulations*. New York: Semiotext(e), 1983.

Beissinger, Mark R. "Soviet Empire as 'Family Resemblance.'" *Slavic Review* 2 (2006): 294–303.

Benois, Aleksandr. "Zhivopisnyi Peterburg." *Mir iskusstva* 1 (1902): 1–5.

Berdyaev, Nicolas. *The Russian Idea*. Translated by R. M. French. London: Geoffrey Bles, 1947.

Bethea, David. "Brodsky's and Nabokov's Bilingualism(s): Translation, American Poetry, and the *Muttersprache*." *Russian Literature* 37 (1995): 157–84.

———. *Joseph Brodsky and the Creation of Exile*. Princeton, N.J.: Princeton University Press, 1994.

———. *Khodasevich: His Life and Art*. Princeton, N.J.: Princeton University Press, 1983.

Bhabha, Homi K. *The Location of Culture*. London: Routledge, 1995.

Bishop, Elizabeth. *The Complete Poems 1927–1979*. London: Hogarth Press, 1984.

Bitov, Andrei. *A Captive of the Caucasus*. Translated by Susan Brownsberger. New York: Farrar, Straus and Giroux, 1992.

Black, J. L. "Opening up Siberia: Russia's 'Window on the East.'" In *The History of Siberia: From Russian Conquest to Revolution*, edited by Alan Wood, 57–68. London: Routledge, 1991.

Bobyshev, Dmitrii. "Dusha Peterburga v nebesnom i zemnom voploshcheniiakh." In *Moi Peterburg*, edited by Elena Shubina, 102–9. Moscow: Elle/Vargius, 2003.

Boele, Otto. *The North in Russian Romantic Literature*. Amsterdam: Rodopi, 1996.

Boorstin, Daniel J. *The Image; or, What Happened to the American Dream*. New York: Atheneum, 1961.

Boym, Svetlana. *Death in Quotation Marks*. Cambridge, Mass.: Harvard University Press, 1991.

———. *The Future of Nostalgia*. New York: Basic Books, 2001.

Bradbury, Malcolm. "The Cities of Modernism." In *Modernism: 1890–1930*, edited by Malcolm Bradbury and James McFarlane, 96–104. Atlantic Highlands: Humanities Press, 1978.

Bronguleev, V. V. *Posredine stranstviia zemnogo: Dokumental'naia povest' o zhizni i tvorchestve Nikolaia Gumileva; Gody 1886–1913*. Moscow: Mysl', 1995.

Brown, Edward J. *Mayakovsky: A Poet in the Revolution*. Princeton, N.J.: Princeton University Press, 1973.

Buckler, Juliet. *Mapping St. Petersburg: Imperial Text and Cityshape*. Princeton, N.J.: Princeton University Press, 2005.

Burton, Stacy. "Difference and Convention: Bakhtin and the Practice of Travel Literature." In *Carnivalizing Difference: Bakhtin and the Other*, edited by Peter I. Barta, Paul Allen Miller, Charles Platter, and David Shepherd, 225–45. London: Routledge, 2001.

Buzard, James. "The Uses of Romanticism: Byron and the Victorian Continental Tour." *Victorian Studies* 35, no. 1 (1991): 29–49.

Carr, Helen. "Modernism and Travel (1880–1940)." In *The Cambridge Companion to Travel Writing*, edited by Peter Hulme and Tim Youngs, 70–86. Cambridge: Cambridge University Press, 2002.

Chaadaev, Peter Iakovlevich. *Philosophical Letters and Apology of a Madman*. Translated by Mary-Barbara Zeldin. Knoxville: University of Tennessee Press, 1969.

Chekhov, A. P. *Polnoe sobranie sochinenii*. Vol. 12. *Pis'ma*. Moscow: Nauka, 1976.

Clark, Katerina. *Petersburg, Crucible of Cultural Revolution*. Cambridge, Mass.: Harvard University Press, 1995.

Clark, Steve, ed. *Travel Writing and Empire: Postcolonial Theory in Transit*. New York: St. Martin's Press, 1999.

Corten, Irina H. *Vocabulary of Soviet Society and Culture: A Selected Guide to Russian Words, Idioms, and Expressions of the Post-Stalinist Era, 1953–1991*. Durham, N.C.: Duke University Press, 1992.

Crone, Anna Lisa. "Blok's 'Venecija' and *Molnii iskusstva* as Inspiration to Mandelstam: Parallels in Italian Materials." In *Aleksandr Blok Centennial Conference*, edited by Walter N. Vickery, 73–88. Columbus, Ohio: Slavica Publishers, 1984.

Culler, Jonathan. "Semiotics of Tourism." *American Journal of Tourism* 1, nos. 1–2 (1981): 127–40.

Curtis, Barry, and Claire Pajaczkowska. "Venice: Masking the Real." In *Hieroglyphics of Space: Reading and Experiencing the Modern Metropolis*, edited by Neil Leach, 152–63. London: Routledge, 2002.

Debray, Régis. *Against Venice*. Translated by Philip Wohlstetter. Berkeley: North Atlantic Books, 1999.

Deotto, Patrizia. "Impressioni, dipinti, visioni: l'Italia nell'immaginario russo." *Europe Orientalis* 15, no. 2 (1996): 51–76.

Dickinson, Sara. *Breaking Ground: Travel and National Culture in Russia from Peter I to the Era of Pushkin*. Amsterdam: Rodopi, 2006.

———. "Russia's First 'Orient': Characterizing the Crimea in 1787." *Kritika* 3, no. 1 (2002): 3–26.

Doherty, Justin. "Acmeist Perceptions of Italy." In *Literary Tradition and Practice in Russian Culture*, edited by Valentina Polukhina, Joe Andrew, and Robert Reid, 106–21. Amsterdam: Rodopi, 1993.

Dostoyevsky, Fyodor. *The Brothers Karamazov*. Translated by Constance Garnett. New York: Random House, 1950.

Druzhnikov, Yuri. *Prisoner of Russia: Alexander Pushkin and the Political Uses of Nationalism*. Translated by Thomas Moore and Ilya Druzhnikov. New Brunswick, N.J.: Transaction Publishers, 1999.

Eco, Umberto. *Travels in Hyperreality: Essays*. San Diego: Harcourt Brace Jovanovich, 1986.

Epstein, Mikhail, and Alexander Genis. "Appendix: Who's Who in Russian Postmodernism." In *Russian Postmodernism: New Perspectives on Post-Soviet Culture*, edited by Mikhail N. Epstein, Alexander A. Genis, and Slobodonka M. Vladiv-Glover, 469–508. New York: Berghahn Books, 1999.

Epstein, Thomas. Introduction to *Russian Postmodernism: New Perspectives on Post-Soviet Culture*, edited by Mikhail N. Epstein, Alexander A. Genis, and Slobodonka M. Vladiv-Glover, vii–xii. New York: Berghahn Books, 1999.

Erofeev, Viktor. "Pominki po sovetskoi literature." *Literaturnaia Gazeta*, July 4, 1990.

Etkind, Aleksander. "Bremia britogo cheloveka, ili vnutrenniaia kolonizatsiia Rossii." *Ab Imperio* 1 (2002): 265–98.

Etkind, Efim. "Oligarkhicheskaia estetika." In *Peterburg—okno v Evropu*, ed. Natalia Baschmakoff, 47–67. Helsinki: Institute for Russian and East European Studies, 1996.

Etkind, Mark. *Aleksandr Nikolaevich Benua, 1870–1960*. Leningrad-Moscow: Izdatel'stvo Iskusstvo, 1965.

Fedotov, Georgii. *Rossiia i svoboda: sbornik statei*. Edited by M. A. Meerson. New York: Chalidze Publications, 1981.

———. *Sud'ba i grekhi Rossii: izbrannye stat'i*. Moscow: Dar', 2005.

———. *Sud'ba i grekhi Rossii: izbrannye stat'i po filosofii istorii i kul'tury v dvukh tomakh*. Vol. 1. St. Petersburg: Izdatel'stvo Sofiia, 1991.

Flaker, Aleksandar. "Venetsianskie literaturnye veduty." *Russian Literature* 43 (1998): 149–58.

Foucault, Michel. "Nietzsche, Genealogy, History." In *The Foucault Reader*, ed. Paul Rabinow, 76–100. New York: Pantheon Books, 1984.

Frizman, L. G. *Zhizn' liricheskogo zhanra: russkaia elegiia ot Sumarokova do Nekrasova*. Moscow: Izdatel'tsvo Akademiia nauk, 1973.

Frow, John. "Tourism and the Semiotics of Nostalgia." *October* 57 (1991): 123–51.

Fussell, Paul. *Abroad*. Oxford: Oxford University Press, 1980.

Galatskaia, Natalia. "Venetsianskie strofy (1)—smert' v Venetsii?" In *Meddelanden från slaviska institutionen Nr 34/1: Föredrag hållna vid Fjortonde nordiska slavistmötet i Helsingfors, augusti 1997. Häfte 1*, 33–44. Stockholm: Slaviska institutionen Stockholms universitet, 1998.

Gasparov, B. M. "Russkaia Gretsiia, russkii Rim." In *Christianity and the Eastern Slavs*, vol. 2, *Russian Culture and Modern Times*, edited by Robert P. Hughes and Irina Paperno, 245–86. California Slavic Studies 17. Berkeley: University of California Press, 1994.

———. "Tridtsatye gody—zheleznyi vek (k analizu motivov stoletnego vozvrashcheniia u Mandel'shtama." In *Cultural Mythologies of Russian Modernism*, edited by Boris Gasparov, Robert P. Hughes, and Irina Paperno, 150–79. Berkeley: University of California Press, 1992.

Gasparov, M. L. "The Iron Age of the 1930s: The Centennial Return to Mandelstam." In *Rereading Russian Poetry*, edited by Stephanie Sandler, 78–103. New Haven, Conn.: Yale University Press, 1999.

———. *Ocherk istorii russkogo stikha: metrika, ritmika, rifma, strofika*. Moscow: Izdatel'stvo Akademiia nauk, 1984.

———. "Poeziia Goratsiia." Introduction." In *Kvint Goratsii Flakk. Ody, epody, satiry, poslaniia*. Moscow: Khudozhestvennaia literatura, 1970.

———. *Sovremennyi russkii stikh: metrika i ritmika*. Moscow: Izdatel'stvo Akademiia nauk, 1974.

Ginzburg, Lidiia. *O lirike*. Moscow: Sovetskii pisatel', 1964.

Gippius, Zinaida. *Zhivye litsa*. Vol. 2, *Vospominaniia*. Tbilisi: Merani, 1991.

Givens, John. "The Anxiety of a Dedication: Joseph Brodsky's 'Kvintet/Sextet' and Mark Strand." *Russian Literature* 37 (1995): 203–26.

Goldfrank, David M. "Moscow, the Third Rome." In *The Modern Encyclopedia of Russian and Soviet History*, edited by Joseph L. Wieczynski, 119–21. Gulf Breeze: Academic International Press, 1981.

Gorsuch, Anne E. "'There Is No Place Like Home': Soviet Tourism in Late Stalinism." *Slavic Review* 4 (2003): 760–85.

Greenleaf, Monika. *Pushkin and the Romantic Fashion: Fragment, Elegy, Orient, Irony*. Stanford: Stanford University Press, 1994.

Gross, John. "Books of the Times." *New York Times*, May 6, 1986.

Groys, Boris. *The Total Art of Stalinism: Avant-garde, Aesthetic Dictatorship, and Beyond*. Princeton, N.J.: Princeton University Press, 1992.

Haven, Cynthia L., ed. *Joseph Brodsky: Conversations*. Jackson: University Press of Mississippi, 2002.

Hertzen, A. I. *Byloe i dumy*. Vols. 6–8. Moscow: Khudozhestvennaia literatura, 1982.

———. *Sobranie sochinenii v 30-h tomakh*. Vol. 7. Moscow: Izdatel'stvo Akademiia nauk, 1956.

Hinrichs, Paul. *In Search of Another St. Petersburg: Venice in Russian Poetry*. Munich: Otto Sagner, 1997.

Hogan, Patrick Colm. *Empire and Poetic Voice: Cognitive and Cultural Studies of Literary Tradition and Colonialism*. Albany: State University of New York Press, 2004.

Holland, Patrick, and Graham Huggan. *Tourists with Typewriters: Critical Reflections on Contemporary Travel Writing*. Ann Arbor: University of Michigan Press, 1999.

Horace. *The Odes and Epodes*. Translated by C. E. Bennett. Cambridge, Mass.: Harvard University Press, 1968.

Horowitz, Brian. "The Tension of Athens and Jerusalem in the Philosophy of Lev Shestov." *SEEJ* 43, no. 1 (1999): 156–73.

Hulme, Peter, and Tim Youngs, eds. *The Cambridge Companion to Travel Writing*. Cambridge: Cambridge University Press, 2002.

Hutcheon, Linda. "Irony, Nostalgia, and the Postmodern." http://www.library.utoronto.ca/ute/criticism/hutchinp.html [accessed April 10, 2008].

Ignateff, M. "Interv'iu s Oktavio Pasom." In *Iosif Brodskii: trudy i dni*, edited by Lev Loseff and Petr Vail', 256–58. Moscow: Nezavisimaia gazeta, 1998.

Iosif Brodskii: Uraniia; Leningrad-Venetsiia-N'iu-Iork. St. Petersburg: Zvezda, 2003.

Jameson, Fredric. "Postmodernism and Consumer Society." In *The Anti-Aesthetic: Essays on Postmodern Culture*, edited by Hal Foster, 111–25. 1983. Reprint, New York: New Press, 1998.

Kaplan, Caren. *Questions of Travel: Postmodern Discourses of Displacement*. Durham, N.C.: Duke University Press, 1996.

Kara-Murza, Aleksei. *Znamenitye russkie v Venetsii*. Moscow: Nezavisimaia Gazeta, 2001.

Khodasevich, Vladislav. *Stikhotvoreniia*. Leningrad: Sovetskii pisatel', 1989.

Kipling, Rudyard. *Rudyard Kipling's Verse*. London: Hodder and Stoughton, 1973.

Kline, George L. "Variations on the Theme of Exile." In *Brodsky's Poetics and Aesthetics*, edited by Lev Loseff and Valentina Polukhina, 56–88. London: Macmillan, 1990.

Knight, Nathaniel. "Grigor'ev in Orenburg, 1851–1862: Russian Orientalism in the Service of Empire?" *Slavic Review* 59, no. 1 (2000): 74–100.

Könönen, Maija. *Four Ways of Writing a City: St. Petersburg-Leningrad as a Metaphor in the Poetry of Joseph Brodsky*. Helsinki: Department of Slavonic and Baltic Languages and Literatures, University of Helsinki, 2003.

Kovačević, Natašha. *Narrating Post/Communism: Colonial Discourse and Europe's Borderline Civilization*. London: Routledge, 2008.

Kreps, Mikhail. *Poetika Brodskogo*. Ann Arbor, Mich.: Ardis, 1984.

Kristeva, Julia. *Strangers to Ourselves*. Translated by Len S. Roudiez. New York: Harvester Wheatsheaf, 1991.

Krivulin, Viktor. "Pisatel' posle istorii ili Antigona-dva (K voprosu o roli pisatelia v situatsii postmoderna)." In *Modernizm i postmodernizm v russkoi literature i kul'ture*, edited by Jouko Lindstedt, Ben Hellman, and Helena Niemensivu, 67–72. Helsinki: Helsinki University Press, 1996.

Kulle, Viktor. "Iosif Brodskii: novaia Odisseia." In *Sochineniia Iosifa Brodskogo*, edited by Ia. A. Gordin, 1:283–97. St. Petersburg: Pushkinskii fond, 1999.

Kushner, Aleksandr. "1974 god." *Literaturnaia gazeta*, August 22, 1990.

———. *Nochnaia muzyka*. Leningrad: Lenizdat, 1991.

———. *Stikhotvoreniia*. Leningrad: Khudozhestvennaia literatura, 1986.

Layton, Susan. *Russian Literature and Empire: Conquest of the Caucasus from Pushkin to Tolstoi*. Cambridge: Cambridge University Press, 1994.

Lebedev-Kumach, V. *Pesni*. Moscow: Moskovskii rabochii, 1947.

Lekmanov, Oleg. "'Chto zhe pishut v gazetakh?' (Smert' Iosifa Brodskogo v zerkale moskovskoi pressy)." *Novoe liternaturnoe obozrenie* 3 (2004): 233–34.

Lévi-Strauss, Claude. *Tristes Tropiques*. Translated by John and Doreen Wieghtman. London: Pan Books, 1989.

Loseff, Lev. "Home and Abroad in the Works of Brodskii." In *Under Eastern Eyes: The West as Reflected in Recent Russian Émigré Writing*, edited by Arnold McMillin, 25–41. London: Macmillan, 1992.

———. *Opyt literaturnoi biografii*. Moscow: Molodaia gvardiia, 2006.

———. "Politics/Poetics." In *Brodsky's Poetics and Aesthetics*, edited by Lev Loseff and Valentina Polukhina, 34–55. London: Macmillan, 1990.

———. "Real'nost' Zazerkal'ia: Venetsiia Iosifa Brodskogo." *Inostrannaia literatura* 5 (1996): 224–37.

Loseff, Lev, and Petr Vail', eds. *Iosif Brodskii: trudy i dni*. Moscow: Nezavisimaia gazeta, 1998.

Lotman, Yuri M. "Otzvuki kontseptsii 'Moskva—tretii Rim' v ideologii Petra Pervogo." In *Istoriia i tipologiia russkoi kul'tury*, edited by L. N. Kiseleva and M. Yuri Lotman, 349–61. St. Petersburg: Iskusstvo-SPG, 2002.

———. "Simvolika Peterburga i semiotika goroda." In *Semiotika goroda i gorodskoi kul'tury*, vol. 664, edited by A. E. Mal'ts, 30–45. Tartu: University of Tartu (Tartu riikliku ülikooli toimetised), 1984.

Lotman, Yuri M., and B. A. Uspenski. "Rol' dual'nykh modelei v dinamike russkoi kul'tury." In *Istoriia i tipologiia russkoi kul'tury*, edited by L. N. Kiseleva and M. Yuri Lotman, 88–115. Petersburg: Iskusstvo-SPB, 2002.

———. "The Role of Dual Models in the Dynamics of Russian Culture (Up to the End of the Eighteenth Century)." In *The Semiotics of Russian Culture*, edited by Ann Shukman, 30–66. Ann Arbor: University of Michigan Press, 1984.

Lyotard, Jean-François. *Postmodern Condition: A Report on Knowledge*. Minneapolis: University of Minnesota Press, 1984.

MacCannel, Dean. *The Tourist: A New Theory of the Leisure Class*. Berkeley: University of California Press, 1999.

MacFadyen, David. *Joseph Brodsky and the Baroque*. Westport, Conn.: Greenwood Press, 1999.

———. *Joseph Brodsky and the Soviet Muse*. Montreal: McGill-Queen's University Press, 2000.

Mandelstam, Osip. *The Complete Critical Prose and Letters*. Edited by Jane Gary Harris. Translated by Jane Gary Harris and Constance Link. Ann Arbor, Mich.: Ardis, 1979.

———. *Selected Poems*. Translated by Clarence Brown and W. S. Merwin. Harmondsworth: Penguin, 1977.

———. *Sobranie sochinenii*. Vol. 3. Moscow: Art-Biznes-Tsentr, 1994.

———. *Sochineniia*. Vol 2. Moscow: Khudozhestvennaia literatura, 1990.

Mansel, Philip. *Constantinople: City of the World's Desire, 1453–1924*. New York: St. Martin's Press, 1996.

Margolis, Ekaterina, ed. *Venetsianskie tetradi: Iosif Brodskii i drugie/Quaderni veneziani: Joseph Brodsky and Others*. Moscow: OGI, 2002.

Martin, Richard. "The Autonomous Eye of Joseph Brodsky." In *Ethics and Aesthetics: the Moral Turn of Postmodernism*, edited by Gerhard Hoffman and Alfred Hornung, 242–53. Heidelberg: Universitätsverlag C. Winter, 1996.

Mayakovsky, V. V. *Sobranie sochinenii v vos'mi tomakh*. Vol. 4. Moscow: Izdatel'stvo Pravda, 1968.

McCarthy, Mary. *Venice Observed*. Lausanne: R. Bernier, 1957.

Mednis, N. E. *Venetsiia v russkoi literature*. Novosibirsk: Izdatel'stvo novosibirskogo universiteta, 1999.

Mendelson, Edward. *Later Auden*. New York: Farrar, Straus and Giroux, 1999.

Meregalli, Franco. "Venice in Romantic Literature." *arcadia* 18, no. 3 (1983): 225–39.

Meyer, Michael C., and William L. Sherman, eds. *The Course of Mexican History*. Oxford: Oxford University Press, 1983.

Miatlev, I. P. *Sensatsii i zamechaniia gospozhi Kurdiukovoi za granitseiu, dan l'etranzhe*. Leningrad: Sovetskii pisatel', 1969.

Moser, Charles A. "Mayakovsky's Unsentimental Journeys." *American Slavic and East European Review* 19, no. 1 (1960): 85–100.

Muratov, Pavel. *Obrazy Italii*. Edited by V. N. Grashchenkov. Moscow: Galart, 1993.

Nabokov, Vladimir. *Speak, Memory*. London: Weidenfeld and Nicolson, 1967.

Naiman, Anatoli. "Hava Nagila—A Memoir." *Commentary*, July 1997.

Nivat, George. "An Ironic Journey into Antiquity." In *Brodsky's Poetics and Aesthetics*, edited by Lev Loseff and Valentina Polukhina, 89–97. London: Macmillan, 1990.

———. "l'Italie de Blok et celle de Gumilev." *Revue des Études Slaves* 4 (1982): 697–709.

Nixon, Rob. *London Calling: V. S. Naipaul's Postcolonial Mandarin*. Oxford: Oxford University Press, 1992.

Norwich, John Julius. "Did This Man Really Win the Nobel Prize?" *Literary Review*, June 1992.

O'Connor, Katherine Tiernan. "From Kabul to Byzantium and Back," in "Joseph Brodsky, 'On the Talks in Kabul': A Forum on Politics in Poetry." *Russian Review* 61, no. 2 (2002): 208–11.

Offord, Derek. *Journeys to a Graveyard: Perceptions of Europe in Classical Russian Travel Writing*. Dordrecht: Springer, 2005.

Orlov, Raisa. *Heminguei v Rossii*. Ann Arbor, Mich.: Ardis, 1985.

Otradin, M. V., ed. *Peterburg v Russkoi poezii*. Leningrad: Izdatel'stvo leningradskogo universiteta, 1988.

Pamuk, Orhan. *Istanbul: Memories of a City*. Translated by Maureen Freely. London: Faber and Faber, 2005.

Parkes, Henry Bamford. *A History of Mexico*. 1938. Reprint, Boston: Houghton Mifflin, 1969.

Patterson, David. *Exile: The Sense of Alienation in Modern Russian Letters*. Lexington: University Press of Kentucky, 1995.

Pellegrini, Carlo, ed. *Venezia nelle letterature moderne*. Venice: Instituto per la collaborazione culturale, 1955.

Pemble, John. *Venice Rediscovered*. Oxford: Oxford University Press, 1995.

Perloff, Marjorie. *Wittgenstein's Ladder: Poetic Language and the Strangeness of the Ordinary*. Chicago: University of Chicago Press, 1996.

Pertsov, P. *Venetsiia*. St. Petersburg: Gerol'd, 1905.

Pesonen, Pekka. *Teksty zhizni i iskusstva: Texts of Life and Art*. Helsinki: Department of Slavonic and Baltic Languages and Literatures, Helsinki University, 1997.

Pfister, Manfred. "*The Passion* from Winterson to Coryate." In *Venetian Views, Venetian Blinds: English Fantasies of Venice*, edited by Manfred Pfister and Barbara Schaff, 15–28. Amsterdam: Rodopi, 1999.

Piretto, Gian Piero. "Brodskij 'protiv' Venecii." *Russian Literature* 41–44 (1997): 519–32.

Polukhina, Valentina. "Akhmatova i Brodskii (k probleme pritiazhenii i ottalkivanii)." In *Akhmatovskii sbornik*, vol. 1, edited by S. Dediulin and G. Superfin, 143–53. Paris: Institut slavianovedeniia, 1989

———. *Joseph Brodsky: A Poet for Our Time*. Cambridge: Cambridge University Press, 1989.

———. "Khronologiia zhizni i tvorchestva Brodskogo." In *Opyt literaturnoi biografii*, by Lev Loseff, 323–424. Moscow: Molodaia gvardiia, 2006.

———. "Landshaft liricheskoi lichnosti v poezii Iosifa Brodskogo." In *Literary Tradition and Practice in Russian Culture*, edited by Valentina Polukhina, Joe Andrew, and Robert Reid, 229–45. Amsterdam: Rodopi, 1993.

———. "The Myth of a Poet and a Poet of the Myth: Russian Poets on Brodsky." In *Russian Writers on Russian Writers*, edited by Faith Wigzell, 139–60. Oxford: Berg Publishers, 1994.

———. "The Prose of Joseph Brodsky: A Continuation of Poetry by Other Means." *Russian Literature* 41 (1997): 223–40.

Potter, Dennis. *Haunted Journeys: Desire and Transgression in European Travel Writing*. Princeton, N.J.: Princeton University Press, 1992.

Pound, Ezra. *The Cantos of Ezra Pound*. London: Faber and Faber, 1957.

———. *Pavannes and Divagations*. Norfolk: New Directions, 1958.

Prater, Donald. *Thomas Mann: A Life*. Oxford: Oxford University Press, 1995.

Pratt, Mary Louise. *Imperial Eyes: Travel Writing and Transculturation*. London: Routledge, 1992.

Pushkin, A. S. *Eugene Onegin: A Novel in Verse*. Vol. 1. Translated by Vladimir Nabokov. 1964. Reprint, Princeton, N.J.: Princeton University Press, 1975.

———. *Polnoe sobranie sochinenii*. Vols. 1–10. Moscow: Izdatel'stvo Akademiia nauk, 1937–58.

Rabinow, Paul, ed. *The Foucault Reader*. New York: Pantheon Books, 1984.

Ram, Harsha. "Imagining Eurasia: The Poetics and Ideology of Olzhas Suleimenov's Az i IA." *Slavic Review* 60, no. 2 (2001): 289–311.

———. *The Imperial Sublime: A Russian Poetics of Empire*. Madison: University of Wisconsin Press, 2003.

Ramazani, Jahan. *Poetry of Mourning: The Modern Elegy from Hardy to Heaney*. Chicago: University of Chicago Press, 1994.

Ranchin, Andrei. "'Ia rodilsia i vyros v baltiiskikh bolotakh, podle . . .': poeziia Iosifa Brodskogo i 'Mednyi vsadnik' Pushkina." *Novoe literaturnoe obozrenie* 45 (2000): 166–80.

———. *Na piru mnemoziny: interteksty Iosifa Brodskogo*. Moscow: Novoe literaturnoe obozvenie, 2001.

Readings, Bill. *Introduction to Lyotard: Art and Politics*. London: Routledge, 1991.

Rein, Yevgeni. "Moi ekzempliar 'Uranii.'" In *Iosif Brodskii: trudy i dni*, edited by Lev Loseff and Petr Vail', 139–53. Moscow: Nezavisimaia gazeta, 1998.

Reynolds, Andrew. "Returning the Ticket: Joseph Brodsky's 'August' and the End of the Petersburg Text?" *Slavic Review* 64, no. 2 (2005): 307–32.

Richter, Virginia. "Tourist Lost in Venice: Daphne du Maurier's *Don't Look Now* and Ian McEwan's *The Comfort of Strangers*." In *Venetian Views, Venetian Blinds: English Fantasies of Venice*, edited by Manfred Pfister and Barbara Schaff, 181–94. Amsterdam: Rodopi, 1999.

Ridley, Jasper. *Maximilian and Juárez*. London: Constable, 1993.

Rigsbee, David. *Styles of Ruin: Joseph Brodsky and the Postmodernist Elegy*. Westport, Conn.: Greenwood Press, 1999.

Roboli, T. "The Literature of Travel." In *Russian Prose*, edited by B. M. Eikhenbaum and Yury Tynianov, translated and edited by Rey Parrot, 45–66. Ann Arbor, Mich.: Ardis, 1985.

Rosaldo, Renato. *Culture and Truth: The Remaking of Social Analysis*. Boston: Beacon Press, 1984.

Rotkirch, Anna. "Traveling Maidens and Men with Parallel Lives—Journeys as Private Space During Late Socialism." In *Beyond the Limits: The Concept of Space in Russian History and Culture*, edited by Jeremy Smith, 131–49. Helsinki: Suomen historiallinen seura, 1999.

Rozanov, Vasilii. *Sobranie sochinenii: Sredi khudozhnikov: Ital'ianskie vpechatleniia*. Edited by A. N. Nikoliukin. Moscow: Izdatel'stvo Respublika, 1994.

———. "Zolotistaia Venetsiia." *Novoe Vremia*, July 7, 1902.

Ruskin, John. *The Stones of Venice*. Vol. 1, *The Foundation*. New York: Garland Publishing, 1979.

Russell, Alison. *Crossing Boundaries: Postmodern Travel Literature*. Palgrave: New York, 2000.

Sahni, Kalpana. *Crucifying the Orient*. Bangkok: White Orchid Press, 1997.

Said, Edward, W. *Culture and Imperialism*. New York: Vintage Books, 1993.

———. *Orientalism*. 1978. Reprint, New York: Vintage Books, 1994.

———. *Reflections on Exile and Other Essays*. Cambridge, Mass.: Harvard University Press, 2000.

———. *The World, the Text, and the Critic*. Cambridge, Mass.: Harvard University Press, 1983.

Sand, George. *Oeuvres autobiographiques*. Vol. 2. Paris: Gallimard, 1971.

Sandomirskaia, Irina. "Proletarian Tourism: Incorporated History and Incorporated Rhetoric." In *Soviet Civilization between Past and Present*, edited by Mette Bryld and Erik Kulavig, 39–52. Odense University Slavic Studies 10. Odense: Odense University Press, 1998.

Sartre, Jean-Paul. *Situations, IV*. Paris: Gallimard, 1964.

Savitskii, Stanislav. *Andergraund: istoriia i mify leningradskoi neofitsial'noi literatury.* Moscow: Novoe literaturnoe obozrenie, 2002.

Scherr, Barry. "Beginning at the End: Rhyme and Enjambment in Brodsky's Poetry." In *Brodsky's Poetics and Aesthetics*, edited by Lev Loseff and Valentina Polukhina, 180–97. London: Macmillan, 1990.

Schimmenpenninck, David van der Oye. "Orientalizm—delo tonkoe." *Ab Imperio* 1 (2002): 249–64.

Schönle, Andreas. *Authenticity and Fiction in the Russian Literary Journey, 1790–1840.* Cambridge, Mass.: Harvard University Press, 2000.

Schwarzband, Samuil. "Aleksandr Blok and Nikolaj Gumilev." *Slavic and East European Journal* 33, no. 3 (1988): 373–89.

Seaboyer, Judith. "Robert Coover's *Pinocchio in Venice*: An Anatomy of a Talking Book." In *Venetian Views, Venetian Blinds*, edited by Manfred Pfister and Barbara Schaff, 237–55. Amsterdam: Rodopi, 1999.

Seixo, Maria Alzira, ed. *Travel Writing and Cultural Memory.* Amsterdam: Rodopi, 2000.

Shallcross, Bożena. *Through the Poet's Eye: The Travels of Zagajewski, Herbert, and Brodsky.* Evanston, Ill.: Northwestern University Press, 2002.

Shestov, Lev. *Afiny i Ierusalim.* Paris: YMCA-Press, 1951.

Shtern, Liudmila. *Brodski: Osia, Iosif, Joseph.* St. Petersburg: Retro, 2005.

Shur, L. A. *Rossiia i Latinskaia Amerika.* Moscow: Izdatel'stvo sotsial'no-ekonomicheskoi literatury "Mysl," 1964.

Smith, Gerald Stanton. "England in Russian Émigré Poetry: Iosif Brodskii's 'V Anglii.'" In *Under Eastern Eyes*, edited by Arnold McMillin, 17–24. London: Macmillan, 1992.

———. "Some Preliminary Ideas." In "Joseph Brodsky, 'On the Talks in Kabul': A Forum on Politics in Poetry." *Russian Review* 61, no. 2 (2002): 190–93.

Spieker, Sven. *Figures of Memory and Forgetting in Andrej Bitov's Prose: Postmodernism and the Quest for History.* Frankfurt am Main: Peter Lang, 1996.

Spurr, David. *The Rhetoric of Empire: Colonial Discourse in Journalism, Travel Writing and Imperial Administration.* Durham, N.C.: Duke University Press, 1993.

Staël, Mme de. *Corinne, or Italy.* Translated by Avriel H. Goldberger. New Brunswick, N.J.: Rutgers University Press, 1987.

Sterne, Laurence. *A Sentimental Journey through France and Italy.* London: Oxford University Press, 1928.

Stewart, Susan. *On Longing: Narratives of the Miniature, the Gigantic, the Souvenir, the Collection.* Durham, N.C.: Duke University Press, 1993.

Sukhikh, Igor. "Puteshestvie v Stambul (O poetike prozy I. Brodskogo)." In *Iosif Brodski: tvorchestvo, lichnost', sud'ba: Itogi trekh konferentsii*, 232–36. St. Petersburg: Zvezda, 1998.

Suleimenov, Olzhas. *Az i IA.* 1975. Reprint, Alma Ata: Zhalyn, 1989.

Tanner, Tony. *Venice Desired.* Cambridge, Mass.: Harvard University Press, 1992.

Tennyson, Alfred Lord. *The Poems of Tennyson.* Edited by Christopher Ricks. London: Longman, 1969.

Timenchik, Roman. "'1867.'" In *Joseph Brodsky: The Art of a Poem,* edited by Lev Loseff and Valentina Polukhina, 59–67. Houndmills: Palgrave, 1999.

Tolz, Vera. *Inventing the Nation: Russia.* London: Arnold, 2001.

Toporov, V. N. "Italiia v Peterburge." In *Italiia i slavianskii mir: Sovetsko-ital'ianskii simpozium in honorem Professore Ettore Lo Gatto,* 49–81. Moscow: Izdatel'stvo Akademiia nauk, Institut Slavianovedeniia i Balkanistiki, 1990.

———. "Peterburg i peterburgski tekst russkoi literatury." In *Semiotika goroda i gorodskoi kul'tury,* vol. 664, edited by A. E. Mal'ts, 4–29. Tartu: University of Tartu (Tartu riikliku ülikooli toimetised), 1984.

———. *Peterburgskii tekst russkoi literatury: Izbrannye trudy.* Iskusstvo: Petersburg, 2003.

Turoma, Sanna. "Joseph Brodsky and Orientalism: A Russian Moor in Venice?" *Ulbandus, The Slavic Review of Columbia University* 7 (2003): 143–54.

———. "Joseph Brodsky's *Watermark*: Preserving the Venetophile Discourse." *Russian Literature* 52 (2003): 485–502.

———. "Poet kak odinokii poet: Brodskii, Venetsiia i putevye zametki." *Novoe literaturnoe obozrenie* 67 (2004): 164–80.

———. "Poetry as Imperial Discourse: Brodsky, Derzhavin, and Heroic Masculinity." Paper presented at the international conference "Russia in Europe, Europe in Russia," Helsinki, Finland, August 28–30, 2008.

Ungurianu, Dan. "The Wandering Greek: Images of Antiquity in Joseph Brodsky." In *Russian Literature and the Classics,* edited by Peter I. Barta, David H. J. Larmour, and Paul Allen Miller, 161–91. Amsterdam: Hardwood Academic Publishers, 1996.

Urry, John. *The Tourist Gaze: Leisure and Travel in Contemporary Societies.* London: Sage, 1990.

Vail', Petr. "Prostranstvo kak metafora vremeni: stikhi Iosifa Brodskogo v zhanre puteshestviia." *Russian Literature* 37 (1995): 405–16.

Vail', Petr, and Aleksandr Genis. *60-e: Mir sovetskogo cheloveka.* Ann Arbor, Mich.: Ardis, 1988.

———. "Ot mira—k Rimu." In *Poetika Brodskogo,* edited by Lev Loseff, 198–206. Tenafly, N.J.: Ermitazh, 1986.

Valliere, Paul. *Modern Russian Theology: Bukharev, Soloviev, Bulgakov.* Grand Rapids, Mich.: Eerdmans, 2000.

Van Baak, Jost. "Brodsky and the North." In *Neo-Formalist Papers: Contributions to the Silver Jubilee Conference to Mark 25 Years of the Neo-Formalist Circle,* edited by Joe Andrews and Robert Reid, 242–68. Rodopi: Amsterdam, 1998.

———. "'Northern Cultures': What Could This Mean? About the North as a Cultural Concept." *Tijdschrift voor Skandinavistiek* 16, no. 2 (1995): 11–30.

Venclova, Thomas. "Journey from Leningrad to Istanbul." In *Brodsky's Aesthetics and Poetics,* edited by Lev Loseff and Valentina Polukhina, 135–51. London: Macmillan, 1990.

———. "'Keningsbergskii tekst' russkoi literatury i keningsbergskie stikhi Iosifa Brodskogo." In *Brodski w analizach i interpretacjach,* edited by Piotra Fatsa and Joanny Madloch, 7–29. Katowice: Śląsk, 2000.

———. "'Litovskii divertisment' Iosifa Brodskogo." In *The Third Wave: Russian Literature in Emigration*, edited by Olga Matich and Michael Heim, 191–201. Ann Arbor, Mich.: Ardis, 1984.

———. *Neustoichivoe ravnovesie: vosem russkikh poeticheskikh tekstov*. New Haven, Conn.: Yale Center for International and Area Studies, Yale University, 1986.

———. "O stikhotvorenii Iosifa Brodskogo 'Litovskii noktiurn: Tomasu Venclovu.'" *Novoe Literaturnoe Obozrenie* 33, no. 5 (1998): 205–22.

Viazemsky, P. A. *Polnoe sobranie sochinenii kniazia P.A. Viazemskogo*. Vol. 10. St. Petersburg: Tipografiia M. M. Stasiulevicha, 1886.

———. *Polnoe sobranie sochinenii kniazia P.A. Viazemskogo*. Vol. 12. St. Petersburg: Tipografiia M. M. Stasiulevicha, 1896.

Volkov, Solomon. *Conversations with Joseph Brodsky: A Poet's Journey through the Twentieth Century*. New York: Free Press, 1998.

Von Koppenfels, Werner. "Sunset City—City of the Dead: Venice and the Nineteenth Century Apocalyptic Imagination." In *Venetian Views, Venetian Blinds: English Fantasies of Venice*, edited by Manfred Pfister and Barbara Schaff, 99–114. Amsterdam: Rodopi, 1999.

Wachtel, Andrew. "Voyages of Escape, Voyages of Discovery: Transformations of the Travelogue." In *Cultural Mythologies of Russian Modernism*, edited by Boris Gasparov, Robert P. Hughes, and Irina Paperno, 128–49. Berkeley: University of California Press, 1992.

Walicki, Andrzej. *A History of Russian Thought: From the Enlightenment to Marxism*. Oxford: Clarendon Press, 1980.

Walker, Gwen. "Silver-Age Writers on the 'Black' Continent: Russia, Africa, and the Celebration of Distance." PhD diss., University of Wisconsin–Madison, 2003.

Weissbort, Daniel. "Letter from Venice." *Times Literary Supplement* (London), July 7, 2000.

Widdis, Emma. *Visions of the New Land: Soviet Film from the Revolution to the Second World War*. New Haven, Conn.: Yale University Press, 2003.

Wilson, Reuel K. *The Literary Travelogue: A Comparative Study with Special Relevance to Russian Literature from Fonvizin to Pushkin*. The Hague: Martinus Nijhoff, 1973.

Woll, Josephine. *Real Images: Soviet Cinema and the Thaw*. London: I. B. Tauris, 2000.

Wordsworth, William. *The Poems*. New Haven, Conn.: Yale University Press, 1981.

Yukht, Victor V. "K probleme genezisa statuarnogo mifa v poezii Iosifa Brodskogo (1965–1971 gg.)." *Russian Literature* 44 (1998): 409–32.

Zil'bershtein, I. S., and A. N. Savinov, eds. *Aleksandr Benua razmyshliaet. . . .* Moscow: Sovetskii Khudozhnik, 1968.

Index